Designing Modern Childhoods

The Rutgers Series in Childhood Studies

The Rutgers Series in Childhood Studies is dedicated to increasing our understanding of children and childhoods, past and present, throughout the world. Children's voices and experiences are central. Authors come from a variety of fields, including anthropology, criminal justice, history, literature, psychology, religion, and sociology. The books in this series are intended for students, scholars, practitioners, and those who formulate policies that affect children's everyday lives and futures.

Edited by Myra Bluebond-Langner, Rutgers University, Camden

Advisory Board

Joan Jacobs Brumberg, Cornell University, New York City

Perri Klass, Boston University School of Medicine

Jill Korbin, Case Western Reserve University

Bambi Schiefflin, New York University

Enid Schildkraut, American Museum of Natural History

Designing Modern Childhoods

History, Space, and the Material Culture of Children

Edited by
MARTA GUTMAN
NING DE CONINCK-SMITH

RUTGERS UNIVERSITY PRESS

NEW BRUNSWICK, NEW JERSEY AND LONDON

LIBRARY OF CONGRESS CATALOGING-IN-PUBLICATION DATA

Designing modern childhoods : history, space, and the material culture of children /
edited by Marta Gutman and Ning de Coninck-Smith.
    p. cm. — (The Rutgers series in childhood studies)
    Includes bibliographical references and index.
    ISBN 978-0-8135-4195-2 (hardcover : alk.paper)
    ISBN 978-0-8135-4196-9 (pbk. : alk. paper)
    I. Children—History.   2. Children—Social conditions.   3. Children—Social
life and customs.   4. Architecture and children.   5. Children's paraphernalia.
6. Child consumers.   7. Children and adults—History.   I. Gutman, Marta.
II. Coninck-Smith, Ning de.
    HQ767.87.D47 2008
    305.2309′04—dc22

                                2007008416

A British Cataloging-in-Publication record for this book is available
from the British Library.

This collection copyright © 2008 by Rutgers, The State University
Individual chapters copyright © 2008 in the names of their authors

The publication of this volume has been made possible
through the generous support of The Danish Humanities Research Council.

Visit our Web site: http://rutgerspress.rutgers.edu
Manufactured in the United States of America

To our children: Isaac and Nina, Peter and Thomas, with
love–and heartfelt thanks for all that you have taught
us about the design of modern childhoods.

CONTENTS

PART THREE

Space, Power, and Inequality in
Modern Childhoods

PART FOUR

Consumption, Commodification, and the Media:
Material Culture and Contemporary Childhoods

Epilogue: The Islanding of Children–Reshaping the
Mythical Landscapes of Childhood
     JOHN R. GILLIS

FOREWORD

The interest in children and childhood as serious subjects of inquiry has grown dramatically in the last decade. This is the result of a dawning sense of not fully understood changes in childhoods in the globally conscious twenty-first century, from fears about the demise of the childhood we have come to know in the Western world since the early twentieth century, as well as from developments within a variety of disciplines. Together they have made children into the newest subject of study for historians, art and architectural historians, sociologists, philosophers, and anthropologists. For many of us working in this area during this time, the study of children has been an exciting means to understand many of the underpinnings as well as some of the hidden corners of human experience.

Studies of the material culture of children—their spaces, toys, and furnishings—have grown along with this new interest, and museums and other exhibition spaces over the last several years have invited the public into this new world of child studies.[1] This phenomenon suggests that the interest is hardly confined to the academy and that children and their lives have become significant points of a much wider fascination and concern. In fact, spaces and material objects are extremely effective vantages from which to observe the results of the upsurge in scholarly attention to this subject. Schools, children's nurseries, toys, books, clothes, and other material objects—created by adults according to both their understanding of what childhood is like and their commitments to investing in children—are the sites and objects that help to define children's worlds, as well as their experiences and their imaginations. This material world is where childhood (as adults define it) and children (as real participants) intersect. These specially built places and objects have been very much a part of the experience of the middle classes in Europe and the United States since the mid-nineteenth century. How children use their spaces and the objects created for them, by adapting and recreating them, is a large part of what has constituted children's experience. And for observers new to this world of scholarship, seeing (actual objects at exhibitions, or the many illustrations included in this volume) as well as reading is always helpful.

Other societies and earlier periods in the West did not pay as much attention to children's special needs and had fewer resources to build separate spaces and objects exclusively for children. Nevertheless, in these societies and cultures, children have also occupied, shared, and co-created the spaces and objects they used. And throughout history and everywhere in the present, children live, learn, and play in homes, streets, and other places, using the objects that come to hand and the spaces they inherit from adults.

As a contribution to this field of study, *Designing Modern Childhoods* provides an excellent means to introduce new readers to the developing field of scholarship on children and their spaces, while providing scholars already familiar with the new child studies with a wide-ranging set of papers to help satisfy their eager desire for more information and richer forms of analysis. *Designing Modern Childhoods* is wonderfully capacious in providing readers with both historical and ethnographic perspectives on many subjects currently at the forefront of scholarly attention, including matters relating to health, education, and consumerism. The essays cover many important aspects of children's lives as they creatively interact with the spaces developed by adults which they inhabit, such as schools, hospitals, summer camps, the internet, and the streets. And the essays do this on a global terrain, which alerts readers to similarities and differences in the many places and societies of our contemporary world. This feature of the volume is especially noteworthy. In our time, an awareness of the global is becoming more available to children everywhere, while we are becoming much more conscious of all the world's children. Thus, *Designing Modern Childhoods* tells us about children from places as distant from each other as New Zealand, Turkey, Indonesia, and Senegal, while reminding us that not all children even in the United States have had the same experiences, and that race, class, and gender continue to frame children's lives.

This introduction to the spaces of childhood in many places in the world has it origins in a conference held at the University of California at Berkeley in May 2002 that I had the privilege of attending. That conference brought together scholars from many different places and different disciplines who discovered the interests they shared, how much they had to teach each other, and how very much more they wanted to learn. The editors, Marta Gutman and Ning de Coninck-Smith inspired the initial conference, worked to make it a reality, and have now fulfilled the promise of the conference by bringing this field to the attention of a much wider audience, first in a volume of essays drawn from that conference,[2] and here in another volume growing from the insights developed from the conference now expanded to a much wider global expanse. The result will, I expect, tantalize the reader new to the field, and add important dimensions to the understanding of those who have read in this area before. What we are invited to see here is quite literally the new world of childhood.

Paula S. Fass

Margaret Byrne Professor of History

University of California at Berkeley

NOTES

1. For an excellent review of some of these recent exhibitions, see Abigail A. Van Slyck, *"Kid Size: The Material World of Childhood:* An Exhibition Review," *Winterthur Portfolio* 39.1 (2004): 69–77.

2. Ning de Coninck-Smith and Marta Gutman, eds., "Children and Youth in Public: Making Places, Learning Lessons, Claiming Territories," special issue of *Childhood,* 11.2 (2004): 131–141.

ACKNOWLEDGMENTS

Historians often struggle to identify beginnings, but in the case of this book we are able to the pinpoint the precise moment when the idea came to life—over lunch in a garden in Berkeley, California, in the spring of 2001. We had met the previous fall at the Center for Working Families at the University of California at Berkeley, where we discovered a mutual interest in the history of childhood, children's material culture, and interdisciplinary scholarship.

We would like to extend thanks to Arlie Hochschild and Barrie Thorne, directors of the CWF, for their interest in our work and especially for the support offered to the interdisciplinary, international conference, "Designing Modern Childhoods: Landscapes, Buildings, and Material Culture," which we organized at the University of California at Berkeley in May 2002. Several chapters in this collection were presented at the conference. In addition to the Center for Working Families (sponsored by the Alfred P. Sloane Foundation), the Doreen B. Townsend Center for the Humanities, the Center for Childhood and Youth Policy, the History Department, and the College of Environmental Design (all at UC Berkeley) supported the conference, as did the Department of Literature, Cultural, and Media Studies at Southern Denmark University, Odense, and the Kompan Corporation.

Along the way (from conference to book), dear friends and admired colleagues encouraged us to pursue and bring to completion this project. On this count we thank Paula Fass, Randolph Starn, Christina Gillis, John Gillis, Dell Upton, and especially Peter Stearns. Peter read the manuscript not once but twice and at each reading offered insightful comments that improved each essay and the collection as a whole. In 2005, we were invited to present this project to the seminar, "Gendered Passages: The Gendering of Children," sponsored by the Center for Historical Analysis at Rutgers University. We received many valuable comments from seminar participants, especially Jack Spector. Our thanks also to Virginia Yans for making the presentation possible.

Paula Fass and John Gillis brought the book to the attention of Rutgers University Press, where we have been privileged to work with talented editors. Melanie Halkias watched over the book at the beginning, Kendra Boileau helped bring it to completion, and Myra Bluebond-Langner welcomed *Designing Modern Childhoods* to the prestigious Childhood Studies series. The book is the better for their attention and care; and that of Beth Kressel, Alison Hack, Margaret Case,

Donna Liese, and others who shepherded the manuscript through copy-editing, design, and production.

We are very grateful to The Danish Research Council of the Humanities for supporting publication of this volume. The quality and extent of the illustrations are in large measure due to the generous subvention offered by the DRCH. Anne-Marie Châtelet brought to our attention the marvelous photograph, used as the cover illustration, and helped secure permission to publish it from the Archives de la famille Jean Zay. We are indebted to Madame Zay who generously allowed the photograph to be reprinted.

Thanks are also offered to our colleagues, especially to George Ranalli, Jerrilynn D. Dodds, Alan Feigenberg, Michael Sorkin, Achva Benzinberg Stein, and Stephanie Smith at the School of Architecture, Urban Design, and Landscape Architecture, The City College of the City University of New York. Rachel Adams proved to be an admirable research assistant, indispensable in collating the manuscript. Thanks also to Gene Sparling for insights, support, and using the eagle eye of an architect to assist us along the way.

Finally, we offer thanks to the authors—for the quality of the work, patience with the process, and commitment to our shared project: the interdisciplinary, comparative study of children, childhood, and material culture in a global context.

Designing Modern Childhoods

Introduction

Good to Think With–History, Space, and Modern Childhood

MARTA GUTMAN AND NING DE CONINCK-SMITH

Let us start with snapshots of two places recently made for children in Denmark and the United States. In Copenhagen, a new playground opened in the inner-city neighborhood of Oesterbro. Rather than providing a traditional playground, equipped with swings and climbing structures, SLA Landscape Architects filled the play space with grasses of different colors and shapes: green, gray, yellow, and purple; tall, short, and slim; and these were described as gently swaying in a late summer wind when the playground opened. As Stine Poulsen, a young mother and one of the designers, explained, "I want my son to sense the world in all its different colors and textures; I want to create a space open to young children's fantasy when playing."[1]

Across the Atlantic Ocean, the New York City Housing Authority recently announced the opening of the GrandParentFamily Apartments in the South Bronx, one of the poorest neighborhoods in the United States. The low-income housing complex, made possible through collaboration with not-for-profit social service agencies, had been designed by Goshow Architects in response to a growing trend in the United States: grandparents raising their grandchildren. The twelve million dollar facility is the "first-ever" to be purpose built for this use in the United States, according to the Housing Authority. It is equipped for this purpose with fifty-one subsidized apartments, retail space, and many spaces for social services that will be used by children, teenagers, and elderly women of color who make up most of the low-income families in the complex. During a recent visit, one woman explained she took custody of her grandchildren after their father, her son, had been killed and their mother disappeared. As the family explored the apartment, her grandson explained his plans for arranging his bedroom. "I'm going to put my bed in there . . . hook up my PlayStation 2. Put my clothes in the closet. Put the computer in my room." His younger sister planned to decorate her room with dolls and pictures of the cartoon characters Sponge Bob Squarepants and Bratz.[2]

The differences between these places (and the stories written about them) are telling, raising themes—social welfare, nature as a source of health for children, commodification, gender roles, racial inequality—that will be explored in the following discussion of the design of modern childhoods. But, as important as it is to scrutinize the different meanings inscribed in places for children—to recognize difference, broadly speaking—we'd like to step back, for the moment, and start this collection on another note. It is in tune with the collaborative spirit of inquiry that informed this project from its inception over lunch in a garden in Berkeley a few years ago. The stories about the playground in Copenhagen and the public housing project in New York underscore the thesis of this book: that spaces and settings made for children are pivotal to the construction of modernity in global society; and that children are social actors in their own right who use and interpret material culture on their own terms. As these anecdotes suggest, landscapes, buildings, and objects are "good to think" about the history of children with because the architecture of childhood frames, just as it is framed by, culturally constructed views of ideal childhood.[3] Cross-cultural, transnational comparisons are also needed to grasp the different effects of modernity on the lived experiences of children across the globe.

Using interdisciplinary methods, the essays in this collection examine these themes in relationship to children who live on most of the world's continents and in different social and cultural contexts. Although aware that the sense of the terms "children" and "childhood" has changed over time, the authors adhere to contemporary, everyday understandings of them. They broadly define childhood to be the period after infancy and before emerging adulthood—more or less between the ages of three and eighteen. The authors also recognize that the category "childhood" is not homogeneous, but differentiated by age, class, race, gender, and other social identities.[4] These social differentiations come into play as the authors assess the impact of one very influential adult model for "good" childhood on children's places. This model came to dominate thinking about children in Western industrial democracies by the early twentieth century, and continues to shape childhood and youth culture across the globe. The model says that because children are different from adults, they should have a childhood that is in at least some manner protected, nurturing, and playful; that a child's education ought to be centered on mental, emotional, and physical development; and that a specialized material culture is needed to make possible the "good and happy childhood" as lived experience.

Understanding the effects of this model of childhood, we argue, is key to grasping the structure and experience of modernity, historically and in contemporary society.[5] In elucidating this concept we are indebted to the thinking of Sharon Stephens, Peter Stearns, and Paula Fass, because our concern in this volume is with modernity and childhood not only as ideals but also as they are embodied in the material culture and thus the lived realities of children. As these and other students of globalization and global history insist (along with students of social class, gender relations, and race), modernization has not been a homogeneous process; the world's children experience modernity differently, due to historical, economic, social, geographical, and other circumstances. "Modernity generated a crucial new version of childhood," Stearns has written. "Initially [it] spread, very unevenly, as part of adjustments to the Western model, in a common though definitely not blindly homogeneous pattern of change."[6] A network of buildings and spaces, as well as experts (doctors, architects, engineers, and teachers), volunteers (mainly women), journals, books, and conferences facilitated the diffusion of this ideal.[7]

To grasp the diversity of spaces, practices, and experiences, the essays in this collection historicize the creation of children's spaces. The settings are examined in varied cultural and regional contexts so that local sensibilities may be brought to bear on understanding global change. The term "material culture" is also defined broadly, in keeping with the sense of the expression as used in recent, interdisciplinary studies of children's spaces.[8] Material culture is thus taken to include the landscapes, buildings, rooms, furnishings, clothes, toys, and many other objects and things that children wear and use, designed by adults with children in mind: the stuff of childhood, as one historian calls all these things.[9] The material culture of children is also defined to include what one geographer refers to as "the inter-spaces of adult society," meaning structures and objects not necessarily made for children but which children, teenagers, and young adults have claimed and made an integral part of youth culture.[10] In other words, the authors accept what has been argued to be the duality of children's material culture and cultural landscapes: children's settings include those made for them by adults and defined by adult values as well as the sites where children use space and design artifacts to develop what sociologists call "children's own culture."[11]

Inventing the Good Childhood

Philippe Ariès brought to the forefront the mutual dependence between the social life and material culture of modern children in *Centuries of Childhood: A Social History of Family Life*, which when published in 1960 as *L'enfant et la vie familiale sous l'Ancien Régime* launched postwar research into the history of childhood and family life in the West.[12] Ariès argued that among well-born families in early modern Europe, a new sentimentalized concept of children developed, accompanied by a new interest in nurture and education. Because the beginning of this sentimental construction of childhood (for the privileged classes) intersected with the development of the modern concept of public and private life, special objects and places were created for children in these realms. These objects helped to define these spheres and embodied the sense that a child's life world ought to be different from an adult's. In domestic life, the stuff of childhood came to include distinct clothes, toys, and furniture, like highchairs and walking stools. The demarcation of public places for children began with the provision of new institutions for them, mainly primary schools.[13] In due course, schools and school buildings would become "a defining experience of childhood," to borrow a phrase from the historian of childhood Hugh Cunningham.[14]

Despite Ariès's point about the centrality of material culture in modern childhoods, historians have only recently shown interest in examining objects, buildings, and landscapes made for children.[15] With industrialization, the quantity of things made for children expanded, and the built environment, especially in cities and large towns, became even more specialized, in conjunction with the development of middle-class ideals for a good childhood.[16] In industrializing democracies, a broad consensus developed that children should not work, but rather learn and play in settings that were designed and built with those specific purposes in mind. Spaces unregulated by adults—streets, alleys, stoops, and yards—were no longer deemed suitable spaces for children to be.[17] With middle-class parents, educators and philanthropists, architects and urban planners, social workers and politicians advocating spatial differentiation, authorities shaped a highly regulated (in theory at least) public landscape for urban children. Schools,[18] kindergartens,[19] and playgrounds,[20] for example, were sited at the center of cities and towns with other institutions; orphanages,[21] hospitals,[22] and open-air schools were set at the periphery.[23] Further out, summer camps would be built for children.[24] In addition to embodying the ideals of the good childhood, these spaces were used to socialize children;[25] the places were ingrained with the effects of race prejudice and other inequalities,[26] and they furthered imperialist objectives, for example by training future soldiers and imprinting European values on colonial landscapes.[27]

The construction of this public landscape for children was not harmonious or smooth, even though new state-sponsored institutions (often monumental), stately buildings, and clearly defined play spaces delimited by fences and walls made it seem as if powerful processes were at work, assigning children to distinct places in cities and towns. In industrializing cities, the working classes challenged the differentiation of the built environment, perceiving the results to be riddled with upper-class values and expectations for boys and girls. As the historian Anna Davin has shown, this contestation was enacted by children: in London; for example, boys rioted in poorhouse schools in the middle of the nineteenth century; in board schools, girls resisted gendered programs of instruction intended to turn them into docile servants; and boys and girls wrestled with each other, their parents, and civic authorities as they laid claim to streets as their public territory well into the twentieth century.[28] Heated debates also exploded in the late nineteenth and early twentieth centuries between advocates for children and public authorities about the design of playgrounds, orphanages, and other purpose-made settings. Their ideals clashed, because they too linked physical forms with different social and political agendas for children.[29]

The material culture of private life also changed for children in the nineteenth century as the ideals of the good childhood diffused in Europe, the United

States and, with colonization and new forms of communication, other areas of the world. In private life (as in public life) spaces were used to socialize children, and the experience of the good childhood was not homogenous with respect to class, gender, race, or national origin.[30] Predictably, privileged children in the West were the first to experience the impact of these new ideals in private life. In the first half of the century, domestic interiors were differentiated, first with separate bedrooms and then separate beds for children becoming the norm in middle-class homes. Middle-class gender norms shaped the design of these spaces, especially in homes of well-off families, where it was deemed necessary for boys and girls to sleep in separate bedrooms. This would not be the case in many working-class homes until the middle of the twentieth century, and remains unrealized in homes in many parts of the developing world. Children also came to be dressed in special clothing; it would be argued these garments were appropriate to age, gender, and stage of development, especially in the case of young children.[31]

In addition and as important, the symbolic value of childhood shaped the commodification of objects made for children in this period. Abigail A. Van Slyck, an architectural historian, has given close scrutiny to the physical elevation of children in daily life and argues that making children visible marked their importance in an expanding consumer economy. Although children may have been culturally constructed as innocent, pure, and angelic, the design of highchairs and strollers in the second half of the nineteenth century allowed adults to display children; to interact with (and discipline) them, all the while keeping physical contact to a minimum. In second half of the twentieth century, the same items were redesigned because experts and parents wanted children to participate in family life. In either situation, owning objects designed to express ideal childhood was important for parents who were engaged in "conspicuous leisure for whom children served as important accessories."[32]

The Islanding of Contemporary Childhood

The creation of a specialized material culture for children, the demarcation of differentiated buildings for them, and the separation of the lives of children and adults constituted a radical change to customary life in Western society. In thinking about long-range impact of these changes, the sociologists Helga Zeiher and Hartmut Zeiher have argued that this specialization of space and material culture is deeply problematic in that it systematically excludes the lives of children and adults from one another. They characterize the result as the "islanding of children," taking this state of affairs to be detrimental and destructive of the potential for a socially integrated life world in modern society.[33] Other sociologists argue that an added effect of these changes is to infantilize children, reversing the sense of children as responsible human beings to constructing them as infants, not accountable for their actions.[34]

According to the anthropologist Sharon Stephens, this model of insular infantilized childhood reached the climax of its effect during the Cold War. Especially in
the United States, she argues, a consensus developed about childhood that was
rooted in "the vision of the socially fortified, sexually charged, gender-segregated
and consumer-oriented home at the heart of American post-war settlement." One
result was to try to contain children within the limits of "normal childhood"; what
Stone casts as the mythic "'walled garden' of 'Happy, Safe, Protected, Innocent
Childhood'" (borrowing some terms from John Holt).[35] Although seeming to be
apolitical, this vision of childhood was deeply politicized, based on a sense of the
child being the "atom" of nuclear society and thus in need of protection. In the
United States, physical infrastructure (roads, schools) and small houses in segregated suburbs shaped the protective shield, as well as consumption, psychology,
and Cold War public policy.[36]

As the example shows and as Stephens reminds us, "discursive regimes" and
"discursive fields" are rhetorical constructs that have "very real material effects
on physical environments and bodies" of children.[37] These effects are not homogeneous because children are born into existing material worlds, shaped by history, culture, power relations, and inequalities. In the 1950s, the model of the
insulated childhood did not exist for every American child, including Native
American children, whom Stephens argues were intentionally exposed to fallout
from nuclear tests by the U.S. government. The model of insulated childhood was
also challenged by the exigencies of daily life for other children, by the rapid
expansion of consumer society, and in no small measure by the social movements of the 1960s. Since then, and as essays in this book discuss, youth culture
has conquered the lives of both children and adults, and children have come to
be understood as competent social actors in their own right. The use of toys is
declining, and it is no longer obvious when childhood ends and youth begins.
Kindergartens are designed as schools; young children dress in street wear; cell
phones and computers are part of most children's lives; and piggy-banks and saving accounts are being replaced by special credit cards for children.[38]

Some will argue that children grow up too fast and that youth is undermin-
ing childhood; or to paraphrase Gary Cross, cool has replaced cute in styling children and their childhoods.[39] Others warn that the privatization of public space
has dire consequences for democracy, restricting children's access to civic
amenities and reifying social stratification on the basis of class, race, and ethnicity.[40] Still others remind us of the uneven distribution of wealth in global society,
and the consequences of ingrained material inequalities on the present-day and
future lives of children.[41] But no matter what stand one might take in the contemporary debate about children and their lives, the dream about a childhood
unaffected by the adult world remains. According to the cultural historian John R.
Gillis, author of the concluding essay in this book, this dream materializes as
islands. They have become the ideal mythical landscape for adult thinking about
modern childhood. Calling on the Zehirs' arguments and ideas put forth in his

Islands of the Mind: How the Human Imagination Created the Atlantic World, Gillis argues that we impart our "thinking with islands" to children and their settings. He maintains that islands are central to our hopes and dreams about a better life and our fears and anxieties about modern society.[42]

The points are well taken, and the essays in this collection show that the separation of the worlds of children and adults has been threaded with adult hopes for children as well as with their worries about them. Although childhood may have come to be imagined as a heavenly island, we see that specific islands are connected to adult worlds, interests, and settings, for the better and the worse. Children also take charge of their material culture, creating objects and spaces, and claiming and putting to unexpected uses the things and settings adults have given them.

About the Collection

The authors in this collection take inspiration from the work mentioned above, while adding new perspectives to the study of spaces, buildings, and objects made with children in mind. The collection draws from groundbreaking work in the field, including some of the papers presented at "Designing Modern Childhoods: Landscapes, Buildings, and Material Culture," a conference organized by the editors at the University of California at Berkeley. With chapters written by architectural and urban historians, social historians, and social scientists, the study of children's architecture and material culture is historicized and located within an international, interdisciplinary, interpretative framework. The book is organized thematically to facilitate cross-cultural comparison and direct attention to crucial processes and conditions shaping childhood in global society: child saving and social welfare; education and play; power and inequality; and consumption and commodification.

Part I, "Child Saving and the Design of Modern Childhoods" introduces the historical, comparative framework used in this collection by analyzing the effect of the ideal childhood on different spaces for children: summer camps in the United States, hospitals also in the United States, sick rooms in private homes in Canada, and an experimental park in New Zealand. The settings discussed in this section were made as adult concerns about the deleterious effects of industrialization, urbanization, and immigration on childhood exploded in the late nineteenth and early twentieth centuries. As the authors show, adults turned to a variety of child-saving mechanisms, including exposure to nature as a route to health and the use of architecture and design to promote the social welfare of children. The use of space for socialization and enculturation in childhood is also examined in these chapters, especially with respect to gender.

By the end of the nineteenth century, adults had come to believe that contact with nature would save children from the problems of the industrial city and offer them healthier lives, physically as well as mentally. Summer camps were one of the specialized settings created for children, where these ideals could be enacted. Abigail A. Van Slyck analyzes three episodes in the history of summer camps in the United States, focusing on the use of the campfire (one aspect of a child's experience of nature at camp) in creating and maintaining youth culture. The chapter relates changes in the campfire and its place in the camp landscape to adult anxieties about gender and the nature of childhood in modern society. A paradigm shift occurred in the 1930s, when camps were stripped of the anti-modernist rhetoric and replaced by the idea of the summer camp as a modern environment in its own right, directed by professional experts.

Adults also interpreted child-saving ideals, especially the desire for healthier children in relationship to widespread calls for order, regularity, and cleanliness in the built environment. This resulted in the creation of new institutions, including special hospitals for children. Professional interests were at stake in configuring these institutions as engineers, architects, doctors, and educators tried out new ideas and invoked their expertise to establish control over the built environment. Ideas about good childhood, good motherhood, and care-giving networks were also professionalized in these institutions (as they were places where women could find paid work outside the home).

David C. Sloane, a cultural and social historian, draws on these ideas in his discussion of children's hospitals in the United States. The female physicians who created the first children's hospitals in the middle of the nineteenth century intended them to be places for comfort, cure, and moral and spiritual education. The metaphor of the home was a practical reality, since most facilities were located in former houses. As science, hygiene, and medical expertise replaced domesticated ideals, female directors lost out to male colleagues. By 1920s the connection between women's philanthropy and children's hospitals no longer existed. Future hospitals would be located in purpose-built structures, embodying medical expertise.

Sick children were also cared for in private homes, as Annmarie Adams, an architectural historian, and Peter Gossage, a social historian, show in their case study of upper middle-class homes in late-nineteenth-century Montreal. This chapter introduces another theme important in this collection, children's voices and experiences, because the authors use letters, photographs, and drawings to examine the importance of health concerns and the role of gender in family life. Adams and Gossage uncover remarkable spatial fluidity in privileged homes as mothers and daughters translated concerns about health into action.[43] The designs of children's most private spaces were shaped by medicine, hygiene, and new ideas about medicalized motherhood; and children invented spatial strategies to cope with threats to health and death of beloved siblings.

Anéne Cusins-Lewer and Julia Gatley return the discussion of child saving to the public realm with their analysis of an ambitious urban renewal project in New Zealand launched at the beginning of World War I. Construing architecture and urban design to be useful for physical and moral conditioning of children, planners included in the park a playground, a purpose-built kindergarten, and a school for disabled children. Each site was infused with hygienic, militaristic, nationalistic, and imperialistic metaphors. Cusins-Lewer and Gatley, architects and architectural historians, draw analogies between New Zealand, an "infant in the civilization process," and ideas about childhood, the body of the child, and the association of mothers and children. The authors argue planners construed children, schools, playgrounds, and parks to be malleable entities, capable of molding each other and New Zealand into a modern, "garden" country.

Cross-cultural analysis of adult concerns and children's spaces continues in Part II, "The Choreography of Education and Play." The discussion of schools and playgrounds in France, Turkey, Senegal, and England makes clear that adults bring normative, disciplinary, and didactic expectations to bear on the design of settings for learning and play.[44] The chapters in this section also show the importance of transnational cultural exchange in school and playground design, an issue explored in new interdisciplinary research. School and playground design is now studied in relationship to gender and modern architecture;[45] to social reform, urban reform, and social welfare;[46] and in light of nation building, as well as Foucauldian arguments about order and discipline in modern institutions.[47] Most recently, interest in the materiality of discipline in schools has turned to objects and technologies used in instruction (blackboards, desks, pencils, notebooks, light fixtures, and uniforms).[48]

Anne-Marie Châtelet, an architectural historian, shows the movement for open-air schools to have been a true child of the "The Century of the Child," as the Swedish educator Ellen Key called the twentieth century.[49] The first open-air school opened in Berlin in 1900, established as a day school for impoverished children in poor health (usually in the early stages of tuberculosis). Health improved immediately, as did performance in school, and the reform cause spread quickly, leading to the construction of open-air schools in major urban centers in Europe and the United States. Châtelet argues the open-air school movement had a lasting impact on modern architecture, including school design; the concern with social reform and hygiene, which were part and parcel of the program, appealed to progressive architects, planners, and educators.

The other essays in this section show that concern with the choreography of education and play is tied to more than the state's interest in healthy children. Zeynep Kezer, an architectural historian, analyzes the material connections forged between the state, schools, and children during the formative years of the Turkish Republic. After World War I, when the war-torn ruins of the Ottoman Empire developed into a modern nation-state, school buildings, textbooks, processions, and pedagogical techniques, consciously imported from the West, were used to make children into "humble components" of the new Republic. Pointing to the role of environmental memory in knowledge acquisition, she emphasizes that the uniform design of new public schools was intended to cultivate nationalist sensibilities in children and inspire loyalty to the new regime's understanding of modernization. Other spatial strategies taught children to imagine themselves as part of a modern Turkish nation.

Kristine Juul, a geographer, tells a different story about the relationship of school building to children and state authority in northern Senegal. Drawing on fieldwork from the 1990s, she contests the assertion that in postcolonial societies formal education is the preferred means to transform migrant agricultural workers into citizens. Itinerant pastoral groups rejected the rigid educational structure (inherited from colonial authorities in French West Africa) because their children worked and spoke a different language from that used in school. Although investing in children's labor proved more beneficial than investing in education, the construction of schools proceeded because schools were valued symbols of modernity. The buildings also established signs of permanent presence in the landscape, as habitation patterns changed due to climatic crises (drought) and state-mandated resettlement of formerly nomadic peoples. In point of fact, the schools were empty; prized as symbols of modernity but not used to educate children.

The discussion of junk playgrounds by Roy Kozlovsky turns to the choreography of play in modern childhood. Kozlovsky, an architectural historian, draws on the Foucauldian concept of governmentality to analyze the ways in which changes in adult understandings of children's needs and social roles shaped playground design in the 1930s and 1940s. At the beginning of the century, organized play on dedicated spaces was intended to socialize immigrant and working-class children, to inculcate gender norms, and to create a foundation for citizenship in democratic societies.[50] In the interwar years, however, a concern with traumatized children and asocial behavior began to displace preoccupation with social control and hygiene. Instead of arguing that play spaces ought to embody adult authority, educators and play leaders advocated alternatives like the junk playground, where self-regulation and creativity ruled. In war-torn Europe, junk playgrounds, opened on bombed sites, vividly underscored the importance of free play, emotional health, and the creativity of children to democratic society.

As shown in the first two sections of the book, the symbolic importance of children's spaces becomes especially visible in times of political struggle and cultural crisis. The chapters in Part III, "Space, Power, and Inequality in Modern Childhoods" enrich understandings of the symbolic role of children's spaces by probing this theme in relationship to social inequalities, prejudices, and privileges. The authors show that domestic space in South Africa, schools in the American South, and streets in Indonesia are sites where children experience the social construction of space and learn who they are through these spatial experiences and memories of them. They also learn to use space to contest inequality. Race, gender, and class are the locus of concern.[51]

Rebecca Ginsburg, an architectural and urban historian, draws on adult recollections of childhood in the apartheid era to show that perceived relationships between buildings, material culture, and people established a white child's understanding of racial privilege in South Africa. Children did not grasp the racial differentiation of space in suburban backyards (where their caretakers lived), until middle childhood, when black and white spaces started to seem different from one another, and parents encouraged children to break ties with caretakers. Domestic service and apartheid complemented each other in suburban space, with children learning both how the social world operates and their own places within it. Access to black domestic spaces, inscribed with material evidence of inequality, and the subsequent denial of contact brilliantly imparted the benefits of racial privilege to white children.

Mary S. Hoffschwelle, a social historian, uses architectural analysis, archival research, and oral history to explain the meanings invested in settings purpose-built for the education of black children—the Rosenwald schools in the American South. Booker T. Washington, the African American leader, collaborated with Julius Rosenwald, the wealthy philanthropist, and school boards in African American communities to build schools for black children between 1912 and 1932. With standardized plans, the schools appeared to be plain and functional, yet the innovation embedded in the designs offered African American children and their families hope for social advancement. Although race prejudice took its toll on these sites, Hoffschwelle argues the schools established the rights of black children to a public place in the civic landscape of the modernizing South.

Extensive fieldwork in Yogyakarta is used by Harriot Beazley, a cultural geographer, to explore how street girls are pushed to the margins of street culture in this Indonesian city. Harassed by state agents, street boys, and other men because they are seen to be committing a "heretical geography" by living on the street, girls articulate strategies of resistance through language, style, methods of earning money, leisure activities, and uses of urban space. By negotiating social and personal spaces for themselves, street girls enact gendered "geographies of resistance" that create a positive self-identity for themselves as a subjugated social group. The spaces also are sites of liberation for street girls, where they are relatively safe and able to behave as they choose, free from the gaze of male authority.

The chapters in Part IV, "Consumption, Commodification, and the Media: Material Culture and Contemporary Childhoods" discuss the explosion of children's consumption in the postwar world. With the spread of consumer society, the quantity of things made for kids grew to new heights as children became consumers in their own right. Ethnographers and curators have a long tradition of dealing with children's stuff, especially clothes and toys, although these things are often not studied in an interdisciplinary or spatial context.[52] New critical dimensions have been added to understanding this aspect of children's material life from consumer studies, the history of consumption, and youth culture, although often the spaces where children use consumer objects are not examined.[53] Recent sociological, anthropological, and geographical studies of children's spaces offer other new perspectives, usually without an historical perspective.[54] The ethnographic perspective in this section presents children as carriers and creators of culture who claim interspaces of adult society and make them part of modern childhood. The examples range from toys in England to food in Sweden, snowboards in Norway, and *Yugioh* cards in Japan.

Children's gift giving in north London is examined by Alison J. Clarke, historian of design and material culture. She contextualizes the acquisitive behavior of contemporary children and their preferences for specific commodities. While recognizing that corporate-controlled toy culture exploits children, Clarke argues that children generate dynamic relationships with adults and friends through making known their gift preferences. This study demonstrates the importance to parents of their children having the right toys—and the troubles parents experience if they do not purchase the "right" gifts. The exchange of information, occurring largely in domestic sites, becomes the means by which households take part in a broader public culture of the child, as parents and children project their values on each other.

Helene Brembeck, an ethnographer, examines the meanings of the McDonald's "Happy Meal" in Scandinavia. The application of Bruno Latour's actor-network theory to her fieldwork shows that adult constructions of ideal childhood cannot be separated from goods designed for children. The materiality of the toys and food included in the familiar red boxes affords a range of actions, makes certain trajectories possible, and thus plays an active part in shaping childhoods. Her fieldwork shows that children transform the stuff of childhood, as they call on familiar stories and categories of knowledge related to play culture.

Olav Christensen, an ethnographer, also draws on fieldwork, in this case with Norwegian snowboarders. Christensen, who became a skilled snowboarder during his research, offers telling examples of his engagement with young Norwegians and his discovery of the ways in which they adopt and alter dominant American expressions of their sport; he also describes how snowboarders understand their identity in terms of the kinds of tracks their boards imprint on the snowy slopes of Norway. His observations of Norwegian teenagers demonstrate that the forming of personhood is an embodied process in modern childhoods, where social contexts, gender, and material cultures blend in unpredictable ways.

Mizuko Ito, a cultural anthropologist, also uses ethnographic fieldwork to describe and analyze the new media mixes of *Yugioh*, a *manga* (comic) and *anime* (animation) series in contemporary Japan. After situating these media mixes in children's media culture, Ito describes three ethnographic "sitings" where the imaginary world of Yugioh intersects with the everyday lives of children and adult players. In addition to making the fantasy world of Yugioh tangible, the practices render palpable different interpretations of childhood, gender, and economic relations. Although the symbolic separation of childhood is as much of an obsession in Japan as it is elsewhere in the modern world, this cultural construction is challenged by everyday intersections between the worlds of children and adults. In Japan, as in other Western democracies, the sense of childhood as being at risk is ever present; ironically, though, adults "consume" childhood, as they adopt childhood as an alternative form of identity.

John Gillis's essay on the islanding of contemporary childhood brings the collection to a close, with a provocative analysis of this theme in relationship to each chapter in the collection. It is our hope that the intersection in this book of contemporary and historical research topics, the embrace of interdisciplinary perspectives (from architectural and social history to the sociology of childhood), and the varied research methodologies (from discourse analysis to actor-network theory, archival research, and ethnographic field work) will make visible the complex processes behind the so-called insularization of modern childhood. As the chapters show, and as Gillis underscores, the idea of the good and happy childhood and its ideal physical surroundings has been exchanged and negotiated through space, over time and across continents, and between different social classes.

In line with Gillis (and Ariès, Cunningham, and Miller), we argue that materiality matters, when it comes to the history of childhood.[55] The history of modern childhood is a material process, engaged with the making of cultural landscapes, buildings, toys, and other stuff and things for children. Taking a material approach to the history of childhood helps us see different things, tell different stories, and question assumptions. In the history of architecture and design, for example, schools and other settings purpose-made for children are a relatively new topic; the chapters in this volume also underscore the importance of discussing ordinary architecture as well as high-style buildings, designed by well-known architects, and considering the social construction of space. For social historians, concerned with the history of childhood, thinking about childhood as a material matter makes visible a variety of new social actors—adults as well as children. Other lessons may also be gleaned: lessons of method (the importance of calling on diaries, fieldwork, drawings, photos, and memoirs as evidence) as well as lessons about the significance and limits of theories and models of the good childhood. As the chapters in this collection make clear, the existence of one model of the good childhood—the Western model, enacted for and by privileged children—is correct in one sense, but also highly questionable, rendered so by the heterogeneous, lived experiences of modernity by the world's children.

NOTES

1. Lea Kathrine Bahnsen, "Shh . . . Kan Du Høre Græsset Gro? [Hush . . . Can You Hear the Grass Grow?]," *MetroXpress,* September 19, 2005, 4.

2. Timothy Williams, "A Place for Grandparents Who Are Parents Again," *New York Times,* May 21, 2005, B6.

3. The phrase, "good to think," is borrowed from Claude Lévi-Strauss, *Totemism,* translated by Rodney Needham (Boston: Beacon Press, 1963), 89.

4. Anna Davin, "When Is a Child Not a Child?," in *Politics of Everyday Life: Continuity and Change in Work and Family,* edited by Helen Corr and Lynn Jamieson (New York: St. Martin's Press, 1990), 37–39.

5. See Sharon Stephens, "Children and the Politics of Culture in 'Late Capitalism,'" in *Children and the Politics of Culture*, edited by Sharon Stephens (Princeton: Princeton University Press, 1995), 6.

6. Peter N. Stearns, "Change, Globalization, and Childhood," *Journal of Social History* 38.4 (2005): 1043.

7. See Catherine Burke and Ian Grosvenor, "Designed Spaces and Disciplined Bodies: E. R. Robson's Architectural Tour," paper presented at the European Social Science History Conference, Amsterdam, 2006.

8. Recent interdisciplinary studies of children and the built environment include *Children in the City: Home, Neighbourhood, and Community*, edited by Pia Christensen and Margaret O'Brien (London: Routledge, 2003); Sarah L. Holloway and Gill Valentine, eds., *Children's Geographies: Living, Playing, Learning* (London: Routledge, 2000); Karen Fog Olwig and Eva Gulløv, eds., *Children's Places: Cross-Cultural Perspectives* (London: Routledge, 2003); Tracey Skelton and Gill Valentine, eds., *Cool Places: Geographies of Youth Cultures* (New York: Routledge, 1998), as well as Ning de Coninck-Smith and Marta Gutman, "Children and Youth in Public: Making Places, Learning Lessons, Claiming Territories," *Childhood* 11.2 (2004): 131–141. For the renewed historical interest in the material culture of the children, see Annmarie Adams and Abigail A. Van Slyck, "Children's Spaces," in *Encyclopedia of Children and Childhood in History and Society*, edited by Paula S. Fass (New York: Macmillan Reference, 2004), 187–194, and many other entries in that volume.

9. Gary Cross, *Kid's Stuff: Toys and the Changing World of American Childhood* (Cambridge: Harvard University Press, 1997).

10. Herb Childress, "Teenagers, Territory, and the Appropriation of Space," *Childhood* 11.2 (2004): 195–206; Hugh Matthews et al., "The Unacceptable *Flaneur*: The Shopping Mall as a Teenage Hangout," *Childhood* 7.3 (2000): 279–294.

11. Coninck-Smith and Gutman, "Children and Youth in Public"; Marta Gutman, "Adopted Homes for Yesterday's Children: Intention and Experience in an Oakland Orphanage," *Pacific Historical Review* 73.4 (2004): 541–618; Karen Fog Olwig, "'Displaced' Children? Risks and Opportunities in a Caribbean Urban Environment," in *Children in the City: Home, Neighborhood, and Community*, edited by Pia Christensen and Margaret O'Brien (London: Routledge, 2003), 46–65; Kim Rasmussen, "Places for Children and Children's Places," *Childhood* 11.2 (2004): 155–174.

12. Philippe Ariès, *Centuries of Childhood: A Social History of Family Life*, trans. Robert Baldick (New York: Vintage Books, 1962). For this point also see Hugh Cunningham, *Children and Childhood in Western Society since 1500*, 2nd ed. (New York: Pearson Longman, 2005), 3–15; Hugh Cunningham, "Histories of Childhood," *American Historical Review* 103.4 (1998): 1197–1202; Stephens, "Children and the Politics of Culture in 'Late Capitalism,'" 4–5.

13. Also see Patrick H. Hutton, *Philippe Ariès and the Politics of French Cultural History* (Amherst: University of Massachusetts Press, 2004); Michael McKeon, *The Secret History of Domesticity: Public, Private, and the Division of Knowledge* (Baltimore: Johns Hopkins University Press, 2005), 238.

14. Hugh Cunningham, "Childhood in One Country (Review of Steven Mintz, *Huck's Raft: A History of American Childhood*)," H-Childhood@h-netmsu.edu, February 25, 2006. For disputation of Ariès, see Nicholas Orme, *Medieval Children* (New Haven: Yale University Press, 2003); and Nicholas Orme, *Medieval Schools: From Roman Britain to Tudor England* (New Haven: Yale University Press, 2006).

15. Also see Cunningham, "Histories of Childhood," 1197–1202.

16. See Coninck-Smith and Gutman, "Children and Youth in Public."

17. For the general case, Viviana A. Zelizer, *Pricing the Priceless Child: The Changing Social Value of Children* (New York: Basic Books, 1985). For Denmark, see Ning de Coninck-Smith, Bengt Sandin, and Ellen Schrumpf, eds., *Industrious Children: Work and Childhood in the Nordic Countries, 1850–1990* (Odense: Odense University Press, 1997). For New York, see Timothy J. Gilfoyle, "Street-Rats and Gutter-Snipes: Child Pickpockets and Street Culture in New York City, 1850–1900," *Journal of Social History* 37.4 (2004): 853–882; David Nasaw, *Children of the City: At Work and at Play* (Garden City, N.Y.: Anchor Press/Doubleday, 1985); Christine Stansell, "Women, Children, and the Uses of the Streets: Class and Gender Conflict in New York City, 1850–1860," *Feminist Studies* 8.2 (1982): 309–336.

18. For France, see Anne-Marie Châtelet, *La naissance de l'architecture scolaire: les écoles élémentaires parisiennes de 1870 à 1914* (Paris: Honoré Champion, 1999); Anne-Marie Châtelet, *Paris à l'école, "Qui a eu cette idée folle ..."* (Paris: Éditions Picard, 1993); for England, see Malcolm Seaborne, *The English School: Its Architecture and Organization*, vol. 1: 1370–1870 (London: Routledge and Kegan Paul, 1971); Malcolm Seaborne and Roy Lowe, *The English School: Its Architecture and Organization,* vol. 2: 1870–1970 (London: Routledge and Kegan Paul, 1977); Deborah E. B. Weiner, *Architecture and Social Reform in Late-Victorian London* (Manchester: Manchester University Press, and New York: St. Martin's, 1994); for the United States, Marta Gutman, "School Buildings and Architecture: United States," in *Encyclopedia of Children and Childhood in History and Society*, edited by Paula S. Fass (New York: Macmillan Reference, 2004), 726–728.

19. Norman Brosterman, *Inventing Kindergarten* (New York: Harry N. Abrams, 1997); Mark Dudek, *Kindergarten Architecture: Space for the Imagination* (London: E & FN Spon, 1996). Also see Roberta Wollons, ed., *Kindergartens and Cultures: The Global Diffusion of an Idea* (New Haven: Yale University Press, 2000).

20. Dominick Cavallo, *Muscles and Morals: Organized Playgrounds and Urban Reform* (Philadelphia: University of Pennsylvania Press, 1981); Galen Cranz, *The Politics of Park Design: A History of Urban Parks in America* (Cambridge: MIT Press, 1982); Susan G. Solomon, *American Playgrounds: Revitalizing Community Space* (Lebanon, N.H.: University Press of New England, 2005); Suzanne M. Spencer-Wood, "A Survey of Domestic Reform Movement Sites in Boston and Cambridge, ca. 1865–1905," *Historical Archaeology* 21.2 (1987): 7–36; Suzanne M. Spencer-Wood, "Feminist Historical Archaeology and the Transformation of American Culture by Domestic Reform Movements, 1840–1925," in *Historical Archaeology and the Study of American Culture*, edited by Lu Ann De Cunzo and Bernard L. Herman (Winterthur, Del.: Winterthur Museum, and Knoxville: University of Tennessee Press, 1996), 397–445.

21. Anne-Marie Châtelet, Dominique Lerch, and Jean-Noël Luc, eds., *Open-Air Schools: An Educational and Architectural Venture in Twentieth-Century Europe* (Paris: Éditions Recherches, 2003); Anne-Marie Châtelet et al., "L'école de plein air de Suresnes: Un cas d'école," *Archiscope* (May 2006): 4–32; Marta Gutman, "Entre moyens de fortune et constructions spécifiques: les écoles de plein air aux États-Unis à l'époque Progressiste (1900–1920)," *Histoire de l'éducation* 102 (May 2004), 157–180.

22. Children's hospitals are discussed in David Sloane and Beverly Conant Sloane, *Medicine Moves to the Mall* (Baltimore: Johns Hopkins University Press, 2003); and Annmarie Adams and David Theodore, "The Architecture of Children's Hospitals in Toronto and Montreal, 1875–2010," in *Children's Health Issues in Historical Perspective*, edited by Cheryl Krasnick Warsh and Veronica Strong-Boag (Waterloo: Wilfrid Laurier University Press, 2005): 439–478.

23. Kenneth Cmiel, *A Home of Another Kind: One Chicago Orphanage and the Tangle of Child Welfare* (Chicago: University of Chicago Press, 1995); Marta Gutman, *What Kind of City: The*

Charitable Landscape That Women Built for Children in Oakland, California (Chicago: University of Chicago Press, forthcoming); Lydia Murdoch, *Imagined Orphans: Poor Families, Child Welfare, and Contested Citizenship in London* (New Brunswick: Rutgers University Press, 2006); Nurith Zmora, *Orphanages Reconsidered: Child Care Institutions in Progressive Era Baltimore* (Baltimore: Johns Hopkins University Press, 1994).

24. Abigail A. Van Slyck, *A Manufactured Wilderness: Summer Camps and the Shaping of American Youth, 1890–1960* (Minneapolis: University of Minnesota Press, 2006).

25. Elizabeth A. Gagen, "Play the Part: Performing Gender in America's Playgrounds," in *Children's Geographies: Playing, Living, Learning,* edited by Sarah L. Holloway and Gill Valentine (London: Routledge, 2000), 213–229; Marta Gutman, "Inside the Institution: The Art and Craft of Settlement Work at the Oakland New Century Club, 1895–1923," in *People, Power, and Places: Perspectives in Vernacular Architecture VIII,* edited by Sally McMurry and Annmarie Adams (Knoxville: University of Tennessee Press, 2000), 248–279; Abigail A. Van Slyck, "Kitchen Technologies and Mealtime Rituals: Interpreting the Food Axis at American Summer Camps, 1890–1950," *Technology and Culture* 43.4 (2002): 668–692. Also see Barrie Thorne, *Gender Play: Girls and Boys at School* (New Brunswick: Rutgers University Press, 1993).

26. Mary S. Hoffschwelle, *Rebuilding the Rural Southern Community: Reformers, Schools, and Homes in Tennessee, 1900–1930* (Knoxville: University of Tennessee Press, 1998); Rena Swentzell, "Conflicting Landscape Values: The Santa Clara Pueblo and Day School," in *Understanding Ordinary Landscapes,* edited by Paul Groth and Todd W. Bressi (New Haven: Yale University Press, 1997), 56–66.

27. Anna Davin, *Growing up Poor: Home, School, and Street in London, 1870–1914* (London: Rivers Oram Press, 1996). Also see Ann Laura Stoler's chapter, "A Sentimental Education: Children on the Imperial Divide," in her book *Carnal Knowledge and Imperial Power: Race and the Intimate in Colonial Rule* (Berkeley: University of California Press, 2002), 112–139.

28. For London, see Davin, *Growing up Poor*; Ellen Ross, *Love and Toil: Motherhood in Outcast London, 1870–1918* (New York: Oxford University Press, 1993); and Weiner, *Architecture and Social Reform in Late-Victorian London.*

29. Our own research, for example, engages these points with respect to playgrounds in Denmark and orphanages in the United States. Ning de Coninck-Smith, "Where Should Children Play? City Planning Seen from Knee-Height: Copenhagen, 1870–1920," *Children's Environments Quarterly* 7.4 (1990): 54–61; Gutman, "Adopted Homes for Yesterday's Children."

30. See Annmarie Adams, *Architecture in the Family Way. Doctors, Houses, Women, 1870–1900* (Montreal and Kingston: McGill-Queen's University Press, 1996); Elizabeth Cromley, "Transforming the Food Axis: Houses, Tools, Modes of Analysis," *Material History Review* 44 (Fall 1996): 8–22; Bryn Varley Hollenbeck, "The Littlest Ones at Home: The Material Culture of the Youngest Americans in the Early Twentieth Century," Ph.D. dissertation, University of Delaware, forthcoming; Mary Jo Maynes, Birgitte Soland, and Christina Benninghaus, eds., *Secret Gardens, Satanic Mills: Placing Girls in European History* (Bloomington: Indiana University Press, 2004).

31. Karin Calvert, *Children in the House: The Material Culture of Early Childhood, 1600–1900* (Boston: Northeastern University Press, 1992); Elizabeth Collins Cromley, "A History of American Beds and Bedrooms," in *Perspectives in Vernacular Architecture IV,* edited by Thomas Carter and Bernard L. Herman (Columbia: University of Missouri Press, 1991), 177–188; Elizabeth Collins Cromley, "A History of American Beds and

Bedrooms, 1890–1930," in *American Home Life, 1880–1930*, edited by Jessica H. Foy and Thomas J. Schlereth (Knoxville: University of Tennessee Press, 1992), 120–161.

32. Abigail A. Van Slyck, *"Kid Size: The Material World of Childhood*: An Exhibition Review," *Winterthur Portfolio* 39.1 (2004): 72–73. Also see Alexander von Vegesak, Jutta Oldiges, and Lucy Bullivant, eds., *Kid Size: The Material World of Childhood* (Milan: Skira editore, and Weil am Rhein: Vitra Design Museum, 1997).

33. Helga Zeiher, "Children's Islands in Space and Time: The Impact of Spatial Differentiation on Children's Ways of Shaping Social Life," in *Childhood in Europe*, edited by M. du Bois-Reymond, Heinz Sünker, and Heinz-Hermann Krüger (New York: Peter Lang, 2001), 139–160; Helga Zeiher and Hartmut Zeiher, *Orte und Zeilen der Kinder: Soziale Leben im Alltag von Grossstadtkindern* (Weinheim/Munich: Juventa, 1991).

34. Jens Qvortrup, *Childhood as a Social Phenomenon: An Introduction to a Series of National Reports* (Esbjerg: Sydjysk Universitetscenter, 1990); Jens Qvortrup and M. Sgritta, eds., *Childhood Matters: Social Theory, Practice, Politics* (Aldershot: Avebury, 1994).

35. Sharon Stephens, "Nationalism, Nuclear Policy and Children in Cold War America," *Childhood* 4.1 (1997): 110, citing John Holt, *Escape from Childhood* (Harmondsworth: Penguin Books, 1975), 22–23.

36. Stephens, "Nationalism, Nuclear Policy and Children in Cold War America," 113. Also see Amy F. Ogata, "Designing Education in Postwar American Schools," paper presented at the European Social Science History Conference, Amsterdam, 2006.

37. Stephens, "Nationalism, Nuclear Policy and Children in Cold War America," 121.

38. Ning de Coninck-Smith, "Ej Blot Til Lyst. Refleksioner over Dansk Byggeri Til Born Gennem 250 År [Not for Fun: Reflections on Children's Buildings in Denmark over the Past 250 Years]," in *Arkitektur, Krop, Pædagogik* [*Architecture, Body, and Education*], edited by K. Larsen (København: Hans Reitzels Forlag, 2005), 69–88; Ning de Coninck-Smith and Bengt Sandin, "Social Welfare: Comparative Twentieth-Century Developments," in *Encyclopedia of Children and Childhood in History and Society*, edited by Paula S. Fass (New York: Macmillan Reference, 2004), 767–770; John R. Gillis, "A World of Their Own Making: Families and the Modern Culture of Aging," in *Childhood and Old Age*, edited by J. Povlsen, S. Mellemgaard, and N. de Coninck-Smith (Odense: Odense University Press, 1999), 109–124; Jan Kampman, ed., *Beyond the Competent Child* (Roskilde: Roskilde University Press, 2004).

39. Gary Cross, *The Cute and the Cool: Wondrous Innocence and Modern American Children's Culture* (New York: Oxford University Press, 2004).

40. Cindi Katz, "Power, Space, and Terror: Social Reproduction and the Public Environment," in *The Politics of Public Space*, edited by Setha Low and Neil Smith (New York: Routledge, 2006), 105–121.

41. Paula S. Fass, "Children in Global Migrations," *Journal of Social History* 38.4 (2005): 937–953.

42. John Gillis, *Islands of the Mind: How the Human Imagination Created the Atlantic World* (New York: Palgrave/Macmillan, 2004).

43. Also see Jean-Louis Flandrin, *Familles: Parenté, maison, sexualité, dans l'ancienne société* (Paris: Editions du Seuil, 1976), 213–229. Also see Rima Apple, *Mothers and Medicine: A Social History of Infant Feeding, 1890–1950* (Madison: University of Wisconsin Press, 1987); Julia Grant, *Raising Baby by the Book: The Education of American Mothers* (New Haven: Yale University Press, 1998).

44. The title of this section is borrowed from Betty Eggermont, "The Choreography of Schooling as a Site of Struggle: Belgian Primary Schools, 1880–1940," *History of Education* 30.2 (2001): 129–140. See also Michel Foucault, *Discipline and Punish: The Birth of the Prison*, translated by Alan Sheridan (New York: Vintage Books, 1975); Michel Foucault, "Governmentality," in *The Foucault Effect: Studies in Governmentality*, edited by Graham Burchell, Colin Gordon, and Peter Miller (Chicago: University of Chicago Press, 1991), 87–104. Also see "Containing the School Child: Architectures and Pedagogies (Double Special Issue)," *Paedagogica Historica* 41.4/5 (2005).

45. Nicholas Bullock, "Reconstruction, School Building, and the Avant-Garde," paper presented at the Team 10—Between Modernity and the Everyday, Faculty of Architecture, TU Delft, June 5–6, 2003; Châtelet, Lerch, and Luc, eds., *Open-Air Schools*; Andrew Saint, *Towards a Social Architecture: The Role of School-Building in Post-War England* (New Haven: Yale University Press, 1987).

46. Gutman, "Entre moyens de fortune et constructions spécifiques"; Roy Kozlovsky, "Reconstruction through the Child: English Modernism and the Welfare State," Ph.D. dissertation, Princeton University, forthcoming; Ken Worpole, *Here Comes the Sun: Architecture and Public Space in Twentieth-Century European Culture* (London: Reaktion Books, 2000).

47. For example, Ning de Coninck-Smith, "The Panopticon of Childhood: Harold E. Jones Child Study Center, Berkeley, California, 1946–1960," *Paedagogica Historica* 41.4/5 (2005): 495–506; Thomas A. Markus, *Buildings and Power: Freedom and Control in the Origin of Modern Building Types* (London: Routledge, 1993); Stoler, "A Sentimental Education"; Dell Upton, "Lancasterian Schools, Republican Citizenship, and the Spatial Imagination in Early Nineteenth-Century America," *Journal of the Society of Architectural Historians* 55.3 (1996): 238–253.

48. Martin Lawn and Ian Grosvenor, "Imagining a Project: Networks, Discourses, and Spaces: Toward a New Archaeology of Urban Education," *Paedagogica Historica* 35.2 (1999): 381–393; Martin Lawn and Ian Grosvenor, eds., *Materialities of Schooling: Design, Technology, Objects, Routines* (London: Symposium Books, 2005).

49. Ronny Ambjörnsson, "Key, Ellen (1849–1926)," in *Encyclopedia of Children and Childhood in History and Society*, edited by Paula S. Fass (New York: Macmillan Reference, 2004): 522–523; Denise Hagströmer, "A 'Child's Century' at Last?," in *Kid Size: The Material World of Childhood*, edited by Alexander von Vegesak, Jutta Oldiges, and Lucy Bullivant (Milan: Skira editore, and Weil am Rhein: Vitra Design Museum, 1997), 183–195. Also see Cunningham, *Children and Childhood*, 171–172.

50. For example, see Cavallo, *Muscles and Morals*; Gagen, "Play the Part: Performing Gender in America's Playgrounds."

51. For houses, schools and streets, see Davin, *Growing up Poor*; Hoffschwelle, *Rebuilding the Rural Southern Community*.

52. Calvert, *Children in the House: The Material Culture of Early Childhood, 1600–1900*, with the principal focus being clothing and toys used by (and to identify) children before the twentieth century. Also see Anthony Burton, *Children's Pleasures: Toys and Games from the Bethnal Green Museum of Childhood* (London: V & A Publications, 1996); Vegesak, Oldiges, and Bullivant, eds., *Kid Size*.

53. Cross, *Kid's Stuff* is an excellent example; toys, consumption, and changing notions of American childhood are discussed, although not in relationship to children's spaces. Also see Miriam Forman-Brunell, *Made to Play House: Dolls and the Commercialization of American Girlhood, 1830–1930* (New Haven: Yale University Press, 1993).

54. Christensen and O'Brien, eds., *Children in the City*; Holloway and Valentine, eds., *Children's Geographies*; Olwig and Gulløv, eds., *Children's Places*; Skelton and Valentine, eds., *Cool Places*. Also see the journal *Children's Geographies*.

55. In addition to works cited above (by Aries, Cunningham, and Gillis), see Daniel Miller, *Material Cultures: Why Some Things Matter* (Chicago: University of Chicago Press, 1998); Daniel Miller, "Materiality: An Introduction," in *Materiality*, edited by Miller (Durham: Duke University Press, 2005): 1–50.

Child Saving and the Design of Modern Childhoods

1

Connecting with the Landscape

Campfires and Youth Culture
at American Summer Camps, 1890–1950

ABIGAIL A. VAN SLYCK

We are all so fond of council fire that we can't express it in words.

–Barbara Fuller, "Council Fire"

When young Barbara Fuller wrote these words for the pages of her camp newspaper in 1936, she was referring specifically to the campfires that she and her fellow campers—all girls between the ages of five and twelve—had experienced that summer at Hilloway-on-Ten-Mile-Lake, in Hackensack, Minnesota. Yet she could well have been speaking for generations of children who had attended (or would go on to attend) one of the hundreds of overnight camps that had sprung up in the North American landscape since 1890. An evening ritual in which campers and camp staff assembled around an open flame to sing songs, perform skits, tell stories, and listen to serious talks, the campfire was designed to build campwide camaraderie, provide an outlet for intercabin rivalries, and foster individual introspection. It was, in short, the symbolic heart of the summer camp experience.[1]

Aimed at removing children from the family home for a period that ranged from a few days to eight weeks or more, summer camps fit firmly within the larger cultural trend examined throughout this volume: the modern tendency to create a wide range of spaces devoted exclusively to the use of children. As John Gillis notes in the last chapter, this "islanding" of children is a complex phenomenon. Often explained as a way of protecting children from real and apparent danger, it can also be seen as a means of providing anxious adults with visible reassurance that childhood itself—its boundaries blurred by global capitalism's restructuring of time and space—continues to exist.[2]

A close consideration of the cultural landscape of summer camps deepens our understanding of this phenomenon in several important ways. First, it reminds us that anxieties about the disappearance of childhood date back at least to the end of the nineteenth century. Psychologist G. Stanley Hall—whose ideas inspired many early camp organizers—gave these worries scientific credence with his recapitulation theory. Positing that each human being repeated (or "recapitulated") the evolution of the species, he saw children quite literally as savages who were best served when allowed to develop naturally and gradually into a state of civilization. Implicit in this theory was the fear that childhood itself was under threat, especially in genteel households where children were encouraged to adopt civilized behavior at too early an age.[3] Not only did Hall call into question the Victorian conviction that the private family home was the best setting for child rearing, but his theories also confirm what many scholars now believe: that childhood has always been an unstable concept, even during the Victorian era once enshrined in the scholarly literature as a sort of Golden Age of childhood.[4]

Second, the study of summer camps demonstrates the extent to which the islanding of children has been fraught with concerns about gender, particularly with anxieties about the role of women as primary caregivers. Hall, for instance, was chiefly interested in the psychological health of boys and laid the blame for their developmental derailment squarely on female shoulders. As he wrote in 1908, "the callow fledging in the pin-feather stage of the earliest 'teens whom the lady teacher and the fond mother can truly call a perfect gentleman has something the matter with him."[5] Informed by such views, nineteenth-century summer camps catered exclusively to boys, removing them from comfortable, feminized homes and immersing them in rustic, all-male environments. Even when private girls' camps were instituted in the early twentieth century, they embraced the opportunity to reform gender roles; rather than reproducing modes of femininity familiar in Victorian homes, these institutions encouraged campers to develop into capable and fun-loving women who would help raise the next generation of vigorous men.

Finally, a systematic look at summer camps calls attention to the fact that islanding often has a temporal aspect as well as a spatial one. As we will see, the goal of camps was not just to remove youngsters from the spaces that adults occupied but also to distance children from the modern moment, taking them back in time to the primitive past, or even extracting them entirely from the march of history in order to cocoon them in an ahistorical, antediluvian natural state. These differences highlight one other point: although islanding is an overarching theme in the construction of modern childhood, there are nonetheless significant historical variations, even among childhood settings designed to serve similar functions. At summer camps (as in the schools, parks, and hospitals discussed elsewhere in this volume), adults made and remade the cultural landscape as they continued to refine their design of modern childhood.

In order to investigate both these historical changes in the camp landscape and their relationship to gender anxieties and concerns about the nature of childhood itself, this chapter will look closely at three different episodes in the history of American summer camps: the campfire at early twentieth-century camps sponsored by the Young Men's Christian Association (YMCA) and its role in reforming Victorian gender roles; the Indian council ring popularized by Ernest Thompson Seton between the First and Second World Wars and its role in reinforcing white privilege in gender-appropriate ways; and the de-Indianized campfire circle of the postwar period and its role in insulating children from the adult world. In each case, a close reading of the campfire's material trappings will confirm the extent to which adults used the cultural landscape in an attempt to shape the behaviors and attitudes of campers, while a consideration of campers' views—recorded both at the time and in retrospect—will demonstrate the degree to which adults were successful in their attempts.

Modeling Christian Manliness at the Early YMCA Campfire

Although the earliest camps had been founded in the 1880s to serve the sons of elite families, the YMCA began to extend the camping experience to middle-class boys in the 1890s, launching a camp-building boom that resulted in the establishment of 178 camps by 1905. Explicitly intended to foster Christian conversion, these early YMCA camps also implicitly aimed at intervening in Victorian gender roles. In addition to extracting boys from their mother-centered homes, these camps sought to introduce young campers to muscular Christianity, a new mode of manhood that melded masculinity (a new term in the late nineteenth century) and religious sentiment (reclaimed from the feminine sphere).[6]

Campfire rituals were central to these goals. Yet camp leaders devoted little attention to describing the physical arrangement of the evening campfire, presumably because middle-class Americans were already quite familiar with the concept. Indeed, in the last half of the nineteenth century, images and descriptions of many kinds of campfires were widespread, whether in Winslow Homer's Civil War depictions of military campfires, many of which appeared as engravings published in mass-circulation periodicals like *Harper's Weekly*; images of sportsmen's campfires in the Adirondacks, produced by artists such as Arthur Fitzwilliam Tait, and reproduced in engravings by Currier and Ives in the 1850s and 1860s (Figure 1.1); literary descriptions of Indian campfires in the novels of James Fennimore Cooper or the poetry of Rudyard Kipling; or even in bonfires that became a ritual of American collegiate life at the end of the nineteenth century.[7]

Early published advice suggests that camp leaders had many, if not all, of these sources in mind when they built fires at camp. Henry W. Gibson drew upon his experience as director of YMCA Camp Becket in western Massachusetts when he described campfires in *Camping for Boys*, a 1911 book that served as the Bible of the early camping movement both within the YMCA and beyond. According to Gibson, camp leaders should introduce a wide range of campfire stories into the evening ritual: "Indian legends, war stories, ghost stories, detective stories, stories of heroism, the history of fire, a talk about the stars." The music he suggested was equally varied, ranging from "college songs [that] always appeal to

FIGURE 1.1 *Camping in the Woods: "A Good Time Coming,"* Currier and Ives lithograph, after a painting by A. F. Tait, 1863.

Courtesy of the Adirondack Museum, Blue Mountain Lake, New York.

boys" to ballads like "My Old Kentucky Home." Even his firemaking advice embraced both the Indian method of rubbing two sticks together and the more modern technique of using a match to light kindling doused in kerosene.[8] In short, early camp leaders were free to evoke several types of campfires.

Having declined to fix the symbolic meaning of the campfire by specifying any single source, early camp leaders were equally free to use the evening program to highlight aspects of the camp experience they found most significant. Thus, in early YMCA camps, the campfire was deployed to aid in the process of religious conversion. *Association Boys*, a YMCA journal established in 1902, served as a clearing house for the most effective campfire strategies, and by 1905, YMCA campfires followed a similar progression: popular songs were followed by patriotic songs and then a few hymns. Finally "when the right time . . . arrived," according to one account, "the leader or an assistant step[ped] forward, and in the beautiful silence of the night, deliver[ed] a short, pointed, religious talk."[9] Built into this program was a gradual transition from the boisterous activity of the day to a quieter moment of introspection. At the same time, because the choice of the particular songs emerged from the boys themselves, the campfire retained an air of spontaneity that may have allowed campers to see it as an event they had initiated.

Even in the early period, the fire itself was an important prop in the evening program. At Camp Tuxis in Connecticut, one Sunday evening campfire ended with the leader's observation that camp kindles a fire in the heart of each boy that he carries back to the city to light other hearts. At the close of the campfire, "Each boy was then handed a candle and long line was formed from the top of the hill to the cottage." The light was passed from boy to boy until "finally the light was passed into the dark parlor of the cottage and boys filed in one by one and took their places in a semi-circle around the fire place . . . As the leader resumed his talk he leaned over and touched the long flame to the material in the fire place, and in a moment the entire room was beautifully illuminated. As the talk proceeded and the fire died down, the intensity of feeling deepened and the testimonies given must have gladdened the very host of heaven."[10] In addition to contributing to the event's aesthetic component, fire was integral to its religious content as well.

The passing of the sacred light from the campfire to the parlor fireplace is particularly telling in that it upsets Victorian formulations of the relationship between gender, piety, and the domestic setting. Rather than suggesting that religious sentiment emanated from the woman seated at the domestic hearth (as Victorians had done), this ritual situated the origins of religious feeling in the wilder parts of nature, and placed responsibility for bringing piety into the home in male hands. Indeed, we see here one example of a much larger fin-de-siècle tendency to reverse what Ann Douglas has dubbed "the feminization of American culture," which had begun in the first half of the nineteenth century.[11]

Tapping Primitive Authenticity at the Indian Council Ring

In the interwar period, both the form and the meaning of the campfire changed dramatically, as many camps began to build permanent campfire rings and to associate them specifically with Indian culture. The intellectual background for this change had begun earlier in the century with thinkers such as nature writer Ernest Thompson Seton; in 1902 he founded the Woodcraft Indians, an early forerunner of the Boy Scouts, which celebrated Native American culture as a model of simplicity, nobility, and respect for the environment. As Seton explained in his 1912 work, *The Book of Woodcraft*, the campfire was closely associated with the very emergence of Man. According to Seton, "When first the brutal anthropoid stood up and walked erect—was man, the great event was symbolized and marked by the lighting of the first campfire. For millions of years our race has seen in this blessed fire, the means and emblem of light, warmth, protection, friendly gathering, council."[12]

Although his language was deeply informed by evolutionary theory, Seton rejected Darwinian notions of early man as inherently competitive. In fact, like Hall and other of his antimodernist contemporaries, Seton valued the campfire for its ability to connect boys with a harmonious primitive past. As he went on to write, "Only the ancient sacred fire of wood has power to touch and thrill the chords of primitive remembrance. When men sit together at the campfire they seem to shed all modern form and poise, and hark back to the primitive—to meet as man to man—to show the naked soul." For Seton, then, the campfire was the portal to premodern authenticity.

In order to unlock the magic of the campfire, Seton paid close attention to its material manifestations, including the method used for lighting the fire itself. Well known for his mastery of the Indian technique of making fire by rubbing two sticks together, Seton even claimed to have set the world's record by starting a fire in this manner in thirty-one seconds. In *The Book of Woodcraft*, he provided detailed step-by-step instructions, so that every boy could follow his example. Seton also specified the use of a neat stack of horizontal logs in order to achieve a fire that was easy to start and that gave a steady, bright light with little heat; he objected vehemently to the high pyramid used in bonfires, as it "goes off like a flash, roasts everyone, and then goes dead."[13]

The Book of Woodcraft also provided Seton's specifications for building a "council-fire circle," the term he used to signify an Indian fire ring. The form is one that Seton himself had used earlier in the century on his estate at Cos Cob, Connecticut, where he ran short-term camps for members of the Woodcraft Indians, one of which was photographed in 1908 (Figure 1.2).[14] As described in 1912, it was to be "a perfectly level circle twenty-four feet across . . . [with] a permanently fixed circle of very low seats," eight inches high with low backs, and additional rings of progressively higher seats in sufficient numbers to provide a fixed seat for each person in camp.

FIGURE 1.2 Council and War Dance at Wyndygoul, Cos Cob, Connecticut, 1908.
Prints and Photographs Division, Library of Congress.

Beyond these basics, Seton emphasized three qualities that accorded with his own view of Indian culture. The first was orderliness, evident not only in the precise measurements but also in Seton's admonition that "the place should be carefully leveled and prepared, and kept always in order, for it will be used several times each day, either for councils or for games, dances, and performances."[15] Second, Seton emphasized the council ring's community orientation, noting that each band or clan in camp should make its own seat, fitted out with two loops of wire to allow them to display their standard. Finally, Seton's council ring was acutely hierarchical, including a throne for the chief to be positioned "at one side of the ring in a conspicuous place" with totem poles placed opposite.

Both the term *council ring* and the form advocated by Seton became widespread at North American summer camps after World War I, thanks in large part to Seton himself, who maintained a grueling travel schedule for several summers, as he went from camp to camp teaching Indian lore, bestowing Indian names on sympathetic leaders, laying out council rings, and fashioning the ritual elements to be used during Indianized council ring ceremonies. For Seton, who advocated adopting "the best things from the best Indians," authenticity was not a priority. On a 1915 visit to Camp Greenkill (near Kingston-on-Hudson, New York), for instance, he made a so-called Indian drum from a lardpail and a calfskin. Nonetheless, a charismatic personality helped secure Seton's reputation as an expert on all aspects of Indian life.[16]

By the 1920s, Seton's impact on the form of campfire circles was widespread. In 1927, the Boy Scouts of America published *Camp Site Development Plans*, which included a hypothetical layout for a divisional camp, in which each division would focus on themed activities. The Indian group included a simplified but clearly labeled council ring. The same publication featured the plan of Camp Siwanoy in Dutchess County, New York, where even a schematic depiction suggested Seton's influence by hinting at logs stacked in the approved manner and a rudimentary ritual axis created by the entrance. Camp Mishawaka, a private boys' camp near Grand Rapids, Minnesota, featured a campfire ring near the center of campus in the late 1920s, and in the early 1930s, had erected tipis for the "big chiefs," campers who lead the camp athletic teams, the Chippewa and the Sioux (Figure 1.3). Although by this time they had also adopted Seton's term, council ring, the conical arrangement of the firewood suggests that they had forgotten some of the fire-making lessons he sought to instill.

The form of the campfire circle was becoming somewhat standardized in the interwar period, but its symbolic meaning was still open to debate. Issues of gender were particularly important, as camp supporters and interpreters of Indian life understood themselves as deeply involved in the ongoing cultural project of reforming manliness. Seton, for instance, explained the program for the Woodcraft Indians in the following terms: "Realizing that *manhood, not scholarship*, is the first aim of education, we have sought out those pursuits which develop the finest character, the finest physique, and . . . which in a word, *make for manhood*."[17]

FIGURE 1.3 Council Ring, Camp Mishawaka, Grand Rapids, Minnesota, c. 1933.
Courtesy of Camp Mishawaka.

Two years later, Charles A. Eastman (Ohiyesa)—himself a highly assimilated Santee Sioux raised by traditional Dakota people and then educated at Dartmouth and Boston University medical school—also emphasized what he saw as the natural connection between the campfire and manhood. In his 1914 book, *Indian Scout Talks: A Guide for Boy Scouts and Camp Fire Girls*, Eastman wrote: "As fire is the symbol of enthusiasm, energy, and devotion, and is with the Indians a strictly masculine emblem, it is fit that the young men gather about it before going upon a journey or 'war-path.' " Whereas Eastman encouraged Boy Scouts to participate in evening ceremonies centered on the fire, his version of "The Maiden's Feast" was a noontime ritual focused on "the 'Sacred Stone,' a rudely heart-shaped or pyramidal boulder, which has been touched lightly with red paint."[18] In Eastman's view at least, playing with fire at night was a male prerogative.

This interpretation of the campfire as inherently masculine was contested by Luther Halsey Gulick and Charlotte Gulick. Friends and admirers of Seton's, the Gulicks took the campfire as the chief symbol of the Camp Fire Girls, a national organization they launched in 1910, using programming ideas they had developed earlier at their own camp, Wohelo, in Maine.[19] Both campers' memories and period photographs make it clear that the weekly council ring—with its associations of community spirit—was a central component of camp life (Figure 1.4). According to Lydia Bush Brown (who had first camped at Wohelo in 1913), the program of each council ring followed a similar pattern.

Silently we filed up to the tennis court, our moccasined feet making no noise in the twilight woods. There we swung out in a great circle and sat

FIGURE 1.4 Council Fire, Camp Wohelo, Sebago Lake, Maine, c. 1915.
Courtesy of Wohelo—The Luther Gulick Camps.

cross-legged singly softy "Rolling, rolling, rolling, Keep the fire sticks quickly rolling, rolling," while Hiiteni [as Charlotte Gulick was known at camp] bent over the rubbing sticks. On dry, clear evenings how quickly the spark came, but when mist rose from the lake into trees about us, it was a long time before Hiiteni stopped and carefully fed the spark with the fragrant wood-dust. Sometimes she would blow it into flame, sometimes call on one of us to blow it and light the fire. Then came "Burn, fire, burn" [a Wohelo song written by Florence Converse in 1912] and then—one never knew what, for Hiiteni had some new thing planned each week. . . . Even the ceremonial was not always in the same place. It could be in the Indian tepee, or some other place in the woods. I shall never forget the time I became fire-maker. We sat in a little clearing in the woods purple with pine needles, and dark with their branches meeting overhead. Hiiteni gave me a fire-set for my own. I can see her now at that ceremony.

Written fifteen years after her first summer at camp, Brown's vivid description suggests the importance of such council fires in the life of Wohelo.[20]

Although the Gulicks freely acknowledged Seton's impact on this element of the camp program and especially in teaching them the Indian method of making fire, Wohelo council fires differed from those of the Woodcraft Indians in important ways. For one thing, the Gulicks themselves interpreted the Wohelo council fire not as the blaze at the center of a war dance but rather as the flame of the domestic hearth and a reminder that (in Luther Gulick's words) "the bearing and rearing of children has always been the first duty of most women, and that must always continue to be." (They conveniently ignored the fact that child-rearing responsibilities were not universally associated with women among Native American tribes.)[21]

Likewise, the material trappings of the council circle were also quite different. With its rock throne and permanent seating assigned by tribe, Seton's council ring used the material world to reinforce his own ideal of organizational hierarchy. In contrast, Wohelo eschewed permanent council ring fixtures and used the human ring of seated campers to demarcate the special space. The difference is significant, for not only did it allow Hiiteni to change the location of the council ring with ease—and thus heighten the memorable quality of what might otherwise have become a routine occurrence—but it also emphasized the inclusive nature of the event. Rather than fixing campers in their ranks around the council ring, the Wohelo council ring allowed Hiiteni to share the firemaking honors with campers and gently to expand the circle of insiders. No more authentic than what took place at Wyndygoul, this was a distinctly non-hierarchical performance of council ring activities.

These gendered interpretations of the campfire coexisted throughout the interwar period, and may have had some impact on council ring locations. In boys' camps, for instance, there was a tendency to situate the council ring in clear view, as we have already seen at Camp Mishawaka. At Camp Wigwam, a boys' camp in Harrison, Maine, three council rings were in use by 1930, two of which were in very visible locations: one on the edge of the camp's main clearing and the other near the middle of camp, on axis with the theater and a natural amphitheater, for ceremonials that involved the entire camp. The third was set near the nature museum and arts and crafts studio, useful adjuncts for the teaching of Indian lore at this council ring.

In contrast, council rings at girls' camps tended to be either hidden from view or divested of their hierarchical arrangements. At Camp Mary Day, a Girl Scout camp in the Boston area, the council bowl, as it was called, was on the margins of the camp grounds but close to the craft house, a location that may have suggested itself because of the heavy use of Indian-inspired crafts in council ring ceremonies (Figure 1.5). Brochures for Camp Alanita for Girls in northern Alabama hint at the distant location of the council ring used for "weekly 'pow-wows'" when they mention "memories of the trail up the hills at night, lighted only by the dancing flashlights."[22] In contrast, the preliminary layout for Camp Ojiketa, a Camp Fire Girl camp in Minnesota, included two campfire locations, each at the hub of a half-circle of camper cabins. While obviously visible from the main part of camp, they lacked the chief's throne or any other indication of a ritual axis, suggesting that these were less for ceremonial use and more for intimate gatherings.

In many ways, debates about the gendered meaning of the Indian campfire took the focus off its racial implications. As comparative literature scholar Shari Huhndorf has argued, antimodernist celebrations of Native American cultures

FIGURE 1.5 Site plan, Camp Mary Day, Natick, Massachusetts, c. 1925.
Courtesy of the Girl Scout Museum at Cedar Hill, Patriots' Trail Girl Scout Council.

did nothing to challenge European-American domination, and instead left "stereo-typed visions of Native life intact and the radically unequal relations between European American and Native American unquestioned." By encouraging campers to find their authentic selves by temporarily adopting Indian ways, summer camps encouraged white children to see themselves as rightful inheritors to North America, thus downplaying the violence involved in the conquest of Indian lands and erasing white responsibility for that violence. Individual campers may well have played Indian at the summer camp council ring with the best of intentions, but the Indian campfire nonetheless served to reinforce white privilege.[23]

Fostering the Natural Child at the Postwar Campfire Circle

By the end of the 1930s, camp-planning professionals had begun to strip the campfire circle of its Indian associations. This is particularly apparent in the influential three-volume work *Park and Recreation Structures*, published in 1938 to

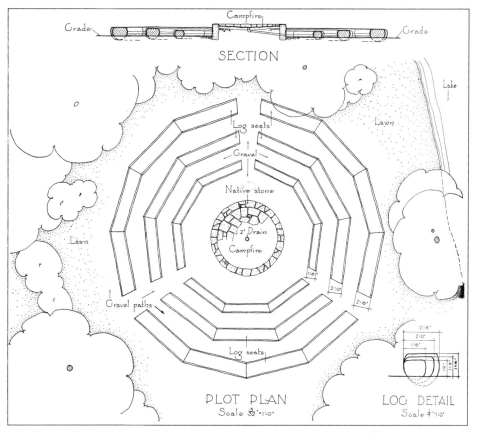

FIGURE 1.6 Campfire circle, Lassen Volcanic National Park, California, c. 1935.

From Albert H. Good, *Park and Recreation Structures*, vol. 2
(Washington, D.C.: National Park Service, 1938).

document and celebrate the achievements of the National Park Service, working under the aegis of the New Deal. Illustrated in the second volume was the campfire circle at Lassen Volcanic National Park in northern California, in a familiar arrangement of low log seats around a ring of stone for the fire (Figure 1.6). Although the forms were familiar from Seton's writings, the meanings attached to them were quite different. Not only was the term *council ring* de-emphasized, but the text itself also avoided any mention of Native American parallels. In fact, author Albert H. Good asserted that in planning the campfire circle "there are no fixed principles, no time-revered traditions to be pressed"; instead he encouraged camp planners to select "surroundings that suggest . . . the glories of Nature unmodified."[24] Construed as an extension of the natural environment, the campfire seemed devoid of previous cultural connections. Elsewhere in the publication were plans for organized camps, which showed the council ring banished to the edges of the camp landscape.

This de-Indianized campfire circle dominated the flood of camp-planning literature that emerged at the end of World War II. When the YMCA published *Layout, Building Designs, and Equipment for YMCA Camps* in 1946, it included a council ring modeled very closely on the National Park Service example, described as "an attractive setting for special ceremonial programs of the camp," without any allusion to Indian cultural practices. On the idealized camp layout included in the same publication, the council ring was located in the woods, out of sight from the rest of camp, divorced from the visible symbolic role it played in the interwar period (Figure 1.7). In *Camp Site Development*, a 1948 camp-planning manual prepared for the Girl Scouts, the council ring was included on the layout for a two-unit tent camp, but not in the masterplan for a larger camp. Nowhere did the text describe the specifications for a permanent campfire area. The council ring was entirely absent from *When You Plan Your Camp*, a 1946 Camp Fire Girl publication.[25]

The de-Indianizing of the campfire circle and the rest of the camp landscape is a complex phenomenon driven by multiple forces. Among them is the emergence of camp directing as a profession, which had a decisive impact on how camp leaders assessed their own effectiveness. Especially after the establishment of the American Camping Association in 1935, camp directors came to base their professional status on their quantifiable impact on campers (like improving posture and muscle tone, changes some camp directors documented in before-and-after photos) and less on intangible qualities of their own character (like a deep knowledge of Indian lore). Indeed, in the postwar period camp directors also signaled their professional aspirations by distinguishing themselves more self-consciously from campers. Early in the twentieth century, the head of the camp had been called a leader, someone who led the campers by example, showing them how to light a fire without matches, for instance. Forty years later, the head of the camp was a director, someone who directed the paid staff from an administration building connected to the dining lodge.

These changes had an impact on campfire activities themselves. Indian ceremonials enacted around the council ring had often been highly scripted performances, but ones in which campers played important roles. In the late 1930s, advice literature began to focus instead on elaborate campfire spectacles produced by the camp director for the amazement of campers. Henry W. Gibson, still a force in the summer camp movement, published *Recreational Programs for Summer Camps* in 1938. Although he briefly mentioned a rubbing-stick fire (albeit without any reference to Indian practices), he described in greater detail what he called a "fire from heaven," in which the campfire was to be lit from a flaming wad of kerosene-soaked burlap sent shooting down a wire stretched between the fire circle and a tree. Even more daring was the tunnel fire, in which kerosene-soaked burlap was pulled quickly by cable through a tunnel of boards in order to light the campfire in "a mysterious manner."[26] Far from involving the camper directly, these campfires depended for their effectiveness on the campers' ignorance of the preparations.

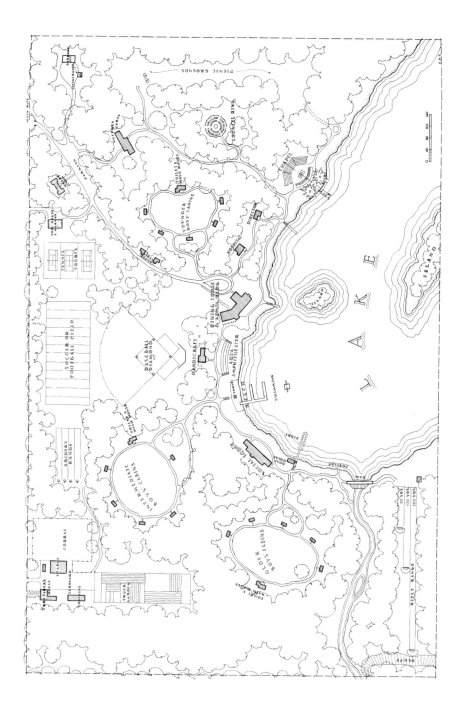

Campers' Perspectives on the Campfire

The question of how children experienced campfire events in the past is a difficult one to answer, given the dearth of campers' firsthand accounts of their daily activities. (Letters home are potentially rich resources, but in practice are frustratingly silent about the daily routines of camp, highlighting instead events that upset that routine.) We know, for instance, that campers were often directly involved in campfire activities, making up and performing their own skits, writing and singing their own songs. At Camp Ahmek (a private boys' camp in Ontario and one of the camps where Seton built a council ring), the weekly council ring centered on The Chief (as director Taylor Statten was known at camp). "This was 'his show,'" according to a recent camp history, and the general shape of the event "remained virtually unchanged down through the years." Yet within this well-established pattern, campers were allowed to arrange the details, with one camp section taking responsibility for the specific content of each week's council ring. But no records exist to tell us what meaning early Ahmek campers attached to their council ring activities.[27]

Certainly, there was room for campers to imbue these events with their own meaning. The boys who danced around the campfire at Wyndygoul, for instance, may have thought of themselves as enacting a ritual of community (as Seton saw it). But they might have also cast themselves in more violent, but equally Romantic, roles as bloodthirsty savages—a version of Indianness that would have been familiar to them from Buffalo Bill Cody's Wild West Shows or from camp games like White Man and Indian (described in Gibson's *Camping for Boys* as a "battle royal" between one team representing "white people . . . traveling over the prairie," and the other the Indians who attempt to capture the whites after they lie down to sleep for the night).[28]

Adult reports of camper behavior can also be read as evidence that youngsters had their own ideas about the character of the campfire. In the fall of 1927, for instance, Miss Ray Mitchell reported to the New York headquarters of the Girl Scouts on a weekend camp she had organized for rural girls from Virginia. From Mitchell's point of view, "the first camp fire was terrible" because the girls' "idea of a camp fire consisted of poor jokes and ukuleles." It is not clear whether the leader objected more to the low-brow tone of the girls' contributions or to the introduction of instruments and music that celebrated modern vigor instead of timeless spirituality; she may not have been able to disentangle the two sins. Diagnosing the root of the problem as rural ignorance, Mitchell provided her charges with copies of *The American Girl* (a Girl Scout periodical she evidently

FIGURE 1.7 (*opposite*) Layout for a YMCA camp with a capacity of 125.
From *Layout, Building Designs, and Equipment for Y.M.C.A. Camps*, 1946.
Courtesy of YMCA of the USA and Kautz Family Archives,
Andersen Library, University of Minnesota.

brought with her to camp) and was delighted with their improvement. "Sunday night camp fire was lovely," she reported. "We learned songs and told Bible stories." In Mitchell's own eyes, her lessons on the right way to camp were a success with the girls. "They asked me if it were possible for me to come back and take them camping again next year."[29]

If Mitchell's report documents one incidence of campers interpreting the campfire very differently from their leader, it also confirms the extent to which adults attempted to maintain their control of the event's form and meaning. Indeed, this is borne out by the few firsthand accounts written by campers. When young Betty Ann Webster described a 1934 council fire at Hillaway-on-Ten-Mile-Lake, her consistent use of the passive voice ("When we were taken to our first council fire this year, we were led to an entirely new place") suggests that campers had little opportunity to initiate or direct council ring activities.[30] Likewise, Lydia Bush Brown's fond remembrances of Wohelo council fires make it clear that campers participated in the fire-making ceremony only at Hiiteni's explicit invitation.

Yet each of these accounts—Mitchell's report, Webster's story for her camp newspaper, Brown's memories written some fifteen years after the fact—can also be read as evidence that campers often adopted the respectful, reflective, pious attitudes their leaders expected of them at the campfire. Barbara Fuller's comments quoted at the start of this chapter are another case in point. At a superficial level, her words offer one explanation of why campers' commentaries on the campfire are so rare. Yet, by hinting at the depth of feeling that the campfire triggered in Fuller and her peers, her comment also provides evidence that many Hillaway campers accepted the evening ritual as a deeply meaningful shared experience that helped forge bonds among them and between them and the place. While hardly conclusive, the evidence suggests that campers—particularly the ones who loved camp enough to become the kind of seasoned campers whom historians seek out for comment—experienced the campfire much as their leaders expected them to do.

The Lessons of the Campfire

Notwithstanding Ernest Thompson Seton's assertion that the meaning of the campfire has held steady since the ascent of Man millions of year ago, the campfires built at American summer camps changed dramatically in form and meaning in the first half of the twentieth century. At the turn of the century, these evening events were somewhat flexible, both in terms of where they were held and metaphors they embraced. Recalling both historical and contemporary modes of masculinity, campfires invited boys to see themselves as soldiers, as Indians, as sportsmen, as college football heroes—and at YMCA camps to use those roles to reclaim religion from the female sphere. In the interwar period, the material trappings of the campfire evoked a much narrower range of symbols. Not only were the sites permanently fixed and the forms more likely to adhere to a standard lay-out, but the meanings of these forms were also now firmly associated with Native American culture. Boys and girls were encouraged to use the campfire to step back in time to a more primitive state of being, to reconnect with an authentic self that was not necessarily accessible through conventional religion. By the post-war period, the campfire had been stripped of its Indian associations and relocated to a secluded spot where campers could imagine themselves in a completely natural state, without reference to any particular temporal framework.

Ultimately, this history of the summer camp campfire offers two lessons to scholars concerned with the design of modern childhood. First, it helps pinpoint the late 1930s as a time of significant change in thinking about how the built environment might support the process of child development. Earlier in the twentieth century, the campfire had been shaped by antimodernist convictions that the modern world was harmful to children who needed (Hall and others argued) the opportunity to develop in a premodern setting. Only in the late 1930s did advice literature strip the campfire of its antimodernist associations and begin to position summer camps as modern environments in their own right. Indeed, despite their rustic forms, mid-century summer camps adopted many trappings of the modern world, particularly the use of professional expertise (on the part of camp directors, camp planners, and park administrators) to manufacture the sort of wilderness setting that other professionals (like child psychologists) had identified as conducive to the development of healthy, well-adjusted children.

Second, this history alerts us to some of the methodological difficulties of interpreting child-centered environments, among them the fact that form and meaning are not always linked in consistent ways. The formal differences between the Woodcraft council ring of the interwar period and the de-Indianized council ring of the late 1930s and 1940s were small indeed. Yet the meanings attached to them were significant. Formal analysis alone is not enough to understand these settings in all their complexity. Although the tendency with summer camps and other child-centered spaces is to supplement formal analysis with recollections of our own encounters with similar environments, such an anachronistic process can be deeply flawed. Accepting that our own childhood experiences are not universal may be the biggest challenge to understanding the design of modern childhood.

NOTES

1. For the history of other aspects of the summer camp landscape, see Abigail A. Van Slyck, *A Manufactured Wilderness: Summer Camps and the Shaping of American Youth, 1890–1960* (Minneapolis: University of Minnesota Press, 2006); Abigail A. Van Slyck, "Kitchen Technologies and Mealtime Rituals: Interpreting the Food Axis at American Summer Camps, 1890–1950," *Technology and Culture* 43.4 (2002): 668–692, and Abigail A. Van Slyck, "Housing the Happy Camper," *Minnesota History* 58.2 (2002): 68–83.

2. Elsewhere I have argued that such concerns may also account for the current popularity of museum exhibitions focused on the material culture of childhood. Abigail A. Van Slyck,

"*Kid Size: The Material World of Childhood*: An Exhibition Review," *Winterthur Portfolio* 39.1 (2004): 69–77.

3. Hall is also credited with coining the term "adolescence," the title of his best-known work, *Adolescence: Its Psychology and Its Relations to Physiology, Anthropology, Sociology, Sex, Crime, Religion and Education*, 2 vols. (New York, 1904). Dorothy Ross, *G. Stanley Hall: The Psychologist as Prophet* (Chicago: University of Chicago Press, 1972); Gail Bederman, *Manliness and Civilization: A Cultural History of Gender and Race in the United States, 1880–1917* (Chicago: University of Chicago Press, 1995), chapter 3.

4. The idea of the Victorian era as a Golden Age of childhood is implicit in many books on middle-class domesticity, especially those that rely on advertisements and prescriptive literature featuring doting mothers and their angelic offspring. See, for example, Harvey Green, *The Light of the Home: An Intimate View of the Lives of Women in Victorian America* (New York: Pantheon Books, 1983). The counterpoint to this view has come from historians (such as Anna Davin) who focus on the lived experience of children. Anna Davin, *Growing up Poor: Home, School and Street in London 1870–1914* (London: Rivers Oram Press; Concord, Mass.: Paul and Company, 1996).

5. G. Stanley Hall, "Feminization in School and Home," *World's Work* 16 (May 1908): 10240.

6. The term "muscular Christianity" was first introduced in England in the 1850s to describe the fiction of Thomas Hughes and Charles Kingsley. It became widespread in the last decades of the nineteenth century when "droves of Protestant Ministers in England and America concluded that men were not truly Christians unless they were healthy and 'manly.'" Clifford Putney, *Muscular Christianity: Manhood and Sports in Protestant America, 1880–1920* (Cambridge: Harvard University Press, 2001), I, II. According to historian Gail Bederman, "masculinity" was a term used to distinguish a new mode of manhood—associated with physical strength and aggressive behavior—from "manliness," the Victorian ideal that had emphasized high-minded self-restraint. Bederman, *Manliness and Civilization*, 16–23.

7. For Homer's Civil War engravings, see Lloyd Goodrich, *The Graphic Art of Winslow Homer* (New York: Museum of Graphic Art; Washington, D.C.: Smithsonian Institution Press, 1968), and Philip C. Beam, *Winslow Homer's Magazine Engravings* (New York: Harper and Row, 1979). For images of sportsmen's fires in the Adirondacks, see Georgia B. Barnhill, *Wild Impressions: The Adirondacks on Paper* (Blue Mountain Lake, N.Y.: Adirondack Museum; Boston: David Godine, 1995). Rudyard Kipling evoked the Indian campfire in "The Feet of the Young Men" (1897). For collegiate bonfires, see Helen Lefkowitz Horowitz, *Campus Life: Undergraduate Cultures from the End of the Eighteenth Century to the Present* (New York: Alfred A. Knopf, 1987).

8. Henry W. Gibson, *Camping for Boys* (New York: Association Press, 1911), 124–125.

9. Frank H. Streightoff, "Summer Camps," *Association Boys* 4 (June 1905): 133–134. The year before, another article described a very similar program held at Camp Tuxis in New York. Irving Cobleigh and Harvey L. Smith, "Some Interesting Things about Camp Tuxis," *Association Boys* 3 (June 1904): 122–123.

10. Cobleigh and Smith, "Some Interesting Things about Camp Tuxis."

11. Ann Douglas, *The Feminization of American Culture* (New York: Alfred A. Knopf, 1977).

12. Ernest Thompson Seton, *The Book of Woodcraft* (1912; reprint, Garden City, N.Y.: Garden City Publishing, 1921), 5.

13. Seton, *Book of Woodcraft*, 191.

14. Ernest Thompson Seton, *Trail of an Artist-Naturalist: The Autobiography of Ernest Thompson Seton* (New York: Charles Scribner's Sons, 1940), 376–385.

15. Seton, *Book of Woodcraft*, 183.

16. Seton's travels to camps are recorded in his diaries, especially in vols. 22–25. The lard-pail drum is mentioned in vol. 23: 42. Seton's diaries are preserved in the American Museum of Natural History in New York, although photocopies are also available in the Seton Memorial Library on the Philmont Scout Ranch in Cimarron, New Mexico.

17. Seton, *Book of Woodcraft*, 5. Emphasis in the original.

18. Charles A. Eastman, *Indian Scout Talks: A Guide for Boy Scouts and Camp Fire Girls* (1914; reprint, Boston: Little, Brown, 1920), 138, 147.

19. Quoted in Philip Deloria, *Playing Indian* (New Haven: Yale University Press, 1998), 113. For the early history of the Camp Fire Girls, see also Helen Buckler, Mary F. Fiedler, and Martha F. Allen, eds., *Wo-He-Lo: The Story of Camp Fire Girls* (New York: Holt, Rinehart and Winston, 1961), 3–49; and Charlotte Gulick Hewson, *Wohelo: Down through the Years* (South Casco, Maine: Wohelo Press, 2000).

20. Writing in 1928, Lydia Bush Brown is quoted in Hewson, *Wohelo Down through the Years*, 43.

21. Gulick is quoted in Buckler, Fiedler, and Allen, *Wo-He-Lo*, 22.

22. *Camp Alanita for Girls*, 1927 brochure, 17.

23. Shari M. Huhndorf, *Going Native: Indians in the American Cultural Imagination* (Ithaca: Cornell University Press, 2001), 4–5.

24. Albert H. Good, *Park and Recreation Structures* (Washington, D.C.: Department of the Interior, National Park Service, 1938), vol. 2: 197.

25. John A. Ledlie, ed., *Layout, Building Designs, and Equipment for Y.M.C.A. Camps* (New York: YMCA, 1946); Julian Harris Salomon, *Camp Site Development* (New York: Girl Scouts of the U.S.A., 1948); Camp Fire Girls, *When You Plan Your Camp* (New York: Camp Fire Girls, 1946).

26. H. W. Gibson, *Recreational Programs for Summer Camps* (New York: Greenberg, 1938), 5–6.

27. Liz Lundell, ed., *Fires of Friendship: Eighty Years of the Taylor Statten Camps* (Toronto: Fires of Friendship Books, 2000), 23–34.

28. Gibson, *Camping for Boys*, 217.

29. Minutes of the Girl Scouts of the U.S.A. Camp Committee, September 15, 1927, Girl Scout Archives.

30. Betty Ann Webster, "Ceremony at Council Fire Strengthens Hillaway Sprit," *Hillaway Wave* 6.1 (August 12, 1934): 6.

2

A (Better) Home Away from Home

The Emergence of Children's Hospitals in an Age of Women's Reform

DAVID C. SLOANE

Children were a special concern of women reformers in the Gilded Age and Progressive Era. Women were, as Mary Odem has written, "especially active in efforts that aimed to protect women, children, and the home from the harmful effects of rapid urban growth and industrial capitalism."[1] Poor children were at risk due to industrial accidents, epidemics, and the stress of simply surviving in crowded tenements and polluted cities. Daphne Spain has suggested that women "saved the city" by starting political coalitions, improving neighborhood environments, and fighting for protective legislation.[2] Among those reforms was the nationwide movement to establish pediatric wards and children's hospitals, intended as places of comfort and cure as well as moral and spiritual education for the "little sufferers" and their parents.[3]

The urban institutional safety net was minimal prior to the nineteenth-century child-saving enterprise.[4] In cities, charity dispensaries (clinics) with sparse facilities provided outpatient care, while almshouses, poorhouses, and general hospitals offered inpatient care. Adults and children in general hospitals were unsorted in the large wards, where ambulatory patients served as assistants to an overworked nursing staff. Between 1866 and 1869, up to 14 percent of patients at Massachusetts General Hospital were children, but the hospital did not have a separate pavilion or ward for them.[5] Physicians and reformers wondered whether such a hospital was a suitable place for a child.

After the first North American children's hospital was founded in Philadelphia in 1855, others gradually appeared in Chicago, Boston, Washington, St. Louis, Toronto, and additional cities primarily in eastern and midwestern states. By 1890, about thirty North American independent children's hospitals had opened.[6] Physicians organized some hospitals in an effort to buttress their claim to professional status and their specialty's importance in the emerging health care system. Orthopedic and maternity hospital founders argued that in their facilities patients would receive care from physicians trained to know the patient's needs. The French had used a similar justification for the establishment of Europe's first children's hospital in 1804, and the claim reverberated when Germans, Poles, Turks, and the British followed suit over the next half century.[7]

Some children's hospital advocates argued that children were being killed by the city and their parents' inability to protect them from its ravages. As one reformer argued about slum children: "The child has a right to a fair chance in life. If parents are delinquent in furnishing their children with this opportunity, it is the clear duty of the state to interfere."[8] Reformers criticized poor parents, chastised industrialists, organized private organizations, and reformed public institutions to ensure the safety and security of these most valuable members of society. They believed that the new institutions would better protect the children by inculcating them with middle-class values.

The new hospitals embodied the physicians' hope for increased status and the reformers' desire to save the children and thus to heal the nation's future. The facilities were strictly regulated medical spaces where physicians and reformers could domesticate parents, educate and cure children, and socialize families. The social reform mission meshed with the medical purpose, albeit sometimes uneasily, to create a fictional parentless home managed by professionals for the purpose of saving children physically and spiritually.

The Formative Generation of Children's Hospitals, 1855–1890

Although male physicians established several early hospitals, women were the primary boosters of children's hospitals. Women physicians viewed them as an institutional sanctuary from gender discrimination in medicine, while women reformers sometimes viewed them as an institutional setting for female leadership. In Chicago, Dr. Mary Thompson established Women's and Children's Hospital in 1865, at a time when the city's two hospitals would not allow women to "utilize their facilities and one did not accept women patients." In San Francisco, Drs. Martha Bucknell and Charlotte Blake Brown called the meeting where seventy women incorporated the Pacific Dispensary for Women and Children that later became Children's Hospital of San Francisco. Their mission explicitly recognized the role of women in every element of the organization: "To provide for women the medical aid of competent women physicians, and to assist in educating women for nurses, and in the practice of medicine and kindred professions."[9] In such institutions, women physicians could practice medicine and nurses could care for the sick.

Founders of the formative generation of children's hospitals during the Gilded Age experimented with the components that would become the coherent designs of the Progressive Era. Since most adult Americans viewed the hospital as a desolate place where poor people died, founders cloaked early children's hospitals in the metaphor of home. The combination of home and hospital served as a welcome transition from the home-based health care system to the modern institutional system. Particularly for children, leaving home must have been traumatic. Mary Rogers, superintendent of Children's Hospital of the District of Columbia (CHDC), reported in 1894 that mothers had repeatedly told her, "they would bring the child where so many other children were, because he would not be lonely, but would never take him to a 'big' hospital."[10] No one needed to worry, as they would have had to in Massachusetts General, that the adjacent patient would be an adult.

The metaphor of home was a practical reality, because most children's hospitals opened in converted residences. As Rogers noted, each organization seemed to go through "a repetition of this small beginning," as illustrated in Figure 2.1 by the first building of St. Louis Children's Hospital. The two-story half-Georgian house with crenellated chimney flutes and an attic was sited slightly off-center to the lot, leaving a large area for trees and a yard surrounded by a white picket fence. The house had a second-floor screen porch along its side. No plan of the interior survives, but contemporary descriptions suggest that the founders maintained a conventional house plan.

Poor children going to a children's hospital in Boston, Chicago, and Toronto, founders believed, would experience a home such as they had never before in

FIRST HOSPITAL LOCATED AT 2834 FRANKLIN AVENUE
1879-1884

FIGURE 2.1 St. Louis Children's Hospital, Franklin Avenue Building, 1879.

From St. Louis Children's Hospital, *Annual Report* (1915). Courtesy of Becker Medical Library, Washington University School of Medicine.

their short lives imagined: "Within the first few days, the irritable, querulous cry of our patients, their filthy, rude, or disorderly habits, yield before the potent, because firm, kind, and faithful attention of our ladies [nurses]."[11] Lady visitors noted with pleasure the "fat and rosy faces, the happy frolics, the improved manners." CHDC's Lady Visitors reported in 1883 that the institution proved for many "poor destitute" children "the happy home" "to which they have been strangers" outside the hospital. In the imaginations of the Lady Visitors, the hospital had become for patients "the *one* bright spot of earth which they have learned to call *home*."[12]

Inside, managers and trustees went to elaborate lengths to shape the facility into a model home imbued with their values. The wards were the places that children spent most of their time, and they were intended to serve as stark contrasts to the patients' homes. Early photographs show wards that resemble small bedrooms, although crowded with extra beds and with the children carefully posed in obedient positions, typically staring into the camera. Most wards were quite small, with four to eight beds. In one literary portrait of Boston Children's Hospital, "neat little beds with white spreads were arranged along the sides of the room." The wards were decorated with paintings and furnished with small lamps and other symbols of a middle-class home.

Founders may have aspired to more order than they were able to achieve. In a lithograph from *Frank Leslie's Illustrated Newspaper* from 1881, four Boston Children's Hospital nurses cope with nineteen children in a "large ward."[13] The room is a rectangle with high ceilings; protruding chests provide some relief from the long room. A fireplace is on a short wall of the rectangle, a rug covers much of the floor, and paintings of children hang from the walls. Some patients are in bed, others appear to be appealing for attention, and some simply are amusing each other. The beds are not aligned along the walls, but scattered throughout the room. Other furnishings, such as chairs and a small table sit haphazardly amid the beds.

The position of the children, the furnishing, and the nurses throughout the space suggest that here, at the beginning of the children's hospital movement, the need for order lost out to the desire to create a home. The spaces were rarely purpose-designed, but were rather adapted to new uses. Further, the women who organized and furnished those spaces filled them with their values, from quilted bedspreads to ice cream treats.[14] One writer established a iconic portrait of the hospital as healthy home when he wrote that in the ward "the sun was shining brightly in at the window; some fresh flowers were on the tables; and some pictures of the children and horses and dogs were on the walls."[15] The ward was filled with sunlight, not the grim shadows of the urban slum; flowers, not the withering trees and shrubs of the urban street; and art, not the commerce and poverty of the urban household. He could have continued by mentioning the wood paneling, high ceilings, carpets, high-backed chairs, and other elements the women incorporated from their vision of the ideal home to the reality of their hospital (Figure 2.2).

The contemporary medical treatment might be a "merry frolic, a pleasant smile," since these were the methods the "wise physician strives to employ in his care of children's diseases, and regards as more potent than drugs."[16] Medicine only gradually offered more effective interventions, as surgical techniques were improved and diagnostic technologies invented. The children were placed in the care of "Christian ladies" and professional physicians who could be trusted to strengthen "their bodily condition."[17] The first Lady Superintendent in Boston was hired for her "faith, patience, and self-denial." Nursing was gradually being professionalized, but the women were expected to work for little or no salary— just room, board, and the experience. In addition, the Lady Visitors in Washington made daily visits and weekly inspections to ensure communication between physicians and the managers and to see that the physical plant was in good condition.[18]

Managers' definition of "children" was influenced by the inability of physicians to treat contagious disease and of architects to develop needed isolation techniques, as well as by reformers' desire for the institutions to be viewed as a success. Mary Rogers wrote in 1894 that few of the early hospitals accepted children suffering from contagious, chronic, and incurable illnesses. The focus was on curable, acute-care medical illnesses such as an abscess, burn, or fracture. They feared that a patient developing an infectious disease could mean multiple

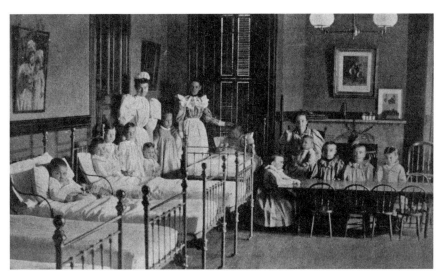

FIGURE 2.2 Christmas in the Children's Ward, 1891. The ornate decorations remind one of home, while the nurses represent order in the medical space.

From *Harper's Young People* (December 1891), author's collection.

deaths among the sicker children, since the spaces in the hospitals were not differentiated sufficiently to isolate emerging illnesses. Still, the hospitals constantly were filled with children who had infectious and contagious illnesses.[19]

Early children's hospitals rarely accepted babies under the age of two or children beyond the age of thirteen or fourteen. They refused babies because most physicians associated infant care with their mothers, and they worried that babies would not thrive among the older ill children. Specialty institutions, such as Babies Hospital in New York City, were organized for infants, while many general hospitals admitted mothers and their children.[20] As for the older children, hospitals such as CHDC did not admit patients above the age of twelve "for reasons recognized by the physicians in charge as necessary for the maintenance of a proper moral standard in the Institution." While physicians feared that infants might be exposed to further disease, apparently managers were equally worried about social issues when they placed the upper age restriction.

This first generation of hospitals provided care for the suffering in hopes of "quickening their intellects, refining their manners, and softening and encouraging their hearts."[21] They may have been "short in scientific output, but [they were] long in the intelligent and personal care and attention . . . given suffering humanity."[22] Founders designed the medical homes to provide children with amenities and services unknown to them in their own homes. Through the giving of the charity, the women hoped to reform and mold their young charges into healthy and respectable citizens. With new intellects, refined manners, and softened hearts they would influence their families, and therefore improve their society.

The Progressive Impulse, 1890–1917

The next generation drew upon these formative models to create sophisticated medical enterprises housed in nostalgic domestic environments where children and their families were taught middle-class manners and morals. The institutional goals of curing disease and healing the spirit would increasingly conflict as children's hospitals became medical necessities for all children, not just the poor. Still, even as the male physicians and administrators began to marginalize the female pioneers, children's hospitals continued to use elements of domestic life to soothe patient fears and comfort new patient populations.

The number of children's hospitals at least tripled in the United States and Canada between 1890 and 1920. They were not just in large cities such as Buffalo (1892) and Denver (1910), but also in Winnipeg (1907) and Fort Worth (1918). Two hospitals would open in Montreal, one for English Canadians (1903), the other for French Canadians (1907). Three hospitals would be established in the emerging cities of Texas during the 1910s. A new hospital would even be established off the mainland in Honolulu (1906).

The hospitals sometimes started as pediatric nurseries, dispensaries, and clinics. In 1895, a group of Los Angeles women opened the King's Daughters Day Nursery, which cared "for the unfortunate children of mothers who had to work outside the home." Two years later, Denver women, led by suffragist Dr. Minnie Love, opened an outdoor tent clinic for gastrointestinal disorders during the summer months.[23] When desperate poor mothers overran the nurseries and clinics searching for help for children who were very sick, the women took the next step, the establishment of a children's hospital. In Los Angeles, the hospital opened in 1902, Denver in 1910.

The dispensaries provided a transitional space for many families who continued to fear the hospital. In 1899, St. Louis Children's Hospital's president, Mary W. McKittrick, noted that many poor people in that city continued to have "a prejudice against Hospitals, but gladly bring their sick children to be prescribed for [at the dispensary], and then in some cases are induced to leave them where they can have better care."[24] The 1908 St. Louis Children's Hospital annual report showed the dispensary as a plain, functional room with two sets of two windows of differing styles, suggesting it was a corner room. A nurse stands over an examination table, next to a chair and industrial-looking desk. Along one wall, a short shelf holds a variety of bottles and other items, just above a wire wastebasket. Pipes are visible on the ceiling, the walls are bare of decoration, and the windows are without shades or curtains—a far cry from the homey feeling designed for the earlier wards or, as we shall see, for the private rooms just beginning to be built into hospitals.

Many hospitals quickly replaced their converted residences with purpose-built facilities. Buildings designed as hospitals had been constructed as early as the 1880s, but this generation of hospitals signaled a different balance between medicine and social mission. The designs largely emulated similar ones for general hospitals. In 1913 Sarah Morris Children's Hospital, a component of the Michael Reese Hospital in Chicago, opened its $300,000 four-story hollow clay tile fireproof structure, built of reinforced concrete, with a basement; its designer, Richard Schmidt, and his coauthor of a hospital architecture book, John Hornsby, considered it "the last word in children's hospital construction."[25] The V-shaped structure had a slightly protruding cornice, flat roof, and basket porches on the upper floors; the first floor opened on to a street corner (Figure 2.3). Passing through the vestibule and rotunda, one came to two corridors. One corridor took the prospective patient to the admission waiting room, off of which were isolation and examination rooms. The other corridor led to treatment rooms and small wards. At the back of the structure was the second floor of a square ground-floor playroom. The basic V-pattern of the first floor was followed on upper floors, where surgical and treatment wards of various sizes intermingled with specialty examination rooms and, on the fourth floor, with the surgical operating suites.

FIGURE 2.3 Children's Hospital, Los Angeles, circa 1912.

Courtesy of the University of Southern California, on behalf of the USC Specialized
Libraries and Archival Collections.

Sarah Morris and other new facilities symbolized the delicate ballet that managers, architects, and physicians were dancing as they tried to maintain the home-
like character of the hospital even as medical interventions were increasingly
sophisticated and successful.[26] X-rays and other diagnostic equipment allowed
more precise diagnoses of illnesses. Improved anesthetics and the implementation of aseptic procedures greatly improved surgical results. Designers were now
aware that glass partitions between beds might dramatically lower rates of infection, as long as medical practitioners followed appropriate procedures.

The prime example of medicine's prominence was the surgical suite. Many
nineteenth-century hospitals were built without an operating room. In 1881,
Boston Children's Hospital's proposed building included two pavilions of twenty
beds located on either side of a central structure. A rudimentary operating room
was set off behind the entry rooms (Figure 2.4). In 1914, the hospital dedicated
a new complex, with its main administration building, nurses' home, outpatient
facility, four pavilion wards, and the operating rooms "in a special building." The
building held four small operating rooms with galleries for twenty-four observers
ringing the tables. Surrounding the operating rooms were additional rooms for
dressing the wounds, etherizing, recovery, and sterilizing instruments.[27]

At Sarah Morris, the surgical suite became the most modern, functional, and
sterile space within the hospital, now without the wooden galleries of the previous generation. On the fourth floor, a short hallway brought one into the suite,
which was divided into two operating rooms as well as separate spaces for instrument sterilization, anaesthetizing, and nose and throat examinations. The rest of
the corridor's rooms were devoted to support functions, such as rooms for the
doctors and nurses. Operating tables sat in front of a mass of windows, since
natural light was still the preference for this generation of surgeons. The windows rose through the entire wall up to the building's roof, providing side and

FIGURE 2.4 Operating Rooms, Sarah Morris Hospital for Children, 1915.
From *American Architect* 108.2077 (October 13, 1915), 244.

overhead light that was then augmented with artificial light fixtures directly
above the operating table. Enamel-topped metal tables on wheels and medical
instruments surrounded the metal operating table in a room devoid of ceiling
moldings, paintings, or carpets.

The other corridor on this floor held private patient rooms. Whereas ward
patients who had to have surgery would be prepped on their floor and brought
up to the operating suite by an elevator directly next to the suite, only private
patients began and finished their stay on this floor. This spatial arrangement
ensured the separation of private and public patients, comforting paying
patients who hoped to use the services of the hospital without mixing with
poorer patients.

As was true with general hospitals, the children's hospitals' wards were the
institutions' heart and soul, the "living rooms" of the modernized buildings.
Hospitals began inserting photographs of their orderly and carefully regulated
wards into their annual reports in the late nineteenth century. At Sarah Morris,
a high-ceiling room with almost wall-length windows was home to twelve beds,
six on a side, set along the long walls of the rectangular space. The northern,
shorter wall held a glass entrance to the sun porch. Three inset wall-length windows were on the eastern wall, and the door to the ward was in the center of the
western wall. Overhead lights and smaller wall lights above the beds provided
additional lighting. In the center of the space sat a lone nurse's desk, the place of
authority regulating the activities of the patients. Save for the ceiling moldings

and inset shelves beside each bed, the walls were bare of decoration. The room shouts of medical authority, illness, and institutional life. The homey ward of the formative generation has been replaced by the more sterile efficiency of the medical workplace.

However, women reformers strove to maintain the social mission of the institution. Sarah Morris, for instance, was different from the typical general hospital in that it included a milk production station in the basement, isolation wards near admissions, a variety of small wards, and a large playroom. These design elements, and kindergartens and other educational rooms in other hospitals, reflected the special nature of children as patients. In addition, whereas some general hospitals had a porch for tuberculosis and other respiratory illnesses, porches were considered an essential element of children's hospitals. These elements symbolize the tenacity with which the women managers sought to maintain their vision even as they adapted to the new era.

Sarah Morris had large porches off the second- and third-floor fifteen-bed wards as well as smaller ones off the five-bed and two-bed wards. Then, on the fourth floor, which held mainly private rooms, each room had a small protruding basket porch for the use of that patient. The porches served as a therapeutic environment where sick children were exposed to fresh air and sunlight, and were a physical reminder of a gracious home—a beautiful North American home almost always included a porch. Here, the porches were another "beneficial influence" that managers hoped could reeducate children away from old habits and inculcate new ones. As the CHDC managers asserted in their 1895 annual report, "Instances are not uncommon of the beneficial influences that have been exerted upon families by children who have been treated in our hospital for comparatively short periods."[28] Managers needed an environment that mirrored the values they hoped to inculcate.

The porches were physical manifestations of the children's hospital as a fictional home in which parents gave up their children to the scientific expertise and moral superiority of hospital physicians and managers. As Figure 2.5 illustrates, the first purpose-built hospital facility at CHDC included porches on three floors, two of which are joined in a soaring arch. These porches had two purposes. First, they were used to ensure that sick children, such as the patients visible on the second-floor porch in the illustration, got sufficient sun and fresh air. Second, while their children were sunning, parents could stand below and see them.

Managers carefully regulated patient-parent interactions. In 1918, a leading hospital administrator, Dr. Stanford McLean, wrote: "Of course it would disrupt a hospital if mothers were allowed to visit their children more than once a week." Before 1882, Boston Children's Hospital allowed one relative at a time to visit sick children from eleven to twelve o'clock each day of the week. Then it restricted visiting to three days a week. Starting in 1894, visiting was allowed just on Wednesday from eleven to twelve.[29] Sick babies were not to be touched by the

FIGURE 2.5 Porches, Children's Hospital of the District of Columbia, 1928.

From Edward F. Stevens, *The American Hospital*, third edition, 1928, 211.

mother, visits were to be only one or two hours a day, one or two visitors at a time, and all gifts were strictly monitored to ensure that no contraband, such as ice cream and candy, was brought into the building. Parents unable to hold their children in their arms were allowed to stand below them while they were on the porch and, if possible, converse.

McLean would have never considered limiting the right of medical personnel to hold, touch, or physically manipulate the patients. In an age when nurses lived in homes adjacent to the hospitals, and patients were hospitalized for long periods, such a physical distance would have been unthinkable. Hospitals regularly published photographs in their annual reports of nurses holding children and staff standing among the children in their wards. In one, staff and children at Chicago's Children's Memorial Hospital celebrate Christmas on one of the hospital's porches. Floor-length casement windows with transoms create doors that provide easy access to the porches for beds and patients. A rocking chair suggests the transformation of the space into a living room, much like those in real homes. The nurses casually hold the children, who are themselves holding presents, presumably from the hospital. Christmas is one of the iconic moments in domestic bourgeois life, here lived with the smiling nurses and paternal physician. Parents were figuratively and literally outside the tight family of the children's hospital.

Mother's milk is as associated with a nurturing family as the porch is synonymous with the gracious home. During the Progressive Era, children's hospitals played an important role in focusing public attention on the issue of milk, educating parents of their patients about the concern, and establishing exemplars of how to raise children. Many children's hospitals either opened milk production facilities or allied themselves with milk depots. The Women's Auxiliary Board of the African American Provident Hospital in Chicago "took over leadership of [the hospital's] infant feeding program in order to provide free pure milk to babies in poor black neighborhoods." Children's Hospital of San Francisco opened a milk laboratory in 1893, while the managers in St. Louis sold 4,500 bottles through their dispensary in 1908.[30]

In 1913, Hornsby and Schmidt praised the "milking station" at Sarah Morris (Figure 2.6).[31] In a large room on the hospital's ground floor, staff conducted the three steps of pasteurization, sterilization, and formulation by prescription. The authors encouraged architects to separate the pasteurization process, which they distrusted, from the other two stages. The milk stations were manifestations of the efforts that managers took to employ science and innovative medical practices in service of their aspirations to change children, and through them society. Faced with the refusal, in reformers' minds, of poor parents to ensure that their children were fed proper milk, the children's hospitals proved a vehicle for education as well as healthy milk distribution. And, of course, it offered an opportunity to teach parents about other nutritional and hygienic issues.

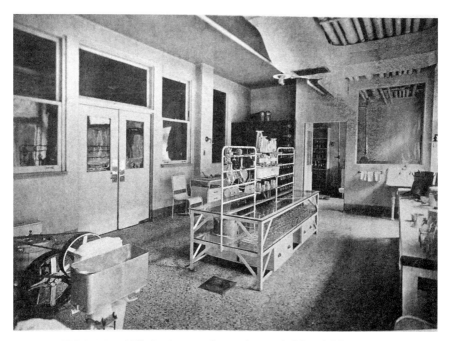

FIGURE 2.6 Milk Station, Sarah Morris Hospital for Children, 1915.
From *American Architect* 108.2077 (October 13, 1915), 242.

As early as 1898, St. Louis Children's Hospital published a photograph of a corner of its Laura Weil Kindergarten. A wooden table with twelve chairs sits in the center of the room, surrounded by a piano, a cabinet filled with what appear to be demonstration items, a small screen holding children's drawings, and a blackboard filled with words ending in "at." An ornate clock and a metal shield grace the walls, while paper strings drape down from the room's high ceiling. The room combines the size and grace of a large family sitting room with the typical items of a middle-class tasteful education in music and art.

Hospitals opened kindergartens in keeping with Progressive emphasis on both education and the hospital's mission to transform the children, and through the children, their families and society (Figure 2.7).[32] In 1895, the president of CHDC argued that wealthy residents should support the institution for reasons beyond the actual saving of lives. The institution was inculcating "habits of cleanliness, order, and deportment" that led to the "beneficial influences that have been exerted upon families by children who have been treated in our hospital for comparatively short periods."[33] The hospital was not simply a place for the physically ill; it was also a place for normative training and moral education.

Within the new hospitals, reformers strove to establish the atmosphere of the middle-class home by exposing poor children to the proper manners of play.[34] The plan for Sarah Morris shows a large two-story "Exercise and Play Room," with a clerestory showering the room with indirect light. No drapes, paintings, or other decorations adorn the room. Children are playing with a

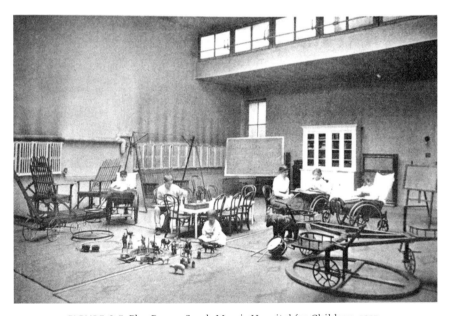

FIGURE 2.7 Play Room, Sarah Morris Hospital for Children, 1915.
From *American Architect* 108.2077 (October 13, 1915), 241.

variety of toys amid what appears to be examples of physical and occupational therapy equipment. The equipment reminds us that professionals started overseeing exercise in the same way they managed other components of the hospital.[35] Toys seem scattered around the floor in front of the seated child, but they are actually carefully orchestrated and isolated from other activities. Several children are in wheelchairs, two interacting with an adult. Convalescent children might use play therapy rooms and playgrounds as a way to strengthen their bodies for recovery and to learn the social skills of organized recreation. In other words, the moral playground was becoming a medical therapeutic space, which was reinforced by the hiring of occupational and physical therapists to supervise these areas.[36]

A Place for the Privileged as Well as the Poor

Around 1920, Dr. Adelaide Brown, daughter of a founder of Children's Hospital of San Francisco and on the staff of the same hospital, wrote a history of her hospital. She noted that since 1875 the staff had grown dramatically, the endowment was increasing, and the complications of running this enterprise with its multiple buildings and numerous services had led the hospital to affiliate with the University of California, an example of the integration of children's hospitals into the maturing health care system.[37] Even more representative of the change were the marginalization of women within the hospitals' administration and the shift in design that placed increasing importance on homelike spaces for privileged.

In 1918, Dr. McLean asserted the need for a "model children's hospital" with a social service taken seriously by the medical staff, "not relegated, as it is in most cases at present, to the sporadic efforts of a well-meaning board of women managers." Further, only men should superintend a children's hospital, since women offered "too much Christmas tree and not enough bookkeeping."[38] He gave little credit to the women who had established, sustained, and defended the children's hospitals. Women, the founding force and sustaining power of children's hospitals, were now being marked as meddling busybodies who should leave the direction of these institutions to men. Actually not just any men—McLean clearly meant that the time had come for the children's hospital to be governed by physicians.

New hospital buildings embodied this emphasis on medical expertise. The extent of the shift is apparent in a 1974 history of the Department of Surgery at Children's Hospital of San Francisco. Even though the hospital had offered surgical services almost from its inception in 1875, Dr. Victor Richards argued that the "modern history" of the department started in 1955, "when it was decided to admit men, as well as women and children, to the Hospital, thus permitting the commencement of Services in General Surgery for both adults and children." Richards then dismissed the previous generations of activities by elaborating that "up to that time," the hospital "had been largely devoted to the care of children and women, and general medicine and surgery were not part of the scene."[39] Male physicians treating adult, male patients was, by definition, modern medicine.

Confident medical professionals transformed the public charity for the poor into a medical service for all children. Although children's hospitals had had paying patients in private rooms for decades, managers now embraced and celebrated their presence. In 1922, Boston Children's Hospital opened a four-story plus basement private ward designed by the architectural firm of Coolidge and Shattuck as an annex to their neoclassical administration building. Managers argued that the pavilion was necessary, given the demand that "a place be provided where patients, who could pay for the privilege, could enjoy all the technical and other advantages bestowed on those in the public wards of the Hospital."[40] Ironically, persuading the wealthy to use the hospital's resources meant once again clothing the scientific workplace in the atmosphere of home.

The five floors of the private pavilion at Boston Children's contained all the services that the patients would typically need, meaning that their care could be isolated spatially from that of the public wards. A total of forty-six private beds were available, ranging in price from $35 a week for the two-bed wards to $200 a week for a single room with adjoining bath and a second room for mother or a private nurse. The pavilion included a sitting room for the patients and their families, a dining room for mothers, and sun porches for each patient floor. A photograph of "one of the bedrooms" showed two beds in a small undecorated room with curtains and shades on the windows, hardwood floors, and a leather sitting chair in the corner. The two beds are perpendicular to one another, with one between the two double-hung windows and the other against the inner wall next to the outer door. The pavilion's operating room was a high-ceilinged, plain room with a large central window between two double-hung smaller yet almost wall-length windows, through which one can see a balustraded balcony. As at Sarah Morris, a variety of wheeled metal carts surrounded the operating table and overhead lighting augmented the natural light from the windows.

The introduction of sumptuous private wards signified an important change in the role of the children's hospital within the American health care system. In St. Louis, shortly after their private corridor opened, Physician-in-Chief McKim Marriott noted, "parents are coming to realize the advantages of hospital care for the diagnosis and treatment of disease in children." He went on to say that the "home-like surroundings" and the "convenient arrangement for mothers who desire to stay with their children" had made the private services quite popular, even drawing a "fair proportion" of private patients from out of town.[41] In the same annual report, the chief of the ambulatory services, primarily used by the poor, complained that many poor children from outside St. Louis needed hospital services, but hospital rules prohibited them from being served. Further, although the hospital had long served African Americans, the women Board of Managers ruled that African Americans should be excluded from the new pavilion. After some members objected, the board decided that the "motion be not recorded without some expression of regret."[42] The managers were protecting the spaces reserved for wealthier children and their parents.

In 1876, Reverend Chandler Robbins of the Boston Children's Hospital Board of Managers had written that the new institution was "not designed merely to heal or alleviate physical diseases" in children, but also for the "moral benefit of its little patients."[43] Although the metaphor of the home was essential in each of the three successive generations of children's hospitals constructed between 1855 and 1920, the meaning of "home" shifted with each generation. The first hospitals were hospital homes for the poor, who distrusted institutions and feared them. Then, in the Progressive Era, managers and designers maintained elements of the home within the more sophisticated medical workplace. Finally, designers used the home metaphor to convince wealthier Americans to admit their children to the hospital. This time, however, instead of the home serving as a vehicle of education to train poor children in the values of the middle class, the spaces were used to accentuate the differences between the children. The redesigned hospitals thus reinforced the two-tiered approach to American medicine that the original children's hospitals hoped to alleviate by offering poor children medical treatments equal to those that wealthier children expected as due course. The hospitals continued to heal children, but increasingly they were simply cogs in the American health care system.

NOTES

Portions of this chapter appeared in a different form in the October 2005 edition (Vol. 4.4) of the *Journal of the Gilded Age and Progressive Era*. I thank Alan Lessoff, editor of that journal, for his support; Beverlie Conant Sloane, Greg Hise, Annmarie Adams, and David Theodore for their helpful reviews of earlier drafts; and Paul Anderson and Philip Skroska at the Becker Medical Library at Washington University, Rob Medina at the Chicago Historical Society, as well as Dace Taube and Ruth Wallach at the University of Southern California for aid with the illustrations.

1. Odem, *Delinquent Daughters: Protecting and Policing Adolescent Women's Sexuality in the United States, 1885–1920* (Chapel Hill: University of North Carolina Press, 1995), 99–100.

2. Daphne Spain, *How Women Saved the City* (Minneapolis: University of Minnesota Press, 2001). Also see, among many possible sources, Maureen A. Flanagan, *Seeing with Their Hearts: Chicago Women and the Vision of the Good City, 1871–1933* (Princeton: Princeton University Press, 2001).

3. Janet Golden, ed., *Infant Asylums and Children's Hospitals: Medical Dilemmas and Developments, 1850–1920, An Anthology of Sources* (New York: Garland, 1989), and Annmarie Adams and David Theodore, "Designing for 'the Little Convalescents': Children's Hospitals in Toronto and Montreal, 1875–2006," *Canadian Bulletin of Medical History* 19.1 (2002): 20–22. The issue of children's health has recently been discussed in Alexandra Minna Stern and Howard Markel, eds., *Formative Years: Children's Health in the United States, 1880–2000* (Ann Arbor: University of Michigan Press, 2004), and Janet Golden, Richard A. Meckel, and Heather Munro Prescott, eds., *Children and Youth in Sickness and Health: A Historical Handbook and Guide* (Westport, Conn.: Greenwood, 2004).

4. Le Roy Ashby, *Saving the Waifs: Reformers and Dependent Children, 1890–1917* (Philadelphia: Temple University Press, 1984).

5. Benjamin S. Shaw in a letter to the *Boston Daily Advertiser* in April 1869, quoted in Helen Hughes Evans, "Hospital Waifs: The Hospital Care of Children in Boston, 1860–1920," Ph.D. dissertation, Harvard University, 1995, 51.

6. I have not included institutions that served birthing mothers and foundlings or asylums and orphanages, even though they may have served children, nor children's wards in general hospitals. The most difficult category is "homes"; see Ashby's discussion, *Saving the Waifs*, xi. The basis of my selection is descriptions of the hospitals; see James Clark Fifield, *American and Canadian Hospitals* (Minneapolis: Midwest Publishers, 1933).

7. Sandra Lee Barney, *Authorized to Heal: Gender, Class, and the Transformation of Medicine in Appalachia, 1880–1930* (Chapel Hill: University of North Carolina Press, 2000), 38–39. For English children's hospitals, see Elizabeth M. R. Lomax, *Small and Special: The Development of Hospitals for Children in Victorian Britain* (London: Welcome Institute for the History of Medicine, 1996).

8. Viviana Zelizer, *Pricing the Priceless Child: The Changing Social Value of Children* (Princeton: Princeton University Press, 1985), 27.

9. On Thompson, see Beulah Cushman, "Early American Hospitals: The Women and Children's Hospital," *Surgery, Gynecology and Obstetrics* 60.3 (1935): 753. On Bucknell, Brown, and the Children's Hospital of San Francisco (CHSF), see Brown, "The History of the Children's Hospital in Relation to Medical Women," 1, and the hospital's certificate of incorporation as reprinted in March 1875, Folder 60, CHSF Collection, University of California at Berkeley.

10. Rogers, "Children's Hospitals in America," in J. S. Billings and H. M. Hurd, editors, *Hospitals, Dispensaries and Nursing: Papers and Discussions in the International Congress of Charities, Correction and Philanthropy, Section III, Chicago, June 12th to 17th, 1893* (Baltimore: Johns Hopkins University Press, 1894), 378.

11. Boston Children's Hospital, *First Annual Report* (Boston: privately printed, 1869), 12; *Second Annual Report* (Boston: privately printed, 1870), 10.

12. CHDC, *12th Annual Report* (Washington, D.C.: privately printed, 1883), 13; the emphasis is in the original.

13. Lithograph of Boston Children's Hospital, *Frank Leslie's Illustrated Newspaper* (December 10, 1881), 252.

14. Clement A., Smith, *The Children's Hospital of Boston: "Built Better Than They Knew"* (Boston: Little, Brown, 1983), 44 note.

15. Annie Birnie, "How Edie Wallace Cured a Little Girl's Broken Leg," *Christian Register*, August 5, 1869, in the Francis H. Brown Scrapbook, Countaway Library.

16. Boston Children's Hospital, *First Annual Report*, 10. CHDC annual reports show how little was spent on medicines; between 1872 and 1877, the hospital budget skyrocketed from $8,178 to $22,336, while "Medicine and Supplies" declined from $926 to $643.

17. Boston Children's Hospital, *First Annual Report*, 8–9.

18. CHDC, *9th Annual Report* (Washington, D.C.: privately printed, 1880), 14.

19. Among the early examples in Milwaukee were children with tuberculosis, typhoid fever, scarlet fever, and measles; Children's Hospital of Wisconsin, "100 Years of Caring, 1894–1994" (Milwaukee: privately printed, 1994), 4. A diphtheria outbreak is chronicled in CHDC, *20th Annual Report* (Washington, D.C.: privately printed, 1892), 11.

20. Rogers, "Children's Hospitals in America," 375.

21. Boston Children's Hospital, *First Annual Report*, 13.

22. Brown, "The History of the Children's Hospital in Relation to Medical Women," 5.

23. Los Angeles: Harriet Dakin and Mary L. McNamara, compiler, *History of the Children's Hospital of Los Angeles* (Los Angeles: privately published, no date), 7; Denver: Rickey Hendricks, "Feminism and Maternalism in Early Hospitals for Children: San Francisco and Denver, 1875–1915," *Journal of the West* 32.3 (1993): 66.

24. St. Louis Children's Hospital, *9th Annual Report* (St. Louis: privately printed, 1881), 13.

25. The dollar figure comes from, Sarah Gordon, ed., *A Centennial History of Michael Reese Hospital and Medical Center, 1881–1981* (Chicago: privately published, 1981); the quote is from "A System of Pediatrics." John Hornsby and Richard E. Schmidt, *The Modern Hospital: Its Inspiration, Architecture, Equipment, Operation* (Philadelphia: W. B. Saunders, 1913), 132; see also Richard E. Schmidt, "The Sarah Morris Hospital for Children, Chicago, Ill.," *American Architect* 108.2077 (October 13, 1915): 248 and 251; and Oliver H. Bartine, "Hospital Construction: The View of a Hospital Superintendent," *American Architect* 108.2077 (October 13, 1915): 241–246.

26. Joel Howell, *Technology in the Hospital: Transforming Patient Care in the Early Twentieth Century* (Baltimore: Johns Hopkins University Press, 1995).

27. Boston Children's Hospital, *Thirteenth Annual Report for 1881* (Boston: privately printed, 1882), prior to the "Report of the Board of Managers," and *46th Annual Report for 1914* (Boston: privately printed, 1915), 17–18.

28. CHDC, *24th Annual Report for 1895* (Washington, D.C.: privately printed, 1896), 9.

29. The changes in Boston's visiting hours are recorded on the back covers of the annual reports from 1869 to 1894.

30. Susan Smith, *Sick and Tired of Being Sick and Tired: Black Women's Health Activism in America, 1890–1950* (Philadelphia: University of Pennsylvania Press, 1995), 24; Children's Hospital San Francisco, "Summary of Events at CHSF, 1875–1918," 12, folder 30, CHSF Collection; St. Louis Children's Hospital, *Annual Report for 1908* (1909), in the report of the Dispensary Attendant.

31. Hornsby and Schmidt, *The Modern Hospital*, 412–424. On milk reforms, see, Richard Meckel, *Save the Babies: American Public Health Reform and the Prevention of Infant Mortality, 1850–1929* (Baltimore: Johns Hopkins University Press, 1990), chapter 3.

32. St. Louis Children's Hospital annual reports in 1882, 1895, and 1896 discuss educating the patients. Children's Hospital San Francisco opened a kindergarten in 1890, according to its annual report for that year, "Summary of Events at CHSF, 1875–1918," 10.

33. CHDC, *24th Annual Report for 1895*, 9.

34. Paul Boyer, *Urban Masses and Moral Order in America, 1820–1920* (Cambridge: Harvard University Press, 1978); Dominick Cavallo, *Muscles and Morals: Organized Playgrounds and Urban Reform, 1880–1920* (Philadelphia: Temple University Press, 1981). For a recent discussion of play and politics, see Sarah Jo Peterson, "Voting for Play: The Democratic Potential of Progressive Era Playgrounds," *Journal of the Gilded Age and Progressive Era* 3.2 (2004): 145–175.

35. Bartine, "Hospital Construction," 241–249.

36. For instance, St. Louis Children's Hospital, *40th Annual Report* (St. Louis: privately printed, 1919), 17, for a discussion of the new occupational therapy program.

37. Brown, "The History of the Children's Hospital in Relation to Medical Women," 9.

38. McLean, "Standards for a Children's Hospital," 325.

39. Victor Richard, "History of the Department of Surgery, Children's Hospital of San Francisco—Report for Public Relations Department" (1974), Folder 37, CHSF Collections.

40. "New Private Ward of Children's Hospital of Boston," 1922 brochure at the Frances A. Countway Library at Harvard University, Boston Children's Hospital materials, 3.

41. "New Private Ward of Children's Hospital of Boston," 13.

42. The discussion is noted in the Board of Managers minutes, May 23, 1912.

43. Children's Hospital of Boston, *8th Annual Report* (Boston: privately printed, 1876), 5–6; quoted in Helen Hughes Evans, "Hospital Waifs," 129.

3

Sick Children and the Thresholds of Domesticity

The Dawson-Harrington Families at Home

ANNMARIE ADAMS AND PETER GOSSAGE

Sir John William Dawson was a remarkable man. As a geologist, he is best known for his early fossil plants and his identification (later disproven) of *Eozoön canadense* ("dawn animal of Canada"), the oldest nonplant fossil known in 1864, as a coral.[1] Dawson was the only individual ever to serve as presidents of both the American and British Associations for the Advancement of Science; he was knighted in 1884 and he was the first president of the Royal Society of Canada (founded in 1882). As principal of McGill University from 1855 to 1893, he is credited with establishing the foundations of modern science in Canada. His administration admitted women to McGill and established the university as a leading research institution. Not surprisingly, he is the subject of several detailed biographies and of numerous scholarly articles.[2]

The Dawson name and legacy are also ubiquitous on the McGill University campus. The family's residence until the late 1870s was in the East wing of the Arts Building, later renamed Dawson Hall.[3] Dawson's personal collection of shells, fossils, and other objects still comprises the core of the Redpath Museum's remarkable inventory. And as a record of the varied accomplishments of its best known principal, the university archives boast an astonishing fifteen linear meters of *Dawsonia*.[4]

Our chapter sidesteps this official, public side of Dawson's life. Instead, we draw on his vast archival legacy to explore a subject only tangentially related to his work as a geologist, collector, and educator: sick children at home. Scholars have paid some attention to the Dawsons' private life. It is well established, for example, that the couple met in Edinburgh in 1840, when Dawson was studying at the University of Edinburgh, and married against the wishes of her mother.[5] But Dawson's retirement years are so thoroughly neglected that when, in the early 1960s, McGill University purchased as an investment property the house in which he had lived his last six years, university administrators were unaware that it had ever been his home.[6]

With children and their health squarely in the foreground, our essay probes the thresholds of the Dawson family's private spaces in retirement, as well as the photos and very detailed letters written by his wife, Lady Margaret Ann Young Mercer Dawson, and by their children and grandchildren. Both visual and textual sources for this study abound in the McGill collections. Many images reveal the family's life beyond the university. A stunning photograph (Figure 3.1), for example, extracted from grandson George "Eric" Harrington's photo album, shows Dawson's daughter (and Eric's mother), Anna Harrington, bathing her two daughters Lois and Constance, in February 1892.[7] Likewise, the archival record and architectural evidence of the Dawsons' life in their nine-room, three-story townhouse in Montreal, 293 University Street (Figure 3.2) is an extraordinarily detailed record of extended family relations in the English Protestant elite of Canada's largest city at the turn of the twentieth century.[8]

Sir William and Lady Dawson commissioned their retirement house from architect Andrew Taylor in 1893 or 1894.[9] Also in 1893, when Dawson retired, the couple purchased the much larger, sixteen-room house next door, at 295 University Street (Figure 3.3), which was probably built in 1873 or 1874.[10] The building was acquired as a home for Anna, her husband, the chemist Bernard Harrington (married 1876), and their eight children, who lived in a home called Walbrae Place on the university campus.[11] The Dawsons clearly conceived of their purpose-built retirement home as an addition to their daughter's house, a relationship most evident from the design of an unusual outdoor passageway, which

FIGURE 3.1 Anna, Lois, and Constance in the bath, at Walbrae Place, with rocking horse, February 1892.

McGill University Archives PA027196.

FIGURE 3.2 293 University Street, 1893. Note the upper railing, which may indicate that the roof was used as an outdoor living area.

McGill University Archives PA027196.

probably also linked the houses internally.[12] Lady Dawson described the proximity of the new house to Anna's in a letter to her son George Mercer Dawson in May 1893: "Papa at the same time has secured a small lot adjoining lest he should decide to add a few rooms for our use, these wd have a separate entrance from the street and a private door by which we could enter into A's house so that we cd take our meals with her."[13] Today the internal link between the two houses is unclear, and none of the surviving architectural evidence allows us to clarify these spatial relationships any further. In any case, the passageway and the shared garden to which it led make the two houses an especially good spatial source on how two generations lived together and separately simultaneously,

FIGURE 3.3 295 University Street (now 3641 University). Note the unusual passageway between the Harrington and Dawson houses, leading to the shared back garden.

Photo by Ricardo L. Castro.

even though the plans of both houses were typical Victorian arrangements, featuring a myriad of isolated, use- and gender-specific rooms accessible from a central hall or corridor.[14]

The major arguments of this chapter stem directly from the fluidity of these household arrangements. This case study of the Dawson-Harrington families showcases the supreme importance of health concerns at this time and the role of privileged mothers like Anna and older children, especially daughters, in translating such concerns into action. Montrealers at the turn of the twentieth century had good reason to be concerned about health, and particularly the health of children. In the first five years of the new century, the city had infant mortality rates of 275 per thousand live births, among the highest on the continent.[15] Congenital and contagious diseases carried off thousands more children each year, leaving a strong sense, at least in the social-history literature, that children were the most tragic victims of the public-health problems linked to rapid urban and industrial development.[16]

Without contesting the health risks associated with urban life in Victorian Canada, especially for those less privileged than the Dawsons, our essay places the emphasis elsewhere: on children's active role in the use of spatial strategies to deal with health risks. In so doing, it also calls into question the cultural construction of rural places as necessarily healthier than city houses and the passivity and helplessness of children, even privileged teenaged children in this period.

Finally, the example of the Dawson-Harrington enclave provides an exception to historian John Gillis's concept of the "islanding" of children with respect to an often-dramatic situation, illness, where one would expect the concept of spatial segregation to be rigidly enforced. When did the islanding of modern children begin? Was being sick an opportunity to escape the realm of childhood described by architectural historian Abigail A. Van Slyck as "the performance of childness"?[17] We will argue that young Clare Harrington, the eldest child of Anna and Bernard Harrington, born in 1880, acted more as an isthmus than an island. She not only cared for her siblings and reported on their health but also managed servants and acted as a link to other Montreal households. In this respect, Clare was the human complement to the extended family's remarkably supple living arrangements.

This case study of the Dawson-Harringtons, moreover, is intended to challenge several assumptions expressed in various ways by historians of the family and medicine: that the Victorian house and family were insulated; that, as mentioned, children were islanded or separated from their parents; that middle-class mothers with sick children were largely confined at home; and that domestic medicine lagged behind or differed significantly from that practiced in the urban hospital.

The chapter is also intended to confirm and alter some of the hypotheses we and other scholars have made from normative and nominative sources. In her 1992 dissertation and subsequent 1996 book, *Architecture in the Family Way*, Annmarie Adams explored the female regulation of the healthy house, including the special accommodations made for sick family members, and the spatial confinement of women following childbirth.[18] One limitation of the book was that it relied almost exclusively on prescriptive sources, rather than specific accounts of sickness at home, such as the Dawson archives. Detailed letters to and from the Harrington children suggest that late nineteenth-century prescriptive literature in general actually contradicted rather than reflected reality. Were Victorian mothers warned to keep sick children at home, for example, because it was an infrequent practice? New research on hospital architecture, too, shows how sick children were largely invisible rather than segregated or islanded in the general hospital until about World War I. Even purpose-built hospitals for children in the interwar period provided few technologies or medical spaces that differed from those of purpose-built hospitals for adults, reflecting the ambiguous relationship of pediatrics to the scientific ambitions of other medical specialities.[19]

This chapter also builds on one of the arguments in Peter Gossage's book-length study of families in Saint-Hyacinthe, Quebec, a small manufacturing and market town located fifty kilometers east of Montreal.[20] In a chapter built around links from local marriage registers to manuscript census returns from 1871, 1881, and 1891, he found that young married couples, most of them French Canadian, chose to live very near to their parents, without "doubling up" in the same dwelling.[21] *Families in Transition*, however, did not move beyond the routinely generated sources of historical demography to explore the spatial contours of this widespread practice (as reflected, for example, in house plans and photographs) or the social and psychological dimensions accessible only through diaries, letters, and other private papers. The richly documented Dawson-Harrington family lends support to those earlier findings, while permitting close attention to the ways in which residential propinquity allowed extended families to cope with both daily tensions and major crises such as illness and death.

Ultimately, this chapter represents the second case study in an interdisciplinary, multiyear project by Adams and Gossage to explore the intersection of architectural and family histories in nineteenth- and early twentieth-century Quebec. Following the publication of a first example, which dealt with the issue of remarriage and focused on the Dessaulles house of 1854–1857 in Saint-Hyacinthe, our working hypothesis is that as family tensions rise, girls and women gain control of domestic space. In the wake of her father's remarriage, the young Henriette Dessaulles took an extremely active part in reordering her domestic space, thus predating Virginia Woolf's emancipatory call for a "room of one's own" by several decades.[22]

The Sick Child at Home

Sick children were a constant concern to Anna Harrington. Particularly worrisome was the health of her firstborn son, Eric, who eventually died at the age of seventeen. Eric had suffered from a number of ailments during his seventeen years, and there is strong circumstantial evidence that he died of tuberculosis. But none of the many family letters that speculate on Eric's prognosis state explicitly that the teenager had the disease. In June and July 1893 he was described as suffering from rheumatism.[23] One letter refers to a "family inheritance" with regard to Eric's condition, as diagnosed by Anna's physician-brother Rankine, perhaps an allusion to a genetic condition. In a letter dated July 21, 1894, from Lady Dawson to Anna's brother George, she wrote, "Rankine I fear is only too likely to be correct in his opinion of the family inheritance. His diagnosis of Eric's case is confirmed by Bernard now that he has joined Anna & Eric & has heard the opinion of a nice painstaking, sensible & sincere local medicine man who has made an examination of Eric's lungs—he finds disease well established & in an advanced stages."[24] A month earlier, George Dawson (not a physician) apparently said Eric had tubercular deposits in the lungs.[25] And to confuse things even more, Anna says, "I don't know what to say about Eric, this whole disease is new to me & I cannot understand what the doctors mean by what they say."[26] The letters also reveal that many individuals offered money to Anna for Eric, including her brother George who offered "unlimited cash," insisting that Anna get a nurse for Eric, at his expense.[27]

Much of Anna's domestic life in 1893 and 1894 was spent away from home, with Eric, due to his deteriorating condition. The family tension around Eric's illness affected the way Anna understood the house, and the way she wanted it organized. Her domestic environments, that is, were determined by the decisions made about Eric's illness and where he should be. Fortunately for us, because Eric's illness meant that Anna was often away from Bernard, she wrote lengthy letters to him about how the Montreal house should be organized to make Eric more comfortable. From an architectural perspective, Anna's letters also reveal that she believed certain spatial arrangements (mostly separation and fresh air) would mitigate the spread of illness in the house. For example, on October 24, 1894, she worried to Bernard: "I hope dear baby is better, & that he goes out twice a day & his room is well aired. I don't like his sleeping in the nursery—for I know it mean[s] bad air for all. . . . Please don't forget about Clare's window having a proper ventilator & I think R's suggestion as to a room to herself very useful. They [might?] sleep [better?] open window in any case, if a curtain or shade interposed to prevent draughts."[28] The Harrington children also wrote frequently to their absent mother articulating the minutiae of healthful living. Twelve-year-old Ruth wrote to Anna on November 18, 1894: "Was it Grandma that told you that our windows were not open for our window is open all day and Miss Bakers and the boys, and the nursery is open at intervals as often as possible."[29] The documentation of daily practices such as room ventilation by children is extremely rare.

In the fall of 1894, when Anna's letters to her mother anticipate Eric's death, she instructs Lady Dawson: "Will you please have Eric's own blankets & pillows put on our bed & ours on his—I will sleep in the dressing room & I wd like a fire laid ready in my room. If there is lime it ought to have a thorough surfacing to avoid the necessity of its being done soon again. If you cd order a few oysters in the shell & new laid eggs & if your cook is equal to it have her make a little chicken jelly—with no pieces of chicken, or flavoring in it. . . . He can swallow the jelly better than fluid or solid. . . . Don't make the children realize the sorrow of the home coming."[30] From Saranac Lake, where she had gone with Eric for his health, Anna warned her husband to be vigilant about the servants, whom she never relied on to make decisions regarding health: "Do be sure the children are out as much as possible especially baby & the little ones—I don't think Kate is at all so keen about that as Florence was & when the weather changes warn the older ones to be careful about warm clothing."[31] In early December 1894, she ordered Eric's room at home thoroughly disinfected ("if the authorities here are right in confining possible infection") and some furniture in the drawing room recovered.

Life outside the house also meant outside the city, and the country. Both the Dawsons and the Harringtons traveled regularly to their adjacent summer homes in the anglophone summer enclave of Little Metis, on the lower St. Lawrence River, about 340 kilometers downstream from Quebec City.[32] Remarkably, the houses at Little Metis illustrate a second situation in which the two families lived in close association, here separated only by a gate.[33] William Dawson was a fervent believer in the health-giving properties of the area, claiming that the ozone was superior.[34] He purchased his house, Birkenshaw, apparently to escape the heat of Montreal in the summers.

The Dawsons purchased the cottage next door to theirs for Anna and Bernard in about 1891.[35] Although Anna's strong belief in the healing powers of the rural environment is clear in her letters—this is particularly evident in her letters about her son Conrad's illness after Eric's death—it is equally apparent that the country house acted as an extension of the city situation, rather than as a contrast to it. Daily routines and the families' social circles were simply transposed east, confirming the widely held notion that a physical (not social) change was understood as restorative. When part of the family was at Little Metis and part in Montreal, there was occasion for further correspondence. But in nearly every way life in the Dawson-Harrington country houses functioned as an extension of the families' urban lives. "The cottage cultures that have proliferated throughout the Western world all show the same characteristics: a desire for the simpler, slower life," notes Gillis in his book-length study of islanding.[36] But family letters suggest that life was neither simple nor slow in Little Metis, although the area's dramatic natural landscape was obviously a significant change from the density of University Street in central Montreal, as was the children's holiday from school.

In addition, Anna stayed with Eric for nearly two months in Saranac Lake, New York, in the fall of 1894. That same year, the town saw the construction of the Saranac Laboratory, the first lab for the scientific study of tuberculosis in the United States.[37] Five days after she wrote about bad air in the nursery, Anna disclosed to Bernard in a letter that Eric's kidneys were affected; he had albumin in his urine, his liver was enlarged, and there was thickening in his throat. By then, doctors, including the world-famous tuberculosis expert Edward Livingstone Trudeau, had declared him a "hopeless case."[38] Since Trudeau's sanatorium only accepted patients in the early stages of disease, it is unlikely that Eric was ever admitted to this hospital.[39] Still, Lady Dawson sent Anna a "fur cloak" for "this sitting out business," suggesting that he was subject to Trudeau's famous fresh-air cure.[40]

Anna writes, too, about the reasons to come home and how, through renovation, their University Street house might be as good as the hospital: "I do believe we cd make as good a sitting out-place on Grandmama's roof as here, for the price of one week's board, or perhaps on mother's little gallery."[41] These are lessons that Anna may have learned from her stay at Saranac Lake, where hotels and houses sported generous sleeping/cure porches.[42] She may have imagined the intriguing forty-by-four-foot passageway between the two houses, like Lady Dawson's rooftop, as a channel of fresh air between the two houses. It led to the all-important and shared back garden. Although it is evident from the letters that the two families conceived of the compound as two separate residences—the Harringtons would be invited, for example, to come to tea with Lady Dawson—the two buildings also functioned as a single place. This situation was highlighted when a child was sick. The presence of one sick child might temporarily dislocate the others. Here is Anna's description of how the two houses—theirs and her parents—functioned as one: "If Eric goes home it seems to me Clare ought to go. Mother wd take her, but that wd only be a half separation."[43]

Still, the younger family clearly used the house next door as a space for quarantining both sick and healthy children. In 1906, for example, daughter Lois had the measles and was sent to stay with Lady Dawson. When Eric was gravely ill, however, as in December 1894, this "half separation," as Anna called it, did not suffice. At that time, the other children were banished from the house altogether. In the letters, there is much discussion of the girls boarding at nearby Trafalgar School for a few weeks; or at the home of Louisa Goddard Frothingham Molson, a close family friend. This was a common strategy, especially for the middle class, for keeping siblings out of harm's way in times of crisis. Poorer people might use an orphanage for temporary boarding, as historian Bettina Bradbury has shown for Montreal's working class.[44] Comparisons between their home and other public institutions abound in the family's letters. Following Eric's death, when several of the other Harrington children had high fevers, Lady Dawson referred to her daughter's house as "a veritable private hospital."[45]

The Child as Connection

Important in probing the way the two houses functioned as a health-driven enclave is the ubiquitous figure of Clare (Figure 3.4), a young teenager when her brother died on January 24, 1895. Clare was the human counterpart to the passageway and an excellent example of how a child might act as a connection between spaces, or an isthmus, to follow Gillis's geographical metaphor. Like the passage between the houses, Clare served as a bridge among the three generations, between the family members and the servants, and from her own extended family to other households. From the perspective of preventive medicine, Clare was also the hub of an information network that kept absent adults, especially her mother, informed as to the health and well-being of Lady Dawson, the Harrington children, and the servants, both during Eric's illness and long afterward.

Even as a fourteen year old, Clare managed the everyday affairs of her younger siblings, as is evident from her charming letters. "Loise's boots will not nearly meet round her instep or anchel & Eva cannot get hers on. I tried Loise's on Eva but they are ever so much to long. . . . They need new boots very badly at once. . . . I think I could teach Ruth music if she would promise to practice & not take it as play."[46] She also reported regularly to her mother regarding her siblings' growth, weight, and eating habits, comparing her younger brother to a sailor: "The children all look very well, Lois is getting too stout for beauty, but I suppose not for health. Bernard looks like a regular 'Jack-Tar,' as solid as can be. Eva is very well, and rosy, but particular and cranby. . . . Poppy is as merry

FIGURE 3.4 Clare Harrington in living room, c. 1915.
McCord Museum, Montreal, MP–1981.35.5053.

& as well as can be."[47] Indeed, the younger children frequently reported back to their mother on the effectiveness of Clare, even referring to their sister as a mother or "muddie." In 1900, Clare transcribed a letter from her younger brother: "My own dear Muddie, Hope you be back soon, & hope Grandmama be well too. . . . Dear Muddie we be quite lonely without you. . . . Clare been quite a good Muddie, quite sweet and kind. We love one another & me & Loie never forget to say our prayers—."[48]

As young adults Clare and her sister Ruth (born 1882) served as crucial sources of medical information on her grandmother's situation, describing the condition of the older woman and communicating the advice of Lady Dawson's Montreal-based physicians. On May 18, 1907, Clare listed Lady Dawson's symptoms to Anna: "Grandmama is not well—Yesterday she did not feel herself but had nothing definite the matter with her. She went to bed early. This morning she had a slight pain in her right side."[49] Three weeks later, Ruth reported: "Just a line to tell you that Dr Blackader finds it absolutely necessary that they should tap Grandmother's lung tomorrow because of the amount of the fluid there is. Dr Findley & Dr Roddick both agree that it must be done."[50] Clare was clearly a comfort to her grandmother: "I do feel that G.M. really wants me at present. I seem to be the only person that she makes no effort for—She was sat up yesterday in the arm chair for about 20 minutes—Dr Bell insisted on this as he thinks the tube drains better that way, but poor G.M. was very, very tired after it."[51]

Clare's remarkable role as an intermediary between physicians and her mother extended to the condition of the other children as well, whom she nursed diligently when they were ill: "Dr Browne came to see Eva, when I was at the Hospital, but Ruth saw him. He said she certainly ought not to be at school, & just to have her be out of doors as much as possible, but never to let her overtire. . . . I got a hammock today & I think she will be able to be out most of the time, I sit up on the top veranda too a lot so that is quite nice, especially as we like the same books."[52]

Helping her father to manage the house, children, and servants while Anna was away was a general responsibility of Clare's by age fourteen, especially taking the younger children to visit other families. Bernard wrote his wife: "Clare and I have had a great hunt to find the garments, tea, that you wanted and will mail them in an old valise that I found in the attic. . . . All of them [the children] except Clare & Baby were at Sunday School this afternoon. Clare took Baby up to the Molson's where he seems to have done his best to show what he could do."[53] Clare describes her visit to the Molson household almost exactly as her father did: "I took Baby to see Mrs Molson, she was *delighted* with him, he was so merry & good."[54]

Clare's responsibilities at age fifteen extended to the scouting of potential employees. Bernard wrote Anna in the fall of 1895: "I do not think there is any chance of getting Millie, as they have succeeded in getting several boarders and she is needed at home. Clare, however, is going to see her to-day. . . . Mrs. J. L. Molson told Clare about some girl who expected to come to town shortly and wanted a housemaids place."[55] Frequently Clare communicated general information from the family's servants to her mother. While her mother was at Saranac, she wrote: "Miss Baker asked me to please tell you that if Florence leaves she would much prefer looking after all the children herself—and if the sewing was too much have her sister come up three times a week like last winter. As it is Miss Baker has the baby as much and more than Florence. Miss Baker *will not* stay after Xmas, she would like to leave *before* if possible."[56]

Anna Harrington constantly worried about Clare's extensive responsibilities, a fact noted by family friends. In August 1898, Louisa Molson comforted Anna from Little Metis: "All goes well at yr cottage. I am watching Clare & have not yet seen the least sign of her being over tired, and I need hardly add she shows great wisdom & kindness to Conrad and the younger children."[57] Not surprisingly, when Molson herself fell ill, it was Clare who helped out: "You must see that Clare is not overtaxed," Anna warned Bernard in a letter concerning the older woman's recovery.[58]

Shared Spaces

Clare was the most significant human connection between the Dawsons and the Harringtons. The shared garden, however, like the passageway between the

FIGURE 3.5 The Dawson-Harrington compound in a 1907 map. Note that this map lists the addresses incorrectly, as 291 and 293 University St. (the unlabeled street on the left, parallel to Oxenden), rather than 293 and 295 University St.

From A. R. Pinsonault, *Atlas of the Island and City of Montréal and île Bizard* (Montreal: Atlas Publishing, 1907), plate 19. Bibliothèque nationale du Québec.

houses, was a crucial spatial link between the grandparents and their grandchildren. The properties were represented as a single compound in a detailed 1907 map (Figure 3.5) of the area. The fact that there was no fence, hedge, or other barrier between them is confirmed in a plan (Figure 3.6) drawn by thirteen-year-old Clare on May 23, 1894. It shows a path extending into the shared space from the passageway, defined on the Dawson side by two beds of tulips. The rest is labeled by the young girl as "Grandpa's garden." On her own parents' side, Clare identifies "Con's little house" (her brother Conrad), a tree and perhaps a swing, and reports that grass seed is coming up. Although the two exterior spaces were somewhat separate, as shown in Clare's plan, the fact that she drew them together speaks to the conceptual unity of the family garden.

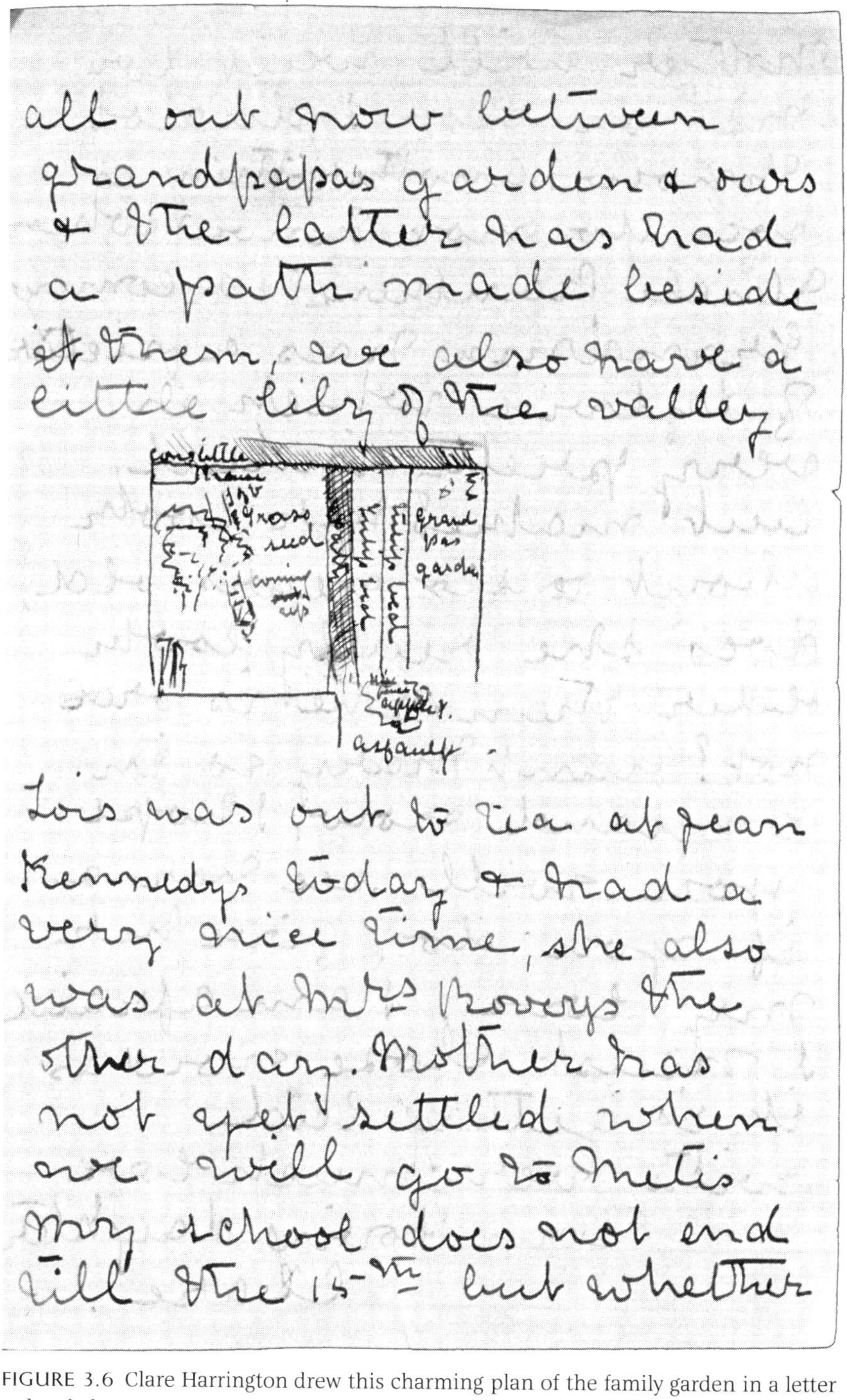

all out now between
grandpapas garden & ours
& the latter has had
a path made beside
it them, we also have a
little lily of the valley

Lois was out to tea at Jean
Kennedys today & had a
very nice time, she also
was at Mrs Bowers the
other day. Mother has
not yet settled when
we will go to Metis
my school does not end
till the 15th but whether

FIGURE 3.6 Clare Harrington drew this charming plan of the family garden in a letter to her father, May 23, 1894.

McGill University Archives MG 1022 Container 66.

As they provided models of scientific classification, the gardens had direct links to both Dawson and Harrington's published work. They also had a connection to Little Metis. In an interesting reversal of the contemporary trend of bringing plants from untouched rural places to the city, the Harringtons sent plants yearly from Montreal to their Little Metis garden. Sometimes the children sent samples back to Montreal to their father, Bernard, for identification.[59] Even today, the path between Birkenshaw and the Harrington cottage in Little Metis is well worn.[60] Both the urban and rural gardens, then, were important spaces of communication and education about health and nature between the children and these father figures, William Dawson and Bernard Harrington.

In addition to its function as an entrance to the shared garden, the passageway and the internal links it likely facilitated allowed Lady Dawson, too, to use her daughter's house as a form of "escape," especially when her son, Rankine, who suffered from depression, would come to visit. The letters to Rankine assured him throughout that there would always be a special room for him in his parents' house. In 1902, however, when he arrived for what was billed as a temporary stay, Lady Dawson moved in with the Harringtons.[61] Rankine also stayed at Little Metis. Clare, who took charge of the family while Anna traveled to Europe in 1902, reported that "one cannot help but notice how they all seem to rub each other up the wrong way," and that Uncle Rankine was "depressed with nothing to do"; Bernard Harrington concurred that his brother-in-law was "giving us a very bad time."[62]

Although the senior Dawsons were happy with the arrangement, their son-in-law, Bernard Harrington, was sometimes frustrated by the proximity of the two houses. "I wish we did not live so near to your mother," he wrote in 1894. "She seems to think that everything in our home is going to the dogs straight and excites herself greatly over it. The fact of the matter, however, is that all things considered we are getting on very well."[63] And again, "I have been in . . . next door and as usual come back cross. My dear Mother-in-law I respect greatly, but I wish she had more tact. She always rubs me the wrong way. Still I know that she does not mean to do so."[64] Perhaps these domestic tensions were exacerbated, too, by the younger couple's constant financial dependence on the Dawsons. This explanation would not be surprising, given the centrality of the breadwinner role in Victorian conceptions of fatherhood and masculinity.

The larger lesson of the Dawson-Harrington compounds in both Montreal and Little Metis for historians of childhood and the family is in the considerable overlap they show between the so-called private and public, urban and rural, healthy and unhealthy spheres. The architect Andrew Taylor represents a human connection among some of these seemingly disparate architectures. In addition to the Dawson house, Taylor designed the building for Harrington's university chemistry department, now home to the Schools of Architecture and Urban Planning. All of these buildings were intricately connected to a medicalization of urban space at this time, especially in this corner of the McGill University campus.

Walbrae Place, where the Harringtons had lived before 1893, was even demolished to make way for a new medical building. The Strathcona Medical Building, constructed in 1907, is directly across University Street from the Dawson and Harrington houses.

The magnificent pavilion-plan Royal Victoria Hospital, modeled after the Royal Infirmary at Edinburgh, opened the same year that the two families moved into their new lodgings. The convenience of the hospital's proximity was not lost on the Dawsons, even though middle-class patients did not frequent the institution until after World War I. "Our new house is only a stone's throw from the Hospital," boasts William Dawson to his son Rankine in 1894.[65] The hospital and the nearby municipal reservoir (another urban space devoted to health) are featured in a splendid photo (Figure 3.7) from Eric Harrington's photo album, perhaps taken by the ailing teenager.

As in the Dawson-Harrington homes, young patients were integrated with adults in the general hospital of the 1890s. In the architectural drawings of the Royal Victoria Hospital produced by London-based hospital specialist Henry Saxon Snell, children are accorded no special spaces or attention. In the institution's first annual report in 1894, there is no separate reporting of children. Few photographs survive of children at the sprawling, castle-inspired hospital. One image by famous photographer William Notman shows the end of an open ward with twelve beds and seventeen children. In this room intended for adults, the arrangement of furniture and patients echoes those found in other adult wards,

FIGURE 3.7 The Royal Victoria Hospital and city reservoir, photographed by Eric Harrington perhaps two years before his death.

McGill University Archives PA027096.

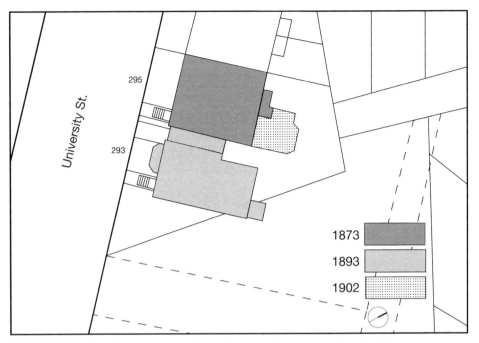

FIGURE 3.8 Diagram showing the evolution of the site, including the Molson apartment added in 1902, based on historic maps and on-site fieldwork.

Drawn by McGill University School of Architecture student Ricardo Vera, 2002.

except for the inclusion of tiny rocking chairs around a tea table especially scaled for children.[66] Echoing Anna Harrington's advice to her children to open the windows of their rooms as frequently as possible, three of the four windows in the hospital ward shown in Notman's photograph are propped open.

The ventilated, connected, and fluid spaces for children and adults at the hospital and the home even reached beyond the extended, three-generational family structure. The Harringtons invited Louisa Molson to move into their home in her old age. In 1902, at age seventy-five, she commissioned a large extension (Figure 3.8) to the Harrington house as her own apartment, but never moved in due to a stroke. This addition, which is shown on a 1912 insurance map, included a breakfast nook, dining room, and "another room," below a large veranda with views of the city and river.[67] The apartment may have been something like what Sir and Lady Dawson had first imagined for their Taylor-designed retirement home, or perhaps what they may have hoped for at the Windsor Hotel—separate sleeping quarters with shared meals.

Outside the Home

Historians have suggested that before sick middle-class Canadian children were admitted to hospitals, they were cared for by parents, mostly mothers, at home, usually in bedrooms. What this real-world case study reveals is the extent of healthcare practices that took place beyond the thresholds of the bedroom and the home, where an extended family network was crucial to the regulation of healthy children. "Home" to Anna Harrington, and presumably to other mothers (though few would have the means or the depth of scientific knowledge she had at her disposal), meant a constellation of city and country houses, health resorts, hospitals, and university buildings. The passageway and garden, as architectural evidence, parallel the important role played by daughter Clare as an agent of domestic change and a hub of medical information. Like Henriette Dessaulles in our earlier study, the teenaged Clare seemed to gain control of her surroundings as family tensions around sickness increased, actively participating in reordering her domestic spaces. Here is a child, albeit a child of privilege, whose active role in the Victorian drama of maintaining a healthy home should push us to rethink notions of children as passive victims, whether of decisions made by their elders or of the public health risks run by young and old alike in this period.

Gillis suggests, finally, that the islanding of children is part of an effort to preserve certain notions of childhood cherished by adults struggling with unprecedented change.[68] Similarly, Van Slyck asks whether the intense interest in the material culture of childhood on the part of museum curators and scholars today might arise from anxiety that childhood itself is on the verge of extinction.[69] Perhaps in the late-Victorian era, when sickness and mortality were seen as normal, inevitable aspects of family life, these distinctions between age groups were less necessary or even conceivable. As childhood illnesses came to be viewed as curable or preventable, sick children were increasingly islanded. Along with the emergence of pediatrics came the proliferation of purpose-built hospitals for children, in which distinctive procedures were undertaken by specialist physicians and nurses in the interwar period. Anna and Clare Harrington's detailed communication explains how the Victorian house and family were not separated like islands, but were often connected to other households and institutions in unexpected and scientific ways. In the case of the Dawson-Harringtons, indeed, sick children inspired travel and self-education, reinforcing this family's connection to the worlds outside their homes.

NOTES

We are grateful to the Fonds FCAR for financial support, and for research assistance to Anna Bradbury, Ricardo Castro, Valerie Minnett, David Theodore, Ricardo Vera, Suzanne Williams, and especially Vanessa Reid, who left no Dawson-Harrington source untouched. Also thanks to Gordon Burr, Anne Byers, Derek Drummond, Conrad Graham, Nora Hague, Jill Harrington, and Victoria Solan. Robert McDonald made insightful comments on an earlier version of this paper, presented at the conference of the Canadian Historical Association, Toronto, 2002. Thanks also to Stanley B. Frost for his helpful comments and kind encouragement.

1. Donald J. C. Phillipson, "Sir John William Dawson," *Canadian Encyclopedia*, 2nd edition (Edmonton: Hurtig Publishers, 1988), vol. 2: 574.

2. See especially. Phillipson's entry on Dawson in the *Canadian Encyclopedia*. Biographies
    of Dawson include Susan Sheets–Pyenson, *John William Dawson: Geologist and Educator*
    (Montreal: McGill–Queen's University Press, 1998); also her *John William Dawson: Faith,
    Hope and Science* (Montreal and Kingston: McGill–Queen's University Press, 1996). See
    also Rankine Dawson's edition of his father's memoirs, entitled *Fifty Years of Work in
    Canada, Scientific and Education, Being Autobiographical Notes by Sir William Dawson*
    (London: Ballantyne, Hanson, 1901). Dawson himself wrote more than 400 books and
    articles. He also figures prominently in histories of women at McGill, of the field of nat-
    ural history, of the Royal Society of Canada, and of the Geological Society of Canada.

3. For Dawson's description of Dawson Hall, see William Dawson, *Fifty Years of Work in
    Canada*, 98–99. A brief history of the building is presented in Stanley B. Frost, "When
    Rocks Hit the Roof," *McGill News* 83.4 (2003/2004): 52.

4. The estimate of fifteen linear meters is from Gordon Burr of the McGill University
    Archives, where John William Dawson's family can be traced through four generations.
    Anna Dawson Harrington is further represented in the McCord Museum's collections,
    which include her illustrations and some personal artifacts.

5. See "Sir John William Dawson," in *Dictionary of Canadian Biography*, vol. 12 (Toronto:
    University of Toronto Press, 1990), 230; Stanley Frost discusses their early relationship
    in "A Transatlantic Wooing," *Dalhousie Review* 58.3 (1978): 458–470.

6. *McGill News* 62.2 (1961): 20.

7. The photo album from which this image was extracted includes many images of
    the Dawson family, as well as photographs of the Royal Victoria Hospital and of two
    university buildings under construction (Redpath Library and the Physics Building).
    The handwritten captions match that of the name and date on the inside cover,
    "George Eric Harrington, Xmas 1892"; McGill University Archives PA027196. Eric was
    rarely identified by the name George, although it does appear on his gravestone.

8. The current address of the property is 3641 University Street, now the Off–Campus
    Housing office. In 1944 an apartment building was erected in its rear yard. A good
    description of the property in 1952 is in building inspector Alfred Trottier's report,
    McGill University Archives RG 12 Container 12.

9. The relations between Taylor and the Dawsons are numerous. He designed at least six
    buildings at McGill University, and Taylor's wife's sister married William Bell Dawson.

10. 293 University first appears in the Lovells' Street Directory in 1873–1874. *Montreal
    Directory for 1873–74: Containing an Alphabetical Directory of the Citizens, and a Street
    Directory, with Subscribers and Advertisers, Classified Business Directories and a
    Miscellaneous Directory* . . . (Montreal: J. Lovell, 1873).

11. The wedding is described in Peter Ward, *Courtship, Love, and Marriage* (Montreal and
    Kingston: McGill-Queen's University Press, 1990), 108. Anna Harrington gave birth to
    nine children, and all but a daughter (Edith, who died in 1890) survived infancy. When
    they obtained the University St. house on July 6, 1893, she had just given birth to her
    youngest child, William, born May 17 or 19, 1893.

12. The Dawsons also considered the Windsor Hotel and the apartment building called the
    Sherbrooke. Their son George Mercer Dawson offered them a house in Ottawa, but
    William Dawson felt he needed to remain in Montreal for his work.

13. Margaret to George, May 16, 1893; McGill University Archives MG 1022 Container 55.
    Lady Dawson's comment about taking meals together suggests that an internal connec-
    tion was included in the original house as designed by Taylor. Sheets-Pyenson, however,
    says the link was only added following the death of William Dawson in 1899 (*John*

William Dawson, 96). George Mercer Dawson became one of Canada's pioneering geologists. See Lois Winslow-Spragge, *No Ordinary Man: George Dawson, 1849–1901* (Toronto: Natural Heritage, 1993). His own health was as complex as young Eric Harrington's, as at age nine Dawson contracted tuberculosis of the spine, or Pott's disease, which stunted his growth and left him hunchbacked.

14. The house remained in the Dawson family until 1920, at which time Clare and Conrad Harrington sold it to Phi Kappa Pi McGill Limited.

15. Denyse Baillargeon, *Un Québec en mal d'enfants: La médicalisation de la maternité, 1910–1970* (Montreal: Les éditions du remue-ménage, 2004), 40.

16. See, for example, Terry Copp, *The Anatomy of Poverty: The Condition of the Working Class in Montreal, 1897–1929* (Toronto: McLelland and Stewart, 1974), and Jean-Claude Robert, "The City of Wealth and Death": Urban Mortality in Montreal, 1821–1871" in *Essays in the History of Canadian Medicine*, edited by Wendy Mitchinson and Janice Dickin McGinnis (Toronto: McLelland and Stewart, 1988), 18–38.

17. Abigail A. Van Slyck, "*Kid Size: The Material World of Childhood*: An Exhibition Review," *Winterthur Portfolio* 39.1 (2004): 71.

18. Annmarie Adams, *Architecture in the Family Way: Doctors, Houses, and Women, 1870–1900* (Montreal and Kingston: McGill-Queen's University Press, 1996).

19. Annmarie Adams and David Theodore, "Designing for 'the Little Convalescents': Children's Hospitals in Toronto and Montreal, 1875–2006," *Canadian Bulletin of Medical History* 19.1 (2002): 201–243.

20. Peter Gossage, *Families in Transition: Industry and Population in Nineteenth-Century Saint-Hyacinthe* (Montreal and Kingston: McGill-Queen's University Press, 1999).

21. This is in contrast to what Howard Chudacoff found in selected New England cities, where young couples did live with their parents. See, for example, Chudacoff, "New Branches on the Family Tree: Household Structure in Early Stages of the Life Cycle in Worcester, Massachusetts, 1860–1880," in *Themes in the History of the Family*, edited by Tamara K. Hareven (Worcester: American Antiquarian Society, 1978), 55–72.

22. Annmarie Adams and Peter Gossage, "Chez Fadette: Girlhood, Family, and Private Space in Late Nineteenth-Century Saint-Hyacinthe," *Urban History Review* 26.2 (1998): 56–68.

23. See Margaret to George, June 13, 1893, McGill University Archives MG 1022 Container 55, and William to Bernard, July 3, 1893, McGill University Archives MG 1022 Container 66.

24. Margaret to George, June 13, 1893, McGill University Archives MG 1022 Container 55.

25. Anna to Bernard, June 4, 1894, McGill University Archives MG 1022 Container 66.

26. Anna to Bernard, June 8, 1894, McGill University Archives MG 1022 Container 66.

27. George to Anna, January 6, 1895, McGill University Archives MG 1022 Container 62. The phrase "unlimited cash" occurs in a letter from Anna to Bernard, [no day] 1894, McGill University Archives MG 1022 Container 66. Jill Harrington, the daughter of Conrad F. Harrington and Joan Hastings Harrington, also reports that the family lore includes a story that Eric choked on a cherry stone and died. Jill Harrington, personal communication, June 2002.

28. Anna to Bernard, October 24, 1894, McGill University Archives MG 1022 Container 66.

29. Ruth to Anna, November 18, 1894, McGill University Archives, MG 1022 Container 62.

30. Anna to Lady Dawson, November [no day] 1894, from Saranac Lake, McGill University Archives MG 1022 Container 52.

31. Anna to Bernard, October 29, 1894, McGill University Archives MG 1022 Container 66.

32. Alice Sharples Baldwin, *Metis wee Scotland of the Gaspé* ([Montreal], 1960).

33. All three of the families' houses were, in fact, closely linked. While the older Dawsons lived at Dawson Hall, the Harringtons resided at Walbrae Place, just to the east of Dawson Hall on the McGill campus.

34. Winslow-Spragge, *No Ordinary Man*, 43.

35. We are grateful to Jill Harrington, who reports that Birkenshaw was left by Lady Dawson to Clare, who left it to her surviving sisters (Lois and Eva), and then to a group of nieces and nephews. The Harrington house became the property of Anna's siblings and later, their children. It is still owned by Joan Hastings Harrington, the widow of Conrad Fetherstonhaugh Harrington (1912–2000), the son of Anna's second son, Conrad Dawson Harrington, and Muriel Fetherstonhaugh. Jill Harrington, personal communication, June 2002.

36. John R. Gillis, *Islands of the Mind: How the Human Imagination Created the Atlantic World* (New York: Palgrave Macmillan, 2004), 152.

37. "Fate of Trudeau's Saranac Laboratory Uncertain," *Newsletter Adirondack Architectural Heritage*, May 1992, 1.

38. On Trudeau, see "Edward Livingston Trudeau: A Biographical Sketch," *Journal of Outdoor Life* 7.6 (1910): 157–178.

39. Anna's letters are quite detailed on their various activities and the therapies tried by doctors there. This should perhaps be the topic of a separate paper.

40. The letters reveal that Eric enjoyed photography, sketching, and reading science journals when he felt well.

41. Anna to Bernard, November 7, 1894, from Saranac Lake, McGill University Archives MG 1022 Container 66.

42. Mary B. Hotaling, "Porches That Cured," *Adirondack Life*, December 1986, 11–12, 14.

43. Anna to Bernard, November 30, 1894, from Saranac Lake, McGill University Archives MG 1022 Container 66.

44. Bettina Bradbury, "The Fragmented Family: Family Strategies in the Face of Death, Illness, and Poverty, Montreal, 1860–1885," in *Childhood and Family in Canadian History*, edited by Joy Parr (Toronto: McLelland and Stewart, 1982), 109–128.

45. Lady Dawson to George Dawson, on mourning paper, February 21, 1895. McGill University Archives MG 1022 Container 55.

46. Clare to Anna, September 16, 1894, McGill University Archives, MG 1022 Container 62.

47. Clare to Anna, June [no day] 1895, McGill University Archives, MG 1022 Container 62.

48. Poppy to Anna (transcribed by Clare), March [no day] 1900, McGill University Archives, MG 1022 Container 63.

49. Clare to Anna, May 18, 1907, McGill University Archives, MG 1022 Container 63.

50. Ruth to Anna, June 5, 1907, McGill University Archives, MG 1022 Container 63.

51. Clare to Anna, July 2, 1907, McGill University Archives, MG 1022 Container 63.

52. Clare to Anna, June [no day] 1907, McGill University Archives, MG 1022 Container 63.

53. Bernard to Anna, September 16, 1894, McGill University Archives, MG 1022 Container 62.

54. Clare to Anna, September 16, 1894, McGill University Archives, MG 1022 Container 62.

55. Bernard to Anna, September 23, 1895, McGill University Archives, MG 1022 Container 62.

56. Clare to Anna, September 16, 1894, McGill University Archives, MG 1022 Container 62.

57. Louisa Molson to Anna, August 17, 1898, McGill University Archives, MG 1022 Container 62.

58. Anna to Bernard, June 6, 1902, McGill University Archives, MG 1022 Container 66.

59. Bernard [Jr.] to Bernard, November [no day] 1900, McGill University Archives, MG 1022 Container 66.

60. Jill Harrington, personal communication, June 2002.

61. Anna to Bernard, September 2, 1902, McGill University Archives, MG 1022 Container 66.

62. The three quotations in the previous sentence are from the following letters: Clare to Anna, July 7, 1902; Clare to Anna, July 12, 1902; Bernard to Anna, August 23, 1902; all are from McGill University Archives, MG 1022 Container 63.

63. Bernard to Anna, November 11, 1894, McGill University Archives, MG 1022 Container 62.

64. Bernard to Anna, December 14, 1894, McGill University Archives, MG 1022 Container 62.

65. See William to Rankine, April 8, 1894, McGill University Archives, MG 1022 Container 68.

66. Adams and Theodore, "Designing for 'the Little Convalescents,'" 205.

67. Alterations were also made to the existing house at this time. See Winslow-Spragge, *No Ordinary Man*, 9–10.

68. The concept is discussed by John R. Gillis in the epilogue, "The Islanding of Children: Reshaping the Mythical Landscapes of Childhood."

69. Van Slyck, *"Kid Size,"* 72.

4

The "Myers Park Experiment" in Auckland, New Zealand, 1913–1916

ANÉNE CUSINS-LEWER AND JULIA GATLEY

Myers Park is an inner-city park in New Zealand's largest city. Opened in 1915, it was an early, influential, and thus significant urban renewal project, requiring the removal of nineteenth-century cottages and houses that were at the time described as slums. A kindergarten and playground were then built within the park (1915–1916). Myers Kindergarten was the Auckland Kindergarten Association's fourth facility, but it soon became its "showpiece,"[1] because it was centrally located, architect designed, purpose built, and a landmark within the environs of Myers Park. The playground was the first supervised public playground in Auckland.

This chapter examines the formation of this infant-focused site. The initiatives cannot be considered in isolation from the Great War that so dominated all aspects of life in this the farthest flung of Britain's "white dominions" during the period under consideration. New Zealand, colonized in 1840, had achieved dominion status as recently as 1907. It was considered to be a "young country," an "infant" in the civilization process, and one still loyal to its Mother Country.[2] By default, its cities were young too.

The chapter pursues the conceptualization, promotion, and realization of Myers Park and the associated kindergarten and playground, as well as the objectives thereto, for child, city, dominion, and, indeed, empire. It reveals perpetual recourse to slum rhetoric and to the desire to shape, to mold, to improve both the urban environment and ultimately the young citizens using the facilities. As a result, the site provides fertile ground for reflection upon the deployment of architecture and urban design in the physical and moral conditioning of children.

Myers Park also held a privileged position within New Zealand's nascent town-planning movement during and immediately after the war. Ideas about childhood, the body of the child, and the mother-child association, entrenched in the Myers Park project from the outset, were recurrent within town-planning rhetoric more generally. Infused by hygienic and militaristic metaphors, these ideas assumed a catalytic role in the discourse on urban development. Within such discourse, the physical environment was imbued with properties of agency, shaping "the habits and nature of humankind."[3] The garden, brimful with health-giving properties, was considered the most potent space in this regard, molding New Zealand, it was hoped, into "one whole garden country."[4] Comments about gardens hold particular resonance in this chapter, concerned as it is with both an urban park/garden and a kindergarten, that is, in Froebelian thinking, a metaphorical garden in which preschool children were the unfolding plants.[5]

Modern Town Planning

At the opening of Myers Park in January 1915, C. J. Parr, M.P. and president of the Federated Town-planning Associations of New Zealand, claimed that Auckland had "witnessed there the fruition of an experiment new to Australasia. True, in other cities slum areas had been reclaimed and transformed for commercial and utilitarian purposes. In the present instance a noisome gully, an unwholesome spot, had been converted into a park for the people of Auckland for all time. . . . Consequently, Auckland might claim to be a pioneer in town-planning."[6] Four years later, at the First New Zealand Town-planning Conference and Exhibition in Wellington, the park was referred to as the "Myers Park experiment."[7] The repeated framing of this urban renewal project as an experiment is indicative of the desire to establish a scientific footing for the new discipline of town planning. The central tenet was "the growth and development of town life on lines of health and beauty."[8]

New Zealand's town-planning advocates were aware of contemporary British, American, and European developments, including the Garden City and City Beautiful movements. These new ideas were diffused through imported books and journals, by recent immigrants, and by New Zealanders who traveled or studied abroad. They were discussed in the popular press and debated in architectural publications.

Much of New Zealand's early town-planning activity occurred in Auckland, the dominion's largest and fastest-growing city.[9] It was there that Charles Reade's 1909 book, *The Revelation of Britain: A Book for Colonials*, essentially a denigration of British slums, was published. In newspaper articles and lectures, Reade then identified the existence of slums in New Zealand towns and cities and called for more extensive town-planning legislation to prevent further deterioration. Historian Ben Schrader has shown how Reade used slums as "agents of mobilization,"[10] "exposing," and even exaggerating, the existence of overcrowding, "horrible conditions," miscegeny, and prostitution to trigger support for the introduction of more extensive town planning.[11]

Reade found an ally in Arthur Myers, a successful businessman, former mayor of Auckland, and Liberal M.P., who drafted New Zealand's first town-planning bill in 1911.[12] A second, more extensive bill was debated in parliament later that year but was not enacted, possibly because of a change of government. In the wake of these legislative initiatives, the British Garden Cities and Town Planning Association's Australasian Town Planning Tour, conducted by Reade and William Davidge in 1914, did much to promote town planning in New Zealand and Australia.

Out with the Old, In with the Young

The Grey Street Gully, an inner-city valley behind the Auckland Town Hall, attracted the attention of local planning advocates. Parr, then mayor of Auckland City, formulated the park project in 1913. It required eight acres of land to be acquired from twenty-five different owners and cleared of fourteen houses and other outbuildings (Figure 4.1). Myers, a generous benefactor with a particular interest in the area, was approached, and he agreed to fund the project. The Town Hall had been erected during Myers's mayoralty, and the park would adjoin a piece of land he had suggested should be developed into a civic center.[13]

FIGURE 4.1 The four cottages in the foreground were among the Grey Street Gully houses that were assumed to be slums and were cleared in 1914.

Special Collections A5177, Auckland City Libraries.

As was the case with many urban parks in nineteenth- and early-twentieth-century America, Britain, and Europe, social and moral reform motivations are apparent in the discourse surrounding the transformation of the Grey Street Gully into Myers Park.[14] Parr described the gully as a "veritable eyesore," and claimed that it had "degenerated into a squalid and miserable quarter ... filled with ancient and slumlike buildings."[15] Myers added that "well-kept parks and open spaces, clean and well-built streets, buildings which, instead of disfiguring, added beauty and dignity to the surroundings, not only inspired the people with a justifiable civic pride, but also helped them to realise in themselves a truer and more wholesome life."[16]

There is, however, little evidence to support the slum-clearance premise. The houses may have been "old and dilapidated,"[17] and the vegetation overgrown and unkempt, but these did not constitute slum conditions and, with only fourteen houses in its eight acres, it was not congested. Rather than calling it a slum, a *New Zealand Herald* editorial suggested that it "would have probably become 'slum,'" had it not been cleared and converted into a park.[18] Further, the Council's letters of eviction to the occupants specified that the houses would be "sold for removal" rather than demolished. Initially, two of the houses were retained, a single-storied one for use by the park caretaker and a two-storied one for possible reuse as a crèche or kindergarten.[19]

It would later be recalled that the old houses had been "largely occupied by Chinese," but evidence does not support this claim, either.[20] The tenant occupants were predominantly laborers and pensioners. Several were in poor health.[21] No consideration was given to their relocation, even though both Parr and Myers were interested in the provision of worker housing. Myers, for example, had during his mayoralty proposed a densification of worker housing near the city center.[22] In the case of the Grey Street Gully, however, the creation of a park for Auckland's inner-city children took priority over housing concerns, including the housing of the aged.

Improving Fitness, Health, Efficiency

Linked to slum conditions were fears about the physical and moral deterioration of the populace. Early twentieth-century British town-planning advocates in particular argued that improved housing conditions, lower population densities, and more open space would benefit the physical fitness, health, and morality of the populace and thus contribute to increased industrial efficiency, military strength, and national prosperity.

Similar arguments were put forward by New Zealand planning advocates, notably Myers. In 1907 he suggested that workers living in crowded inner-city rental cottages "suffer both physically and morally. Nor are they the only sufferers; a reduction on the efficiency of labour affects the interests of the whole community; and the rearing of increasing numbers of children in unhealthy surroundings must tend to the gradual decline of the race both in physique and in number. The home of the individual is among the most important factors in the prosperity of the nation and the strength of the Empire."[23]

Hygienic concerns, fundamental to the principles and rhetoric of town planning, focused specifically on the figure of the child. Myers used the public forum of the 1915 opening of Myers Park to promote town planning, including the impact it would have on children, to the crowd, predominantly women and children. He used potent metaphors to describe overcrowding ("The 'Land-Sweating' Evil") and the park itself ("Auckland's Additional 'Lung'" and "an invaluable breathing place for the children").[24] These were reiterated at the 1919 town planning conference, when the "Myers Park experiment" was touted as a miniaturized model for future urban development. Open spaces, parks, and playgrounds were described as "the lungs of a city" and "the anti-toxin of tuberculosis,"[25] deemed necessary in countering a range of diseases from "catarrhal conditions of the nose and throat, to middle-ear diseases, deafness, mental dullness, backwardness, and other conditions most detrimental to the State,"[26] and to "reduce delinquency."[27] Indispensable to these therapeutic and moral underpinnings was the call for a return to nature and for the exposure of children to fresh air and sunshine. Medical science had identified these as beneficial in the restoration and regeneration of "deficient" and/or "diseased" bodies. Indeed, the open space of parks and playgrounds was claimed to be "absolutely essential to the growing frame of childhood."[28]

Molding the Citizens of Tomorrow

In addition to funding the park, Arthur Myers and his wife, Vera, initiated and funded the construction of the Myers Kindergarten building and the children's playground within the park (Figure 4.2).[29]

Given that it was New Zealand's largest city, Auckland was a surprising latecomer in the establishment of kindergartens. The 1877 Education Act had established free secular schooling for all New Zealand children from the age of five, with compulsory attendance for those over seven. New Zealand's first kindergarten opened in Dunedin in 1889, followed by Christchurch (1904), Wellington (1906), and Auckland (1910).[30] The Myers Park amenities, discussed in more detail below, along with their counterparts in New Zealand's other main cities, were the local variation on overseas models, established as international ideas on child care and education were modified in response to local realities. Concurrently, additional laws for the protection of children were introduced, and the idea that the physical health of children was a state investment became widely accepted. The latter meant a shift in the perception of children from family "chattels" or parental possessions to "social capital."[31]

Women played a key role in the realization of this shift, involving themselves in every aspect of children's—and, indeed, women's—welfare concerns and issues. As historian Linda Bryder has commented, the control of women's and children's

FIGURE 4.2 Myers Kindergarten and the Myers Park Playground shortly after their 1916 opening. The tributary pathway exits to Grey Street can be seen in the foreground and, uphill from the kindergarten building, the caretaker's residence.

Photo by F. G. Radcliffe. F. G. Radcliffe Collection G6213½,
Alexander Turnbull Library, Wellington.

welfare services was performed "as an act of citizenship, in the firm belief that, as educated women and mothers, such control was their duty and their right."[32] There was also a redefinition of childhood and motherhood in this period, informed by the assumed management of early childhood by emergent fields of study: pediatrics, sociology, and psychology. The focus upon parameters of "normalization" in the physical, psychical, and social development of children went hand in hand with a perception of mothers as both "agents" and "obstacles" to child development.[33]

Scholars have also recognized that the "adult colonization" of the children's lives, and minds, was done in the interest of nation and empire.[34] New Zealand shared this attachment of national and imperial significance to the act of child-rearing with Britain and its other white dominions. In discussing the British situation, Anna Davin has identified a "surge of concern about the bearing and rearing of children—the next generation of soldiers and workers, the Imperial race."[35]

In early-twentieth-century New Zealand, the key "child-saving" organization, the Plunket Society, was overtly imperialist. Its founder, Dr. (later Sir) Truby King, argued that the future health and thus efficiency of the family, the nation, and the empire were dependent upon the care of babies and infants.[36] He linked "racial degeneracy" to the changing role of women in industrialized societies and, more specifically, to the "unpreparedness and ignorance" of (working-class) mothers, arguing that the secret to rearing "a strong and healthy race" lay with educating mothers.[37] King's publications on child-rearing methods, in particular *Feeding and Care of Baby* (1910, republished many times), were internationally read, widely cited, and very influential.

Proponents and benefactors of the Myers Park, kindergarten, and playground projects would have been familiar with notions regarding the teaching and training of children as means of raising standards of physique. Vera Myers was an enthusiastic supporter of the Plunket Society, and one of Arthur Myers's brothers, Bernard, was a London doctor specializing in children's medicine. Like King, he produced books on the subject, including *Home Nursing* (1903) and *The Care of Children from Babyhood to Adolescence* (1909). Furthermore, the Myers family had close connections with the Auckland Kindergarten Association: it had been set up in 1908 by Arthur's American sister-in-law Martha Myers, who, as a San Francisco journalist, may have been familiar with Sarah B. Cooper's work there and/or the Golden Gate Kindergarten.[38] Vera Myers was a member.[39] Moreover, the Association's first kindergarten, the Campbell Kindergarten in Victoria Park (1910), had been funded by and named after Arthur Myers's business partner, John Logan Campbell.

Members of the Auckland Kindergarten Association framed the child as materially plastic, a moldable entity. In the 1909 campaign for Auckland's first free kindergarten, for example, Martha Myers claimed:

> the children's futures must be moulded in their plastic youthfulness. By the provision of instructive toys and development of an appreciation of flowers and colours, training in melody and numerous other ways the children are made useful and intelligent, truthful, moral, decent and self-respecting. It is the young child placed in the sunshine of its proper environment. Auckland is a growing city with many neglected children whose school is the street and whose playground is the gutter. It is for these children that we want free kindergartens.[40]

This call for the removal of children from the "dirt" and immorality of the streets and their placement in kindergartens echoed statements and initiatives made by Froebelian enthusiasts across the Western world.[41]

The perceived benefits for children who attended kindergartens were extended to the women who worked in the facilities. The kindergarten movement evolved out of feminist activism, taking aspects of child rearing out of the home and into the public realm. It is relevant, in this regard that New Zealand was the first country in the world to enact women's suffrage, doing so in 1893. But the employment and teacher-training opportunities that kindergartens provided for young women were still closely associated with women's domesticity, being construed as an education applicable to motherhood, child rearing, and "home life." In her submission to the 1912 Cohen Commission on Education, Martha

Myers promoted the value of kindergarten work and its repercussions thus: "It trains young women towards home life—not away from it. It is a profession full of depth and dignity, far better and far more developing to their womanhood than an office, shop or tearoom. It is at the very heart and soul of women's work. In making the profession of a kindergarten teacher possible to the young women of this Dominion . . . you are setting the keystone of a higher social and civic life."[42]

Mind and Body

Upon the November 1916 opening of Myers Kindergarten, the Auckland Kindergarten Association assumed use of the building's lower level, attracting thirty-three pupils, boys and girls aged one to three.[43] Whether these children were from the city or suburbs is unknown. Their ethnicity is also unrecorded, but in general early New Zealand kindergartners tended to be Pakeha (of British descent), not Maori (indigenous) (Figures 4.3, 4.4).[44]

That New Zealand's Pakeha children "grew up knowing themselves to be British"[45] in this period was readily apparent at the November opening

FIGURE 4.3 Consistent with the Froebelian foundations of the Myers Kindergarten program, photographs show early kindergartners playing with the colored building blocks developed by the nineteenth-century educationalist as educative toys for young children.

NZMS 1275, Auckland Kindergarten Association.
Special Collections, Auckland City Libraries.

FIGURE 4.4 Women staffed the kindergarten, taking aspects of child-rearing out of the home and into the public realm. Photographs such as this also support the suggestion that the first kindergartners are likely to have been Pakeha (of British descent).

NZMS 1275, Auckland Kindergarten Association.
Special Collections, Auckland City Libraries.

ceremony. King George V's New Zealand representative, the governor general, the earl of Liverpool, described the children who would use the facilities as those who would "carry on the good name, work, and cause represented by the British flag."[46] The British national anthem, "God Save the King," was sung, and Arthur Myers claimed that the facilities were intended to counteract the effects of war: "The child of to-day was the citizen of tomorrow, and the great wastage of our manhood that now was on made it necessary to give all the more attention to motherhood and childhood. On economic grounds alone it was a sound policy to do everything that was possible for the future citizens of the Empire."[47] Further, teachers made sure the daily routine for the Myers Kindergarten pupils included singing the British national anthem and saluting the Union Jack (the British flag).[48]

The upper level of the Myers Kindergarten building was occupied by the Education Board, rent free, for use as a kindergarten teacher training center and a school for "backward children."[49] Educationalists used the latter term to describe children with an intellectual capacity two or three years behind their age. Such children were considered educable, but in need of "special schools" with liberal floor space and suitably equipped rooms for the educational activities, mainly manual occupations. This school was consistent with Arthur Myers's intention that Myers Park "should be specially equipped in many directions for the amusement and instruction of the children."[50] He expressed his hope that the inclusion of the school would stimulate the creation of other similar facilities.[51] More than this, Reverend Beatty, president of the Auckland Kindergarten Association in 1916 when Myers Kindergarten was opened, added: "The country that did most for the unfit and deficient exhibited the noblest of national characteristics. Such institutions were capable of counteracting hereditary or other defects to an extent that a generation ago was not considered possible."[52] Thus the inclusion of the School for Backward Children in the Myers Park precinct ensured that future citizens, deemed "other" were also provided with opportunities to be molded.

It was accepted that the kindergartners' learning experiences would be enhanced through outdoor play. Inspired by American precedents, New Zealand's early public playgrounds were generally located in working-class areas, with "lady supervisors" appointed to oversee the children. The focus was on inculcating a mode of discipline and self-control by means of "organized play."[53] Activities, including sports, for the "little citizens" were identified by early educationalists as significant in the physical and psychological development of the child to "enlarge their imagination, have healthy impulses, with a desire to excel, a spirit of wanting to win."[54] The importance to the community and the state was explicit: the playground was deemed of "wider importance than merely a place of recreation; it becomes the nursery in which good citizenship is cultivated."[55]

While some aspects of playground advocacy and imagery were concerned with physical and moral improvement, others were nationalistic, imperialistic, and even militaristic. For example, in addition to using play equipment and playing sports, children also practiced and performed marching, filing, and flag salutes within playground confines. As Australian historians of physical education David Kirk and Barbara Spiller have suggested of the late-nineteenth/early-twentieth-century practice of military drill in schools, such activities were "quite explicitly concerned with the shaping of pupils' bodies and movements, and the training and installation of a particular repertoire of behaviours, sentiments and responses."[56] In the United States, children of different ethnicities were united under the Stars and Stripes; in Britain's "white dominions," imperialist fervor underpinned the rituals.

Furthermore, and particularly in times of war, a parallel was drawn between child and soldier. Both figures were considered impressionable, responsive to external factors, and thus predisposed to the influential forces of an environment constructed for hygienist and militarist procedures. In 1919, for example, lawyer F. A. De La Mare claimed that the "spirit of war" was evident in the "mimic warfare" of children in playgrounds and the competitive warring of sports teams on playing fields.[57] The playing of games, in his opinion, allowed for the release of inherent barbaric tendencies and was thus psychologically beneficial. The physical training of boys was seen as a precursor for the military training of young men and thus for an assumed future in the military.

For girls, it was child bearing and rearing that were presumed to lie ahead. Girls were to participate in organized play and team games and use playground appliances to increase their fitness for childbirth and motherhood. This objective was more subtly expressed than that for boys and the military, but it underpins the proponents' oft-repeated claims that the benefits of playgrounds would be moral. In girls, morality referred specifically to sexuality. It meant childhood innocence followed by marriage, motherhood, and domesticity.

Ornamenting the City

At the opening ceremonies for the park (1915), and the kindergarten and playground (1916), public gratitude for Arthur Myers's munificence overshadowed the contribution made by designers. However, the records show that Myers valued the collaborative relationships he shared with members of the design professions. Indeed, his own language regarding the creation of a civic center and his concern with civic pride were consistent with City Beautiful discourse. But Myers Park does not conform to the Beaux-Arts classicism favored by proponents of that movement. No grand vistas were created, and the most prominent civic structure, the Auckland Town Hall, was visible only from the park's lower reaches—and even then, only its rear end. In fact, the park is largely hidden from public view by buildings lining the four perimeter streets: Pitt Street, Grey Street, Queen Street, and Karangahape Road.

The project of transforming the Grey Street Gully "from an ugly wilderness into a thing of beauty" fell to Auckland City's landscape gardener, T. E. Pearson.[58] He advocated tropical plantings for the wind-sheltered site. The primary design feature, an "irregular winding" pedestrian pathway, traversed the quarter-mile length of the site (Figure 4.5). This picturesque element echoed the forces and forms of nature, tracing the course of an old waterway below the raised valley floor.[59] Similarly, the "rock and water garden" suggested by Pearson had aesthetic, practical, and educational intentions. It was a fashionable garden feature that also allowed for the storage of water runoff from the site's steep slopes.[60] Myers and Pearson were in agreement upon the educative potential of the park, with Pearson noting that his proposal would provide "a happy hunting ground for all students of plant life."[61]

Five tributary pathway exits to the four perimeter streets passed between buildings. All pathways were lined with exotic palms. The more gently sloping lower end of the park was planted with native New Zealand shrubs. Pergolas with blooming creepers would later provide shade for seating alongside the exit pathways for those women (mothers and supervisors) overseeing playground activities.

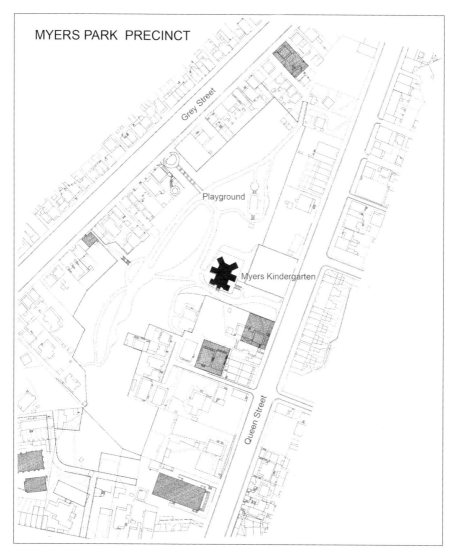

FIGURE 4.5 The eight-acre site was a quarter mile in length with a width varying between 140 and 390 feet. The kindergarten building, easily identifiable as a result of its splayed plan, was set back from Queen Street.

City of Auckland Map, Sheet H12, Series ACC 014, 1919. Auckland City Archives.
Redrawn by Ruth Wivell, 2004.

As mentioned above, during the formation of the park, a two-storied house was considered for reuse as a crèche or, Myers suggested, a kindergarten. However, the City Engineer, C. E. Bush, deemed the old building unsuitable for use by infants and suggested it be replaced by "a more ornate building, and one designed to better fulfill the special requirements of a kindergarten."[62] A second floor for use as a kindergarten teacher-training center and school for "backward children" was added to the initial proposal for a single-storied replacement building.

The new kindergarten building was designed by the recently formed partnership of Chilwell and Trevithick in 1914–1915.[63] Located on the embankment, the brick edifice was described as "an ornament to the city" (Figure 4.6).[64] Its elevated position afforded views across the playground, extending to the city and harbor beyond. In contrast to the established urban pattern, it was set back some distance from the street. This gesture was consistent with the desire to remove children from street life. Pathways to the building were at split levels, announcing to visitors the spatial separation of the two pedagogical programs. The narrow unmarked entrance to the upper level was located on the south (colder) face of the building.

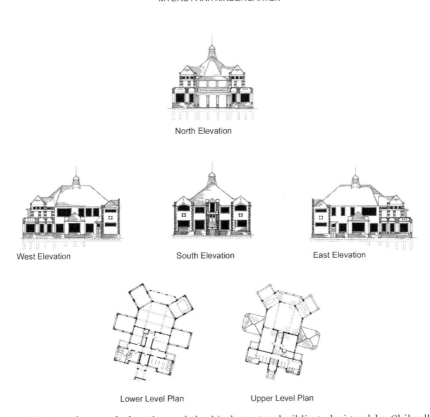

MYERS PARK KINDERGARTEN

North Elevation

West Elevation   South Elevation   East Elevation

Lower Level Plan   Upper Level Plan

FIGURE 4.6 Plans and elevations of the kindergarten building, designed by Chilwell and Trevethick, dated May 1915. They show the building's splayed plan and the use of Queen Anne decorative details, including contrasting bands of red brick and render and the use of segmental arches in conjunction with pointed gable ends.

Building Permits 72 Greys Avenue, Erect Kindergarten P. 7885 1915 AKC 305 Item 8 Box 129, Auckland City Archives. Redrawn by Ruth Wivell, 2004.

The building has a formal affinity with institutional buildings of the era, such as sanatoria. This is evident in spatial planning and detail: the splayed plan, segregation of functional units, isolation of ablution blocks, recessed balconies, gabled wings, and the use of red brick in conjunction with cement render. The building's name, "Myers Kindergarten," is boldly inscribed on exterior wall surfaces adjacent to separate entries off the street and park. Bulky columns and beams allowed for voluminous internal spaces. These were well ventilated by top-hung windows and large bifolding external doors (huge and heavy from a child's perspective). The north-facing aspect of the building allowed for sun saturation of the interior. These architectural solutions were commensurate with heliotherapeutic principles (exposure to fresh air and sunshine) evident in discussions on the park and employed, more generally, in the design of therapeutic environments.

In plan, the lower-level kindergarten comprised a large "circle room" girdled by three classrooms,[65] a covered verandah equipped with a sand pit, and a director's room. The "circle room," a semi-octagonal space, was an important symbolic feature of the Froebelian program, as it was intended to facilitate the gathering of children in circle formation for group activities (Figure 4.7).[66] The centralized planning had the added advantage of unobstructed circulation

FIGURE 4.7 Chilwell's own photograph of the ground-floor "circle room" shows a circle drawn on the floor of the semi-octagonal space to assist with the positioning of children for group activities. Also visible are the large windows and folding doors that allowed for the penetration of fresh air and sunlight.

Photo by Benjamin Chilwell. Sheppard Collection C538, Architecture Library, University of Auckland.

between the various internal spaces and the exterior. The building's upper level comprised two rooms for teacher training and the classroom for "backward children." The spatial planning physically fortified the abstract utopian principle of a harmoniously structured social environment.

As with the Froebelian "gifts," interior fixtures and furnishings were intended to stimulate "self-instruction" among the infants. The kitchen arrangement, the lowered positioning of all sanitary fixtures, and the adaptation of hardware fittings and moveable furniture were intended to help children become self-sufficient in their immediate environment, "thereby forming habits of cleanliness and tidiness."[67]

Internally, smooth surfaces and coved junctions were praised for their "hygienic properties," emphasizing the association between the kindergarten and a hospital: "there are no square angles in the building where dust can be collected, all external and internal angles of the walls, floors and ceilings are rounded, not with the usual attempt at rounding angles but one that can be seen which leaves no excuse for the accumulation of dirt."[68]

Interior decorations and outdoor activities maintained the key metaphorical link between the school/garden and the "growth" of the child/plant.[69] The kindergarten's upper floor was given a green-and-white color scheme and window boxes replete with variegated plants. Externally, the colors and textures of the kindergarten building were continued into the park's pathway surfaces, and the "sprouting" of sixty-five small flowerbeds in front of the building extended the educational aspects of the complex.[70] Ironically, however, given his earlier statements on the educative potential of the park site, Pearson objected to the cultivation of additional plots by kindergartners, as he considered them too young to be educated in the tenets of gardening. Although he had instructed a caretaker to assist teachers in "explaining plant life, etc" to children,[71] this objection contradicted a key aspect of Froebelian kindergartens.

New Zealand Building Progress described the overall aesthetic effect of the building and landscape as "picturesque" and identified this as important for mental hygiene: "The building, beautifully situated on a rising portion of the ground in the park surrounded by grassy slopes, shrubs and foliage gives the whole effect a picturesqueness which must bear a wholesome influence on the minds of the children . . . and here the little ones are taken from the playground of the street and taught to live the beautiful."[72]

It was typical for public playgrounds of this period to combine equipment areas and open space, the latter often used for sports fields. Myers Park did not include any sports fields; the slope of the land precluded them. Thus the playground comprised only an equipment area. Typically, such areas segregated children by both sex and age. Historical geographer Elizabeth Gagen suggests that segregation was not to prevent "subversive bodily acts" but rather "to legitimize the logical separation of girls and boys," and thus to encourage the "correct" conditioning.[73] There is no evidence of any segregation by either sex or age at the

Myers Park Playground—simply the provision of playground equipment such as swings, slides, climbing frames, and a maypole. The proximity of the kindergarten, and thus the greater number of adults on hand than would have staffed a playground in isolation, may have compensated for lack of segregation.

Growth and Development

Prior to the development of Myers Park, welfare organizations, churches of various denominations, hotels, housing, a crèche, and businesses jostled cheek by jowl along the Grey Street Gully's perimeter streets.[74] Following the completion of the Myers Park complex, other organizations with a specific interest in children, youths, and women initiated building programs in the vicinity, including a Young Women's Christian Association (YWCA) headquarters (1918) and hostel (1928), a Salvation Army congress hall (1928), and a Jewish synagogue and college complex (1960s). All were spatially orientated toward the park and incorporated its amenities into their programs.[75] These later facilities reinforced the moralist, nationalist, militarist, and hygienist agendas underpinning the park, kindergarten, and playground projects.

For all the moral objectives expressed by the protagonists of the park, its facilities, and the later buildings, however, the "Myers Park experiment" was beset by reports of vandalism, bullying, and molestation. The Auckland City Council received requests for park lighting near the neighboring YWCA building to deter "men prowling" around the hostel; an ambulance for children injured in park accidents; and closer supervision of children at play in the park to prevent breakages of kindergarten windows.[76] From 1916 on, various surveillance methods and deterrent devices were installed for the controlled and safe use of the park.

Grey Street continued to be thought of as a slum for many years after the completion of Myers Park. A name change to Greys Avenue in 1927 was to no avail in transforming its character. In the 1940s the Auckland City Council and New Zealand's first Labour Government embarked on a joint project of land acquisition and slum clearance in Greys Avenue. Modernist blocks of state-owned rental flats were erected on the west side of the street. The later and more haphazard redevelopment of the east side, adjoining Myers Park, included the Jewish synagogue and college complex, complete with the Kadimah kindergarten in its basement. The relocation of the Jewish community to this site complemented the initiatives made in an earlier era by the Myers family: Arthur Myers was of German Jewish descent, and Vera Myers of English Jewish descent (Figure 4.8).

From the 1980s on, Myers Park and the associated kindergarten and playground were increasingly overshadowed by high-rise apartment and office blocks erected on Queen Street. Consistent with increased concern for child safety and protection, a high security fence was erected at the north end of the kindergarten building. Unlike many twenty-first-century public playgrounds, however, the

FIGURE 4.8 A statue of Moses casts a sweeping gaze down the main palm-lined pathway of Myers Park. The trees too have grown and developed since the park's completion.

Photo by Julia Gatley, 2001.

Myers Park Playground remains unfenced. Of reduced size and with replacement play equipment, the facility continues to be used on a daily basis by children from the Myers and Kadimah kindergartens and the general public, under the watchful eyes of kindergarten staff, parents, and guardians.

Developments occurred at the national level, too. New Zealand's Town-planning Act, passed in 1926, required for the first time that local authorities prepare town-planning schemes for every town with a population of 1,000 or more. The New Zealand Kindergarten Union was formed in the same year. Its primary focus was the continued establishment of free kindergartens nationwide.[77] Although neither of these developments was a direct repercussion of the Myers

Park, kindergarten, and playground projects, the Auckland facilities were a well-known reference point for both town planning and kindergarten protagonists, in part because of their association with high-profile politicians and Auckland's social elite; but, in addition, the kindergarten building was architect designed and purpose built, and thus provided a physical model to which others could aspire. Furthermore, photographs captured model kindergartners—girls with ribbons in their hair and white socks, boys with shirts buttoned to the top and trousers tightly buckled—their smiles, their educative toys, and the food and drink with which they were provided, all in contrast to the assumed misery, filth, and immorality of the children ("larrikins") who did not have access to such facilities and continued to play on the streets. An increased number of kindergartens and public playgrounds opened in New Zealand cities and towns in the 1920s. Thus for preschoolers, organized activities in formalized spaces increasingly replaced imaginative, unsupervised play and the associated exploration of not only streets but also the natural environment of bush and beach.[78]

The "Myers Park experiment" is a socially and historically specific exemplar of an infant-focused site where urban, landscape, and architectural design, underpinned by notions of beauty, health, and efficiency, were deployed at a range of scales from the urban to the domestic as effective means of shaping and molding the physical condition and moral character of children. This is not to deny the public and civic-mindedness of the benefactors but also to look beyond their altruism by considering a range of motivating factors and complexities. In the realization of Myers Park and its facilities, ideas on "the child" were drawn into alignment with those on the city by a metaphorically infused discourse on "plastic," malleable bodies and the "growth" potential of the garden. The continued recourse to the mythic presence of the "slum" served to preserve a moral encoding in this alignment. Indeed, the idea of childhood as the fecund territory of the civilization process was reinforced by the morally encoded constructions of the modern city of Auckland and, particularly, the infant-focused environments of the Myers Park precinct.

NOTES

Portions of this chapter were originally published as "The 'Myers Park Experiment' (1913–1916) and Its Legacy in Auckland" in *Fabrications: The Journal of the Society of Architectural Historians, Australia and New Zealand* 12.1 (2002), 59–80. Reprinted with permission.

1. Helen May, *The Discovery of Early Childhood* (Auckland: Auckland University Press with Bridget Williams Books and the New Zealand Council for Educational Research, [1997] 2004), 80.

2. Arthur M. Myers, *Report on Workers' Homes* (Auckland: City of Auckland/Berry Press, 1907), 11–12; and Arthur M. Myers, *Town Planning* (Auckland: n.p., 1911), 1.

3. A. M. Myers, "Paper on Town-planning," *Official Volume of Proceedings of the First New Zealand Town-planning Conference and Exhibition, Wellington, 20–23 May 1919* (Wellington: Marcus F. Marks, Government Printer, 1919), 47.

4. Myers, "Paper on Town-planning," 50.

5. Mark Dudek, *Kindergarten Architecture: Space for the Imagination* (London: E & FN Spon, 1996), 1.

6. "Myers Park Opened: The Formal Ceremony," *New Zealand Herald*, 29 January 1915, 7. Parr was a former chairman of the Auckland Education Board. See Graham W. A. Bush, "Parr, Christopher James (1869–1941)," in *Dictionary of New Zealand Biography, Volume 3, 1901–1920*, edited by Claudia Orange (Wellington: Auckland University Press with Bridget Williams Books and Department of Internal Affairs, 1996), 384–385.

7. C. J. Parr, "Paper on Parks, Playgrounds, and Open Spaces," *Official Volume of Proceedings*, 238–239.

8. Myers, "Paper on Town-planning," 46.

9. In 1906 the population of the Auckland urban area was 82,000 (of Auckland city, 38,000); in 1916 the figures were 134,000 (65,000); in 1921, 158,000 (82,000); and in 1926, 193,000 (88,000). See G. T. Bloomfield, *New Zealand: A Handbook of Historical Statistics* (Boston: G. K. Hall, 1984), 57–58.

10. Phrase quoted from Alan Mayne, *The Imagined Slum: Newspaper Representation in Three Cities, 1870–1914* (Leicester: Leicester University Press, 1993), 137.

11. Ben Schrader, "Avoiding the Mistakes of the 'Mother Country': The New Zealand Garden City Movement, 1900–1926," *Planning Perspectives* 14.4 (1999): 398–399.

12. Myers was a member of the British Garden Cities and Town Planning Association and, from 1915, patron of the Auckland Town-planning League. See Kenneth Myers, "The Myers Family," in *Identity and Involvement: Auckland Jewry, Past and Present*, edited by Ann Gluckman (Palmerston North: Dunmore Press, 1990), 101–113; R.C.J. Stone, "Myers, Arthur Mielziner (1867–1926)" in *Dictionary of New Zealand Biography, Volume 3, 1901–1920*, 353–354; and Julia Gatley, "Jews, Breweries and National Efficiency in Early 20th Century Auckland," in *Southern Crossings: Proceedings for the Sixth Australasian Urban History/Planning History Conference*, edited by Errol Haarhoff, et al. (Auckland: School of Architecture and Department of Planning, University of Auckland, 2002), 263–284.

13. In 1911, Myers commissioned architect Benjamin C. Chilwell to prepare a plan for a civic center in front of (north of) the Town Hall, but this excluded the area south of it that would later become Myers Park. See "The Ideal City and How to Plan It: What to Avoid and What to Emulate," *Weekly Graphic and New Zealand Mail*, March 8, 1911, 33–37, 60–61; and "Auckland's Town Hall: An Attractive Scheme," *Weekly Graphic and New Zealand Mail*, March 8, 1911, 61.

14. See Paul Boyer, *Urban Masses and Moral Order in America, 1820–1920* (Cambridge: Harvard University Press, 1978); Galen Cranz, *The Politics of Park Design: A History of Urban Parks in America* (Cambridge: MIT Press, 1982); Nan Hesse Dreher, "Public Parks in Urban Britain, 1870–1920: Creating a New Public Culture," Ph.D. dissertation, University of Pennsylvania, 1993; and David Schuyler, *The New Urban Landscape: The Redefinition of City Form in Nineteenth-Century America* (Baltimore: Johns Hopkins University Press, 1986).

15. "New Park: Gift of Mr Myers, MP," *New Zealand Herald*, September 30, 1913, 8; Parr, "Paper on Parks, Playgrounds, and Open Spaces," 238.

16. "Myers Park Opened: The Formal Ceremony," 7.

17. "New Park: Gift of Mr Myers, MP," 8.

18. "The Myers Park," *New Zealand Herald*, January 28, 1915, 6.

19. Letter, T. E. Pearson, Auckland City Landscape Gardener, to C. E. Bush, Auckland City Engineer, August 6, 1914, City Engineer's (hereafter CE) Series, Parks and Reserves 219/12/13/588, Auckland City Archives (hereafter ACA).

20. "Former Mayoress," Unreferenced newspaper article. Copy in "New Zealand Biographies" 1 (1956): 123 in the collection of the Alexander Turnbull Library, Wellington. For the names and occupations of the occupants of houses on Adams Lane, Lancelot Terrace, Queen Street and Scotia Place, see Town Clerk's (hereafter TC) Series 275/5/1913/304 and 275/5/1917/1219, ACA; *Cleave's Post Office Directories*, 1913–1916; and *New Zealand Electoral Rolls*, 1913–1916.

21. Mary Cooper was nearly seventy in 1914 when she was evicted; Caroline Jowsey was sixty-two; and Sarah Ann Cain, Mary Downing, and Sarah Black were all in their late fifties or early sixties, but died in 1916, 1917, and 1918, respectively, suggesting that their health was poor. See Biographies Index, Auckland City Library Local History Room.

22. Myers, *Report on Workers' Homes*, 3.

23. Myers, *Report on Workers' Homes*, 4. See also Myers, *Town Planning*, 2.

24. "Myers Park Opened: The Formal Ceremony," 7.

25. Parr, "Paper on Parks, Playgrounds, and Open Spaces," 237.

26. Dr. C. Monro Hector, Comments, *Official Volume of Proceedings*, 108.

27. Parr, "Paper on Parks, Playgrounds, and Open Spaces," 237.

28. Dr. Colquhoun, "Paper on 'Fresh–Air Schools,'" *Official Volume of Proceedings*, 256.

29. Sarah Fields has suggested an international pattern in public park and playground formation, comprising the involvement of women, philanthropic donations, rezoning, and the appointment of supervisors. See Sarah K. Fields, "Sports," in *Encyclopedia of Children and Childhood in History and Society*, edited by Paula S. Fass (New York: Macmillan, 2004), 783. New Zealand conformed to this pattern, and Myers Park exemplified it.

30. Jane Matthews and Antony Matthews, *Myers Park Kindergarten, 381 Queen Street, Auckland: Conservation Plan* (Auckland: Auckland City Council, 1998), 7.

31. May, *The Discovery of Early Childhood*, xv–xvi.

32. Linda Bryder, *A Voice for Mothers: The Plunket Society and Infant Welfare, 1907–2000* (Auckland: Auckland University Press with History Group, Ministry for Culture and Heritage, 2003), xiii.

33. May, *The Discovery of Early Childhood*, xv.

34. May, *The Discovery of Early Childhood*, xvi. May refers to James Belich, "Taming the Wild Colonial Child," lecture, October 1995.

35. Anna Davin, "Imperialism and Motherhood," first published 1978, reprinted in *Tensions of Empire: Colonial Cultures in a Bourgeois World*, edited by Frederick Cooper and Ann Laura Stoler (Berkeley: University of California Press, 1997), 90.

36. Erik Olssen, "Truby King and the Plunket Society: An Analysis of a Prescriptive Ideology," *New Zealand Journal of History* 15.1 (1981): 4. See also Bryder, *A Voice for Mothers*.

37. Truby King, "A Plea for the Drawing up and Circulation . . . of Simple Reliable Consistent Standards for Guidance in the Rearing of Normal Infants," *Report of the Proceedings of the Imperial Health Conference held at the Imperial Institute, London, May 18th to 21st, 1914* (London: Victoria League, 1914), 211, 218.

38. Sarah B. Cooper corresponded regularly with members of the Dunedin Kindergarten Association. For an analysis of her influence on the development of New Zealand kindergartens, see May, *The Discovery of Early Childhood*, 80–82. See also Matthews and Matthews, *Myers Park Kindergarten*, 6–7.

39. See Linda Bryder, *Not Just Weighing Babies: Plunket in Auckland, 1908–1998* (Auckland: Pyramid Press, 1998), 5.

40. *New Zealand Herald*, October 29, 1909, quoted in Matthews and Matthews, *Myers Park Kindergarten*, 8.

41. For example, see Ning de Coninck–Smith, "Where Should Children Play?: City Planning Seen from Knee–Height, Copenhagen, 1870–1920," *Children's Environments Quarterly* 7.4 (1990): 54–61; Dudek, *Kindergarten Architecture*, 41; Dominick Cavallo, *Muscles and Morals: Organized Playgrounds and Urban Reform, 1880–1920* (Philadelphia: University of Pennsylvania Press, 1981), 2; and Michael Steven Shapiro, *Child's Garden: The Kindergarten Movement from Froebel to Dewey* (University Park: Pennsylvania State University Press, 1983), 85.

42. Quote in May, *The Discovery of Early Childhood*, 76. Original in *Cohen Report on Education* (Wellington: Department of Education, 1912), 189.

43. Matthews and Matthews, *Myers Park Kindergarten*, 15.

44. May, *The Discovery of Early Childhood*, 151.

45. Jeanine Graham, "New Zealand," in *Encyclopedia of Children and Childhood in History and Society*, 625.

46. "Myers Kindergarten: Opening by Governor," *New Zealand Herald*, November 16, 1916, 9.

47. "Myers Kindergarten: Opening by Governor," 9.

48. "Myers Kindergarten: Training of Children," *New Zealand Herald*, November 15, 1916, 9.

49. Letter R. Crowe, Auckland Education Board, to Town Clerk, Auckland City Council, "Myers Park Kindergarten," May 17, 1917, TC Series 275/8/15/26, ACA. The Education Board and the Auckland Kindergarten Association were jointly responsible for building maintenance.

50. "Opening Myers Park," *New Zealand Herald*, January 25, 1915, 5.

51. "Myers Park Opened," *New Zealand Herald*, January 29, 1915, copy on CE Series, Parks and Reserves 219/12/13/588, ACA.

52. "Myers Kindergarten: Opening by Governor," 9.

53. For information on the American playground movement, see Cavallo, *Muscles and Morals*.

54. Mrs. N. E. Ferner, Comments, *Official Volume of Proceedings*, 246.

55. Parr, "Paper on Parks, Playgrounds, and Open Spaces," 240.

56. David Kirk and Barbara Spiller, "Schooling for Docility-Utility: Drill, Gymnastics and the Problem of the Body in Victorian Elementary Schools," in *Child and Citizen: Genealogies of Schooling and Subjectivity*, edited by Denise Meredyth and Deborah Tyler (Brisbane: Institute of Cultural Policy Studies, Griffith University, 1993), 118.

57. F. A. De La Mare, Comments, *Official Volume of Proceedings*, 242–243.

58. "Clearing Myers Park: Work of Transformation; Making a Beauty Spot; Hopes of City Gardener," *New Zealand Herald*, May 7, 1914, copy on CE Series, Parks and Reserves 219/12/13/588, ACA. Thomas Edward Pearson was an expatriate British landscape gardener, trained in Philadelphia and Hobart. See *Cyclopedia of New Zealand* (Christchurch: Cyclopedia Co., 1902), 801.

59. The waterway was Waihorotiu Creek. The valley site had been filled in and drainage systems installed before 1911. See Simon Best, "The Myers' Park Excavation, Dam Wall Site: Final Archaeological Report" (Auckland: Metro Water, January 1998), 28.

60. Letter, Pearson to Bush, September 29, 1913, CE Series, Parks and Reserves 219/12/13/588, ACA.

61. Letter, Pearson to Bush, September 29, 1913.

62. Letter, Parr to Bush, October 13, 1914; and letter, Bush to Mayor's Office, October 20, 1914, CE Series, Parks and Reserves 219/12/13/588, ACA. Bush mentioned Myers's intention to "fit up the Big Building as a Kindergarten."

63. Benjamin C. Chilwell and Cecil Trevithick were both expatriate British architects.

64. "The Myers Kindergarten, Auckland," *New Zealand Building Progress*, June 1917, 975.

65. Matthews and Matthews, *Myers Park Kindergarten*, 13.

66. Ellen L. Berg, "Kindergarten," in *Encyclopedia of Children and Childhood in History and Society*, 524.

67. "The Myers Kindergarten, Auckland," 975. Like the building, the furniture was influenced by that designed for hospitals. See Kirsten Hegner, "Furniture," in *Encyclopedia of Children and Childhood in History and Society*, 375–376.

68. "The Myers Kindergarten, Auckland," 975. The coved detailing was attributed to overseas precedents encountered by Myers on his travels. See Matthews and Matthews, *Myers Park Kindergarten*, 27. However, the architects too may have been familiar with such detailing, common in institutional buildings, especially hospitals and sanatoria.

69. See Dudek, *Kindergarten Architecture*, 1; and Brosterman's use of Virginia Woolf's quote "Seed Pearl of the Modern Era" in Norman Brosterman, *Inventing Kindergarten* (New York: Harry N. Abrams, 1997), 7.

70. See "The Myers Kindergarten, Auckland," 975; and Matthews and Matthews, *Myers Park Kindergarten*, 15.

71. Letter, Pearson to Wilson, September 12, 1919, TC Series 275/15/17/29, ACA.

72. "The Myers Kindergarten, Auckland," *New Zealand Building Progress*, June 1917, 975.

73. Elizabeth A. Gagen, "Play the Part: Performing Gender in America's Playgrounds," in *Children's Geographies: Playing, Living, Learning*, edited by Sarah L. Holloway and Gill Valentine (London: Routledge, 2000), 220.

74. Welfare organizations in the vicinity included the Pitt Street Methodist Church, the Baptist Tabernacle, the Sunday School Union, and the Young Men's Christian Association.

75. Anéne Cusins-Lewer and Julia Gatley, "The 'Myers Park Experiment' (1913–1916) and Its Legacy in Auckland," *Fabrications: The Journal of the Society of Architectural Historians, Australia and New Zealand* 12.1 (2002), 59–80.

76. See letters on TC Series 275/5/1917/1219, ACA.

77. May, *The Discovery of Early Childhood*, 61.

78. Mary Trewby, The Best Years of Your Life: A History of New Zealand Childhood (Auckland: Viking, 1995), 12.

PART TWO

The Choreography of Education and Play

5

A Breath of Fresh Air

Open-Air Schools in Europe

ANNE-MARIE CHÂTELET

One imagines open-air schools to be more cheerful places than other schools—places with more trees, where children spend more time out of doors. All of this is true, but does not tell the full story. The open-air school, rare today, was a specific kind of establishment: the schools admitted children at risk from tuberculosis at a time when that disease was an ever-present scourge.[1] Often described as a social disease, tuberculosis especially affected anyone living in unhygienic conditions or poor housing, including city dwellers for whom development had failed to keep pace with the high level of migration from the countryside. Medicine could do little against this blight. Although two discoveries—the identification of the tuberculosis bacillus by Robert Koch (1843–1910) in 1882 and the discovery of the X-ray by Wilhelm Conrad Röntgen (1845–1923)—had opened up new prospects, the real turning point in combating the disease came with the arrival of streptomycin in 1944. Until then, no drug treatments were available; the preferred form of therapy was the open-air cure.

Doctors formulated solutions that went beyond medical treatment. They emphasized patient hygiene and improvement in living conditions, including those in both health establishments and housing. Their idea was to create the conditions for cure through exposure to air, making each room and each house a potential place of treatment. This understanding of the problem led to solutions such as those proposed by the physician David Sarason, who in 1907 suggested constructing stepped buildings with wide terraces on every floor.[2] Terraced buildings, villa-style hospitals, roof terraces, deep balconies, large windows—in fact, any arrangement that would let in great masses of air and light—became the aim of the designers of a new kind of hygienic architecture. This trend continued and in due course affected the architecture of schools in the form of the open-air school concept. The creation of this institution on the fringes of the traditional school system gave its promoters a freedom of action that enabled them to devise innovative solutions in the educational and architectural spheres. In this chapter I shall examine the nature and scope of those innovations.

The Open-Air Suburban Cure Stations of Berlin (1900)

The open-air school was born in Germany. The movement began in Berlin in the late 1890s, following an investigation by the physicians Rudolf Lennhoff (1866–1933) and Wolf Becher (1862–1906) into the living conditions of workers with tuberculosis. Lacking the means to improve these conditions, they came up with another solution: the creation of open-air cure institutions, which, unlike sanatoria, would be accessible and cheap. The first cure station (*Erholungstätte*) for men was opened in May 1900 northwest of the city.[3] It consisted of prefabricated Doecker sheds, generally used by the army and supplied by Christoph und Unmack, specialists in timber prefabrication, which were placed in the middle of a pine forest, near a railway station. Its success was immediate and led to the creation of more establishments in the Berlin suburbs and in other German cities.[4]

Similar institutions were set up for women, and according to Lennhoff these were the basis for the creation of children's cure stations (*Kindererholungsstätte)*, intended for children whose mothers were unable to leave home during the treatment. Becher opened the first one in May 1902 at Schönholz in northeast Berlin, and Lennhoff the second at Sadowa in the southwestern suburbs.[5] They admitted girls and boys aged three to fourteen. Like adults, children arrived by tram and spent the day there. They were well fed and their health was monitored. The small patients played, did gymnastic exercises, and had a two-hour rest, but they could not keep up with their schoolwork. So after a few weeks, a couple of hours of teaching were introduced daily. Originally founded by doctors, the cure station thus opened its doors to teachers, prefiguring the reversal that followed: a school open to doctors.

The Charlottenburg *Waldschule* in Germany (1904)

The impetus for the creation of the first open-air school came from an educator, Hermann Neufert (1858–1935). He was an education councilor (*Stadtsschulrat*) in Charlottenburg, in Berlin's eastern suburbs, and worked in collaboration with a school physician, Bernhard Bendix. Both were convinced that the brisk air of the nearby Grünewald forests would be good for weak children and felt that the Schönholz open-air cure station, less than ten kilometers from Charlottenburg, was the right example to follow in developing their proposal. The location they chose was a one-hectare wooded plot owned by a property development firm that agreed to make the site available free of charge for several years.[6] The Ladies of the Red Cross (a patriotic association) offered to supply a free Doecker-type cabin to house the amenities.[7] Once the proposal was ready, events moved very fast. It was approved on the seventh of June 1904 by the school doctors; on the ninth by the local authority; on the tenth by a delegation from the school board.[8] On the fifteenth of July, the municipal council ratified it, granting a subsidy of 32,000

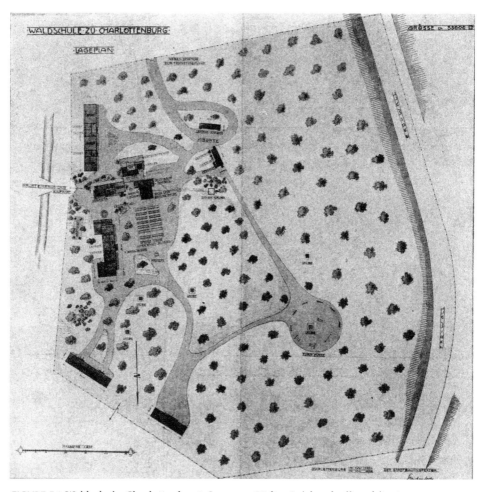

FIGURE 5.1 Waldschule, Charlottenburg, Germany; Walter Spickendorff, architect, 1904.
From A. Kraft, *Waldschulen* (Zurich: Orell Füssli, 1908).

marks.[9] Construction had already begun (immediately after the royal license was
issued on the fifth of July). The open-air school, founded therefore by the municipality, opened on the first day of August.

The name given to the school was *Waldschule* (forest school), because it was
situated in the heart of a pine forest, as the open-air cure stations had been. A
tramway ran to the site. The school was designed by the city architect Walter
Spickendorff; he had three objectives: to maintain visibility for the purpose of
surveillance; to retain the irregular form of the existing landscape and all of the
tall pine trees; and to provide maximum exposure to the sun.[10] He created a
slight hollow in the middle of the plot, which constituted the heart of the school:
a space with plants and shelter, surrounded by activity areas, overlooked by the
rest galleries, classrooms, kitchen, and toilets (Figure 5.1). To the right of the

FIGURE 5.2 Waldschule, Charlottenburg, Germany. Classroom and dining sheds.
From A. Kraft, *Waldschulen* (Zurich: Orell Füssli, 1908).

entrance was the schoolhouse: a wooden Doecker cabin housing two six-by-eight-meter classrooms and two small offices for the principal and teachers. Since they were used as playrooms and refectory in bad weather, they were furnished with easily transportable birch tables and chairs, in three sizes.

The facilities—kitchen, storerooms, and two other rooms, one of them serving as a medical room—were located south of the school in the Doecker cabin provided by the Red Cross. The kitchen had a hatch in the northern wall where the children went to collect their food, and long lunch tables and benches of a suitable size were situated opposite. This area formed an open-air dining room, installed under two shelters amid the pine trees (Figure 5.2). The service courtyard housed further storerooms and a wooden bath cabin that contained two washrooms, a shower, two bathtubs, and six changing rooms. A little way to the west was the gymnastics apparatus, and to the north an open rest gallery with an overhanging roof. Around the site were benches under bowers of woven branches. In the first year of operation, the school admitted between 95 and 120 children, selected from local Charlottenburg schools by the school physicians. The teaching staff consisted of one female and three male teachers, two of whom were former tuberculosis patients who had been cured in a sanatorium. Employed by the Charlottenburg school authority, the staff was assigned to work at the Waldschule during the summer and until it closed on the first of November. This date was chosen because of the shortness of the days, rather than the cold.

On the children's admission, a doctor examined them. At the end of their stay, most of them had improved markedly. The school grew quickly. In subsequent years, it admitted a growing number of pupils for increasingly long periods. It took about 1 percent of the pupils of the local Charlottenburg schools, although this was well below the 4 percent targeted by the school physicians.[11] This increase demanded new teachers and a second three-classroom cabin. In 1908, the school principal, Lange, mentioned the installation of an "air and sun bathing area"—a mound of earth some twenty meters long and eight meters wide, surrounded by a two-meter-high wooden fence.[12] The children came to this place in swimming costumes and straw hats, to lie in the sand and soak up the sunshine; the session ended with a shower. Lange also referred to school gardens, where children were offered plots to cultivate.

Half School, Half Open-Air Cure: New Layout

Modest as it was in scale, the Waldschule might have faded into oblivion. As well as proving therapeutic effectiveness, however, it was also an innovative educational experiment. Boys and girls were educated together, contrary to normal practice in the primary schools of the time. According to Neufert, the results of this departure were entirely positive.[13] Class size averaged twenty pupils, instead of the usual forty or fifty. Lessons lasted for two or three hours a day, depending on the level of the class, with breaks every half hour. Practical lessons and singing and gymnastics took place outside, as did games, meals, and the two-hour rest periods. The children gardened, learning about the principal local species.[14] In one of the lunch shelters, a notice board showed daytime temperature, wind direction, barometric pressure, and cloud conditions, teaching the children about the weather.

Lange stresses the modernity of this educational approach, with its emphasis on direct observation rather than "indirect" studies of stuffed animals and dried plants (the norm in primary schools).[15] In addition, teachers remained in school from 7:45 A.M. to 7 P.M., dedicating all their time to the children. They were asked to adapt their methods and the "tone" of their teaching to the children's behavior, replacing irony and sarcasm with encouragement. In the first year, Neufert evaluated the experiment using information provided by the Charlottenburg schools. While twelve children still appeared weak, most had not fallen behind in their schoolwork, and some of them had even improved.[16] In certain respects, such as its emphasis on the bond with nature and respect for the children's living patterns, the school's approach resembled that of certain rural boarding schools (*Landerziehungsheim*) based on the experiment set up by Hermann Lietz, in 1898, at Ilsenburg in the Harz mountains. However, in one respect it differed greatly: the Waldschule was for working-class children, while the rural boarding schools were private institutions exclusively for children of the middle classes.

The other feature that made the school modern was its design. The term might seem exaggerated given its basic and temporary character; however, the design gave a foretaste of things to come. To begin with, it was distinctive in its remoteness from the city center, which meant that the children had to commute every day. In return, they enjoyed cleaner air and a quieter location than they would have found in the center. Next, there was the size and nature of the plot: the external area of a normal Prussian school had two square meters per pupil, whereas Waldschule children enjoyed almost forty square meters.[17] In addition, while the spaces in most schools were bounded by the compulsory separation of boys and girls, here there were no boundaries other than those of the plot itself.

Finally, the ground was sandy and planted with pine trees, whereas most school playgrounds had asphalt surfaces.

Because it was a medical establishment dedicated to the care of pretubercular children, the Waldschule included a cure gallery. This was the "nucleus of treatment for tuberculosis."[18] This item was defined in 1899 as a wooden structure, free on all sides, open on the south and with windows on the north.[19] It thus introduced a principle of geographical orientation previously neglected in teaching establishments, which, like many public buildings, were generally aligned along main roads. The Waldschule was different; Spickendorff says that he chose for the different buildings "the most appropriate solar exposure": east for the classrooms, south for the cure gallery.[20]

Spread of the Waldschule Concept

This experiment was backed by the Prussian government which, in 1906, sent a circular to educational leaders encouraging the creation of similar establishments.[21] It was publicized by its promoters at international conferences, especially the successive conferences on school hygiene held in Nuremberg in 1904, London in 1907, Paris in 1910, and Buffalo in 1913. As a result, numerous open-air schools were created in Germany—in Mulhouse,[22] Mönchengladbach,[23] Strasbourg,[24] Elberfeld, Lübeck,[25] and Dortmund[26]—and also all around the world. In Europe, they were generally founded by municipal authorities. In 1904, the inaugural year of the Charlottenburg Waldschule, a similar experiment, the "Diesterweg School Villa," was launched in Flanders for children from the city of Anvers.[27] In 1907, the mayor of Lyon, Edouard Herriot, founded the first school in France, and similar establishments also opened their doors in Padua in Italy, near London in Great Britain, and in Lausanne in Switzerland.[28] The next year, the first Spanish experiment began in Barcelona.[29] Then, in 1912, came a school in the Netherlands in Den Haag, followed in 1914 by one in Stockholm in Sweden.[30]

The propagation of the open-air school did not stop at the borders of Europe. The movement very quickly extended across the Atlantic Ocean to the United States. Open-air schools were built in cities along the East Coast and sponsored by anti-tuberculosis associations. Their role was even more crucial in the United States than in Europe due to the low level of municipal involvement as compared with some European countries. According to Kingsley and Dresslar, the first American open-air school was founded in 1908 in Providence, Rhode Island, at the instigation of the Providence League for the Suppression of Tuberculosis.[31] Six years later the open-air school idea reached the shores of Australia. Here again, the movement spread rapidly and extended to the whole country: between 1910 and 1925, hundreds of establishments were created.[32] And this round-the-world tour is not exhaustive.[33]

In fourteen years, the Waldschule spread widely. Rooted in different cultural contexts, it also underwent changes. The first was the name. Although the term

Waldschule remained common in Germany, it rarely was literally translated. True, in Spain, the Catalans chose "escuela del bosque," an expression taken up in Madrid in 1918. In French, we also find the terms "école sous bois"[34] or "école forestière,"[35] but "école de plein air" is the one that has stuck. The Swiss initially adopted "école de la forêt," but then also opted for "école de plein air."[36] As for the English, they quickly opted for "open-air school," the name that has been retained in English-speaking countries.

From the 1920s onward, this expansion was sustained by the development of an international movement. The first congress was held in 1922 at the Faculty of Medicine in Paris, reflecting the founding role played by the medical community.[37] More than two hundred participants from many countries attended. Germany, uninvited following its defeat in World War I, was notable for its absence. The second congress took place in Brussels at Easter 1931, and the proceedings were published. This was significant not only as that country's first involvement in the conferences but also as an indication that the balance of influence was shifting from the medical to the educational establishment.[38] The third conference, the last before World War II, was held in Bielefeld and Hanover, Germany, in 1936.

The Birmingham Open-Air School (1911)

The first open-air schools were, like Charlottenburg, modest constructions: a few marquees or temporary cabins set up on an available plot, and simple in design. However, the new type of establishment aroused interest and in subsequent years began to attract greater investment for the creation of "permanent open-air schools." This aspiration involved contradictory imperatives: a building that would provide necessary protection from the weather together with internal spaces that would offer an open-air experience. In other words, the challenge was to build a protective envelope, while making its substance as immaterial as possible.

One of the first responses was formulated near Birmingham, England, by the architect F. Barry Peacock of Cossins, Peacock and Bewlay. The instigators of the open-air school scheme were Barrow and Geraldine Cadbury, of the famous chocolate family. One of their sons, Paul, had contracted tuberculosis and was treated, on their doctor's advice, through open-air living. This cure and the almost simultaneous creation of the first open-air schools in the London suburbs had convinced the couple of the advantages of this type of establishment.[39] In 1910, they put forward a proposal to Councilor Norman Chamberlain of the Birmingham Education Committee: "We have pleasure in offering to the Education Committee the free use of a field of five acres . . . opposite Uffculme, which is 500 feet above sea-level with an open view. . . . The Kings Heath trams pass the gate. We are prepared to provide the simple buildings and furniture required for such a school which we understand will cost about £400."[40] They therefore financed the building, and the municipality funded the school.

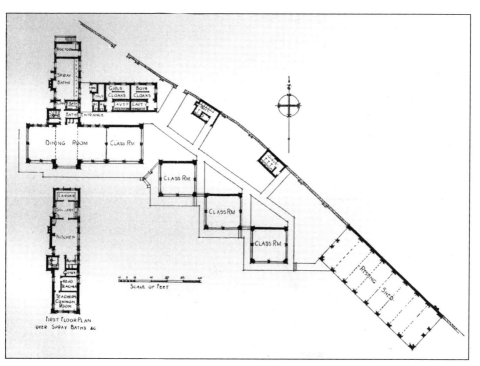

FIGURE 5.3 Uffculme Open-Air School, Birmingham, Great Britain; Barry Peacock, architect, 1911.

From Felix Clay, *Modern School Buildings, Elementary and Secondary*
(London: Batsford, 1929), ill. 102.

Like the Charlottenburg Waldschule, the school was sited in the suburbs on a plot of some two hectares; it was also made up three types of buildings: classrooms, service rooms, and an open gallery.[41] However, it differed from the German predecessor in two respects: first, the site was not in the middle of a forest, and more important, the buildings were not cabins—a situation that required the principals and their architect to look in detail at the precise architectural layout. The most thought was given to the essence of the school: the classrooms. Whereas the Waldschule classrooms, installed in one of the Doecker cabins, were only used occasionally, with most teaching taking place outside, in Uffculme, Peacock took up the challenge of building true open-air classrooms. The outcome comprised three square wood and brick villas, which opened on three sides by means of folding glass doors; they were topped by a pavilion roof (Figures 5.3, 5.4). Only on the northern side was there a solid brick wall, where the blackboard was hung. "Geraldine Cadbury is credited with the ingenious idea of the central heating system whereby under-floor hot water pipes ran around the sides of the classroom beneath a grille; the theory being that the cold air entering the room would be tempered by the rising heat."[42] A similar change was applied to the eating area: Charlottenburg's outdoor refectory was replaced in

FIGURE 5.4 Uffculme Open-Air School, Birmingham, Great Britain, classroom.
From Felix Clay, *Modern School Buildings, Elementary and Secondary*
(London: Batsford, 1929), ill. 96.

Uffculme by a dining room designed in the same way as the classrooms, with folding glass doors on three sides and under-floor heating. Both classrooms and dining room faced south. Finally, Charlottenburg's cure gallery became a rest gallery at Uffculme, with similar construction materials and layout, but larger in its proportions and with a southeastern exposure.

On September 18, 1911, the school opened its doors to eighty children, boys and girls, chosen from the city's ten thousand schoolchildren by Dr. Auden, Birmingham's School Medical Officer.[43] His 1911 report gives an idea of the children's day-to-day routines:

> They receive a breakfast of porridge, milk or cocoa, and bread and butter. It has been found necessary to give some of the children an additional morning meal of hot milk at 11 o'clock. On arrival each child dons a jersey and a pair of clogs, and during the cold weather a knitted cap as well. When sitting at their desks in cold weather the children wrap up their legs and feet in a rug. A two-course meal at 12.30 is followed by one-and-a-half hours sleep. At 4.40 pm the children have their third meal and leave for home at 5.30 pm. Each child is provided with a toothbrush, which is used before they leave for home.[44]

The medical results exceeded all expectations.[45] The success was probably due as much to the quality and quantity of the food as to the fresh air, which was an aspect of the "hygieno-dietetic" cure defined by the founder of the sanatorium movement, Hermann Brehmer. The educational practices were in some respects similar to those of Charlottenburg: coeducation, open-air practical lessons and gymnastics, gardening, weather observation. However, the discipline may have been too strict, and the children lacked freedom and autonomy, if the annual report of the assistant superintendent of special schools in 1914 is to be believed.[46] It is harder to know what the children themselves thought, although an account by a former pupil who attended the school between 1915 and 1918 is positive and full of the pleasure of being in the country, among the "flowers and buttercups."[47]

Built with ordinary materials and traditional techniques that were standard in the English countryside, the architecture is nevertheless surprisingly bold. The plan shows a freedom of layout tempered by the need to face the sun, as at Charlottenburg. The most striking thing is permeability to the environment. Made of brick, wood and glass, the protective envelope could nonetheless become almost invisible. The classrooms were like independent units, level with the surrounding fields. Their walls could be folded back to let in light, wind, smells, and the countryside. And yet they were more than just shelters. The children enjoyed amenities similar to those of a traditional classroom. Under-floor heating modulated the temperature of the fresh air around them. The folding glass doors could be fully or partially closed to protect them from the rain or wind. True, it might be pointed out that the technical solutions were not completely successful. The classroom floor was actually raised one step above the surrounding level, the corners were supported by massive brick columns, the French doors were only centrally folding, and finally, the heating apparently did not fulfill expectations.[48] Nonetheless, the building as a whole, represented an inventive and tailored response in light of the available financial resources.

Architectural Layout

After a two-year interruption caused by World War I, interest in the design of open-air schools quickly resumed, prompted by difficult living conditions and deprivations suffered by children. However, financial difficulties were such that nothing was built for the next few years. Construction only began again at the end of the 1920s. It was usually financed by socially committed local authorities and carried out by municipal architects. These schools differed from ordinary schools in the size of their plots, the extent of their health amenities, the complexity of their lighting and ventilation systems, and their close links with nature. The best-known constructions are those in Arnhem (H.B. van Broekhuizen, 1930) and Amsterdam (Jan Duiker, 1927–1930) in Holland; Saint-Quentin (Germain Debré, 1931), Roubaix (Jacques Greber, 1931) and Suresnes (Beaudouin and Lods,

1931–1935) in France; Cottbus (Schroeder, c.1930) and Dresden (Paul Wolf, 1931) in Germany; and Copenhagen (Kaj Gottlob, 1938) in Denmark. Others were built in Great Britain, Austria, and even Morocco.[49] If certain accounts are to be believed, the number of open-air schools ran into the hundreds, but most of them are little known or have not been identified.[50]

The early Uffculme design suggested the adoption of a villa layout that would fulfill both medical and educational requirements, with each classroom designed as an independent unit opening into nature. It represented an idealized version of the Waldschule cabin classroom, and was indirectly inspired by the development of detached hospital units, promoted at the time as the ideal in terms of hygiene. Similar adaptations to school architecture had actually been proposed as early as 1907 by the Staffordshire County architect John Hutchings, at the prompting of the physician Georges Reid. For him, the essential thing was that the classrooms should be ventilated on two sides, hence the access via an open gallery. After the Uffculme experiment, the villa design persisted in England, as may be seen from the open-air school built in North Shields in 1925. Its two classrooms are small, detached villas, with all sides other than the northern made up of folding glass doors.

In the rest of Europe, however, many architects sought compromises to reduce the financial costs associated with plot size and to resolve the difficulties involved in heating and watching detached villas. They tried solutions that would retain the advantages of the villa classroom design, especially the openness to nature, but with a denser construction. In Dresden, for example, Paul Wolf joined two classrooms together; standing level with the wide outdoor terraces, they were lit and ventilated on two sides. In Arnhem, Van den Broekhuizen combined three classrooms within a single structure, while retaining partial openness on three sides by offsetting the rooms in relation to each other. In Copenhagen, Gottlob employed an octagonal layout to group classrooms while retaining the glass walls on the three sides.

The most radical design, in terms of density and openness, was by the architect Jan Duiker (1890–1935) for the Amsterdam open-air school, which was atypical in other ways. First, it was designed for children in good health, with the intention of extending the educational benefits of this type of establishment to all schoolchildren. And second, it was to be built in the city, on a 2,000-square-meter plot in the middle of a housing block in the South Amsterdam district, then being built by H. P. Berlage. Duiker responded to the challenge by grouping the classrooms in pairs, with a terrace of equivalent dimensions between them for open-air activities. These were superimposed on one another to form three floors in a diagonal layout, with the blackboard in a corner recess. The concrete construction removed the need for weight-bearing corner columns, all four sides had long continuous strips of windows, and the heating was filtered through the ceiling (Figure 5.5). The result is remarkable: the classrooms are more open than in the villa design; it is what Duiker calls "a glass wardrobe," an architecture that

FIGURE 5.5 Open-Air School for Healthy Children, Cliostraat, Amsterdam, Holland. Jan Duiker, architect, 1930.

Netherlands Architecture Institute, Rotterdam.

fulfils contradictory requirements: high permeability to air and light together with great compactness.

The Suresnes Open-Air School (1931–1935)

Diametrically different was the open-air school built by Eugène Beaudouin (1898–1983) and Marcel Lods (1891–1978) in Suresnes, west of Paris.[51] One of the last to be built before World War II, it combined all the knowledge accumulated in some thirty years of experimentation. The decision to build was taken by a remarkable Socialist mayor, Henri Sellier (1883–1943), who became minister of health in 1936. Construction was overseen by the mayor's general secretary, Louis Boulonnois, a former primary school teacher and tuberculosis sufferer. It was situated on a sloping 1.89-hectare plot on the southern flank of Mont Valérien. In their earliest sketches, the architects opted for a villa design, with each classroom flush with and opening onto the surrounding land, and a layout very reminiscent of the classrooms of the Amsterdam open-air school, which they had visited shortly before with Sellier.[52] The project was, however, subsequently redesigned to meet three essential criteria, as Boulonnois explained:

> [The first is that] the design of a school should be a team effort between
> local administrators, educationalists, social workers, and architects. The

second is the theory that, following Lods, we have called the "circulation-school" system. The most important thing in a school is not the body of the building or the way the alveolae are grouped. It is the articulations of the classrooms, the corridors, the changes of level, the actual representation of the movements required by the timetable. And finally, the third is the law of double relaxation. Each school premises should have an "expansion chamber" for ordered exercise and voluntary mental discipline. Rather than resembling a cell or alveola, the classroom should have a proscenium or an enclosed lawn.[53]

The school entrance was marked by a large globe (map of the world), surrounded by a helical stair, which children could walk up (Figure 5.6). They arrived at a long building at the northern edge of the plot, slightly angled toward the park and protected from cold winds (Figure 5.7). This building contained amenities and communal areas: kitchen and dining room, playrooms and showers. The structure as a whole was Janus-like: a blind wall of prefabricated panels set with large blue-black pebbles on the northern side, all transparent glass on the southern side. The shower basins ran along the front of the building, partly in the open air.

The medical service pavilion (infirmary) was situated in the middle of the park, while eight classroom villas, with glass doors on three sides that could be entirely folded back to the corners, were distributed around the site (Figure 5.8).

FIGURE 5.6 Suresnes Open-Air School, France. Eugène Beaudouin and Marcel Lods architects, 1931–1935. The globe marked the entrance of the school.

Postcard, author's collection.

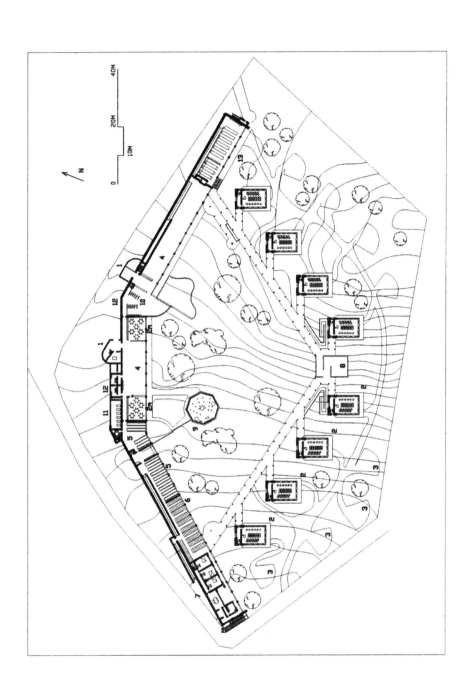

FIGURE 5.8 Suresnes Open-Air School, France, classroom.
Postcard, author's collection.

An under-floor heating system heated the floor slabs and the surrounding air; the warm air emerged through grilles running around the edge of each room, so that children were enveloped in a curtain of warm air. The result is somewhat reminiscent of the Uffculme villas built twenty years earlier. However, the technical solutions are more sophisticated and the architectural language more modern. The entire structure was made of metal and glass, using innovative solutions both for the system of construction and for the window opening mechanisms. The architectural expression, with its emphasis on transparency and oblique views, was of cubist inspiration.

In 1935, the school opened its doors to 211 pupils selected from the Suresnes schools by the schools' medical inspection department headed by the physician

FIGURE 5.7 (*opposite*) Suresnes Open-Air School, France. Eugène Beaudouin and Marcel Lods architects, 1931–1935.

Reconstruction drawing by Dagmar Prasilova, 2003.

Key

1. Entrance	8. Medical service pavilion
2. Classroom pavilions	9. Pavilion for special teaching
3. Open-air class	10. Indoor and outdoor splash basin
4. Recreation hall	11. Therapy
5. Dining room	12. Wash and dressing room
6. Rest room	13. Domestic science and needlework
7. Staff quarters	

Robert Hazemann. There were at least eleven teachers.[54] On arrival, the children would receive a medical examination, have a quick wash, and then go to their classroom. They had no more than four hours of lessons and, as in the other open-air schools, physical activities, afternoon rest, and light meals were alternated throughout the day. There was coeducation, together with other aspects of open-air living: attention to the children's health and bodily development as well as education based on direct observation of nature, drawing on the ideas of the Active School and of Célestin Freinet (1896–1966).

Recent interviews reflect the children's pleasure: "It was great, always out of doors, even in winter."[55] The daughter of one of the first principals even remembers that "the children loved their school. They didn't want to leave: in the evening, they cried when they were put on the bus."[56] The adults also seem to have liked the school. In her *Souvenirs de la maison de verre* (*Memories of the Glass House*), Simonne Lacapère, principal from 1954 to 1976, recalls that "educative community," emphasizing how stimulating its unusual and flexible architecture was: "Living here in this hectare and a half of greenery, trees, flowers, and pure lines, sheltered from the prevailing winds by the huge pebble-embedded wall that supports the communal buildings, you find yourself asking how Sellier, his colleagues and his architects, were able to think of everything and to elicit modern and a rational methods of education simply by the disposition of the buildings, the amenities, the material organization."[57]

Influences

Other open-air schools were built after Suresnes, but the discovery of antibiotics at the end of World War II removed their raison d'être. After this, few opened and many closed. Those that still survive have been converted. Uffculme has become one of the principal establishments for autistic children in the United Kingdom, while Suresnes is used by the National Study and Training Centre for Maladjusted Children. Of the three that survive, only Amsterdam, designed for all children from the start, has kept to its original purpose. In 1953, the fifth meeting under the aegis of the International Committee for Open-Air Education was held in Switzerland.[58] This, the second postwar conference, was the last one of the open-air movement.[59] Nonetheless, the disappearance of the schools and of the movement that accompanied their development did not spell the end of the ideas associated with them, which continued to influence education and schools architecture after the 1930s.

An early example of this influence were schools built in Frankfurt. "In spring 1928, "writes the architect Wilhelm Schütte, "it was agreed with the educational authorities that new schools should be built . . . using a villa design, amid green spaces, to meet the demand for open-air education, for a link with nature, the need for light, air and sunshine."[60] Two schools built between 1928 and 1930, one in Bornheimer Hang designed by Ernst May and one in Praunheim by Eugen

FIGURE 5.9 Praunheim School, Frankfurt, Germany. Eugen Kaufmann and Willi Pullmann, architects, 1929–1931.

Institut für Stadtgeschichte, Frankfurt.

Kauffmann and Willi Pullmann, had ground-level classrooms opening onto an outdoor space for use as an open-air classroom (Figure 5.9). While their sanitary amenities were not as sophisticated as those of the open-air schools, the teaching spaces had the same qualities. The decisions, as we have seen, were taken by the educators, but the architects were also seduced by certain aspects of these schools.

In architectural terms, open-air buildings means those with maximum exposure to their environment, the interpenetration of interior and exterior spaces, and a multiplicity of terraces and balconies. These ideas found a receptive audience among architects because they corresponded to a widely shared dual social preoccupation: the prevention of tuberculosis and aesthetic aspirations. Removing the boundaries of the building in order to expose it as much as possible to the outside corresponded to spatial conceptions propagated by cubism and neoplasticism. This convergence between the ideas applied in the experimental context of the open-air schools and those propagated by progressive architectural movements explains their long-standing influence on school construction, which lasted at least until 1960.

After World War II, when many European countries were looking to rebuild bombed schools, the road seemed clear. The open-air school had emerged from the shadow of tuberculosis; it was backed by leading figures of the modern movement. *The New School, La Nouvelle École, Das Neue Schulhaus*, the seminal work of

FIGURE 5.10 Impington School, Great Britain. Walter Gropius and Maxwell Fry, architects, 1939.

From Alfred Roth, *The New School, La Nouvelle École, Das Neue Schulhaus*
(Zurich: Gisberger, 1950), 127.

the Swiss architect Alfred Roth, was published in 1950.[61] His ambition was to "present the basic ideas involved and . . . furnish incentives toward a methodical solution." He cited open-air schools in three cities as models—Suresnes, Amsterdam, and Copenhagen—and single-story schools with classrooms opening at ground level into the open air: Bruderholz School, Basel, designed by the architect Hermann Baur (1938–1939); Impington School, Cambridgeshire, by Walter Gropius and Maxwell Fry (1939) (Figure 5.10); and Crown Island School in Winnetka, Illinois, by Eliel and Eero Saarinen and Lawrence Perkins, Philip Will, and E. Todd Wheeler (1939–1940). It will come as no surprise, therefore, that a considerable number of schools of this type would be built in subsequent years, instilling a breath of fresh air into school architecture. In the midst of the baby boom, at a time when public education was a popular issue, these new designs were well suited to rural schools and brought new criteria to urban schools.

NOTES

This chapter was translated by John Crisp. The title is borrowed from Frances Wilmot and Pauline Saul, *A Breath of Fresh Air: Birmingham's Open-Air Schools* (Phillimore: Chichester, 1998). I would like to thank Marta Gutman and Ning de Coninck-Smith for inviting me to contribute my research on open-air schools.

1. Charles Coury, *Grandeur et déclin d'une maladie: La tuberculose au cours des âges* (Suresnes: Lepetit, 1972), 200.

2. David Sarason, *Ein neues Bauprinzip (Terrassen-System) für Krankenanstalten und Wohnhaüser* (Berlin, Imberg & Lefson, 1907).

3. Wolf Becher and Rudolf Lennhoff, "Über die Kindererholungsstätten vom Roten Kreuz bei Berlin," in *Das Deutsche Rote Kreuz und die Tuberkulose-Bekämpfung: Denkschrift für den Internationalen Tuberkulose-Kongreß* (Berlin: Das Rote Kreuz, 1908), 115–118.

4. Hützer, "Über Walderholungsstätten und Waldschulen," *Centralblatt für allgemeine Gesundheitspflege* 25.1–2 (1906): 73.

5. Becher and Lennhoff, "Über die Kindererholungsstätten," 115–118.

6. Bernhard Bendix, "Über die Charlottenburger Waldschule," *Deutsche Vierteljahrsschrift für öffentliche Gesundheitspflege* 39 (1907): 308; W. Lange, "Die Waldschule," *Pädagogische Warte* 20 (October 15, 1908), 1096–1107.

7. Vaterländische Frauenverein in German. The association of nurses of the Prussian Red Cross was created in 1866.

8. Hermann Neufert and Bernhard Bendix, *Die Charlottenburger Waldschule im ersten Jahre ihres Bestehens* (Berlin: Urban & Schwarzenberg, 1906), 7.

9. Hermann Neufert, "Charlottenburger Waldschule," *Jahrbuch für Volks- und Jugendspiele* 14 (1905): 72.

10. Walter Spickendorff, "Die Charlottenburger Waldschule," *Zentralblatt der Bauverwaltung* 26.83 (October 13, 1906): 528.

11. Bendix, "Über die Charlottenburger Waldschule," 307.

12. Lange, "Die Waldschule," 1100, 1102

13. Neufert, "Charlottenburger Waldschule," 78.

14. Lange, "Die Waldschule," 1100–1101.

15. Drawing on the ideas of Immanuel Kant, some educators distinguished indirect from direct studies (referring to learning from direct observation of nature or indirect study of it in a classroom). For the notion "Anschauung," see Kant's *Kritik der reinen Vernunft* (1787), translated as *Critique of Pure Reason.*

16. Neufert, "Charlottenburger Waldschule," 79, 86–87.

17. Prussian Ministerial Order, dated February 23, 1882, quoted by H. Th. Matthias Meyer, *Die Schulstätten der Zukunft* (Hamburg und Leipzig: Leopold Voss, 1903), 47.

18. Flurin Condrau, *Lungenheilanstalt und Patientenschicksal. Sozialgeschichte der Tuberkulose in Deutschland und England im späten 19. und frühen 20. Jahrhundert,* (Göttingen: Vandenhoeck & Ruprecht, 2000), 125.

19. Josef Durm, Hermann Ende, Eduard Schmitt, and Victor von Weltzien, *Handbuch der Architektur, Vierter Teil, 5. Halbband, Heft 2: Verschiedene Heil- und Pflegeanstalten;Versorgungs-, Pflege- und Zufluchts-häuser* (Stuttgart: A. Kröner, 1903), 132, 135, 137.

20. Spickendorff, "Die Charlottenburger Waldschule," 528.

21. Karl König, "Die Waldschule," *Beiträge zur Kinderforschung und Heilerziehung. Beihefte zur Zeitschrift für Kinderforschung* (Langensalza: Hermann Beyer & Sohne, 1912), vol. 89: 16.

22. König, "Die Waldschule"; Bienstock, "Die Waldschule in Muelhausen," *Straßburger Medizinische Zeitung* 1 (1907): 1–9; Nancy Aubry and Dominique Lerch, "L'école de plein air de Mulhouse: Pfastatt et son évolution (1906–2001)," *Revue d'Alsace, Fédération des sociétés d'histoire et d'archéologie d'Alsace* 129 (2003): 195–225.

23. Schaefer, "Zur Eröffnung der Waldschule der Stadt M.-Gladbach," *Centralblatt für allgemeine Gesundheitspflege* 25.7/8 (1906): 311–315.

24. A. Kraft, *Waldschulen* (Zürich: Art. Institut Orell Füssli, 1908), 219; Lange, "Die Waldschule," 1099.

25. Toni Benda, "Waldschule Wesloe bei Lübeck," *Kind und Kunst* 1 (1908): 2–5.

26. König, "Die Waldschule," 118–122; Sherman C. Kingsley and Fletcher B. Dresslar, *Open Air Schools* (Washington, D.C.: Government Printing Office, 1917) 105–132.

27. Marc Depaepe and Frank Simon, "Open-Air Schools in Belgium," in *Open-Air Schools: An Educational and Architectural Venture in Twentieth-Century Europe*, edited by Anne-Marie Châtelet, Jean-Noël Luc, and Dominique Lerch (Paris: Recherches, 2003), 80–95.

28. The following are in Châtelet, Luc, and Lerch, eds., *Open-Air Schools*: Anne-Marie Châtelet, "From Ideas to Building: The Rise of Open-Air Schools in France (1907–1940)," 168–189; Andrew Saint, "Early Days of the English Open-Air School (1907–1930)," 56–79; Geneviève Heller, "Intensive Hygienic Treatment Cures in Switzerland," 211–221.

29. Javier Rodriguez Méndez, "Architectural Renewal and Open-Air Education in Spain (1910–1936), in *Open-Air Schools*, edited by Châtelet, Luc, and Lerch, 148–167.

30. Dolf Broekhuizen, *Openluchtscholen in Nederland* (Rotterdam: Uitgeverij 010, 2005); Ed Taverne and Dolf Broekhuizen, "Doctors, Teachers and Open-Air Schools in the Netherlands (1905–1931)," in *Open-Air Schools*, edited by Châtelet, Luc, and Lerch, 96–116; Ning de Coninck-Smith, "A Danish Open-Air School by Kaj Gottlob (1935–1938)," in *Open-Air Schools*, edited by Châtelet, Luc, and Lerch, 346–353.

31. Kingsley and Dresslar, *Open Air Schools*, 15–17; Marta Gutman, "Entre moyens de fortune et constructions spécifiques: Les écoles de plein air aux Etats-Unis à l'époque progressiste (1900–1920)," *Histoire de l'éducation* 102 (May 2004): 157–180.

32. Grant Rodwell, "Australian Open-air School Architecture," *History of Education Review* 24.2 (1995): 21–41.

33. "Requests for information on open-air school work have come from Japan, China, India, and South America, but no definite undertakings have been reported," Kingsley and Dresslar, *Open Air Schools*, 166.

34. Henri Schoen, "Les nouvelles écoles sous bois (*Waldschulen*) en Allemagne, en Angleterre et en Suisse," *L'Éducation. Revue trimestrielle illustrée d'éducation familiale et scolaire* 1.3 (1909): 389–420.

35. Robert Dinet, "Les conceptions modernes concernant l'architecture scolaire," *L'hygiène à et par l'école* 4 (April 1913): 40.

36. Heller, "Intensive Hygienic Treatment Cures in Switzerland," 212.

37. *Premier congrès international des écoles de plein air en la faculté de médecine de Paris, 24–28 juin 1922* (Paris: A. Maloine, 1925).

38. Karl Triebold, ed., *Die Freiluftschulbewegung, Versuch einer Darstellung ihres gegenwärtigen internationalen Standes* (Berlin: R. Schoetz, 1931), 1 (Proceedings of the 2nd International Congress on Open-air Schools).

39. Saint, "Early Days of the English Open-Air School," 73–75.

40. Frances Wilmot and Pauline Saul, *A Breath of Fresh Air: Birmingham's Open-Air Schools* (Phillimore: Chichester, 1998), 18.

41. Lange, "Die Waldschule," 110.

42. Wilmot and Saul, *A Breath of Fresh Air*, 22.

43. Wilmot and Saul, *A Breath of Fresh Air*, 23.

44. Wilmot and Saul, *A Breath of Fresh Air*, 25.

45. Wilmot and Saul, *A Breath of Fresh Air*, 31.

46. Wilmot and Saul, *A Breath of Fresh Air*, 37.

47. Wilmot and Saul, *A Breath of Fresh Air*, 43.

48. Wilmot and Saul, *A Breath of Fresh Air*, 22.

49. R. Pradeaux, "Le Jardin du Soleil, école de plein air à Rabat," *La technique des travaux* 1 (January 1935): 18–20.

50. Triebold, *Die Freiluftschulbewegung*, 9–10.

51. Nicolas Pairault, "The Suresnes Open-Air School by Eugène Beaudouin and Marcel Lods (1931–1935)," in *Open-Air Schools*, edited by Châtelet, Luc, and Lerch, 333–345.

52. Bernard Barraqué, "L'école de plein air de Suresnes, symbole d'un projet de réforme sociale par l'espace?" in *La banlieue Oasis. Henri Sellier et les cités-jardins, 1900–1940*, edited by Katherine Burlen (Saint-Denis: Presses Universitaires de Vincennes, 1987), 221–231.

53. Louis Boulonnois, "Architecture serment reel," *Œuvres et maître d'œuvre*, 10 (1948): 1–3. In French *alvéole* means the individual cell in a beehive; the term was used to describe individual classrooms in schools.

54. Florence Laufman, "Open-Air Schools in Suresnes (1921–1944)," in *Open-Air Schools*, edited by Châtelet, Luc, and Lerch, 383–390.

55. Mr. Raboisson, who entered the open-air school in 1945 at the age of 5; my thanks to Marie-Pierre Deguillaume, curator of the municipal museum of René Sordes in Suresnes, who conducted this interview in 2004 and brought it to my attention.

56. Mrs. Guillon (née Miss Boudert) who entered the school at the age of six; interview by Marie-Pierre Deguillaume.

57. Simonne Lacapère, *Souvenirs de la maison de verre. L'école de plein air de Suresnes, communauté éducative* (Blamont: L'Amitié par le livre, 1978), 8, 9.

58. *Pro Juventute* 34.7/8 (1953): 243–302.

59. For the 1949 conference, see: *La nuova scuola italiana. Relazioni del Convegno italo-germanico, maggio 1942, XX, per la preparazione del IV Congresso internazionale dell'educazione all'aperto* (Rome: F. Centenari, 1942), 12–16.

60. Wilhelm Schütte, "Grundsätzliches über neue Volksschulen," *Der Baumeister* 18.12 (1930): 466–539.

61. Alfred Roth, *The New School, La Nouvelle École, Das Neue Schulhaus* (Zurich: Gisberger, 1950).

6

Molding the Republican Generation

The Landscapes of Learning in Early Republican Turkey

ZEYNEP KEZER

In "Memory Train at the Elementary School," Cengiz Çakir, a professor at Pamukkale University, fondly recalled his elementary school in Sarayköy, a small town in the province of Denizli in West Central Turkey:

> I attended Sarayköy Gazi Elementary School.[1] It was an impressive two-story masonry structure close to the train station at the end of Station Street, our town's largest thoroughfare. On the street side, its low patio wall was finished with decorative stonework and regularly punctuated with mini-turrets, which framed the wrought iron railings running between them . . . the railings allowed passers-by to see happy little children running around in the schoolyard and allowed us to see the outside. . . . The school building was on the south side of the lot, to the north was the playground. The three-way flight of steps leading up to the main entrance were made of gravel-speckled concrete. Our classrooms had high ceilings and tall narrow windows—they were light and airy. The windows were topped with pointed arches fitted with specially cut triangle- and square-shaped glass. . . . With its zinc rain gutters, dark yellow masonry façade, wide eaves held up by sculpted wood bracings, and soffits ornamented with blue square patterns, our school was very pleasing to the eye.[2]

The school grounds emerge as an integral part of Çakir's learning experience as he mentally traces his memory of his path from the patio into the building, through the hallways, the map room, the science lab, and the equipment depot. Each anecdote Çakir invokes is firmly anchored in place: from how, after a rain, his teacher took the class outside to demonstrate miniature versions of geographic formations—islands, lakes, coves, and peninsulas—in the puddles formed in the patio; to how he and his friends built a mock telegraph system to communicate between classrooms in Morse code. So cherished are these memories that, when he walks past this building as an adult, Çakir explains, "my heart leaps up and I revere this building as if it were a temple."[3]

Çakir's recollections, narrated in highly personalized terms, are part of the larger, shared collective memory of a generation that came of age during the formative years of Turkey's transition from the war-torn ruins of the Ottoman Empire to a modern nation-state. The neophyte state's leaders recognized the transformative capacity of education and deployed it as a primary instrument for forging a polity of loyal citizens, who, above all else, saw themselves as members of the Turkish nation and were committed to the ideals of unity and progress as articulated by their leaders. Çakir, a product of this educational system, appreciates the decision of the republic's founding fathers to prioritize education: "On the building's south side, facing the train station, the name GAZI ELEMENTARY SCHOOL was engraved on a marble plaque with large letters, followed by 1931, the date of completion. . . . In 1931, the Republic was barely eight years old. This monumental school building finished during the hardest economic times in the aftermath of the worldwide Depression is an indisputable testament to the importance placed on education at the time."[4]

Scholars have long acknowledged the strategic role education plays in nation-building processes.[5] In Turkey, educational reforms were integral to the sweeping changes introduced by the country's leaders, who were uncompromising in their desire to bring all schools under government control and standardize and secularize both the contents of their offerings and their administration. To date, most research about the history of educational reform in Turkey has concentrated on the implementation of legal and institutional measures.[6] Recent studies, focusing mainly on textual analysis of instructional materials such as curricula and textbooks, have examined how their ideologically charged content has contributed to the nation-building process.[7] By contrast, the material culture of education has garnered relatively scant attention.[8] With few exceptions, the actual sites of learning and the artifacts used in teaching have not been examined in significant detail, even though they appear to frame just about every personal narrative.[9] In this chapter, I address this gap by drawing attention to the crucial role of the physical environment in transforming school children into modern Turkish citizens. I examine not only what children learned but also where and how they learned, and propose that rather than serving as neutral backdrops to the process of indoctrination, the sites and tools of education systematically framed and ordered the students' relationship with the world around them.[10] Elementary education in early republican Turkey was designed expressly to train children to read the physical and visual clues in their everyday settings as markers of a radically different social and political order from that experienced by the previous generation.

My conclusions concur with environmental memory research, which suggests that spatial practices mobilize aspects of mental processes and memory formation different from those based on words and narratives.[11] For children, as for adults, verbal, visual, and spatial memories are information acquisition processes in their own right and each is acquired, stored, and retrieved differently. They cannot be substituted for one another, but may complement each other during retrieval. More important, memory for spaces and artifacts has a distinctly privileged status, not shared even by visual stimuli. The knowledge of space precedes knowledge of language, and memory of space cannot be reduced to language. Research about the biological basis of memory processes has bolstered these assertions. The officials who authored Turkey's educational policies and made recommendations about pedagogical techniques obviously did not have the benefit of these scientific insights. But space has been recognized as a mnemonic device for centuries. As Frances Yates demonstrated in her classic study, societies have long used spatial memory to facilitate the storage and retrieval of other kinds of information.[12] Hence even in the absence of scientific data by which to assess or fine-tune their interventions, early republican policy makers took advantage of the mnemonic qualities of spaces and artifacts. Thus I argue that exploring how spaces and artifacts were used in the cultivation of nationalist sensibilities in children reveals unexplored levels at which nation-building processes operate, complementing previous studies focusing primarily on text and policy analysis.

Centralizing Education

During the Ottoman Empire, the state was not deeply involved in the administration of education, which remained mostly private and parochial. Until the last century of the empire, education had a relatively narrow focus and was overseen by the empire's different ethnoreligious constituencies.[13] Starting in the 1830s, Ottoman officials initiated a wide range of reforms to modernize the state and render it more effective. These included the establishment of state-sponsored secular institutions of higher learning. The education of younger pupils, however, remained under the jurisdiction of various religious constituencies until the last quarter of nineteenth century, when modern secular schools (*rüstiye* and *idadi*) were opened in several provinces. As with other Ottoman reforms, the new institutions did not eliminate existing ones; rather, they were added on to a complex panoply of choices. Consequently, multiple types of schools and educational systems that were redundant or mutually incompatible coexisted. Unity in the sense promoted by the nationalists was inherently counter to the multicultural, multiethnic constitution of the empire, which continued to tolerate and sustain differences in education—and other areas—even when such diversity could (and did) threaten its authority.

In contrast, the republican leaders, who took office after leading Turkey's War of Independence against the Allied occupation following World War I, favored a single centralized national model for education. They considered education a vital priority, and changing its institutional framework was among the first reforms they introduced. Recognizing the impossibility of accomplishing any meaningful change without severing the manifold historic ties between the Ottoman-Islamic religious establishment and education, the republican leaders eliminated the office of the caliph on the same day they issued the Unification of Education Act (*Tevhid-i Tedrisat Kanunu*). The law brought all formal education in Turkey under the control of the Ministry of Education. Although secular schools were retained, all schools affiliated with Islamic religious institutions were closed down and their premises were sealed or seized.[14] The law also imposed strict controls over schools operated by minorities, foreign missionary organizations, and other private entities. Soon afterward, Turkey's leaders amended the constitution to make primary education compulsory for all children in Turkey. To make this feasible, in 1926 they eliminated all fees from public schools and made schools coeducational.[15] They also created specialized agencies to articulate the overall pedagogical goals and implement a standard educational system. The Instruction and Pedagogy Committee (IPC) was established to formulate the curricula, oversee the contents, design, and production of textbooks, suggest pedagogical methods, and provide continuing education courses for teachers.[16] The government also created a network of National Education Inspectorates with regional offices to oversee the proper coverage of required materials. Education inspectors visited schools to examine activity logs, audit classes, and test students. To ensure constant preparedness, their visits were unannounced—if somewhat predictable—and they remain, to this day, among the most intimidating experiences for teachers and students alike.

The IPC recognized the potential of compulsory mass education as a nation-building tool. The committee published the *Elementary Education Regulations Handbook*, in which it maintained that the basis of all instruction and pedagogy should be inculcating a strong appreciation of Turkishness and the Turkish homeland.[17] This entailed forging a sense of belonging to the larger geopolitical unit that Turkey comprised. Membership in a community of vicarious interactions larger than one could ever meet, belonging to a land that stretched further than one could see, and an existence longer than one's life—in other words, imagining one's membership in the nation—are abstract concepts, especially for the target audience, children entering middle childhood. Republican schools and teachers would have to bring them within grasp and make them into everyday concerns of the heart and the mind. To achieve this, the republican leaders turned to Western precedents. In addition to the Western-educated experts within their own ranks, such as Selim Sirri Tarcan, they sent fact-finding delegations and graduate students abroad. Although, as in other fields, the dominant influence on the modernization of Turkish education was German, other approaches were also considered, at least initially.[18] Notably, in 1924, John Dewey spent two months in Turkey and produced a report for the government.[19] The hands-on pedagogical techniques the IPC endorsed had much in common with Dewey's approach, which emphasized learning by praxis. There was also a crucial difference, however: Dewey explicitly cautioned against excessive centralization, arguing that it could stifle individual autonomy and self-realization. Within the context of the regime's increasingly corporatist tendencies, education evolved as a process geared to generate humble constituents of a larger whole rather than self-directed individuals. As I explain below, for the IPC instilling loyalty to the regime and the specific brand of modernization ideology it espoused was an objective equally important as nation building.

Maps in Minds

In "The Use of Illustrations in Geography Education," written for *Ilkögretim Haftasi* (*Elementary Education Week*), Hakki Izet, professor at the Gazi Teachers' College, underlined the importance of images in conveying messages. Izet praised the use of pictures, graphics, and photographs in textbooks, and also called for a further "exploitation of the magical powers of this means of expression."[20] He argued that students' appreciation of images should be cultivated in order to supplement applied or text-based learning.

Izet was especially interested in improving students' cartographic skills. His essay contained several exercises and tips for teaching elementary school students how to draw a quick freehand map of Turkey (Figure 6.1), how to situate Turkey within its region, and how to estimate the relative proportions of the country's dimensions and those of its neighbors. He outlined various geometric tactics to render the task easy, and mentioned potential problems that might be encountered in the classroom. Izet's instructions also included pointers for drawing the map on the blackboard, which, he warned teachers, presented its own challenges due to the larger scale of the board and the peculiarities of drawing with a light-colored chalk on a dark surface. The main concern was not so much to draw perfectly precise maps, such as one would find in an atlas, as it was to acquire a clear mental image of the country through repeated practice. Thus he recommended drawing quick sketches of the country identifiable "through the articulation of its most recognizable features."[21]

Cultivating a widely shared idea of the nation-state as a discrete geographic artifact, which was demarcated from its neighbors, with well-defined boundaries, and was homogeneous throughout, was essential to Turkey's claim to nation-statehood. Yet forging a simple but distinctive image of Turkey that was easy to remember and reconstruct with a few strokes was a challenge.[22] In the first place, Turkey's boundaries had been in flux since the collapse of the Ottoman Empire—negotiations over its current international boundaries were not finalized until 1939. The process left its trace in schoolbooks and atlases, which, for instance, did not show a boundary line for southeastern Turkey (Figure 6.2). Second, conjuring up an abstraction of Turkey almost as if it were a logo was itself new, and the ability to do so was a desirable skill for teachers to have. Yet, before beginning to teach this skill, the republic's first generation of teachers had to be

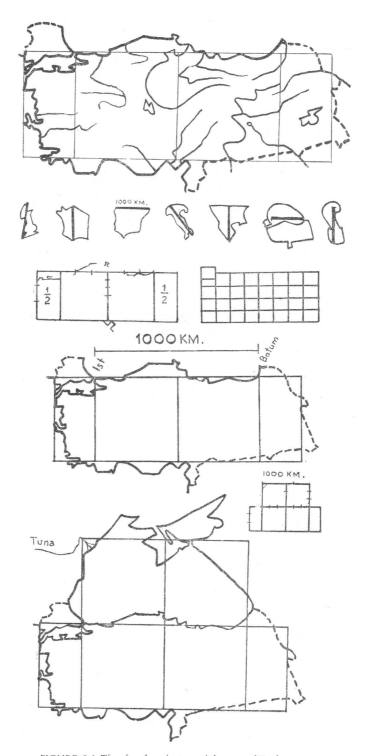

FIGURE 6.1 Tips for drawing a quick map of Turkey.

From Hakki Izet, "Cografya Tedrisatinda Resimden Istifade," *Ilkögretim Haftasi* (January 22, 1939), 262–268. Courtesy of the VEKAM Library.

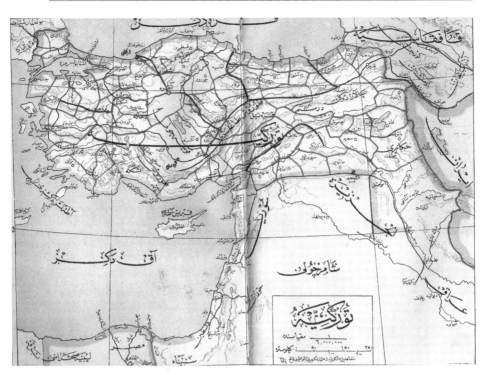

FIGURE 6.2 Map of Turkey from the *Teceddut Atlas* (*The New Atlas*, c. 1925). Note the lack of a boundary between Turkey and Iraq.

From Osman Mükerrem Bin Ismail, *Teceddüd Mekteb Atlası: Cografyaya Mütealik Hülasa Ve Hatıra* (Istanbul: Ikbal Kütüphanesi, 1925). Courtesy of the VEKAM Library.

trained to think in these terms. Consequently, techniques for drawing freehand maps of the country on the blackboard and for teaching elementary school children how to draw the same on paper were incorporated into the geography syllabi at the Gazi Teachers' College. That similar materials were also included in a special illustrated section of the *Study of the Country and Geography: Teaching Methods for Elementary and Middle School Teachers*, distributed by the Ministry of Education, was another indication that this was an important concern.[23]

Students were expected to become familiar enough with Turkey's map to be able to draw the course of rivers, locate mountain ranges, and identify crops grown in different regions. Moreover, they were frequently prompted to put this image to use in other classes. Typical were the textbooks for reading classes, which included a wealth of essays and poems about Turkey's geography, its natural resources, history, and traditions. *Elementary Education Regulations Handbook* recommended that all subjects be infused with nationalistic themes, urging teachers to "take every opportunity to foster and reinforce children's national consciousness." For example, it proposed that mathematics assignments feature

FIGURE 6.3 Children at the Izmir Bayrakli Elementary School learning the units of length on railroad tracks.

From the back cover of the November 16, 1939, issue of *Ilkögretim Haftasi.*
Courtesy of the VEKAM Library.

road problems about traveling times and distances between different provinces, which, albeit indirectly, would invoke the national map. Thus the exercise would not only sharpen children's mathematical skills but also reinforce, by reiteration, their awareness of a larger shared national geography.[24]

Ilkögretim Haftasi (*Elementary Education Week*) also provided practical tips for incorporating these themes into teaching. In one such case, the back cover of an issue of the journal included a photograph of third-grade students at the Izmir Bayrakli Elementary School, supervised by their teacher during a mathematics class field trip (Figure 6.3). The photograph featured a group of children kneeling on the ground, with measuring sticks in their hands, determining the width and length of railroad tracks. According to the caption, the field trip constituted an example of how units of length could be taught through hands-on exercises. This image is remarkable, because if the goal were merely to teach the units of length by actually measuring the sizes of everyday objects, that certainly could have been accomplished in less dangerous places than the railroad tracks. Given the larger concerns about instilling a sense of Turkey as a geographic whole, however, it is possible to think of other motives. As important as engraving Turkey as an image in young minds was the task of getting them to develop the mental agility to move between representation and reality, and to think about the relationship between their everyday environment and its cartographic abstractions.

Dubbed as "weaving an iron web across the country," railroad construction was, by all accounts, one of largest and most important industrial enterprises of the republic. Railroads moved goods, people, and ideas across the country and were, therefore, vital to national integration. Bringing the children to see the railroad and watch its tracks disappear into the horizon allowed them to see for themselves that this iron thread did indeed stretch out and connect them to their compatriots in distant parts of the country. By physically touching the railroad, the students were also touching a part of the abstract railroad maps that appeared in their textbooks, and by implication, connecting the real with the representational.

Standardizing the Learning Environment

The "iron web" was a growing system of paths and nodes centered in Ankara, from whence it fanned out binding the entire country together. Other cartographic depictions of Turkey in textbooks, such as the frontispiece of the fourth-grade geography book, reinforced the notion of Ankara, the capital, as a hub with spokes radiating out to the four corners of the country (Figure 6.4). Despite enormous regional disparities, early republican iconography projected an image of unity and uniformity, with recognizable elements predictably recurring across the national landscape.

School buildings were among the most familiar components of this landscape. Professor Çakir, author of the memoir cited earlier, noted that another Gazi Elementary School, almost identical to the one in Sarayköy, his hometown, was twelve miles down the road, in the provincial seat of Denizli.[25] Both buildings were two stories high, symmetrical in layout, and featured the same plan, organized around a double-loaded circulation spine with classrooms on both sides, entrances on the central axis, and three-window bays protruding on the ends. Their tall narrow windows with pointed arches and wide overhangs with prominent bracings paid homage to the then-popular Ottoman Revivalist style.[26] Both schools were based on a prototypical design produced by the Ministry of Public Works (Figures 6.5, 6.6).[27]

The *Provinces Album* issued by the ministry in 1929 featured dozens of schools based on the same prototype or its variations throughout Turkey. Those at major population centers were usually two stories high, although the number of bays could vary to accommodate larger enrollment. In addition, a smaller type with one to three classrooms was made available for rural settlements. The use of one design to fit various sites with very different topographic and climatic conditions was criticized by members the architectural profession.[28] Nevertheless, given the severe shortage of qualified technical personnel (architects, engineers) and funds in the first few decades of the republic, the policy of relying on prototypes for the mass production of schools was deemed efficient since it streamlined the design process and reduced costs. Also, the schools' uniform appearance

M. BESİM DARKOT   CEMAL ARİF ALAGÖZ

.CUMURİYET ÇOCUKLARINA
Yeni
Coğrafya Dersleri

SINIF: 4

Kuş uçuşu mesəfeler [Kilometre ile]

On Üçüncü Basılış

Kültür Bakanlığı U. Ö. E. Kurulunun 28 numara ve 31 - 7 - 27 tarihli kararıyla İlk Okullara onaylanmış ve 3 - 7 - 1936 tarih ve 83/103185 sayılı emrine göre tadil edilmiştir.

TÜRK KİTAPÇILIĞI LİMİTET SOSYETESİ

İSTANBUL

1936 — 1937

FIGURE 6.4 Frontispiece of the fourth-grade geography textbook, *Cumuriyet [sic] Çocuklarina Yeni Cografya Dersleri, Sinif 4*, by Besim Darkot, Cemal Arif Alagöz (Istanbul: Türk Kitapçiligi Limitet Sosyetesi, 1936).

FIGURE 6.5 Large prototype: Denizli Gazi Ilkokulu.

From *Cumhuriyetin 15. Yilinda Denizli* (Denizli: Cumhuriyet Matbaasi, 1938).
Courtesy of the Turkish Historical Society Library.

FIGURE 6.6 Small prototype: provincial school in Sedirer, Konya.

From *Vilayetler Albümü* (Ankara: Dahiliye Vekaleti, 1929). Courtesy of the
Turkish Historical Society Library.

made them recognizable fixtures in the landscape throughout the country.
Standardization was driven primarily by practical and economic concerns, but it
undeniably contributed to stamping the cache of the newly founded republic on
the physical environment.

Çakir recalled that his school had a prominent location in town, across from the train station, facing the main thoroughfare. Other new institutional buildings, such as the military conscription office and the local middle school were also close by. Like Sarayköy, Denizli Gazi Elementary School had a well-appointed site within the city. Emphasizing the importance of elementary schools by situating them in high-traffic areas, with frontage on a major thoroughfare or square, was common practice during the early republican years. Schools were often built in close proximity to other educational structures and government buildings, which were also based on standard prototypes.

As with the design of schools, the design and construction of government buildings and urban planning were centralized. Between 1930 and 1939, Turkey's leaders had established a number of agencies based in Ankara to oversee the production of designs for buildings and cities throughout the country. Their projects, not surprisingly, showed remarkable similarities, with buildings drawn from a shared repertoire and arranged according to a more or less established template of spatial relationships. The clustering of these structures augmented the effect that the repetition of a single institutional building could have created alone and, importantly, gave early republican towns a recognizable character.

Republican downtowns took their character from a combination of government offices and secular institutions, such as the provincial government house, the courthouse, military or police headquarters, the local offices of the ruling Republican People's Party (RPP), and Halkevi, the party-run community center. Remarkably, the new developments were often built outside existing historic downtowns and the civic and religious landmarks that anchored them. This siting strategy not only eliminated the problem of dealing with a tight urban fabric and complicated ownership patterns but also served important ideological and pedagogical purposes. First, it turned historic downtowns into the perfect foil against which the modernity (read: superiority) of the new developments could be displayed in full. Second, it prevented these spaces from being woven into the collective memory of the new generation. Republican leaders explicitly refrained from taking over and converting any facilities associated with pious foundations and avoided locating new school buildings near them, lest students develop affective ties with such sites in a way that could jeopardize the state's commitment to secularism.[29] Instead, they located educational institutions near the new the public works, which, as fondly invoked in Çakir's recollections of his school in Sarayköy, would form the distinctly secular context of the earliest memories of learning.

Learning by Praxis

Equipping children with the practical skills to recognize and navigate these deliberate and repetitive configurations of the new republican townscape; familiarizing them with the processes that produced them and the institutional structures they engendered; inculcating the official symbolic narratives embedded in that landscape—these were the province of republican schooling. The IPC emphasized the anchoring of meaning and experience in places and artifacts, and strongly advocated complementing book-based learning with hands-on experience. The committee noted that what was learned experientially had "more staying power in children's minds" and added "it is essential that children learn through observation and praxis and that they witness phenomena in situ: this will refine their perspicacity. . . . Providing concrete examples makes the course contents—especially elusive concepts—easier to grasp."[30]

To weave the textual and the experiential together, the IPC suggested using the immediate vicinity of schools as teaching tools by organizing short excursions. Similarly, in *Teaching Geography in Elementary Schools*, Kemal Kaya, an education professor at the Gazi Teachers College, argued that the surroundings of the school building were an indispensable component of the new learning process. Kaya insisted that subjects in the elementary school curriculum stood to benefit from field trips, from mathematics, to science, history, art, and even the Turkish language. He added that only by example and observation could children begin to understand the interdependencies between people and things in their environment and gain an appreciation for their order.[31]

The earliest explorations of surroundings of school grounds appeared in the third-grade curriculum, in which children were taught to navigate the city, specifically, the Turkish city under the republic. By including these field trips in the curriculum, the IPC hoped to ensure that even those children whose schools were further away from the new downtown would have a chance to familiarize themselves with republic's public works program. In a sample exercise, Kaya cited a day-long field trip around the town of Balikesir in western Turkey.[32] In this exercise, developed by an elementary school teacher, children first were asked to walk though the city with the teacher and make notes of their observations. Later, they were to be taken to a hilltop with a bird's eye view of Balikesir. In addition to learning how to read a map and draw diagrammatic sketches, the students were asked to locate and identify prominent buildings. A few written questions rounded out the day's assignments.

Interestingly, in this exercise, with the exception of two mosques and three government offices inherited from the empire, the only structures deemed worthy of mention are the ones built under the auspices of the republic. These include the new main street, the new park and public squares, institutions,and settings for children: the Gazi Elementary School, the birthing center, and the modern playground. Meanwhile, the public spaces that made up the Ottoman city—the hans, bazaars, mosques, dervish lodges, and other sites where the civic, the religious, and the commercial mingled seamlessly—are conspicuously absent.[33] Aspects of the old city that reveal the multiethnic, multireligious makeup of Ottoman society are omitted from this survey (see, for example, Figure 6.7).

Cumhuriyet devrinde Aydın

Saltanat devrinde Aydın

FIGURE 6.7 A typical comparison: the town of Aydin; old (*bottom*) and new (*top*).
From *Cumhuriyetin 15. Yilinda Aydin* (Aydın: CHP, 1938). Courtesy of the TBMM Library.

The list of questions suggested for the written portion of the assignment signal a deeper ideological agenda:

- Observe the settlement patterns from the hill. Which neighborhoods are more orderly? Which ones are more cramped?
- Can you tell the hierarchy of the streets?
- Where are our town's new and most impressive buildings? Why are they clustered together?[34]

These questions were designed to elicit a very specific type of response—one that associated orderliness, elegance, spaciousness, and grandeur with the republic and linked disorder, dilapidation, and overcrowding to the Ottoman legacy. Casting the "failures" of the Ottoman Empire against the "successes" of the republic within a binary matrix of oppositions was part of a broader discursive strategy, which dominated not just textbooks and other instructional materials but also the entire verbal and visual rhetoric of the early republican period.[35] The simple but rather effective method consisted of juxtaposing qualities, practices, institutions, and artifacts associated with the republic against those associated with the empire to reaffirm the accomplishments of the nation under the republican administration. The pairings were coordinated so as to lead the reader to "naturally" conclude that while the republic was the standard bearer of progress, development, and modernity, the empire stood for the mirror-negative versions of these qualities, namely, stagnation, underdevelopment, and tradition. In short, planning strategies that physically distanced the republican downtown from its Ottoman counterpart and pedagogical strategies that rendered the latter as the inferior other complemented one another.

Ideological messages were not conveyed through maps and texts alone. The written materials in the textbooks benefited from the presence of illustrations that reinforced their arguments, providing visual evidence that rendered their claims tangible. Despite serious limitations in reproduction quality and the lack of skilled illustrators, visual materials were indispensable for making a case for the republican agenda. For instance, in a fourth-grade reading book, a chapter titled "Why I Love the Republic" juxtaposed old (Ottoman) and new (republican) schools in an ostensibly representative pair of images (Figure 6.8). The former featured a scene of corporeal punishment known as *falaka*, in which the offending student's feet are tied to a rod and held up by two of his classmates, who appear to be overeager to assist with the punishment. The teacher, an old, bearded, and bespectacled man wearing a turban and a cloak, is shown holding a stick, with which he is fiercely beating the soles of his charge's feet. Infused with a sense of fear and revulsion, the image bolsters the negative image of Ottoman schools. In contrast, the republican school is pictured with girls and boys wearing uniforms, sitting in orderly rows, intently listening to their young teacher. The physical conditions of the two classrooms are also in stark contrast. With the

FIGURE 6.8 Illustrations comparing Ottoman schools and Republican schools included in the fourth-grade reading textbook *Okuma Kitabi Dördüncü Sinif* (Istanbul: Türkiye Cumhuriyeti Kültür Bakanligi, 1935).

Courtesy of the VEKAM Library.

exception of a crooked frame holding an unintelligible sample Arabic script, in the Ottoman school the walls are bare. The missing patches of plaster contribute to its appearance of neglect. The classroom's general state of disrepair hints at the Ottoman Empire's misplaced priorities, lack of organization, and disregard for children and their education. Unlike its dark and dilapidated Ottoman counterpart, the republican school is illuminated with large windows. Behind the teacher is a clearly identifiable map of Turkey, once again invoking the image of the country as a cartographic abstraction. The notes and drawings on the blackboard indicate that a mathematics class is in session, implying that republican schools were well equipped and delivered a modern secular curriculum, focusing on the rational and the scientific rather than obscure religious dogma, which was presented as the focus of Ottoman curricula.

The visual clues identifying the Ottoman and the republican settings are conveyed as incidentals, as though the veracity of those assertions need not be questioned. The illustrations are conveyed as facts, providing a physical context and thereby lending credibility to the texts they accompany, in this case, a conversation between a grandfather and grandchild, in which the former observes:

> Our teacher was a bearded old man. Nobody had ever seen him smile. Sometimes he'd call upon us and make us read things we could not understand. Because we were already overcome by fear, we understood even less of what we read. The teacher would then get mad at us, pull our hair, slap us in the face, pummel us in the back, and if that was not enough, he would punish us with the falaka, whacking our bare feet with a stick.[36]

The grandchild's response paints a strikingly different picture of her experience at school:

> Our teachers are always cheery, they always treat us like we were their siblings or their children. We never have difficulty understanding the lectures they give in our beautiful language. We enjoy working. Let alone beating us up, they get upset if they see us ill-treating an animal.[37]

The pattern of pitting the accomplishments of the republic against the failures of the empire continued as children advanced in further stages of education, with more complex examples that incorporated all aspects of life into this polarized comparison. As a result, Ottoman culture and civilization was presented not on its own terms and merits but rather as an amalgam comprising the opposites of the qualities the republican leadership sought to cultivate in the Turkish nation. Written from a teleological perspective, these comparisons framed history as if it were a long chain of predetermined causal links. Thus the collapse of the empire appeared as if it were a foregone conclusion since the sixteenth century, and just about every historical development since then was presented as a milestone toward the inevitable rise of the modern Turkish state.

A Constant State of Mobilization

In addition to framing the ambitious—and top-down—modernization program as Turkey's manifest destiny, early republican educational policies were intended to recruit a new generation of foot soldiers to take up the cause, and train them to bring the reforms to fruition. To generate the sustained support needed to accomplish this goal, Turkey's leaders tried to hold on to the heightened state of emergency attained during the war against the post-World War I occupation by the Allies. As evidenced in contemporary teaching materials and practices, the authors of the republican educational policy put significant effort into presenting the war as unfinished. Accordingly, armed conflict was but one phase of the struggle against the broader set of circumstances that brought down the Ottoman Empire. In the new phase, the enemy was no longer the Allies or the Greeks; it was ignorance, it was backwardness, it was the Ottoman way of doing things, and the war would not be over until Turkey was thoroughly modernized.

One typical strategy for preserving the sense of continued warlike mobilization was to deliberately blur the boundaries between the past, the present, and the future. Hence in textbooks the coverage of events since World War I was disproportionately more detailed than that of other periods; contemporary events, which would normally be classified as news, were framed as history; and, finally, goals that were yet to be achieved were portrayed as though they had already been accomplished. Moreover, calls for sacrifice and preparedness in the face of Turkey's ongoing struggle permeated almost every textbook in every subject, infusing them with not-so-subtle military overtones. Even first-grade alphabet books reminded students that they were the offspring of fallen warriors and that they too might be asked to make the ultimate sacrifice in the service of the nation.[38]

Common collective classroom activities, such as preparing a "time ribbon," similarly targeted children's sense of time and duration. In an essay penned for *Ilkögretim Haftasi* (*Elementary Education Week*), Hasim Basar, the provincial elementary education inspector of Erzurum (Eastern Turkey), detailed the uses of "time ribbons" in history classes.[39] He recommended that teachers supervise students in the preparation of a blank calendar at the beginning of the academic year and instruct them to fill in important anniversaries in as the year unfolded. Each important date would eventually be illustrated with pictures, charts, and essays, all of which should be prepared in class, by the students. The ribbon could take many forms, but the key was to "engage the students in the making of an artifact of history," rather than "passively memorizing dates and events." The ribbon should become part of the classroom décor and also a collective project, he suggested. Basar also emphasized that the collective and interactive character of the project was crucial to a better learning experience, that it would reinforce the students' sense of ownership over their classroom and make for more lasting memories.

Without a doubt, what generated the most memorable experiences were commemorative ceremonies, performed on the anniversaries of the key events of the republic's history. These brought together everything children learned about the nation and its history, engaged both their bodies and minds, and involved several members of their local communities in large, collectively performed spectacles. Preparations began days, sometimes weeks, before the ceremonies. Supervised by their teachers, children decorated their classrooms, rehearsed for the parades, learned to recite poems, and prepared speeches. The material culture of the pageantry was remarkably uniform. As with urban design, school construction, and curriculum planning, commemorative ceremonies were centrally scripted by government agencies in Ankara. To guarantee the basic uniformity of experience, the Ministry of Culture issued and nationally distributed pamphlets with detailed guidelines about the contents of performances, and instructions about how to set the stage for the pageantry. Floats, flags, and effigies to be used in the events were also made according to specifications. The Ministry of Education, for its part, selected the uniforms and other costumes to be worn by students and scouts as well the accouterments they were expected to use.[40] The similarities between the children's outfits during the parades attest to just how precise these directions were (Figure 6.9).

Commemorative events effectively incorporated urban landscapes across the country into the learning environment. As a general rule, the parades started from the entrance of the town, and if possible at the train station, and continued down the new tree-lined avenues, incorporating the new institutional and administrative

FIGURE 6.9 Children parading at commemorative ceremonies in Yozgat, a small town
in central Anatolia.

From *Cumhuriyetin 15. Yilinda Yozgat* (Yozgat: Vilayet Matbaasi, 1938).
Courtesy of the Turkish Historical Society Library.

buildings to their itinerary, finally reaching the Republic Square. Whenever possible, local places where significant events of the War of Independence had taken
place were also incorporated into the route. As with the textbooks and the urban
exploration exercises, the landmarks that made the Ottoman city, the spaces and
artifacts associated with the Ottoman past, were excluded from the parade route or
downplayed even though they were likely to be better known and more meaningful
to the people.

By standardizing the material culture of the pageantry and synchronizing the
course of events, the republican government tried to instill a sense of unity that
transcended the immediate and the local. The isomorphic layouts for the new
downtowns proved particularly effective in reinforcing this experience. When
woven into the paths of commemorative processions or integrated into the scenario of reenactments, streets, monuments, and other sites that were visited during these events took on new meanings, forming part of a symbolic landscape
where patriotic emotions climaxed. The choreography of the rituals was meant to
introduce a new way of imagining spatial relations between the components of
the urban landscape, based on movement and perception in time rather than evident physical locations. As part of a fixed series of destinations to be visited, these
landmarks could be seen as being arranged linearly over time, even though they
were not situated as such on the map. This peculiar ability to imagine a web of
spatial relationships between physically remote places that were not immediately

visible or accessible was an important sensibility that the republican administration intended to cultivate in the new generation of Turkish citizens.

The cyclical nature of these events and the multigenerational nature of the participation—including those who had actually experienced the war and those who were born after it—pulled the past into the present as a stylized narrative, albeit for a few precious hours. The ceremonies also had an unmistakably reflexive dimension. Children's presence was indispensable for the realization of these events; their participation was heavily featured in textbooks; and, in turn, they studied and discussed these events ad nauseam as part of their education. Hence, children were the performers, subjects, and primary target audience of these commemorations all at once. Their experience merged with what they read in their textbooks and imagined to be happening simultaneously across the country, which they were just beginning to picture.

As teaching tools, the time ribbon and the commemorative pageants fused two distinct—and antithetical—conceptions of time, revealing, by the same token, their promoters' own ambivalence toward historical process. On the one hand, Turkey's leaders embraced the idea of history as a linear process, the possibility of forever leaving behind the Ottoman roadblocks to Turkey's progress. On the other hand, they needed the regular rituals and reenactments that emphasized the cyclical nature of time and preserved the aura of heightened emergency. Merging a linear notion of time with a cyclical one implied a blur between the past and the present. However, and despite its obvious lack of coherence, this was, for all intents and purposes, a desirable effect because it framed recent history—specifically, the cathartic experience of the War of Independence—as if it were suspended in a perpetual present. Remarkably, this framing of the status quo gave license to republican leaders, who violently quashed any form of dissent, to normalize their repressive policies as wartime measures that could not be questioned.

Final Words

Children experience a major cognitive transformation around age six. With the onset of "middle childhood," they begin to develop key conceptual thinking and reasoning skills, which eventually afford them an expanded view of their social world and themselves. Although children already posses these mental capacities at an early age, their maturation becomes especially "salient and conscious" during middle childhood.[41] In modern societies, this is also when schooling begins. Schools provide a structured environment in which they develop lasting ideas about selfhood in relation to a community of peers, individual and cooperative work habits, and the fundamental skills that are valued in their society.[42] Education mediates the internalization of the normative orders and expectations of the society, and the material context of this process is as instrumental to social reproduction as the explicit verbal content of teaching. Spaces and artifacts inculcate the practical taxonomies and orders of everyday life through perform-ance. Children learn about the rules that govern the public presentation of self, gender differences and roles, and social hierarchies by participating in the mate-rial culture of their society.[43]

The pedagogical strategies outlined in this chapter targeted students in middle childhood. To bring the abstract notion of a national community within the reach of children's imagination and make these ideas everyday concerns of the heart and the mind, republican policy makers placed as much emphasis on learning by seeing and doing as on reading. As in the case of the third graders measuring the "iron web," they tried to anchor entities that were elusive, remote, and foreign by focusing on their concrete, immediate, and familiar components that were more accessible. The standardized designs of artifacts, ranging from individual textbooks to school buildings to the new downtowns, bore the recog-nizable cachet of the new republican government—and children were specifically trained to read and interpret these visual and physical cues as part of a shared national landscape.

Republican educational policies were informed as much by a desire to rear a generation adapted to the demands of a modern world as by ideological con-cerns. The republic's founding cadre comprised a diverse group of reformers with different ideas about modernity, politics, and the individual. Many of them were open to progressive methods that encouraged children to experiment with and explore the physical world around them. Not surprisingly, when they were looking for pedagogical models they initially cast their net wide. By 1930, how-ever, those with authoritarian inclinations had gained the upper hand. As with other contemporary corporatist ideologues in Europe, their embrace of moder-nity was only partial. On the one hand they were impatient to import the scien-tific and technological advances and the material comforts these afforded. On the other hand, they were at best uneasy with the enlightenment ideals and morals underpinning modernity, which placed a premium on individual rights. Instead, the republican leadership sought to establish a moral and ethical order in which the self could become meaningful only with reference to the larger national community around it, and the state would serve as the ultimate arbiter of social relations.

Surely, these processes of indoctrination were not unlimited in scope. Given Turkey's lack of means, especially during the early years of the republic, mass education had a limited reach. Children in urban areas were disproportionately privileged over their rural counterparts. Moreover, not all children with access to schooling were convinced by what they saw. Official narrative might have per-suaded them initially, but as their naiveté wore off so did the spell of their indoc-trination. In effect, some of the keenest critics of the centralization and the rigidly ideological republican policies emerged from the generation who were school children at the height of nationalistic fervor.[44] Nevertheless, at least for those who did attend school, the standardized syllabi, textbooks, excursions, and commemorative ceremonies explored in this chapter provided the basic tools for navigating the new order and a common currency of shared experience. In short, they helped transform children into members of a larger national community.

NOTES

I am indebted to Sibel Zandi-Sayek and Marta Gutman for insightful comments. I also would like to thank the VEKAM Archive and its director Zeynep Önen for generously supporting my research in Ankara.

1. The word *gazi* means combat wounded in Turkish. In contemporary use, when capitalized, the term refers to Mustafa Kemal. He acquired the title after his near-death experience in Gallipoli. The word also has religious connotations, as the original Arabic referred to a person wounded fighting for the faith

2. Cengiz Çakir, "Ani Katari Ilkokulda," *Denizlili*, May 14, 2004, 4.

3. Çakir, "Ani Katari Ilkokulda," 4.

4. Çakir, "Ani Katari Ilkokulda," 4.

5. Education as part of nation-building processes is discussed in Ernest Gellner, *Nations and Nationalism* (Ithaca: Cornell University Press, 1983); Eugen Weber, *My France: Politics, Culture, Myth* (Cambridge: Belknap Press of Harvard University Press, 1991); Eugen Weber, *Peasants into Frenchmen: The Modernization of Rural France 1870–1914* (Stanford: Stanford University Press, 1977); Benedict Anderson, *Imagined Communities: Reflections on the Origin and the Spread of Nationalism* (New York: Verso, 1983, 1991); and Francisco O. Ramirez, John Boli, and John W. Meyer, "Explaining the Origins and Expansion of Mass Education," *Comparative Education Review* 29.2 (1985): 145–170.

6. The most widely used surveys of modern Turkish history note that education was among the important modernizing reforms. See Bernard Lewis, *The Emergence of Modern Turkey* (Oxford: Oxford University Press, 1962), and Feroz Ahmad, *The Making of Modern Turkey* (London: Routledge, 1993).

7. Most remarkable among these studies are the following Ph.D. dissertations: Ahmet Eskicumali, "Ideology and Education: Reconstructing the Turkish Curriculum for Social and Cultural Change, 1923–1946" (University of Wisconsin-Madison, 1994); Faith Childress, "Republican Lessons: Education and the Making of Modern Turkey" (University of Utah, 2001); Avonna Deanne Swartz, "Textbooks and National Ideology: A Content Analysis of the Secondary Turkish History Textbooks Used in the Republic of Turkey since 1929" (University of Texas at Austin, 1997); Jessica Selma Tiregöl, "The Role of Primary Education in Nation-State Building: The Case of the Early Turkish Republic (1923–1938)" (Princeton, 1998). For a critical review of the contents of history courses in public education and the official historiography of modern Turkey, see Etienne Copeaux, *Tarih Ders Kitaplarinda (1931–1993): Türk Tarih Tezinden Türk Islam Sentezine* (Istanbul: Tarih Vakfi Yurt Yayinlari, 1998), and Büsra Ersanli Behar, *Iktidar Ve Tarih: Türkiye'de "Resmi Tarih" Tezinin Olusumu (1929–1937)* (Istanbul: AFA Yayinlari, 1992).

8. There is a growing body of literature focusing on the material culture of educational settings. Dell Upton's article about Lancasterian schools is a thoughtful exploration of how space and spatial practices were deployed to instill a particular morality in children: Dell Upton, "Lancasterian Schools, Republican Citizenship, and the Spatial Imagination in Early Nineteenth Century America," *Journal of the Society of Architectural Historians* 53.3 (1996): 238–253. The essays collected in the volume *Silences and Images: The Social History of the Classroom: History of Schools and Schooling*, edited by Ian Grosvenor, Martin Lawn,

and Kate Rousmaniere provide a range of valuable case studies (New York: Peter Lang, 1999). A useful interpretation of standardization of school uniforms maybe found in Inés Dussel, "The Shaping of Citizenship with Style: A History of Uniforms and Vestimentary Codes in Argentinean Public Schools" in *Materialities of Schooling*, edited by Martin Lawn and Ian Grosvenor (London: Symposium Books, 2006), 97–124.

9. Explorations of the material culture of education in Turkey are relatively scarce. For a particularly insightful exploration of Bruno Taut's work and modernist German influence in school design, see Burak Erdim, "Lost in Translation: The Encounter between Bruno Taut and the Turkish Republic from 1936–38," M. Arch. thesis, University of Virginia, 2004. Also see Yael Navaro, "'Using the Mind' at Home: The Rationalization of Housewifery in Early Republican Turkey (1928–1940)," Senior Honors thesis, Brandeis University, 1991. For keen insights about the architecture of the learning environment, see Sibel Bozdogan, *Modernism and Nation-Building: Turkish Architectural Culture in the Early Republic* (Seattle: University of Washington Press, 2001).

10. Daniel Miller, "Introduction," in *Materiality*, edited by Miller (Durham: Duke University Press, 2005), 5–6.

11. For an overview of recent research in spatial memory, see Barbara Tversky, "Remembering Spaces," in *The Oxford Handbook of Memory*, edited by E. Tulving and F.I.M.Craik (New York: Oxford University Press, 2000), 363–379.

12. Frances Yates, *The Art of Memory* (Chicago: University of Chicago Press, 1966), 2–9.

13. Childress, "Republican Lessons," 16–20.

14. Nazif Öztürk, *Türk Yenilesme Çerçevesinde Vakif Müessesesi* (Ankara: Türkiye Diyanet Vakfi Yayinlari, 1995), 66–75; Zeynep Kezer "Contesting Urban Space in Early Republican Ankara," *Journal of Architectural Education* 52.1 (1998): 14–15.

15. Childress, "Republican Lessons," 16–20; Mustafa Ergün, "Atatürk Devri Türk Egitimi II: Egitim Inkilaplari Dönemi" posted at http://www.egitim.aku.edu.tr/ata1.htm, downloaded March 24, 2005. Gender integration in schools was a gradual process. Although legislated in 1924, its implementation, especially in secondary education was not completed until the late 1930s. Schooling of girls always lagged behind, even when facilities became available.

16. Childress, "Republican Lessons," 38.

17. *Türkiye Cumhuriyeti Maarif Vekaleti Ilk Mektepler Talimatnamesi* (Istanbul: Devlet Matbaasi, 1929), 8. In addition to outlining bureaucratic regulations, the handbook provided detailed information about pedagogical priorities and techniques. It also included useful teaching tips regarding rewards and punishments, the objectives of assignments, and the distribution of duties among students.

18. Thanks primarily to the efforts of Ambassador Rudolph Nadolny, German specialists and companies were hired to work on myriad projects. Turkey and Germany maintained a close working relationship until the lead up to World War II. German influence persisted in Turkey afterward, but starting from 1933, most of the contribution came from exiled German (mostly Jewish) academics, hired en masse by the Turkish government to work in universities and other educational institutions.

19. For Dewey's recommendations for Turkey, see John Dewey, "Report on Turkey," *The Middle Works: Essays on Politics and Society, 1923–1924*, Vol. 15 of *Collected Works*, edited by Jo Ann Boydston (Carbondale: Southern Illinois Press, 1983). For discussions of Dewey's influence on Turkish education, see Ernest Wolf-Gazo, "John Dewey in Turkey: An Educational Mission," *Journal of American Studies in Turkey* 3 (1996): 15–42, and Sabri Büyükdüvenci, "John Dewey's Impact on Turkish Education," *Studies in Philosophy and Education* 13.3–4 (1994): 394–400.

20. Hakki Izet, "Cografya Tedrisatinda Resimden Istifade," *Ilkögretim Haftasi* (January 22, 1939), 252.

21. Izet, "Cografya Tedrisatinda Resimden Istifade," 254.

22. For comparison, see Weber, *My France*; Jeremy Black, *Maps and History: Constructing Images of the Past* (Chicago: University of Chicago Press, 2000).

23. Kemal Kaya, *Yurt Tetkiki Ve Cografya: Ilk Ve Ortaokul Ogretmenleri Için Tedris Usulu Kitabi* (Istanbul: Muallim Ahmet Halim Kitaphanesi, 1933), 162–178.

24. Türkiye Cumuriyeti [Cumhuriyeti] Kültür Bakanligi, *Ilkokul Programi* (Istanbul: Devlet Basimevi, 1936), 20–21.

25. Çakir, "Ani Katari Ilkokulda," 4.

26. Bozdogan, *Modernism and Nation-Building*, 40–42.

27. Bozdogan, *Modernism and Nation-Building*, 42.

28. Bozdogan, *Modernism and Nation-Building*, 89–91.

29. *Vakiflar Umum Müdürlüğü Mecmuasi* (Ankara: Vakiflar Umum Müdürlüğü, 1942), 9–13.

30. *Ilkokul Programi*, 104. The same idea is repeated with very similar wording throughout the book, in chapters dealing with various subjects such as history, homeland studies, geography etc.

31. Kaya, *Ilkokulda Cografya Ogretimi*, 51.

32. Kaya, *Ilkokulda Cografya Ogretimi*, 57–60.

33. Kaya, *Ilkokulda Cografya Ogretimi*, 57.

34. Kaya, *Ilkokulda Cografya Ogretimi*, 57–58.

35. Juxtapositions of the old (Ottoman) and the new (Republican) to imply the superiority of the latter were ubiquitous, starting, as in the following example, with illustrated reading books at the earliest stages to more elaborate comparisons of institutions, laws, and arts especially in history and geography books for older students. The same template was used to educate the public at large in outdoor exhibitions prepared for commemorative ceremonies on national holidays. Contemporary government publications, such as city almanacs printed for the fifteenth anniversary of the republic, which outlined progress under the republican administration, had similar comparisons. For a brief sampling and discussion of these juxtapositions also see Sibel Bozdogan, *Modernism and Nation-Building*, 62–65.

36. *Okuma Kitabi Dördüncü Sinif* (Istanbul: Türkiye Cumhuriyeti Kültür Bakanligi, 1935), 7.

37. *Okuma Kitabi Dördüncü Sinif*, 8

38. Tahsin Demiray, *Resimli Alfabe* (Istanbul: Mektep Nesriyat Yurdu, 1929), 29.

39. Hasim Basar, "Bir Ders Vasitasi: Zaman Seridi-Tarih Seridi," *Ilkögretim Haftasi* (October 28, 1939), 294.

40. See for instance T. C. Kültür Bakanligi, *Okullarda Kullanilacak Milli Bayrak Ve Okul Filamasi Hakkinda Talimatname* (Istanbul: Devlet Basimevi, 1938); T. C. Kültür Bakanligi, *Cimnastik Senlikleri Talimatnamesi* (Istanbul: Devlet Basimevi, 1938).

41. Jacquelynne S. Eccles, "The Development of Children Ages 6 to 14," *Future of Children* 9.2 (1999): 32–35.

42. Eccles, "The Development of Children Ages 6 to 14."

43. Miller, "Introduction," 6–8.

44. Notable authors and poets include Adalet Agaoglu (1929–), Mahmut Makal (1931–), Aziz Nesin (1915–1995), Talip Apaydin (1926–), Mehmed Kemal Kursunluoglu (1920–1998), and Cüneyt Arcayürek (1927–).

7

Nomadic Schools in Senegal

Manifestations of Integration or Ritual Performance?

KRISTINE JUUL

What does a state hope to gain from providing schooling to children of itinerant herders in the remotest areas of the nation, and what do the herders hope to achieve by sending their children to school? In colonial and postcolonial understandings, school education constitutes one of the most important means through which peasants, or rural populations as such, are transformed into citizens. For many rural producers, however, children constitute primarily a workforce on which they are painfully dependent. For them the abstract skills taught in the formal education system are considered to be less conducive to future prosperity than the herding skills obtained through daily labor. Schools may, however, also have other functions than simple education. Schools are also sites of modernity and symbols of integration.

This chapter deals with recent change in the attitude toward school and formal learning among Fulani pastoralists in northern Senegal. It discusses whether examples of private investment in education through the creation of small schools in pastoral encampments should be seen as a quest for modernity and a hope for greater integration of pastoral children in a formal educational system, or primarily as a ritual performance, as part of a general manifestation of integration and belonging among pastoral groups.

Formal Education in the Ferlo

Traveling through the flat sandy landscape of the Ferlo region of northern Senegal with its tiny and remote villages, one may be surprised to find some large yellow concrete buildings in the midst of thorny acacia trees and tin-roofed houses. With their standardized structure, reflecting high-quality engineering of the 1980s, the buildings stand out from the rest of the village structures, which are built from local materials and often bear strong imprints of havoc from wind and rain. In contrast to this jumble, the yellow houses are almost uniform throughout the region, consisting of two interconnected parts—one housing the health clinic, the other the primary-school classroom. It turns out that these buildings were constructed in the mid-1980s as a drought-relief activity aimed at improving the formal education of pastoral children. At that time, acquiring basic formal skills was seen by the government as an important prerequisite for their finding employment outside the pastoral sector, perceived to be a production system in decline.

Nonetheless, the promotion of formal education has had limited success in the Ferlo. While the veranda of the health clinic is full of elderly gentlemen in large turbans and ladies in colorful dresses and large golden earrings waiting for the nurse, the school rooms tend to be far quieter and in some cases even empty (Figure 7.1). In other cases children in blue and white school uniforms, struggling to follow what is happening at the blackboard, occupy a few of the school benches and tables. Although most of the local pupils speak Fulani as their mother tongue, the teacher, who usually comes from another region, seldom masters this language, and schoolbooks, if available, are written entirely in French. Hence, basic skills in reading, writing, and arithmetic are taught in either French or Wolof (one of the six national languages of Senegal, spoken by 70 percent of the population).

Although few children are to be found in the confined spaces of the classroom, this is not the case around the mechanized deep-well or borehole that forms the central place in the life of the village (Figure 7.2). In this space and in

FIGURE 7.1 The concrete buildings of the hospital and school are seldom packed with children. These girls are preparing the doctor's lunch.

All photos in this chapter are by the author.

the vast pastures surrounding the villages, one finds many children of different ages engaged in various tasks related to rearing livestock, the central economic activity of the area.

As surface water is inaccessible in the Ferlo region for nine months of the year, the mechanized boreholes, established by the French colonial administration in the 1950s, are indispensable. Because of the centrality of water in pastoral livelihoods, not only economic life but also the social and political spaces of the Ferlo region tend to be structured around these boreholes. The distribution of school attendees also tends to reflect the structuring function of the deep-wells. In contrast to the centralizing intentions of the colonizers, most of the regular borehole users prefer to camp scattered in the bush, where they are closer to the pastures. In many cases, the scattered houses around the borehole can hardly be called a village. They are mainly occupied by the families of the forester, the nurse, the veterinary assistant, and the police officer(s) who together make up the local representatives of the state authorities. Apart from these government servants, a few shopowners reside in close vicinity to the well, although those who own a large number of cattle may prefer to set up their families in dwellings closer to their animal paddocks and thus farther from the village and borehole. The majority of those who attend school live in the houses closest to the well. Apart from the children of the government officials, the regular school attendees may be children of agriculturists who choose to move into the villages during the lean period of the agricultural cycle. In general these children come from families with few or no animals.

As one moves further away from the borehole facilities, the number of children attending school decreases considerably. This is in contrast to the general distribution of wealth. As distance to the school increases, the landscape changes from barren soils, worn by the trampling of many animals, to flat grasslands with woody shrubs. The square tin-roofed adobe dwellings and the planted shade trees of the villagers are replaced by scattered encampments consisting of round

FIGURE 7.2 The borehole is a mechanized pump that draws water from an underground aquifer into a large reservoir. Animals are watered at cement drinking troughs (to the left); water is also carried on donkey carts to the encampment.

grass huts, shaped like beehives and of different sizes. They are often grouped near stands of shading acacia trees and are occupied by relatively sedentary Fulanis, considered to be the first to have settled in the area. These families combine cattle herding with limited agricultural production. They do not engage in larger transhumance movements (seasonal nomadic travel toward better pastures), except in cases of extreme drought.

If one continues even farther, to a distance of twelve to fifteen kilometers from the well, the encampments tend to become even simpler. Often a tree hung with a variety of household utensils to keep them out of reach of the goats, sheep, and cattle roaming around the encampment will first be the first manifestation of the presence of the dwellings (Figure 7.3). Then one can find a grass hut or a provisional shelter made from branches covered with a tarpaulin cloth, or in other cases only with some mats distributed under a shading tree (Figure 7.4). Although these dwellings appear rudimentary, it is in these households that one finds the richest families, those who own enough cattle, sheep, and goats to earn their living exclusively from livestock farming. For these households, staying close to the untrampled pastures largely outweighs any interest in staying close to the village infrastructure, including school, clinic, and borehole. In most cases, the inhabitants of these remote camps will turn out to be relatively recent inhabitants of the area: former refugees from the Fuuta area north of the Ferlo, who moved southward in the 1970s and 1980s to escape the effects of drought.[1]

FIGURE 7.3 An example of provisional shelter. The landlady is sitting in the center of the scene, with the interpreter at her side.

FIGURE 7.4 An example of a temporary shelter of a Fulani family, used in the dry season. The dung on the left side of the dwelling indicates where the animals are kept at night.

Although the yellow school buildings were initially meant primarily to meet the needs of drought victims, the children from these camps seldom attend the public school at the borehole village. These herders depend heavily on the manpower of their children. Moreover, the parents consider the future success of their children to depend more on their ability to become good herders than on the ability to read, write, or do formal mathematics. For the Fulani child of a livestock-rich family, childhood is therefore rarely associated with the strict architecture of the schoolroom, with timetables, school desks, and uniforms. Instead, childhood consists of hard labor and many hot hours spent alone with the animals in a vast landscape of grasslands and bushy shrubs. It is from the practice of herding and the lived experience of coping with a highly variable environment that the Fulani child is expected to acquire basic skills for his future success.

The teaching in the classroom is therefore mainly directed toward the limited number of children of civil servants, shopkeepers, and agriculturalists living in the vicinity of the village. In this perspective, the teaching in Wolof (and French) begins to make more sense, as many agriculturalists are Wolof, and this language is also widely used among the more urban-oriented Senegalese. Nonetheless, talks at the end of the 1980s with young, inexperienced teachers assigned to bring civilization to these remote, hot, and dusty areas revealed that the failure to attract a reasonable number of children to the classroom was a matter of great frustration. Among state administrators, it was seen as a sign of the failure of state integration of pastoral peoples.

Returning to the area twelve years later, it was therefore surprising to find that although the situation in the borehole schools remained largely unchanged, a number of small, private schools were being established on the initiative of particularly wealthy, but also very mobile families in their (wet-season) encampment. What did these pastoral families hope to gain from hiring a private teacher and providing some secondhand school desks? And why was the formal system, as provided by the Senegalese government, unable to fulfill what this alternative and unofficial educational system apparently managed to accomplish? To make sense of this situation, it is useful first to discuss the Fulani pastoralists' perceptions of knowledge and education, and second to look briefly at the origins of the educational system in France's former West African colonies in AOF (Afrique Occidentale Française).

Learning to Be a Herder

As discussed above, pastoral livelihoods are dominated by concern about water and pastures. The rainfall is concentrated in a single rainy season, and its distribution is extremely variable, not only from one year to the next but also from locality to locality. Droughts are frequent but vary in length and hardship. This unequal distribution of precipitation entails important variations in the productivity not only of the cultivated land but also of the bush, which provides grass for the cattle and leaves for the goats and sheep. Pastoral production in semi-arid Africa is thus a highly risky business that often requires a great deal of mobility. Considerable knowledge of soils, pastures, animal health, and so forth is necessary, as well as more informal skills such as the ability to adapt to changing social and political environments if climatic hazards force herding units to move to other areas. The type of skill required for living by constantly improvising is what Claude Lévi-Strauss refers to as *bricolage*, the ability to cobble together odds and ends to find often unpredictable and highly imaginative solutions to pressing problems.[2] Obviously, these skills remain essentially within a science of the concrete, quite different from the highly abstract skills emphasized in the classroom.

For pastoral children, learning to be a good herder starts at their name-giving ceremony, seven days after birth. This is when the child becomes a livestock owner, through the gifts made during the ceremony. From then on, the inculcation of pastoral capabilities continues (Figure 7.5). Training as a herder begins at the age of four to five, when the boys in particular are sent off together with their older siblings to look after the animals. Gradually they extend their responsibilities from surveillance of the lambs and weak animals near the encampment to responsibility for flocks of several hundred sheep and goats. As Paul Riesman observed in his classic ethnographic study of the Fulani, "At about the age of seven, or when the child can understand the important role that cattle are going to play in his life, the father shows him the herd and points out which animals belong to the child. Although the child does not manage his own herd before his

FIGURE 7.5 Training as a herder begins at an early age, with animals integrated into a child's daily life.

majority, the intention is to make the child feel intimately tied to his herd, as his fortune in life depends directly on the health and the fertility of his cattle."[3]

Herders in the Ferlo region seldom live in larger family units, and polygamous households are not the norm. Many families therefore face severe labor shortages, particularly during the dry season, which is the peak season for pastoral activities. In order to ensure proper feeding of the flocks and to limit weight losses as much as possible, the most specialized herders usually set up camps at a distance of twelve to fifteen kilometers from the borehole well. Every second day, young boys are responsible for bringing the animals to fresh pastures located farther from the camp. The next day, the animals are taken the long way to the borehole to be watered. As a result of labor constraints, it is not unusual to see boys only eleven to twelve years old setting off in the early morning for the deep-well with a large flock of several hundred sheep and goats. Keeping such large numbers of animals together makes this a strenuous trip that is likely to take many hours (Figure 7.6).

At the age of fifteen, a boy is expected to be able to carry out the same tasks as a grown-up herder, and thus to take over the herding tasks of his father and older relatives so that the older family members can engage in what Paul Riesman calls "socio-political work."[4] It is therefore young men between fifteen and forty who constitute the most active group when it comes to tending the herd. But younger children also contribute to a significant degree to the survival of herd and family, especially in those cases where households are relatively small.

Pastoral activities involve many different tasks, depending on the season of the year. A large and varied number of skills thus have to be passed on from parents to their children. First, the children must have a great deal of botanical

FIGURE 7.6 Young herders taking a rest and eating a meal of milk and millet.

knowledge to be able to distinguish the most nutritious pastures. They have to learn how to deal with variation in rainfall, where to find places good for digging shallow wells, how to know whether the animals are well nourished, and how to prepare for and safely carry out longer nomadic journeys with the animals (especially in cases of emergency, when the rains fail). To this we can add a large number of more social skills crucial to the itinerant lifestyle, which often calls for quick decisions and improvisations. Most important, they have to know how to negotiate access to crucial resources—such as water, pastures, and labor—in areas in which they cannot rely on kin and family relations.

Although fathers hand down many herding skills to sons, these skills are also to a large extent acquired through practical experience. Fathers often spend a lot of time supervising their sons, but without joining them in the work.[5] In reality, the child spends a very large part of his childhood in the bush separated from his parents. In contrast to the camp, which is mainly the space of the adults, the bush is the space of the children—a space for learning but primarily a "free" space for play and dreaming. Once out of sight of their parents, children will find a place in the shade where they can play and chat with their siblings. Obviously, one consequence of this "freedom" may be that animals are lost in the bush because children have not been paying attention to their whereabouts (Figure 7.7).

According to Riesman, Fulanis do not consider this experience as a transfer or attainment of knowledge. For them, having a successful career as a herdsman and building up a large herd is not so much a question of acquiring skills as of having struck it lucky. Among Fulanis the saying is, "He who is destitute has no recourse, it is God who has given the luck to the one and not to the other."[6]

Although in their daily practice herders are far less fatalistic than this suggests, it is hardly surprising that pastoralists in general show comparatively little interest in formal education. If prosperity and knowledge are "givens," there is little to motivate herders to invest precious labor power in abstract knowledge that is largely unconnected to and inapplicable in their daily lives. As owners of large herds of livestock, pastoralists have no problem sustaining a sense of identity and pride in themselves. For pastoralist children, assuming their role in the division of labor between different age groups seems far more relevant than insulating themselves in the confined realms of formal education. Spending endless hours around the deep-well or in the company of their friends while looking after the animals in the bush makes far more sense. For besides gaining the experience and knowledge that are indispensable to earning a livelihood in these harsh environments, the freedom in the bush and the meeting places around the borehole also involves various kinds of social meetings and relations that may be crucial to their pastoralist careers. As in the case developed by Olga Nieuwenhyus, dealing with fishermen's children in Kerala, schools become a nonplace in pastoralists' perception.[7] What goes on there is largely unconnected to the relationships that lace a local place together. It is associated with "nonwork," that is, activity not regarded as having an economic purpose or a definite social meaning. In contrast to the insulated spaces of the school, the bush and the borehole site are central places of childhood; they are also often liminal places, that is, places through which children enter the adult world (as for example the borehole sites).

FIGURE 7.7 Freedom in the bush. As a group of young herders pose for the photographer, they lose sight of their animals.

The Colonial Experience—Learning to Be a Citizen

The relative indifference toward formal education encountered among the FutankoBe herders of northern Senegal is neither new nor specific to the area. In spite of their many and varied attempts, both British and French colonial administrators have been severely constrained when trying to employ formal education as a means of controlling their subjects and turning them into citizens of their respective nations.

Among the colonizers from republican France, integration was closely related to becoming Frenchmen. The aim was to "create" French *citoyens* out of peasants.[8] This involved affiliation with the French metropolitan education system, mediated through the French language and valorization of French civilization. With the classroom as the secular civic site of Francophony, free and compulsory school became the most appropriate vehicle for the acculturation and grooming of nascent citizens.[9] An ideal for this school system was that at twelve noon, no matter what their geographical location, all children in the French territory would be reading the same texts and following the same lesson plan and speaking the same language (French).

In order to carry out this civilizing mission the colonial administration invited religious organizations such as the Frères de Plöermel to extend their educational activities from France to Senegal. The French state was to cover all costs of the schools, which would be free. The friars were to use the same manuals and the same pedagogical methods as they had been using in their schools in France. By 1841 the Frères de Plöermel had established their first school in St. Louis, Senegal. In a few years their activities had expanded to a total of thirty-two schools all over the Senegambian territory, just as they supplied the great majority of schoolteachers for the future Senegalese school system.[10] After they left Senegal in 1903, their teaching methods continued to be applied over large parts of the territory. The use of "the symbol," a token of shame worn by children who spoke their native tongue in the classroom, can still be observed today.[11]

In the four urban *communes* of Senegal (St. Louis, Gorée, Rufisque, and Dakar) that were granted the status of French overseas territory in 1872, this structure proved fairly successful. Because of the position of Senegal as the political capital of French West Africa, the educational system aimed to prepare administrators to fill the increasing number of civil service posts.[12] Submission to French education thus became an instrument of social promotion.[13]

The inclusion of the urban areas of Senegal in French territory obviously entailed the exclusion of those living beyond the territory of the four communes. Unlike the citoyens of the communes, populations from the rural hinterland were designated as subjects (*sujets* or *indigènes*) whose civil rights fell under the Code de l'Indigenat (native law). This code incorporated the more arbitrary authority of the colonial administration, which mainly relied on traditional chiefs. Control over this vast territory depended on educating a rural elite who could act as *sous-officiers* in charge of implementing the policies of the French colonial administration in the interior territories. In order to "civilize and select the future collaborators for the subordinate tasks of the administration,"[14] the so-called Ecole de Fils de Chefs was created in 1855. These schools were formed to undertake the formal education of descendants of the traditional elite, sons of the Senegalo-Mauritanian chiefs.

An especially difficult task, however, was the integration of nomadic populations of the northern parts of the French territory. In an attempt to gain a foothold in these areas, the authorities tried to set up mobile schools among the encampments of the great nomadic tribes, notably among the Touaregs and the Mauritanian tribes north of the Senegal River. In these areas, traditional Quranic teaching had been carried out by Muslim clerics. Although this education was based primarily on memorizing Islamic knowledge and acquiring some knowledge of Arab language and literature, students also received some basic education in logic, arithmetic, astronomy, and medicine.[15] In an effort to make the schools more attractive to the parents, attempts were made to merge Islamic and colonial education. But the system was quickly abandoned, as Islamic teachers proved unwilling to cooperate with the basic objective of subordination to the new civilization.

The colonial administrators tried out a variety of other methods to attract pupils to the new institutions. The fascinating accounts of colonial civil servants who served in areas dominated by nomadic populations in the early colonial period testify to the immense problems encountered in the attempt to "educate the nomads."[16]

> At the end of 1947 six nomadic schools were established in the *cercle* of Gao (in northern Mali). The administrators insisted that the education should be of good quality, so pupils who were unsuitable for teaching were sent back to their camps, and were to be replaced with pupils more suitable for receiving education. Of the 247 pupils, 46 were sons or nephews of traditional chiefs or religious figures, or other persons from good tents [i.e., of good social standing]. However, the pupils, often recruited very far from the location of the school, had to be lodged and fed by the colonial administration. This did not please the pupils and on several occasions the pupils tried to escape—in some cases with dramatic consequences: three died of thirst during attempts to reach the tents of their families.[17]

To appeal to the pupils, much was done to ensure good standards of living in the school: a school herd was formed, comprising three cows or two camels per pupil, and kept by a herder; milk was prepared and served to the pupils twice a day, together with rice, millet, and mutton. The students slept and studied under comfortable and airy grass shelters. But in spite of these efforts, educational progress remained limited and slow. Many students tried to escape, but were caught by local officials. Others, following the advice of their parents, refused to speak or simulated deafness. Nonetheless, they were kept at the school, as sending them back to their parents would be seen as a sign of weakness.[18]

The great reluctance of the nomadic tribes to send their children to school prompted the colonial administration to set up a quota system whereby each tribe was required to send a number of children of high rank to attend school, a system that was known locally as "educational tax." For the administrators, it was crucial that the children taking part in this civilizing mission be of high social rank, and hence enjoy sufficient legitimacy to form part of a future elite. Nevertheless, this objective proved difficult to achieve. To a great extent traditional chiefs "substituted" the children of lower-ranking relatives, often kidnapped to meet the schooling quota, for their own children. The effects of the quota system can be seen from the following account.

> I was six years old and was living with my paternal grandmother. It was in the rainy season and I was guarding the lambs together with some boys of the same age. We were playing a game which kept us completely absorbed. Suddenly a camel rider came by and took me by the hand and ordered me to get up. While my friends were escaping, the camel rider held me in front of him on the saddle and we rode away. . . . We arrived at a camp where we met the [French] commander of the subdivision and the chief of my tribe, with whom the camel rider had plotted to kidnap me. I tried to escape but was caught, and finally the commander took me away in his jeep. This was the first time I saw a European and the first time I tasted rice.[19]

Results from the educational efforts directed toward the nomadic populations remained meager throughout the colonial period. According to the civil servants interviewed by Bernus et al., the primary aim of the colonial administration was to give the children of the indigènes access to the benefits of French civilization. But the reaction of the nomads was rather what Bernus and his co-authors label "'analphabetism' (illiteracy) as a means of resistance." The failure to use native languages in the schooling system resulted in a psychological resistance to the French system of formal education.[20] By 1954, only 5.3 percent of the population had attended school. Although the number increased to 12 percent after independence, it was still characteristic of large parts of the rural societies that they voluntarily avoided contact with both colonial and independent administrations. In general, the nomadic populations of AOF felt a very limited need for "modern education" and refused to take part in the creation of schools as a place for the diffusion of Francophony, French culture, and French hegemony. As a result, the colonial administrators in the northernmost areas remained in a position where they were "desperately seeking an elite," as expressed by Abdel Wedoud ould Cheick.[21]

This picture was relatively similar among the pastoral populations of Senegal.[22] Even by 1994–1995, 80.5 percent of the rural population had never received any formal education.[23] This picture continued until the two periods of devastating drought in 1972/1973 and 1983/1984 sparked off a genuine explosion of educational demand.

Postdrought Strategies of the Nomad Population of Senegal

In the situation of crisis that followed the drought, the populations of northern herders who had depended on pastoral production were left with very different options. For those herders who still had a number of surviving animals, the opportunity arose to move south to areas less affected by the drought and start building up their herds again. These herders generally took up a labor-intensive herding system based on rearing sheep rather than herding cattle. This system, which called for increased mobility in terms of distance and frequency of movement, was highly dependent on the labor of children, both for watching herds and transporting water to animals over large distances (Figure 7.8). This obviously was not conducive to the development of any interest in place-based formal education. Over the next decade, the labor invested in this new type of herd management turned out to yield very good returns. From being poor, marginalized, drought refugees, camping on what was considered the most marginal pasturelands, the newcomers developed into wealthy herders owning flocks of

FIGURE 7.8 Children form an integrated part of the family's labor force, here shown during vaccination of the sheep.

several thousand sheep and goats and several hundred head of cattle. These are the herders who are now to be found in the bushlands, farthest from the bore-holes of the case-study area.[24]

Although their postdrought settlement has been relatively peaceful, the increasing prosperity of these foreign herders has been a source of conflict and jealousy because they compete for the same grazing lands as the autochthonous herders (the first comers to this community). Even thirty years after the settle-ment of the first refugees from drought, their settlement rights are constantly being questioned. Despite the fact that they enjoy the freedom of movement experienced in the bush, the sphere of contact of their children remains restricted because of the heavy workload placed upon them and the effects of the marginal position implied by their being labeled "foreigners."

Many other herders lost all or most of their stock and were left with no other option than to give up their nomadic lifestyle and settle near larger towns. For these families, education seemed one of very few available means of gaining access to an alternative job market. The result of this process of settlement was therefore that the number of children sent to school increased markedly. As there was no longer any work obligation related to farming or herding, the ambi-tions of parents for the future of their children tended to reach beyond a pastoral livelihood. They were now ready to accept greater separation between adult life and the life of their children.

The strategy of investing in education was not particularly successful, how-ever, because of constraints related to the elitist educational system and the structures of the labor market. Indeed, the goals and ambitions of the educa-tional system remain largely the same as in the times of the Frères de Plöermel, aiming at the creation of an educated elite through a pyramidal system where the primary school tries to select the students who are suitable for secondary educa-tion rather than to connect with the realities experienced by the children.[25] Many students drop out of school without obtaining a diploma, and even for those who succeed the chances of getting a job in public administration or in the private sector are next to nil. In fact, recent figures even suggest that education helps to increase the probability of unemployment. According to a survey carried out in 1995/1996, unemployment rates were 3 percent and 5.3 percent, respec-tively, among those with no education or only primary schooling, while they were as high as 10.7 percent for those who had completed secondary school and 8.5 percent for those with a higher education.[26]

Despite these somber prospects, school education continues to be attractive to a large cross-section of Senegalese youth. This is also the case among the chil-dren of the dispossessed drought victims. For them, schools represent new are-nas where they are able to interact outside the strict generational order of the family and kinship system.[27] For them, attending school may eventually lead to a reconfiguration of the places in society assigned to them and may thus result in a new kind of childhood or youth. The result may well be as expressed by a Yoruba farmer: "Formerly, sons worked for their fathers, but today we have schooling and civilization, and now fathers work for their sons."[28]

In recent years, the two drought rehabilitation strategies described above seem, oddly, to be merging in some ways, while at the same time the dissimilarity of their goals is being confirmed. Because of the limited availability of manpower, the prosperous herders can no longer expand their flocks and are forced to find alternative ways of placing their capital. Setting up shops in borehole villages and larger towns therefore becomes a common strategy for economic diversification. Rich herders (and their children) not only lack the formal skills required for this sort of business but also often distrust their occasionally better-educated autochthonous neighbors. They are therefore increasingly calling upon their destitute but educated kin to run the daily business in stores. In this way, family ties that were loosened by the effects of drought are now being taken up again, as are previously abandoned relations of authority and obligations. Many young men working for a distant uncle have expressed limited enthusiasm for this sort of job, which they feel is badly paid and represents a return to a place in a hierarchy to which they no longer belong. For them, the job embodies a social obligation (pressure from their parents, as they have no other jobs). But it is also an opportunity to earn enough money to fulfill dreams nurtured during their education, first and foremost the dream of trying their luck as migrants in a Western European country. In this sense the shop and the pastoral setting represent a liminal place from which they hope to create new spaces and opportunities for themselves. In itself, the shop does not represent a durable livelihood.

Obviously herders recognize that formal educational skills increasingly become a requirement if these new trading activities are to be developed, but the question is whether this recent need sufficiently explains the efforts made by wealthy herders to create private, informal schooling in their encampments. Are the desks, blackboards, rudimentary yet permanent schoolhouses set up in the encampments, and the private teachers a final surrender of these pastoral populations to modernity and the abstract sciences of "hot societies"? Is this a sign of accommodation to formal education and of recognition of the importance of formal skills such as reading, writing, and arithmetic? Or is it basically part of a quest for modernity and a hope for better integration in the dominant social order?

Although many of these questions may be answered in the affirmative, there are indications to suggest that investment in private and informal schools also performs other functions. For although the new commercial activities of the herders require mastery of new types of skills, acquiring them does not seem to be the main purpose of the schools.

First, the establishment of these schools has involved only the youngest children and has not altered the considerable workloads related to the social division of labor between different age groups. So the older children are unlikely to be able to keep up their education on a regular basis. Indeed, the efficient but more demanding herd management developed after the drought has widened the repertoire of skills that the pastoral children need to acquire. This has led to a reinforcement of the close knowledge-transfer relationships between adult herders and their children—a process which, as shown above, is difficult to reconcile with the requirements of formal educational systems.

Considering the generally poor quality of the teaching, which is carried out without any formal supervision, these private initiatives are hardly better than the programs offered by the state. On the contrary, inasmuch as they are outside the formal educational system, they are not likely to lead to access to higher levels of education. The rationale of the investments is therefore unlikely to be related to the educational output of the schools.

A more realistic interpretation would therefore be that the establishment of private school structures is yet another sign of the perseverance of bricolage among the mobile pastoralist groups of Senegal. Indeed, the building of schoolhouses is not the only presumably irrational investment made by the so-called newcomers in recent years. Other types of permanent buildings have also found their way to pastoral encampments. During fieldwork carried out in 2001, a large number of brick houses were suddenly found in camps occupied by former drought refugees. The digging of private wells, too, had suddenly turned into an issue, where individual herders were willing to invest considerable sums. Considering the mobile herding strategies of these herders and the limited amount of water yielded by these artesian wells, the logic of these investments is hard to grasp. Questioned about the new practices, herders openly admit that buildings and wells have been made primarily in response to continuing rumors that herders would be evicted from legally protected forests in which they have sited their encampments. Although the former postdrought refugees have been living in the area for more than thirty years, they still cannot take their rights in the locality for granted. So true to the spirit of bricolage, where the bricoleur uses whatever items are at hand in new and imaginative combinations, the permanent structures are erected to make a possible ousting more difficult. That the construction activities involve wells and schools is interesting in the sense that, although the schools are attended by very few pupils and the wells appear to play a very limited role as providers of water, it seems that such semipublic institutions best communicate the message of integration and engagement in their role as citizens.

In the words of Appadurai, the schools and the wells have become a means through which the foreigners can embody the locality.[29] As symbols of modernity and integration, they enforce the role of the newcomer herders as local subjects—a role with rights as well as obligations attached. Unlike their destitute but educated urbanized kin, pastoral children and their childhoods remain under the control of their parents. Obviously, integration in the formal education system involves greater separation between parents and children, as parents are now forced to have ambitions that go beyond pastoral livelihoods. In contrast to this, the strategy put forward by the herders in the Ferlo region is rather a mutual strategy or ritual performance aiming at maintaining a pastoral lifestyle by securing children as productive assets.

Conclusion

In both colonial and postcolonial perceptions, school education forms an important part of the strategy of becoming a citizen and being integrated into "modern" society. However, the structures imposed on the pupils in terms of subordination to a well-defined set of disciplinary rules, of surrendering to a new and incomprehensible language, and of engaging in an abstract educational project have seldom been considered attractive by the itinerant pastoral groups of French West Africa. Particularly for the former drought victims, investing in the children's labor instead of in their education has turned out to be far more conducive to future prosperity. As a result of the severe cutbacks in public employment since the 1970s, education cannot be considered a winner's strategy.

This does not imply, however, that the attributes of schools as sites of modernity and symbols of integration have been dismissed. As shown in the case above, the building of schools or other types of permanent infrastructure is not only a sign of submission to new educational standards; these structures are valued just as much as monuments of modernity and civilization among user groups who cannot take their rights in the locality for granted. Although part of a larger process of integration, the education of children still remains under the control of their parents and schools, and therefore serves mainly to ensure that their pastoral lifestyle can be continued.

NOTES

1. The Fuuta is the name of the narrow strip of land along the Senegal River basin that borders the Ferlo region. The Fulani herders originating from this area are sometimes referred to as FuutankoBe. For more information on this process of settlement, see Kristine Juul, "Tubes, Tenure and Turbulence: The Effects of Post Drought Migration on Tenure Systems and Resource Management in Northern Senegal," Ph.D. dissertation, University of Roskilde, Denmark, 1999.

2. Claude Lévi-Strauss draws the distinction between "hot" and "cold" societies: hot societies are those with history and science, while cold societies have myth and bricolage. Bricoleurs are those who work with and reconstitute the odds and ends of available material. See Claude Lévi-Strauss, *The Savage Mind* (Chicago: University of Chicago Press, 1962), 17; Frank Musgrove, *Education and Anthropology, Other Cultures and the Teacher* (Chichester: John Wiley and Sons, 1982), 5.

3. Paul Riesman, *Freedom in Fulani Social Life: An Introspective Ethnography* (Chicago: University of Chicago Press, 1974), 38.

4. Riesman, *Freedom in Fulani Social Life*, 66.

5. Riesman, *Freedom in Fulani Social Life*, 67.

6. Riesman, *Freedom in Fulani Social Life*, 39.

7. Olga Nieuwenhuys, "Places of Work and Non-places of Childhood," in *Children's Places, Cross-cultural Perspectives*, edited by Karen Fog Olwig and Eva Gulløv (London: Routledge, 2003), 106.

    Nieuwenhuys uses Augé's definition of place and nonplace: place is understood as a geographical space endowed with the following qualities: a) relationships among the people who live there; b) a sense of history shared by the same people; c) a place with which one can identify, grounding a shared sense of belonging. In contrast, nonplaces are spaces where one can find oneself regularly and even for protracted periods, but which lack the quality of place. Rather than grounding the shared experience of a stable community, these spaces distance people from meaningful markers of time and place and reinforce solitary individuality. Nonplaces, in Augé's terminology, presuppose that meaningful social relations are grounded and enacted "somewhere else." Marc Augé, *Non-lieux: Introduction à une antropologie de la surmodernité* (Paris: Seuil, 1992), cited in Nieuwenhuys, "Places of Work and Non-places of Childhood," 102.

8. This civilizing mission was directed alike at citizens from the overseas colonies and the non-French-speaking peasants from Bretagne and elsewhere.

9. Nancy Kwang Johnson, "Turning Senegalese 'into Frenchmen'?: The French Technology of Nationalism in Senegal," *Nationalism and Ethnic Politics* 10 (2004): 137.

10. Johnson, "Turning Senegalese 'into Frenchmen'?," 139.

11. In one of the schools in the Ferlo, I witnessed how children who spoke in their mother tongue were required to stand in the corner wearing a large white hat during the rest of the lesson.

12. Michel Carton and Pape N'Diaye Diouf with Christian Comeliau, "Budget Cuts in Education and Training in Sénégal: An Analysis of the Reactions," in *Coping with Crisis; Austerity, Adjustment and Human Resources*, editd by Joel Samoff (UNESCO/ILO, London: Cassell, 1994), 121.

13. Johnson, "Turning Senegalese 'into Frenchmen'?," 136.

14. The phrase is taken from a letter circulated by the colonial authorities in 1933.

15. Abdel Wedoud ould Cheick, "Cherche élite, désespérement; Evolution du système éducatif et (dé)formation des élites dans la société mauritanienne," *Nomadic Peoples* 2.1/2 (1998): 238.

16. The accounts were collected by Edmont Bernus, Jean Clauzel, Pierre Boilley, and Jean-Louis Triaud and published in *Nomades et commandants: Administration et sociétés nomades dans l'ancienne AOF* (Paris: Karthala, 1993).

17. Henri Combelle, "La scolarisation et les écoles nomades au Mali," in *Nomades et commandants*, 135. The translations from French are my own. Combelle served as a school principal in Cercle de Gao.

18. Combelle, "La scolarisation et les écoles nomades au Mali," 135.

19. Testimony of Egleze Ag Fony, in *Nomades et commandants*, 155.

20. Testimony of Egleze Ag Fony, in *Nomades et commandants*, 156.

21. Abdel Wedoud ould Cheick, "Cherche élite, désespérement," 235.

22. It is difficult to get an exact picture of the numbers of pastoralist school attendees in Senegal, as populations here are more mixed than in Mauritania.

23. Abdoulaye Diagne, Dorothé Buccanfoso, and Djibril Gassama Barry, *La rentabilité de l'investissement dans l'éducation au Sénégal*, Working Paper 03–45, CIRPEE (Centre

interuniversitaire sur le risque, les politiques économiques et l'emploi) (Dakar: Centre de recherche économiques appliqués [CREA], 2003), 16.

24. The case area is in the southern part of the Ferlo region, in the southeastern parts of the *département* of Linguère and the southwestern part of the Matam département. See Juul, "Tubes, Tenure and Turbulence," 5, 6.

25. Admittedly, the system worked surprisingly well from the perspective of the local elite of the villages of southern Ferlo during the colonial period. The area counts several centrally located politicians among its former inhabitants, including the former head of the National Assembly and the former minister of education and later of internal affairs.

26. Diagne, Buccanfoso, and Gassama Barry, *La rentabilité de l'investissement dans l'éducation au Sénégal*, 7.

27. See Karen Fog Olwig, "Towards an Anthropology of Children and Place," in *Children's Places: Cross-cultural Perspectives*, edited by Karen Fog Olwig and Eva Gulløv (London: Routledge, 2003), 8.

28. The quotation comes from Sara Berry, *Fathers Work for Their Sons: Accumulation, Mobility, and Class Formation in an Extended Yoruba Community* (Berkeley: University of California Press, 1985), 193.

29. Arjun Appadurai, "The Production of Locality," in *Counterworks: Managing the Diversity of Knowledge*, edited by Richard Fardon (London: Routledge, 1995), 205.

8

Adventure Playgrounds and Postwar Reconstruction

ROY KOZLOVSKY

The history of the playground is marked by an irresolvable contradiction: on the one hand, modernity has conceptualized play as a biologically inherited drive that is spontaneous, pleasurable, and free. It valorized the subjective experience of play as an attribute of the autonomous, individual self. On the other hand, modern societies began to rationalize and shape children's play from the outside to advance social, educational, and political goals. Thus playgrounds are very much about censoring and restricting types of play deemed undesirable and displacing them from places deemed dangerous or corrupting, such as the street. This contradiction is embedded in the 1959 Declaration of the Rights of the Child, which enshrined play as a universal right of the individual and, at the same time, defined it as an instrument of social policy: "The child shall have full opportunity for play and recreation, which should be directed to the same purpose as education; society and the public authorities shall endeavour to promote the enjoyment of this right."[1]

This statement encapsulates the paradox of the modern discourse of play. Enlightened societies take up the obligation to provide children with the means of play, yet children do not posses play as their right, as it is subjected, just like education, to the social and political designs of others. The adventure playground movement, the subject of this chapter, sought to transcend this contradiction by constituting play practices that appeared to be operating from the inside of the subject, from the child's own free will. It intended to enhance and encourage children's own play rather than restrict or shape it from without. Yet this permissive approach was not aimed to liberate play from being an instrument of policy, but rather the opposite, to intensify the effectiveness of policy.

Adventure playgrounds were promoted in England after World War II as the playground for the future, in an explicit critique of the conventional playground with its "four S's": the swing, seesaw, sandbox, and slide. An adventure playground has no readymade play equipment and no predetermined agenda for what should take place in it. Children introduce content and meaning to the playground through their own action. Whereas the conventional playground operates by inciting kinetic modes of pleasure, the adventure playground engages the child through a qualitatively different kind of gratification. It induces the pleasure of experimenting, making, and destroying. Yet while the conventional playground is designed to function without adult intervention, the adventure playground is predicated on the presence of a play leader who administers the use of tools and materials and guides the behavior of children to maintain safety and promote cooperation among them. Thus, while advocates claimed that play activity "must grow from inside and never be directed from outside,"[2] this type of playground required professional guidance, since children had to be taught how to play and become autonomous and free.

Promoters of adventure playgrounds heralded them as being more appropriate to the true nature of children and their play, as well as providing a more pleasurable and meaningful experience than the traditional playground, which they portrayed as boring and sterile.[3] Although its adherents portray the adventure playground as radically different from the traditional playground, its critics tend to flatten the differences between them. Galen Cranz, a sociologist who studied the history of park and playground design in the United States, argued that the two kinds of playgrounds perform the same ideological function, that of social control. According to her, both playgrounds mask class inequalities and enforce social stereotypes by organizing the subjects of a politically weaker class in the supposedly neutral biological category of age.[4] David Cohen, a psychologist, criticized the adventure playground as the instrumentalization of play for social or educational goals. Cohen argued that play ought to be promoted because it is pleasurable, not because it is useful.[5] These positions frame play policies in Marxist terms as social control or in Weberian terms as the rationalization of pleasure. They presuppose that there is a prior condition in which play or subjects are free. Whereas these critics equate power with domination and compulsion, this chapter takes from Michel Foucault the assumption that any social practice involves a relation of power.[6] In the case of the playground, power does not operate by dominating or disciplining subjects who were previously free, but rather by activating subjects and making them aspire to be free. The point is to examine what kind of subjects and truths this type of power produces.

Through the examination of play as a strategy of power, I argue that the adventure playground corresponds with what the sociologist Nikolas Rose identified as the shift from the contractual model of citizenship to one that stresses the subjective aspects of citizenship. In *Governing the Soul* (1990), Rose claimed that during World War II, "Citizenship . . . acquired a subjective form. From this point forth, winning the war, and winning the peace, required the active engagement of the civilian in the social and political process, a shaping of wills, conscience, and aspirations, to forge social solidarity and individual responsibilities in the name of citizenship and democracy."[7] Rose showed that this mode of power operated by studying, measuring, and governing the interiority of the population, constituting a self-regulated, self-improving society made of individuals who internalized the obligation to be free. The adventure playground manifests this model of power: through it, the welfare state brought children's interiority under observation and indirectly shaped it from the outside, while its consenting subjects experienced this employment of power as a space of freedom and agency.

Yet postwar play policy had a complementary symbolic dimension that accounted for its more unusual aspects, such as the legitimization of acts of destruction, the appropriation of junk and waste as desirable play materials, and the practice of establishing adventure playgrounds on bombed sites. This last feature is incompatible with our contemporary belief that childhood ought to be sheltered from the violence and destruction of war. To account for the interplay between play as a social technology and as a narrative of reconstruction, I will examine the historical development of this institution, from its Danish origins to its dissemination into the English context of reconstruction.

Beginnings: The Danish Junk Playground

The Danish landscape architect Carl Theodor Sørensen first suggested the concept of the adventure playground in *Park Policy* (1931). Following his observations of children at play in construction sites and junkyards, Sørensen proposed to enclose a space where children would be permitted to play in ways otherwise prohibited to them: "Perhaps we should try to set up waste material playgrounds in suitable large areas where children would be able to play with old cars, boxes, and timber. It is possible there would have to be some supervision to prevent children fighting too wildly and to lessen the chances of injury but it is likely that such supervision will not be necessary."[8] The idea was first tested in 1943, during the German occupation. The architect Dan Fink commissioned Sørensen to design a junk playground, as these playgrounds were initially named, for the Emdrupvænge housing estate at the outskirts of Copenhagen.

That the idea came out of a landscape discourse rather than a pedagogical or psychological one marks the beginning of the involvement of landscape architects in the design of playgrounds. This development had a contradictory influence on the form, layout, and content of the playground. On the one hand, the impulse of the modernist designer was to endow the playground with the aesthetics of abstraction, as was the case with the artist Isamu Noguchi and the architect Aldo van Eyck.[9] This inclination toward the abstract and the elementary grew out of the idealism of Friedrich Froebel, who offered children toys with simple geometrical forms that represented a harmonic, perfect image of the world. But it also interpreted the playground as a landscape, making art into a useful part of everyday life.

On the other hand, designers inclined toward functionalism, such as Sørensen, sought to constitute the design of the playground upon the analysis of play activity rather than upon formal or compositional concerns. If the modernist imperative was to make play environments "imaginative," it followed that the "imagination" at play should be that of the child, not that of the architect. This understanding was in accord with the pragmatism of John Dewey, who privileged the child's present inclinations over an abstract conception of what he or she should be in the future, and valued learning through experience over repetitive performance of predetermined activities imposed from without.[10]

Sørensen's original scheme employed abstract and symbolic forms that represented the basic elements of the Danish rural landscape—the beach, the meadow, and the grove. Yet children's activities inside the playground's premises did not correspond with the artistic status of the playground as a landscape. Hence Sørensen's admission that "of all the things I have helped to realize, the junk playground is the ugliest; yet for me it is the best and most beautiful of my works."[11] The anti-aesthetic position of the playground was most pronounced in its appropriation of junk as desirable play material. Emdrup's first play leader, John Bertelsen, coined the term *junkology* to describe the activity of children. He defined it as the inversion of social values where "all pedagogical and occupational ideas were quickly turned upside down, becoming junkology."[12] While Bertelsen appraised the creations of children, their towers, caves, and huts as evidence of a primordial human instinct to make and inhabit shelters, akin to nesting, he also represented their work as a critical recreation of the world outside the playground. Emdrup may be seen as the realization of Dada aesthetics, in which the playful and collective reassembling of the leftovers of a machine civilization presented an alternative conception of dwelling, where the unmediated act of building is seen as a direct expression of the values and desires of the subjects. Yet the junk aesthetic was controversial, and the promoter of the playground in England, Lady Allen of Hurtwood, found it necessary to change its name to adventure playground precisely because of the disruptive and degrading connotation of junk, especially after her experience in launching the Clydesdale playground in 1949. The process was delayed for three years because of the intense opposition of neighbors who equated junk with hooliganism.[13]

Although Sørensen's initial proposal did not require an adult play supervisor, the Workers' Co-operative Housing Association employed one as part of its housing policy. This modification of the concept of the junk playground may be gleaned from the play practices initiated by Bertelsen and Agnete Vesteregn, who replaced him in 1947.[14] Bertelsen stressed that the purpose of the leader was not to govern children from the outside and direct their building activity toward a useful goal, but rather to act from within, by allowing them to pursue their own projects. He argued that "the initiative must come from the children themselves. . . . I cannot, and indeed will not, teach the children anything."[15] The hands-off approach had both a social and a political significance. First, children were allowed to play without intervention, so their activity could come under observation as a way of gaining "insight into the mind of the child and his various conflicts."[16] Assuming that children had an emotional interiority points to the role of this playground as part of welfare housing policy. Bertelsen claimed that material differences between economically self-sufficient tenants and those living on welfare had less impact on children's well-being than differences in the emotional investment of parents. The playground provided these children what their homes appeared to be lacking, mainly an emotionally supportive and nurturing environment.

The second purpose of relinquishing authority was to foster children's self-responsibility and promote social skills such as resolving conflicts peacefully. The promotion of democratic values through play coincided with the crystallization of a new educational program, which, to use the words of the progressive pedagogue Inger Merete Nordentoft from the last months of the war, sought to make children into "democratic citizens, humans who can think independently, can be responsible and capable of showing tolerance towards others and have the courage and firmness to defend their own convictions."[17] The use of anti-authoritarian methods was understood to be a challenge to the occupier's Fascist ideology. At the same time, pedagogues were alarmed that children became over-identified with the Resistance and its legitimization of violence and disobedience, which threatened to disrupt the conceptual separation of childhood from adult life. The permissive atmosphere in the playground provided a safe and creative simulation of lawlessness, where children could regain the trust in society through their engagement with a play leader who acted as their advocate and took their side.

Vesteregn advanced play practices that introduced children into a more stable, rule-driven society. Making an implicit critique of her predecessor, she argued that the goal of an adventure playground was not "to make a mess out of everything, ruin things, fight, swear, use rough language or be anti-social. The purpose must be quite the opposite. Children should not remain in this destructive state; they need help to be brought out of it."[18] Each of these strategies of administering play had a corresponding architectural expression. Bertelsen's playground was nomadic, while Vesteregn's was sedentary, with permanent structures added to accommodate organized activities such as painting, clay modeling, and printmaking. Yet despite these differences, both attempted to advance social policies by acting upon children's interiority. The subsequent history of the junk playground in England reaffirms this claim, while demonstrating the flexibility of the concept and its adaptability to local and historical needs.

The English Adventure Playground

The Danish experiment might have remained a local curiosity had it not come under the attention of Allen, who identified with its ethos and became its ceaseless promoter. Like Sørensen, she was a landscape architect, yet her influential role was more dependent on her social status and organizational skills in the voluntary sector than her professional authority. During World War II, Allen became involved in child-centered causes, most notably the campaign to reform the institutional care of orphans and abandoned children, whom Allen defined as "children deprived of a normal home life."[19] Her advocacy led to the Curtis Commission and the 1948 Children Act. This act endowed children with subjective rights, such as the right to happiness and a loving, supportive family environment. After the war, Allen represented England at international conferences that assessed the effects of the war on children. This activity took place between the end of World War II and the beginning of the Cold War, an interim period marked by internationalism and an aversion to violence and nationalism in Europe. Allen, who was associated with the antiwar movement through her husband Clifford Allen, the leader of the Independent Labour Party and a conscientious objector during World War I, advanced the antiwar cause by constituting children as a separate, vulnerable group that transcended divisions of class, nation, or race.[20] She promoted the establishment of the World Organization for Early Childhood Education (1948) and served as its founding president.

In 1946, as part of her international and pacifistic effort to constitute "early child education as the best way of creating peace-loving citizens," Allen was taken to visit Emdrup. In her words, she "was completely swept" off her feet.[21] Allen began to promote the idea in lectures, pamphlets, conferences, and most influentially in an essay she published in the *Picture Post* in 1946. The abundantly illustrated essay galvanized the English public by showing how the Danish model could be used for postwar reconstruction (Figure 8.1). The essay began with a critique of the conventional playground, arguing that it failed to attract children and remove them from the street. Allen claimed that this failure was literally a matter of life and death:

> Juvenile delinquency and the death of young people in road accidents both arise, in part at least, from the inadequate and unimaginative manner in which local authorities try to meet the need for creative play. . . . The best the Borough Engineer can do is to level the ground, surface it with asphalt, and equip it with expensive mechanical swings and slides. His paradise is a place of utter boredom for the children, and it is little wonder that they prefer the dumps of rough wood and piles of bricks and rubbish of the bombed sites, or the dangers and excitements of the traffic.[22]

Allen presented Emdrup as a "revolutionary" playground that could resolve this crisis. The demand for a more creative and intensive play experience reflected the wartime anxiety that the nation's children, schooled in war and destruction, had become insensitive to the amenities of playgrounds and parks.

FIGURE 8.1 Illustration for Lady Allen of Hurtwood's essay, "Why Not Use Our Bomb Sites Like This?," published in the *Picture Post*, November 16, 1946.

Photo by Francis Reiss. Getty Images.

Alongside its preventive functions, Allen stressed the role of the playground in fostering "a democratic community." This goal was advanced not only by providing children with the responsibility for operating the playground by themselves but also by designing it to appeal to all children irrespective of gender or age. Her pragmatic reason for this inclusive approach was that working-class children were often entrusted with the care of their younger siblings and could not play in the playing fields and playgrounds that catered to a particular age and gender group. Creating a variety of play opportunities allowed all children to participate in a play community.

Although Allen provided the impetus for bringing the idea to England, adventure playgrounds were promoted and operated by a coalition of local, national, and international organizations. The first playgrounds at Camberwell (1948) and Clydesdale (initiated in 1949, opened in 1952) were operated with the aid of the International Voluntary Service for Peace. Other sponsors included the University Settlement movement, Save the Children Fund, local councils, and the National Under Fourteens Council.

In the period after the war, children's play with junk became important enough to be the subject of conferences, newspaper articles, and committees. A five-day conference in 1948, sponsored by the Cambridge House University Settlement, examined the first two experimental junk playgrounds, Camberwell and Morden, which had been in operation for less than a year. Junk playgrounds received extensive press coverage, demonstrating that their visibility was in inverse proportion to their quantity. This visibility was not accidental. The Lollard adventure playground was intentionally sited near the Houses of Parliament. Allen, who chaired the playground committee, intended it to be a demonstration playground for visiting members of Parliament (Figure 8.2).[23]

From London the playground spread to other cities such as Liverpool, Hull, Coventry, Leicester, Leeds, and Bristol, where they were opened in blighted or blitzed neighborhoods as a component of urban renewal. They were also built in the new towns surrounding London, most notably Crawly and Welwyn, where they were integrated into Hertfordshire's progressive, child-centered educational infrastructure.

FIGURE 8.2 Lollard Adventure Playground, 1955.

Photo by Brian Brake. Courtesy of Museum of New Zealand
Te Papa Tongarewa (E.004047).

Playgrounds on Bombed Sites

What differentiated Allen's presentation from the Danish precedent was her suggestion that these playgrounds be built on bombed sites. Following her essay, which was titled "Why Not Use Our Bombed Sites Like This?," the first junk playground in England was built on the site of a bombed church in Camberwell, and the third was opened on a destroyed residential property on Clydesdale Road, Paddington (Figures 8.3, 8.4). Likewise, the Lollard Adventure Playground (1955–1960) was built on the site of a bombed school, and was informally known as the "ruins." At the end of the 1950s most of the ten playgrounds operating in London on bombed sites were closed when the properties were returned to their owners for redevelopment.

From the perspective of urban reconstruction, the temporary conversion of bombed sites into playgrounds was part of a broader debate about how to rebuild London, as well as to plan for the return of more than a million evacuated children.[24] This policy went against the grain of the dominant planning ideology, epitomized by Patrick Abercrombie's 1943 County of London Plan. Abercrombie's proposal conceived the blitz as an unprecedented opportunity to rebuild London according to rational, functionalist principles. The plan dealt extensively with the place of the child in the city by dividing the metropolis into self-sufficient neighborhood units organized around the school and the playground.[25] Allen advanced the more modest suggestion that reconstruction ought to be incremental and

FIGURE 8.3 The Clydesdale Road Playground Report for the year 1952 featured two photos on its cover. This one shows the bombed site.

FIGURE 8.4 This photo from the cover of the Clydesdale Road Playground Report for 1952 shows children and volunteers preparing the site.

pragmatic. Yet her truly radical proposition was that reconstruction should be carried out with the participation of the population. Adventure playgrounds were to be developed out of local initiatives by parents and were to be built by children themselves with the help of voluntary organizations. Playgrounds operated as independent associations that were headed by committees, whose members included residents, pedagogues, social workers, local politicians and, in some cases, members of the local clergy.

Such a model for reconstruction reflects to a unique historical moment when English planners experimented with grass-roots democratic planning, most notably the 1946 Middlesbrough rehabilitation plan. In "The Middlesbrough Experiment: Planning from Within," the planner Max Lock argued that a participatory planning process would facilitate the acceptance of the plan because citizens, including children, were involved in the process. He also stated that the plan would meet "the citizen's *personal* and *social* needs such as an outlet for leadership, for creative action, and for the satisfaction of the deep-lying desire for significance, dignity, and freedom. For in supplying such needs, may we not be approaching the heart of the post-war problem—the problem of minimising the *occasion* for the exercise of the totalitarian spirit which arises wherever lives are frustrated?"[26]

Lock's statement demonstrates that reconstruction assumed a psychological and civic dimension beyond that of repairing material damage. Participation has a preventive dimension, as an antidote to totalitarianism as a form of political delinquency. In a similar fashion, the adventure playground was aimed at promoting an active and egalitarian mode of citizenship through the activity of

FIGURE 8.5 Camberwell Junk playground on the site of a bombed church.
Published in "Junk Playgrounds," *Times Educational Supplement,* June 5, 1948.

play, as an antidote to collective and individual misconduct. George Burden, the chairman of the Camberwell playground committee and a psychiatric social worker at King's College Hospital, explained the rationale of building playgrounds on sites of destruction and its relation to citizenship and delinquency: "Playgrounds such as ours set in a district which has suffered much during the war can lead a child away from the tolerance and approval of that destruction which is associated with the war. The child of nine or ten makes few moral judgments. . . . It lies in our power to assist him in choosing what is socially desirable and morally right."[27] Photographic representations of Camberwell stressed the constructive and cathartic aspect of play on bombed sites. The caption describes the children as "postwar builders" providing a metaphor for reconstruction as a redeeming act (Figure 8.5). Why then was it deemed desirable to promote children's play on the ruins of their neighborhoods?

Play, Citizenship, and Violence

In her article, Allen stressed the preventive function of the playground as an antidote to juvenile delinquency. This is, of course, not a new claim, as the prevention of delinquency was one of the main reasons initially used to justify the playground. Yet the adventure playground redefined the relationship between delinquency, democracy, and play. The new role of play may be gleaned by comparing the adventure playground with its English forerunner, the turn-of-the-century play center movement. University settlement houses sponsored play centers in slum areas as child-saving schemes.[28] The preventive strategy was to constitute a separate space for play in order to dissociate working-class youth from the street and its demoralizing influence. Its promoters hoped to install in these children the discipline, character, and vocational skills needed for a respectable way of life. With the enfranchisement of the working classes and later of women, play practices were modified to initiate these populations into a liberal mode of democratic citizenship, encapsulated by the concept of fair play.[29] Yet the play center functioned as a protosocial work institution. It employed play superintendents to manage and direct children's behavior, and more significantly, to observe children's play and evaluate it in relation to the socioeconomic conditions at home, as a method for revealing the underlying causes for poverty and crime.[30]

Play practices evolved with the growing influence of psychology in understanding and treating juvenile delinquency. Classical criminology conceived the criminal act as the result of the subject's rational choice and sought to deter it though punishment. Biological criminology explained it in hereditary or organic defects. The new psychology constituted criminal behavior as a mental illness and sought its etiology in the subject's biography—in unresolved mental conflicts occurring at critical stages of childhood development.[31] From the 1920s onward, English social workers and psychologists working in child guidance clinics began to observe and interpret the unregulated play of children as a way of accessing and assessing the psychic structure of the delinquent.

Moreover, with the advent of psychology, play assumed a therapeutic function. Sigmund Freud argued that the pleasure of play lies in repeating a traumatic experience and mastering it, often by taking revenge upon a substitute.[32] Play, as catharsis, was believed to purge disruptive emotions and provide a safe outlet for dangerous instincts. But the stakes for play were set higher, as psychoanalysis established an analogy between individual aggression and collective political violence. Anna Freud observed the effects of the war on children at the Hampstead War Nursery, reflecting that: "The real danger is not that the child, caught up all innocently in the whirlpool of the war, will be shocked into illness. The danger lies in the fact that the destruction raging in the outer world may meet the very real aggressiveness, which rages in the inside of the child."[33] During World War II, children were no longer conceived as innocent creatures traumatized by the vio-lence of history, but rather as subjects who might identify with it. This pessimistic conception of the child's nature contributed to the revision of the function of playground.

Branch Street: Play as Catharsis

The discourse that equates collective and individual manifestations of violence, and the idea that violence could be healed by returning to the scene of destruction, frame the work of the Austrian artist and pedagogue Marie Paneth. During the blitz, Paneth managed play centers in London's air raid shelters. I will examine her project at length, since Paneth provided an exact blueprint for the adventure playground, including the use of bombed sites and self-building. Her proposal thus illuminates the strategy of power implicit in adventure playground practices, and positions it in relation to the war.

The immediate context for her work was wartime anxiety over the apparent increase in juvenile delinquency.[34] This anxiety reflected the need to single out those who did not identify with the collective war effort, and the concern that the wartime weakening of parental authority would inevitably lead to collapse in discipline and morality. Children's misbehavior became a problem in air raid shelters and evacuation centers, and the government was compelled to introduce play centers to keep the children occupied and content. From 1942 to 1943, Paneth managed a play center for so-called slum children who were too violent to be evacuated. She provided an account of this experiment in *Branch Street: A Sociological Study* (1944).

Paneth dealt with extreme manifestations of aggression, including stealing, destruction of property, and sexual abuse of female volunteers, by taking what she called the "non-resistance line." The rationale behind her refusal to counter or punish violent behavior was twofold. Paneth interpreted the violence directed toward her as the transference of aggression that was addressed to others. Paneth assumed that the root cause of delinquency was in traumatic childhood experiences brought about by overcrowding, poverty, and punitive childrearing techniques. Observing rather than suppressing destructive play provided the play leader an indirect access to the secrets of the home. The refusal to condemn or judge worked as a strategy for winning the children over and gaining their trust. She directed her staff, mostly conscientious objectors, to grant the children full license to act out their aggression until they become, in her words, "sick of their own method," after which they could "start life at the new place with rule and order."[35] The outcome was that the children destroyed the play center, and her staff resigned. This failure brought about a revision of her methods; Paneth began to work with the children on their own turf and accepted their culture of street play, which appeared to diminish their aggression. This development led Paneth to conclude her account with a proposal for a new type of play center, where such children would be provided with a bombed site to build their own play center and in the process heal themselves: "It is a damaged bit. Its very existence is a reminder of damage and destruction. A sore spot and harmful to all of us. But it could be put to good use even before the war is over. It seems to me it could have a very healing effect if one were allowed to build upon the very spot where damage has been done."[36] Paneth concluded her proposal by claiming that slum conditions as existing in Branch Street provided the recruiting grounds for fascism: "We should also remember that the horde which Hitler employed to carry out his first acts of aggression—murdering and torturing peaceful citizens—was

recruited mainly from desperate Branch Street youths, and that to help the individual means helping democracy as well."[37]

The wartime press extensively reviewed her publication, because children's
violent behavior assumed a political significance during this period of conflict.
Paneth's study coincided with the wartime exposure of poverty in surveys such as
the 1943 *Our Towns* report, which made the welfare of children a national concern. Such surveys contributed to the formation of the wartime consensus that
the state should assume responsibility for providing welfare.[38] Even Churchill,
who otherwise sought to postpone the discussion of social services until after the
war, was nevertheless compelled to define children's well-being as the foundation of any future social policy.[39]

Branch Street is an account of using play to build communities on a participatory model of creative citizenship. The act of building playgrounds on bombed
sites established a correspondence between the narrative of reconstructing the
nation and the self, by which marginalized and damaged subjects could integrate
themselves into society. Paneth provided an alternative to both the contractual
mode of citizenship based on a rational model of the subject and the model of
citizenship based on group identification with the nation or the leader, as both
models were brought into crisis by the mass appeal of fascism. Although children
resisted any form of authority, they were patriotic and idolized Churchill. A critic
from the *Times Educational Supplement* was satisfied with this proof of loyalty to
the nation and doubted if Paneth's principle of freedom and autonomy was desirable for the slum population; he assumed that "they wanted a leader whom they
could follow."[40] But such a libidinal tie with the leader was precisely what Paneth
was opposed to, as her goal was to make her subjects accept the responsibility of
freedom rather than delegate it to others.

Branch Street illuminates the rationale behind the domestic activity that
often takes place in adventure playgrounds, such as making fires, cooking mid-
day meals, and dwelling in self-made homes and tree houses. Although these
phenomena are all too readily explained as an expression of the child's desire to
imitate the world of adults, Paneth's work suggests the strategic purpose of defining the playground as a second home. Examination of the daily reports submitted
to playground committees on the play activities of children, such as the one filed
by Clydesdale's play leader Peter Gutkind, demonstrates that the second home
allowed the social worker to access the first, and to pin the pathologies of the
slum child in inadequate mothercraft: "Today one little girl complained bitterly
about her mother who "has no love for me, she always kicks me out." We might
say that as they have no place to play inside in the happy setting of a home they
develop a certain antagonism against the home and later follows boredom and
then delinquency."[41] By reenacting childhood in a permissive and supportive
environment, children's attitude toward society and authority could be rescued
from being a projection, a repetition of their resistance and aggression toward
the imperfect parenthood they experienced at home.

Adventure Playground as Experiment in Anarchy

Paneth employed the strategy of anarchy to allow violence to reach catharsis. Yet Burden provided another conceptual foundation for promoting anarchical play practices, noting that "A bored child is a menace to the community, especially if he has intelligence, for boredom and inactivity almost inevitably lead to delinquency."[42] This strategy implies that social workers began to conceptualize delinquency as a contextual reaction to a given situation, an expression of a lack in the environment to engage and stimulate the subject. This approach is radically different in its empiricism from the stigmatic notion that delinquency has its roots in a social or individual pathological trait. It implied that play had to be more intense and pleasurable than the transgressive experience of delinquency. In our present-day stress on safety, the idea of handing children hammers and axes in public playgrounds would be considered negligent, at best. But in 1946 it was possible for Allen to claim, "even the hammer is an education." The need to intensify the subjective experience of play raised the problem of managing risk. Allen convinced underwriters at Lloyd's to insure the Clydesdale playground by reasoning that children who were deeply engrossed in their own play were less likely to have accidents than those driven by boredom to use conventional playground equipment in ways it was never intended.[43] Allen critiqued functionalism as too rigid to accommodate the agency and will of the user, claiming that imposing authority from without through the design of the play object inevitably led to resistance. The stress on context rather than essence provides an alternative political reading of the experimental nature of the adventure playground. If human behavior was not predetermined by human nature or laws of history, but derived empirically in relation to a situation, then everything became dependent on how the event was set up. The playground assumed the status of an experiment.

This led English critics in the 1960s to regard the adventure playground as a political experiment. For Colin Ward, a left-wing activist and urban theorist, the adventure playground provided a demonstration of how subjects govern themselves when they are not "controlled, directed, or limited." To Ward, it provided an "experimental verification" of the feasibility of an alternative social order in which the absence of external rules and authority allows a more egalitarian and democratic order to arise organically out of the needs of the situation. The playground community was seen as a "free society in miniature," a demonstration that the demand for the "free access to the means of production" was realizable.[44] This discourse conveniently disregarded the crucial role of the play leader in making anarchy work and the usefulness of anarchy in making the interiority of the subjects observable and known.

Play Practices: The Indirect Method of Governing Subjectivity

The two practices of anarchy just discussed—the libertarian and the psychoanalytic—are rooted in different conceptions of human nature and citizenship. However, they both illuminate the strategy of power implicit in the adventure playground in which the internal resources of subjects and their propensity for play are mobilized to constitute their subjectivity. Jack Lambert, a seasoned English play leader, provided a frank account of the use of indirect power to pursue social aims: "One of the great paradoxes in the art of playing with children is that you know you are doing well when you are doing nothing. Doing nothing is one of the hardest things of all. . . . I felt I succeeded in Welwyn because by that time I had found ways of building in controls without the children recognizing them as such. They felt free."[45]

It is not that play leaders do nothing. In that case, they would be redundant. In 1955, play leaders, meeting at a professional conference, defined the adventure playground "as children, a site and a play leader. The play leader makes all the difference. He is the humanizing element, the person who brings the whole thing to life."[46] The role of the play leader is to be there, as his or her mere presence provides the legitimization for children to act out their desires, their imagination, and become active citizens. Their employment of power is much more subtle, since it is predicated on activating rather than limiting children's agency. The ideal is never to say "no" in order that the child would not identify the play leader with parental or pedagogical authority, but would adopt the modern project of self-betterment as its own.

The significance of making play an object of observation and knowledge rather than a subject of direct intervention is demonstrated by Lambert's account of the techniques he developed to deal with aggression. Lambert stated his dilemma in terms of how to accommodate the inclusive and nonauthoritarian ethos of the playground to the problem of rough kids who bully weaker children and destroy their creative work. At first, Lambert expelled them from the playground, after moralizing and reasoning failed. The act of exclusion in itself produced resistance and retaliation, expressed in the dramatic destruction of the playground, and it kept out those who needed it the most. In the next playground he managed, Lambert developed a technique for incorporating the lads, as he called them, by insisting on addressing them as individuals, since "most kids need the gang identity to give them confidence to be aggressive and violent."[47] He then positioned them as helpers with responsibility for managing playground activity. Another technique was to adjust organized play to their interests. Lambert provided an account of a "rough" group he was compelled expel from the playground. He followed them home and observed their intense interest in a broken scooter they were unable to fix. He initiated a scooter club, where the lads salvaged and fixed discarded scooters. This activity became the central attraction of the playground, demonstrating that the openness of the playground to children's interests and what they find pleasurable constituted a productive strategy for allowing social services to penetrate even the most alienated social strata. Inciting children to appropriate and master space, to make it their own—"to identify with it, because it would be theirs"[48]—was intended to attach children at risk to the social body by providing them with a sense of ownership and agency.

Conclusion

The analysis of the adventure playground as a strategy of power and a narrative for reconstruction uncovers the contradictions of the postwar welfare state. The playground was originally part of a utopian project to reconstruct a peaceful and more stable postwar society through policies and practices directed toward each individual child, in his or her capacity as a future citizen. It was predicated upon investing play with the capacity to heal society and purge itself of the wartime manifestation of violence. Postwar society was fascinated with the play of children in ruins and put play on display as a metaphor for regeneration, all the while affirming a tragic and mythical conception of violence as rooted in human nature.

Yet the adventure playground's democratic and participatory model of collectivity, as well as its pacifism, was rooted in a psychological notion of political citizenship. The policy of autonomous free play was predicated on the not-so-liberal notion that society has the right, even the obligation, to know and govern the interiority of its subjects to advance the greater common good, since social cohesion and stability were dependant on the emotional equilibrium of each individual member. In this respect, the adventure playground confirms Rose's claim that the welfare state governs subjects from the inside, by inducing them to change their everyday conduct to act as active citizens, ardent consumers, enthusiastic employees, and loving parents, as if they are realizing their own intimate desires.[49] The playground was one of these institutions where children were made into subjects, precisely because in play they felt themselves to be autonomous and free.

NOTES

1. Principle 7, Declaration of the Rights of the Child, General Assembly Resolution 1386 (XIV), UN doc A/4354 (1959).

2. John Bertelsen, "The Daily Round on a Junk Playground," *Danish Outlook* 6.6 (1953): 690.

3. In the 1960s, American public opinion was hostile to the conventional playground, and newspapers described it as Neanderthal, hideous, or disgraceful. Michael Gotkin, "The Politics of Play," in *Preserving Modern Landscape* Architecture, edited by Charles A. Birnbaum (Cambridge, Mass.: Spacemaker Press, 1999), 64.

4. Galen Cranz, *The Politics of Park Design: A History of Urban Parks in America* (Cambridge: MIT Press, 1982), 192.

5. David Cohen, *The Development of Play* (New York: New York University Press, 1987), 32–33.

6. I draw on the first volume of Michel Foucault's *The History of Sexuality: An Introduction*, translated by Robert Hurley (New York: Pantheon, 1978), which bears on the topic of conceptualizing liberated play as a confessional strategy of subjectivization. I also build

upon Foucault's essay "The Subject and Power," where he states that power, in distinction to violence, is not about dominating or destroying others or taking away freedom, but "a way of acting upon one or more acting subjects by virtue of their acting or being capable of action." Power is productive, "it incites, it induces, it seduces." See Michel Foucault, "The Subject and Power," in *Power: Essential Works of Foucault 1954–1984*, vol. 3, edited by James D. Faubion (London: Penguin, 2000), 341.

7. Nikolas Rose, *Governing the Soul: The Shaping of the Private Self* (London: Routledge, 1990), 32.

8. Lady Allen of Hurtwood, *Planning for Play* (London: Thames and Hudson, 1968), 9.

9. Noguchi's unrealized "Play Mountain" (1933) established the playground as a sculptural landscape. Van Eyck designed more than 700 playgrounds in Amsterdam from 1947 to 1978, using the formal language of de Stijl. Gotkin, "The Politics of Play," 62; Francis Strauven, "Wasted Pearls in the Fabric of the City," in *Aldo van Eyck, the Playgrounds and the City*, edited by Liane Lefaivre and Ingeborg de Roode (Amsterdam: Stedelijk Museum, and Rotterdam: NAi Publishers, 2002), 66–67.

10. Dewey criticized Froebel's use of geometry in education as the imposition of a priori forms. He wrote that for Froebel, "It is not enough that the circle is a convenient way of grouping children. It must be used, 'because it is a symbol of the collective life of mankind in general.'" John Dewey, *Democracy and Education* (New York: Free Press, 1966), 58.

11. Carl Theodor Sørensen, "Junk Playgrounds," *Danish Outlook* 4.1 (1951): 314.

12. Bertelsen, "The Daily Round on a Junk Playground," 688.

13. Petition to the Town Clerk from March 1950, "Clydesdale Road Playground: correspondence and papers 1952–1956," CB 3/310, Public Records Office (PRO hereafter), London.

14. Bertelsen and Vesteregn had been married to one another.

15. John Bertelsen, "Early Experience from Emdrup," in *Adventure Playground*, edited by Arvid Bengtsson (New York, Praeger, 1972), 20.

16. Bertelsen, "Early Experience from Emdrup," 21, 19.

17. Quoted in Ning de Coninck-Smith, "Children, Play, and Democracy: A Contribution to the Designing of Modern Danish Childhood 1943–1960," paper presented at "Stories for Children, Histories of Childhood," Colloque International du GRAAT, Tours, France, November 2005, 6. This statement had its English equivalent in the 1945 Labour Party election manifesto: "Above all, let us remember that the great purpose of education is to give us individual citizens capable of thinking for themselves." See F.W.S. Craig, ed., *British General Election Manifestos 1900–1974* (London: Macmillan, 1975), 129.

18. Coninck-Smith, "Children, Play, and Democracy," 14.

19. It is telling that Allen became aware of the problem upon encountering a group of "institutional children" who "never seemed to join the others in the playground." The absence of play became a signifier for deprivation. Marjory Allen and Mary Nicholson, *Memoirs of an Uneducated Lady: Lady Allen of Hurtwood* (London: Thames and Hudson, 1975), 171.

20. In the aftermath of World War I, Save the Children Fund was established as a challenge to the policy of blockading the defeated nations, on the grounds that it had an irreversible effect on the health of children. Save the Children sponsored the first English junk playground at Camberwell in 1948.

21. Allen and Nicholson, *Memoirs*, 205. Emdrup validated Allen's earlier thoughts about playground design. In 1938 Allen delivered a paper, "The Future of Landscape Architecture," where she described a park in Wales where children were allowed to dig

and dwell. She posed it as the ideal playground for children, as it made them "blissfully happy and engrossingly occupied." Allen's child-centered conception of play was advanced as part of her program to democratize the profession of landscape architecture as a "national service, affecting the character of our people and even our political democracy." MSS 121/HO/7/1/3, Modern Records Centre [MRC hereafter], Coventry.

22. Lady Allen of Hurtwood, "Why Not Use Our Bomb Sites Like This?" *Picture Post*, November 16, 1946, 26–27.

23. Allen disclosed in a memorandum that Lollard was "well placed for use as a demonstration project, since it is within walking distance, across the river, from the House of Parliament." "Lollard Adventure Playground," MSS 121/AP/3/5/14, MRC.

24. The legislation for converting bombed sites into playgrounds was initiated in 1944 by E. H. Keeling in response to the wartime increase in child fatalities in road accidents. "Children's Playgrounds: Local Authorities to Make Suitable Bombed Sites Available 1944–1948," HLG 51/905, PRO.

25. The American sociologist Clarence Perry developed the concept of the neighborhood unit in the 1920s to constitute self-sufficient communities, in which the size and layout of residential development was determined by the centrality of services catering to the family, especially the school. English planners applied the concept in postwar new towns and housing estates.

26. Max Lock, "The Middlesbrough Experiment: Planning from Within," in *Architects' Yearbook* 2, edited by Jane Drew (London: Elek, 1947), 41. Emphasis in the original.

27. George Burden, "The Junk Playground: An Educational Adjunct and an Antidote to Delinquency," *The Friend* 1029 (December 3, 1948): 4.

28. The university settlement movement provided an institutional framework for the middle class to study the realities of urban poverty while offering the working classes educational and cultural programs. According to Timmins, the English welfare state was the intellectual product of the settlement movement: William Beveridge, Clement Atlee, and Richard Tawney all served at Toynbee Hall. Nicholas Timmins, *The Five Giants: A Biography of the Welfare State* (London: HarperCollins, 1995), 12.

29. Walter Wood, a barrister and play theoretician, stated, "Women have not the civic virtues of loyalty and surrender of self to a common cause. . . . Civilisation however, is coming to require more and more the civic virtues from women, and this is one reason why we should encourage team games amongst adolescent girls." Walter D. Wood, *Children's Play and Its Place in Education* (London: Kegan Paul, 1915), 187.

30. With the institution of the juvenile court system in 1907, the first probation officers were recruited from play center workers. Kevin Brehony, "A Socially Civilizing Influence? Play and the Urban 'Degenerate,'" *Paedagogica Historia* 39.1/2 (2003): 103.

31. Claire Valiér, "Psychoanalysis and Crime in Britain during the Inter-War Years," in *Selected Papers from the 1995 British Criminology Conference, Loughborough*, vol. 1, edited by Jon Vagg and Tim Newburn (September 1998), 6–7.

32. Sigmund Freud, *Beyond the Pleasure Principle* (New York: Norton, 1989), 16.

33. Anna Freud and Dorothy Burlingham, *War and Children* ([New York]: Medical War Books, 1943), 24.

34. The sociologist D. C. Marsh argued in retrospect that the statistical rise in delinquency was caused by wartime intolerance toward minor infractions of public order, rather than any real surge in criminal acts. D. C. Marsh, *The Changing Social Structure of England and Wales* (London; Routledge & Kegan Paul 1965), 257–259.

35. Marie Paneth, *Branch Street: A Sociological Study* (London: Allen & Unwin, 1944), 34. Paneth was influenced by August Aichhorn, an Austrian who introduced psychoanalysis into the institutional treatment of delinquents. Aichhorn allowed his subjects to act out their aggressiveness to the point of explosion, since "when this point came, the aggression changed its character. The outbreaks of rage against each other were no longer genuine, but were acted out for our benefit." August Aichhorn, *Wayward Youth* (London: Imago, 1951), 175.

36. Paneth, *Branch Street*, 120.

37. Paneth, *Branch Street*, 120.

38. John Welshman, "Evacuation, Hygiene, and Social Policy: The *Our Towns* Report of 1943," *Historical Journal* 42.3 (1999), 806. Allen was a member of the committee.

39. "Slum Life in Cities: Social Conditions Revealed by Evacuation," *Times*, March 29, 1943, 5; "Mr. Churchill on Post-War Policy: Four Year's Plan for Britain, *Times*, March 22, 1943, 5.

40. "Town Life at its Worst: Social Problems of the Immediate Future," *Times Educational Supplement*, July 29, 1944, 362.

41. Peter C. W. Gutkind, "Report to Clydesdale Road Playground Committee," entry from May 13, 1952. MSS 121/AP/3/2/7, MRC.

42. Burden, "The Junk Playground," 4.

43. Allen, *Memoirs*, 243.

44. Colin Ward, "Adventure Playground: A Parable of Anarchy," *Anarchy* 7 (September 1961): 194, 201 This issue was dedicated to the adventure playground.

45. Jack Lambert, *Adventure Playgrounds: A Personal Account of a Play-leader's Work as Told to Jenny Pearson* (London: Jonathan Cape, 1974), 65.

46. National Playing Fields Association, "Play Leadership on Adventure Playgrounds," April 27, 1955. CB 1/67, PRO.

47. Lambert, *Adventure Playgrounds*, 112.

48. Lambert, *Adventure Playgrounds*, 56.

49. Rose, *Governing the Soul*, 258.

PART THREE

Space, Power, and Inequality in Modern Childhoods

9

The View from the Back Step

White Children Learn about Race in Johannesburg's Suburban Homes

REBECCA GINSBURG

How do children learn social values? This chapter argues that the cultural landscape can serve as a text from which they read how their social world operates and their own places within it.[1] The order of any built environment provides clues to the priorities of those who designed and inhabit it. In apartheid-era South Africa, the nexus between dominant social values and spatial order was especially tight, as the system was premised on space's ability to make meaning. The messages South African youngsters received from their surroundings, then, could be particularly powerful and potent.

South African children learned gradually how apartheid worked, and they learned in and from a variety of different settings. One primary source of white urban children's growing understanding of that system was the landscape of their own back yards. The organization of home ground served as a template for an entire country structured according to race. By observing and participating in the geography of their houses, white children came to make sense of the racialized geography of apartheid and to accept it as natural.

Drawing attention to the role of the landscape in white children's political development accomplishes two important things for those of us interested in the relationship between the built environment and social life. It highlights the bluntness of the concept of "socialization" and encourages us to pinpoint particular institutions and practices within a child's world that bore on her development in specific ways, including the landscape.[2] Second, it disaggregates the notion of reading the landscape by demonstrating that people's interpretations of their surroundings depends on many factors, including their developmental capacities at any given point.

I became interested in the developmental aspects of reading landscapes and the social implications of such processes while researching the conditions of everyday life in the Johannesburg suburbs during apartheid. My focus was the social and spatial relationships between white household members and the female

African servants that typically lived on their properties with them. My interviews with former servants revealed that their relationships with the white youngsters that they cared for were the cause of some of the most rewarding and most painful experiences of domestic service. Curious about white children's perspectives of their relationships with their nannies, I interviewed about fifteen white people who had been children in Johannesburg during the height of apartheid, the 1960s and 1970s. I not only found their memories of their nannies to be equally conflicted but I also came to appreciate that their relationships with their African caretakers were instrumental to their acquisition of environmental awareness.

This chapter is based primarily on those interviews, in which white South African adults recollected their experiences as children in their homes, and on interviews with about fifty former African servants who worked in the same middle- and upper-middle-class area of Johannesburg, known as the Northern Suburbs, during the same time. Other primary sources include novels, autobiographies, and contemporary magazines and newspaper articles that capture a sense of domestic life and the choreography of daily routines in the Northern Suburbs during these, the most repressive years of apartheid. Secondary sources have been less useful. While there is some—not much—research on the experiences of nonwhite children under apartheid, most of which deals with the effects of trauma, violence, and poverty, only a splattering consider the effects of apartheid on white children.[3] There are probably many reasons that white South African literature does a better job acknowledging the pain and costs of growing

FIGURE 9.1 Many houses in the Northern Suburbs sat on lots one-third acre and more.
Photo by the author, 1996.

up in an ostensibly privileged class than does predominantly white South African scholarship. As a nonwhite outsider, it may have been intellectually and emotionally easier for me to observe and research the pathology of middle-class white South African childhood than for white academics from that country.

The Setting

Johannesburg's Northern Suburbs were in many respects an ideal setting for raising a family. Large yards and a flourishing economy permitted the installation of swimming pools, jungle gyms, and playhouses, as well as the companionship of dogs, cats, rabbits, and other pets (Figure 9.1). Most homes were spacious enough that each child could have a bedroom of his or her own, decorated to suit individual taste.

Of the greatest value to couples with children, though, were not the physical amenities of suburbia but the availability of cheap African labor. Almost all

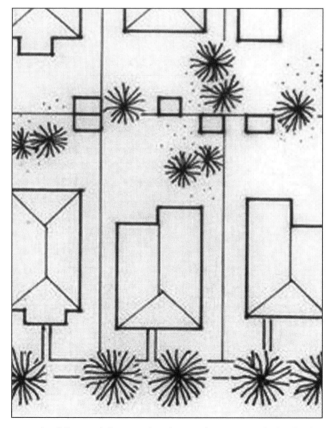

FIGURE 9.2 Standard domestic layout, showing workers' rooms in back of yards, behind main family homes.

Drawing by Sibel Zandi-Sayek. Used with permission.

middle-class urban white properties housed migrant African women who came to South Africa's cities in search of wages to support their families, mostly back in the homelands or on white farms. They slept, typically, in detached rooms in the yards of their employers (Figure 9.2). By city regulation, these rooms could be no smaller than eight by ten feet, and they were rarely larger than that. Adjoining most rooms were toilets and showers for the worker's use.

Domestic workers not only relieved mothers of routine household tasks and so allowed them to spend more time with their children but they often played major roles themselves in raising those youngsters. Some African women were employed specifically as nannies. Others, regardless of their official duties, found that household circumstances, their own maternal longings, or a combination of both factors encouraged them to participate in child care, if not to assume primary responsibility for it. As testament to the degree to which African women, whether employed as nannies or in their general capacity as domestic servants, assumed child-care responsibilities within white homes, in a 1968 study as many as 50 percent of white mothers reported that their social activities and outings had not been restricted at all by the arrival of children.[4] Although mothers usually set rules regarding tasks like bathing, feeding, and playtime, the actual work

FIGURE 9.3 Worker with charges, Johannesburg, undated.
Museum Africa, Johannesburg.

was typically performed by the worker. Maids were usually the most constant presence in a young white child's life (Figure 9.3).

For many African women, the opportunity to form bonds with white children compensated a little for having to spend long years away from their own. Indeed, sometimes the ties between worker and child were very intense, almost desperate. One contemporary white observer suggested that black women "sublimated" their frustrated maternal instincts by throwing their hearts into their relationships with white children.[5] Certainly their degree of attachment could seem extreme even to some workers, in hindsight: "I was overfond of Jane. I had too much time for Jane and no time for anybody else. I've always been with Jane, always, except in her sleeping time. I was her nanny, but in between her and me we were more like mother and child."[6] Or, in the words of another, who assumed primary responsibility for raising an autistic girl after her devastated mother rejected her, "She was just my daughter. I think she was born for me."[7]

Parents were not entirely without concerns about entrusting their children to African servants. According to the same 1968 study, white women cited the "non-reliability" of nonwhites, their "moral inferiority," concerns that the practice was "unhygienic," and the deprivation of "mother love" as drawbacks to the use of nanny care.[8] Significantly, however, they did not include as a problem the close relationships that so often developed between their young sons and daughters and black household servants. The gradual transference of children's loyalty and affection from nannies to parents was an accepted and reassuring fact of life, and few youngsters embarrassed family members by maintaining awkward attachments to African women beyond their early childhood years. While parents hoped that fondness would always remain, as would children's gracious regard for the worker, white adults trusted that their sons and daughters would distance themselves emotionally from nanny by about school-going age, and most did.

The process of disentanglement received guidance from many quarters. White children learned from the offhand remarks of neighbors, explicit discussions with parents and older siblings, books read aloud, and pictures that hung on walls the sanctioned roles of Africans and whites, respectively. One girl, whenever she asked her nanny to come and sit with her at the table, was reminded by her older sister that nanny did not eat with the family.[9] Another remembered being told, "no, don't drink out of that," of the tin cups that her nanny used.[10]

Nonverbal interactions in the home between nanny and family members reinforced those lessons. Indeed, scholars and observers of apartheid life have noted that the institution of domestic service was, ironically, central to a white child's growing ability to distinguish herself from Africans and recognize herself as white, a skill upon which successful acculturation into apartheid society depended.[11] Young whites observed the submissive manners of the worker, her uniform, the nature of her duties around the house, and the way white adults treated her, and from such details began to understand that there were differences between Africans and whites.

Underpinning and reinforcing such observations was the very organization of home ground. The location of things and people revealed their value and status and became the foundation for other racial understandings. Mostly, it supported the ability to view and accept the world in terms of dominant apartheid ideology, which divided all aspects of life—social, economic, and political—into multiple spheres, based on racial classification.

The Stages

Although the means by which humans process, organize, and interpret environmental information are complex and still open to debate, there is general agreement that people are not born with the ability to compose mental maps.[12] Their ability and interest in doing so is a function of their level of cognitive functioning, their degree of environmental experience, and their stage of perceptual development. We know, too, that people similarly situated tend both to have similar engagements with their surroundings and to be at comparable developmental stages.[13] For that reason, it is appropriate to speak of common schemas of white houses held by preschool white children who lived in the middle-class Northern Suburbs, and of shared processes by which those schemas changed over time. My effort to relate white children's growing awareness of racialized space to their developmental stages draws on the work of early twentieth-century Russian psychologists Lev Vgotsky and A. R. Luria.[14] Their emphasis on the social contexts of development and, in particular, its foundation in interpersonal engagement situated in particular historical circumstances strikes me as appropriately sensitive to social forces and change. Piaget's delineation of the stages of development also underpins the following discussion.

White South African infants, like any humans of that age, were unable to form environmental maps. Indeed, within the "blooming, buzzing confusion" that constituted their worlds, they did not even experience themselves as distinct from their surroundings and, in particular, from their primary caretakers. As one woman recalled, perhaps fantastically, in her autobiography, "I remember the rustle and papery starch of Nanny up against my cheek. And a swimming circle around me. Was it face or was it breast?"[15] My informants confirmed that if both parents worked, but often even if they did not, the main presence in a young white life was the black maid. "When you're a small child, they're absolutely constant, from early in the morning until after dinner. . . . There, constantly."[16]

Although of course we cannot know for sure, it is likely that during these years white children were unable to map the spaces of their homes. From their positions on the maid's back or in her arms, babies knew only hunger and satisfaction, cold and warmth, dark and light.[17] These conditions did not relate to the external landscape of their homes. They were located within the rhythms of the intimate connections between themselves and their nannies' bodies.

Developmental research suggests that white South African children probably came gradually to distinguish themselves from their surroundings. Although even prelocomotory infants have some degree of spatial competence, it is when they begin to move around their yards on their own, starting at about the age of twelve months, that toddlers start to construct rudimentary mental maps. As direct dependence on adults declines, they assert their urge to know their surroundings. Cognitive skills also grow, both facilitating their explorations and as a result of them.[18]

By the age of two, then, most healthy white children had entered a new stage. They had become aware that they existed as objects as well as subjects. Expressed another way, they observed that others could have a point of view that was not theirs and that they stood in various relations to those others. With this insight came a new awareness of other people and the beginnings, in the healthy child, of some form of empathy. No longer restricted to seeing the world from the vantage point of self-as-subject, they could begin to consider other perspectives. These were very halting, incomplete, and unsophisticated efforts, but they helped children to produce more sophisticated maps of those parts of the environments through which they moved.[19]

As their curiosity and their cognitive capacities grew, white South African children began to recognize differences between the two homes that stood on their parents' properties. Black spaces, my now-adult informants reported, started to appear different from white ones. For instance, they smelled different—of the paraffin used for heating and of the cornmeal mush that Africans prepared for their evening meal. The absence of electricity made many darker and more mysterious. The music that servants played on their radios had a distinctive sound from the radio programs heard in their parents' homes. The atmosphere in back rooms was closer than in the well-ventilated spaces of the main house. Mildew and cobwebs lined the ceilings (Figure 9.4).

These differences, however, were not associated in the mind of the young child with anything like notions of racial inferiority or superiority. They seem to have made exploration fun, as in the recesses of a loved one's attic, but hinted at no deep or pernicious divide between nanny and self. Indeed, far from being suggestive of the maid's inferiority, the qualities associated with the back room sometimes assumed higher value by virtue of their connection with her. One woman remembers seeing her parents' castoffs in her nanny's room in a new light. "[T]hey became beautiful and shiny and precious [there]."[20] In the same way, a white American child preferred her nanny's cabin in 1960s Louisiana to her parents' large home: "I remember thinking her house was different from mine, but kind of liking it better 'cause there were all those [black] kids around and my house was kind of quiet and nobody else my age."[21]

South African toddlers continued to follow the maid everywhere, and many took their naps lying beside her in her narrow bed. "In a way I think she was my mother. . . . I remember just spending a lot of time in her room," recalled one

FIGURE 9.4 The darkness of a worker's room could cast a sense of enchantment over it. Here, tin pots glimmer in a dim corner.

Photo by author, 1995.

informant of his early boyhood.[22] Another white boy who contracted deadly tick-bite fever around this age caused his mother great distress by calling constantly, in his delirium, for his nanny rather than for her.[23]

Two important developmental shifts take place in most children between the ages of about four and six that had great implications for white children's relations with their nannies and their comprehension of the geographies of race. First, the average child acquires a newfound interest in her own identity. From associating herself with all of her surroundings as an infant, to perceiving that other people exist with independent and sometimes contrary points of view, she comes to perceive that there is a sense of order to it all. She seeks to understand that order, and to learn where she fits into the scheme of things.[24]

The world, she can see, is inhabited by people of varying status and positions. She, too, has a role to play, a position ready made, into which she is expected to fit. She is part of a "we," and that "we" has particular habits, tastes, attitudes, accents, dress, and points of view. Through a process of observation, correction, and direct instruction, she teaches herself the behavior that seems proper for a person in her place. More than that, she begins to see that assuming her role involves acquiring, among other things, a particular way of seeing the world. She studies that as well, striving to see what she believes she should.[25]

At the same time, children during these years develop the capacity to think about race.[26] As they begin to situate themselves in their environments, to be aware of themselves as others might see them, and to discriminate the people and things of their surroundings, children start to note socially relevant categories, those that the people around them, through their words and actions, tell them matter. In apartheid-era South Africa, no category was as salient as race.

There is evidence that most white children at this age tended to oversimplify society in their efforts to organize it. "She recently started talking about Zulus. . . . Whenever she sees a brown person, she says, 'there's a Zulu,'" said one mother of her five-year-old.[27] Reported another, "my child was given a doll with a black face and has given her the same name as the nanny has."[28] That the child would make such a correlation was not surprising. Most white youngsters living in the Northern Suburbs had negligible exposure to any Africans other than their nannies and their nannies' friends. According to a college student who grew up there in the 1970s, "Occasionally, in the car, one would pass black men repairing the road for the municipality . . . or in the more run-down area of Johannesburg . . . one would come across old, sick and crippled black beggars sitting outside shops."[29] Most white children occupied an almost exclusively white world, with the important exception of their primary caretaker.

Attempts to impose order extended to the South African child's physical environment as well, and she perceived that here, too, racial categories helped her efforts. Drives through homelands, with parched earth and unpaved roads, on her way to visit grandparents in the country; the haze of smoke from charcoal, used for cooking and for heat, that overlay distant Soweto township and on occasion floated into the white city; the bus benches down the block marked "whites only"; and the view from her own back step all conveyed the idea that there was a connection between race and place in apartheid society.[30]

Values shifted. As she tried to comprehend better the opinions of those like her, she began to see that not only was the world divided into separate parts but also that the parts were unequal. She revised her mental maps, at various scales, to accommodate race-based distinctions, whose value lay not in what they told her of the world but in what they allowed the world to reflect back of herself. The racial geography that she began to perceive spoke comforting messages of white privilege and superiority. Gradually, she came to regard the back room now as something not just distinct and qualitatively different but also inferior.

Certain features began to acquire significance. She perceived, for instance, that the maid's room and main house did not form an undivided whole. The buildings existed in two separate spheres. In the front stood her family's home, large and permanent. It faced the road and contained features like doorbell, knocker, and mailbox, which enabled connection with the rest of the world. The house screened and filtered outsiders: all visitors and news had to pass through it. It also presented the family, greeting passers-by and announcing to them the status and tastes of the inhabitants. The back room greeted no one. It stood in an inconspicuous corner of the back yard with its face turned to one side and its small entrance obscured (Figure 9.5).

FIGURE 9.5 View of back room, Johannesburg. This room sits in the furthest reaches of the half-acre lot. The roof in the background is of the next-door neighbor's garage.

Photo by author, 2004.

FIGURE 9.6 A hat adorns the crumbling wall of a worker's room.

Photo by author, 1996.

FIGURE 9.7 Mildew and flaking walls were common in back rooms, which employers usually whitewashed once a year, sometimes directly over the bricks. Here, the worker has made some effort to hide the damage by hanging supermarket calendars.

Photo by author, 1996.

The maid's room was actually a ramshackle thing, constructed of cheap materials and furnished with her parents' discards. The roof leaked during the rainy season and water stained the walls. In summer the lack of adequate ventilation made it stuffy and hot. The toilet had no seat, the shower no curtain, the bulb no shade, and the floor no carpet. The items that her parents valued—paintings, books, appliances—were either absent or reproduced in what sometimes appeared gross parody. A give-away supermarket calendar, for instance, took the place of an original watercolor. Old sheets served as curtains. *Mealie* meal sacks were draped over old crates to hide the faded fruit labels (Figures 9.6 and 9.7).

She began to understand, too, that her parents desired distance to be kept between the two structures. Landscaping devices—rows of hedges, trees, a slight grade, perhaps a small wall—separated the servant's quarters from her own home. The scents that had once titillated the child she understood now to be considered unpleasant by those she was learning to associate herself with. The pulsating beats of Radio Zulu to which nanny had once bounced her were, she learned, considered discordant and vulgar. They were unwanted during quiet evenings in the family's lounge (Figure 9.8).

The small back room and the considerably larger house were united in one sense, though. Her parents controlled them both. The back room was the maid's only in the sense that she slept there. White adults had the final word on what she did there, when she did it, whom the maid admitted to the room, and even

FIGURE 9.8 View of back room, Johannesburg, with entrance obscured by tree.
Photo by author, 1998.

the maid's own occupation of the place. The back room, the child could see, was less an independent and equal dwelling than another, "exterior" bedroom affixed to the main house. As her parents held power over the child's room, so they had charge over the maid's. And as the child was a dependent of the household, so was the maid, though of even lesser status.

Many children not only observed these things, but questioned them. One child asked her nanny, "who painted you black?"[31] Another wanted her mother to explain why only Africans worked as domestics.[32] A five-year-old boy sought an explanation for why his nanny lived in an outside room instead of the main house.[33]

A white woman who grew up in the segregated American South remembers her own confused discomfort with that racialized order: "I can remember asking Grandmother one time why Verity had to go outside to go to the toilet. They had a bathroom out under the garage for the help, but I didn't think that was fair. I don't remember her answer, but it was something to the effect that it was just the way it was."[34] Or, from another, "I think as a child I always wondered about the buses. We would take the bus downtown all the time and Ruth [the nanny] had to sit in the back. We sat in the back with her. I remember being confused about that at one time. But no explanation was given, so it just became ingrained—the separation of the races—something you accepted."[35]

White South African and American youngsters grew up in different political and social contexts, but they shared children's desires at this stage to understand things that bore on them and theirs. They shared also the sensibilities that caused them, before they learned to tolerate discrimination, to be affronted or, at least, unaccepting of it. Nonetheless, it seems that with time, increased exposure to racialized distinctions, and a growing need to embrace a socially acceptable identity, acceptance came.

Indeed, by seven or eight, South African children began to use the yard in ways that expressed and reinforced their growing sense of their status as whites, as well as their growing independence as young boys and girls. They were less likely to venture into the maid's room of their own will and, if they found themselves in the vicinity, chasing a runaway ball or having to call her for a task, less likely to stay and talk. As my informants described it, the domestic worker's room became "foreign" and "almost another world." Said one of her later childhood, while acknowledging that her toddler twin sisters wandered freely to the maid's room, "It was her territory. I suppose that was the only place that was sort of off-limits. We [the five older brothers and sisters] didn't go in there. Although no one ever said that. It was just not ours."[36]

Parents encouraged their children to break ties, expressing the expectation that they would spend less time with their nannies and more time with other white people. Said one, approvingly, "my daughter Carol is less attached to the nanny now [at five] than previously because she's getting older and wants more stimulation outside the house."[37] Increased exposure to the world outside the household, especially to peers, was both a result of and a reason for the child's moving away from her nanny. A 1988 study showed that by the time they were five years old, most white children perceived their nannies as distant, peripheral figures.[38] Not only had they become aware of race and of the fact that their nannies were African, they had also learned to value Africans and whites differently.

When younger, [my five-year-old son] would think of her as a family member. Now he'll tell her, "you're not the boss!"[39]

When my child has to tidy up, she responds, "Anna will do it; she's just the maid."[40]

When I ask my child to clean up his mess, he tells me that he's not a nanny.[41]

Fighting Back

Some children responded with resistance to the various pressures to withdraw from the nanny's sphere and enter more fully the life of the white house and the outside world. One six-year-old girl began acting wildly in school, hitting other children and defecating in the classroom, after her mother fired her nursemaid without warning or explanation. She was mute in her pain, unable to explain to others, and possibly even to herself, what was causing her such distress.[42]

Another girl remained close to her nanny long past the time her parents thought she should have begun to disassociate herself. Knowing they disapproved, she used to sneak to the back room on Sunday afternoons while her parents slept.

Eventually, they became so embarrassed of the intimacy between her and the African woman—at the age of six, she would go nowhere without her—that they dismissed the worker.[43]

It was mostly girls who tried to retain close ties to their nannies, in part because boys at this age were trying anyway to distance themselves from their female caretakers and loosen their emotional ties to others in an effort to situate themselves as males.[44] Another girl in the early 1960s used to venture regularly, and surreptitiously, to her maid's room until the woman left the family, when she was about ten. She sneaked up the small flight of stairs at the end of the garden, beyond the avocado trees, making sure first that her parents were away from home. She knew they wouldn't approve, that the woman who had once proved useful for feeding and bathing a small white child was also the possible conveyor of bad habits and manners, of so-called "black ways," like eating with your hands or spitting. She did not even reveal her secret visits to her friends.[45]

Another informant recalled that as a young boy he had come to recognize that an enormous gulf lay between his family's house and the maid's quarters only a few yards away. Unusually sensitive and self-aware as a child, he described the sorrow and frustration he felt toward the expectation that he keep his distance from his nanny. Standing on the back steps of his parents' home, he used to gaze longingly in the direction of her back room, remembering fondly when it had been acceptable for him to visit and yearning bitterly to be able to cross the invisible barriers of race that he was coming to understand governed South African life. Lines and borders appeared on the property where none had before (Figure 9.9).[46]

Other white children dealt with what we can only sensibly or compassionately think of as grief for lost intimacies in less benign ways. Vincent Crapanzano, an American anthropologist who conducted research in the Cape in the 1980s, believes that white children's exaggerated tales about evil exploits of Africans and coloreds were responses to their feeling of abandonment by nannies, who were often abruptly dismissed when children reached school-going age.[47] Children's abuse of domestic workers probably had similar roots. Stories of whites kicking, hitting, spitting at, and taunting African domestic workers are legion in South Africa. One worker tearfully told me that it was at this age that the boy she had raised and, in his infancy, shared her narrow bed with during daytime naps, had stopped calling her by name and started to address her as "kaffir," the South African equivalent of "nigger." Said a five-year-old girl to a contemporary interviewer, laughing, "When Catherine bathes my brother and me I can see her titties. I try to pull her clothes away. I splash her with water. She gets cross with me so I smack her on her titties. It does not matter. She's just the maid."[48] African American domestics coined an expression that captured their own experience of white children's predictable distancing from and rudeness toward them as they grew up: "I never met a white child over twelve that I liked."[49]

FIGURE 9.9 View of domestic workers' rooms from back window of main house.
Photo by author, 2004.

Conclusion

Routine practices and experiences hold a particularly firm place in people's constructions of their worlds. What white children encountered every day they were
unlikely to question. Most grew to comprehend the rules of race that controlled
their back yards, and to understand them as good, immutable, and natural.
As they unconsciously sought ways of reducing the complexity of the world to be
found beyond their garden walls, these rules served as guidelines for making
sense of the geography of their neighborhoods, Johannesburg as a whole, and, as
they got older, South Africa itself. All could be divided into the convenient binary
categories of "white" and "black." Lessons about how space could be divided
among different peoples; about foreign off-bounds territories; about the difference between ownership of land and mere habitation upon it; about "civilized"
versus "uncivilized" ways of living—these were all present in the view from one's
back steps. As Mary Douglas expressed it, adapting an expression from Lévi-
Strauss, the landscape was good for thinking with.[50]

There was no direct correspondence between the institution of domestic
service and apartheid. They complemented each other, however, in ways that
had to do with a child's understanding of space and spatial relationships.
Children learned how apartheid worked, in part, by observing and participating

in the racial geography that they grew to understand as it pertained to their own homes. The almost inevitable change in a child's attitude toward the terrain of her backyard was not incidental to her growing awareness of apartheid, but central to it.

These lessons would be some time in the making. Children are generally not able, before the end of adolescence, to construct an image of a town as a whole. Before that, the image of the city is of a series of disconnected districts.[51] The notion of country cannot be grasped until about the age of eleven.[52] Acquiring mastery of the geography of their backyards did not equip white South African children to develop understanding of geographical hierarchies more quickly than their counterparts in other parts of the world. However, it did mean that the pieces were in place for these white youngsters to understand such concepts, when they were able, in racial terms, and to accept as natural the racialized compartmentalization of their country.

Thankfully, our story does not wrap up neatly with white children's uncritical absorption of apartheid ideology. For the young white South African child, many people and many things in the home were available for helping her to think about and learn how the world was arranged. One such thing, one that affirmed popular apartheid ideology, was the geography of their properties.

However, another source of knowledge about the world was the nanny herself. Indeed, for many white children she was the primary fount of love, encouragement, and wisdom. Memories on this topic often verge on the maudlin, but there can be no doubt that when they were very young, most whites could not help but adore their caretakers. One remembered: "While Nanny existed there was a truth. She was there . . . a face that flowed into a smile, benevolence that was dispensed regardless of this 'good' and 'bad,' that did not measure worth in words but said, 'I'll have you as you are . . . even if you mess the bed, or your white dress, or socks or shoes.'"[53] Another commented: "My mother taught me how to speak and behave. She seldom touched me except for the purposes of discipline. It was my black mother who held me."[54]

All children grow apart from their primary caretakers at about five or six years. Most do not make as sharp or permanent a break as these South African children did. Acquisition of the perspective that allowed the child to see and accept the world according to her society's dominant paradigm, divided along racial lines, necessitated an emotional parting from the person to whom she was often closest. That is the reason, I suspect, that my interviews with whites about their childhood yards and their relationships with domestic workers were very emotional. These memories are strong and often painful ones.

Years after the date of such partings, during the height of South Africa's internal unrest in the 1980s, some groups within the anti-apartheid movement tried to persuade white soldiers, many of them drafted involuntarily into the country's military forces, not to do duty in the African townships, where members of the forces sometimes became involved in violent altercations with young

township residents. It emerged that one of the most successful strategies for persuading young white men to conscientiously object was to suggest that in firing
upon township protesters they were shooting at the children of their nannies.[55]
"We raise your children, you kill ours," read one poster attached to walls throughout Johannesburg. Many men refused to serve. Ideologies, even those long
inscribed on children's earliest awarenesses of identity, nation, and property,
could not trump heart truths. Early memories of embracing a black bosom,
eating from a black hand, and kissing a black cheek were never completely forgotten. Home was not only where apartheid was reproduced but also where the
seeds of many of its contradictions were sown.

NOTES

1. For perhaps the clearest expression of the idea that a landscape can be read, see Pierce
   F. Lewis, "Axioms for Reading the Landscape: Some Guides to the American Scene," in
   The Interpretation of Ordinary Landscapes: Geographical Essays, edited by D. W. Meinig
   (New York: Oxford University Press, 1979).

2. Cf. Alfred Davey, *Learning to Be Prejudiced: Growing up in Multi-Ethnic Britain* (London:
   Edward Arnold, 1983), who argues that "it is plainly inadequate to say that children
   acquire their intergroup attitudes as part of the general process of socialization and
   leave it at that," 55. For a discussion of the limitations of the concept of socialization, see
   Frances Chaput Waksler, ed., *Studying the Social Worlds of Children: Sociological Readings*
   (London: Falmer Press, 1991), especially chapters 2 and 5, written by Waksler.

3. Most contemporary research on white children under apartheid dealt with their atti-
   tudes toward other groups. Key books include Henry Lever, *Ethnic Attitudes of
   Johannesburg Youth* (Johannesburg: Witwatersrand University Press, 1968), and
   I. D. MacCrone, *Race Attitudes in South Africa* (Johannesburg: Witwatersrand University
   Press, 1965), works that set the tone for a generation of research. Important works on the
   lives of nonwhite children under apartheid include Michael Jupp, *Children under
   Apartheid* (Brooklyn: Defense for Children International-USA, 1987) and the numerous
   other reports issued by international NGOs during apartheid; Sean Jones, *Assaulting
   Childhood: Children's Experiences of Migrancy and Hostel Life in South Africa* (Johannesburg:
   Wits University Press, 2001); Peter Kallaway, ed., *Apartheid and Education: The Education of
   Black South Africans* (Johannesburg: Ravan Press, 1984); Baruch Hirson, *Year of Fire, Year of
   Ash: The Soweto Revolt, Roots of a Revolution?* (London: Zed Press, 1979); Muriel Horrell, *A
   Decade of Bantu Education* (Johannesburg: South African Institute of Race Relations,
   1964); G. Straker, *Faces in the Revolution: The Psychological Effects of Violence on Township
   Youth in South Africa* (Cape Town: David Philip Publishers, 1992). Recent research on
   white and nonwhite youth tends to focus on both current problems and issues that arise
   from the dismantling of apartheid in the early 1990s, rather than looking back on historical periods. See, for example, Andrew Dawes and David Donald, eds., *Childhood and
   Adversity: Psychological Perspectives from South African Research* (Cape Town: David Philip
   Publishers, 1994), and N.C. Manganyi, *Treachery and Innocence: Psychology and Racial
   Difference in South Africa* (Johannesburg: Ravan Press, 1991). None of the work cited above
   deals in any substantial way with the everyday domestic life of white South African
   youth.

4. Beryl Unterhalter, "Some Aspects of Family Life in Flatland, Johannesburg," Ph.D. dissertation, University of the Witwatersrand, 1968, 211.

5. Suzanne Gordon, *A Talent for Tomorrow: Life Stories of South African Servants* (Johannesburg: Ravan Press, 1985), xxiii.

6. Muriel Mlebuka, quoted in Gordon, *Talent*, 143.

7. Mogumutsi, quoted in Gordon, *Talent*, 187.

8. Unterhalter, "Some Aspects of Family Life," 214–215.

9. Unidentified white mother, quoted in Diane Rosemary Wulfsohn, "The Impact of the South African Nanny on the Young Child," Ph.D. dissertation, University of South Africa, 1988, 170.

10. Nadine Gordimer, quoted in B. Lipman, *Women in South Africa* (London: Pandora Press, 1984), 108–109, cited in Wulfsohn, "South African Nanny," 29.

11. On the role of the institution of domestic service on white children's acculturation into apartheid society, see G. Straker, "Violence against Children: Emotional Abuse," in *People and Violence in South Africa*, edited by B. McKendrick and W. Hoffmann (Cape Town: Oxford University Press, 1990); Michael G. Whisson and William Weil, *Domestic Servants: A Microcosm of "the Race Problem"* (Johannesburg: SAIRR, 1971), 46; Hilda Bernstein, *For Their Triumphs and for Their Tears* (London: International Defence and Aid Fund for Southern Africa, 1985), 187; Jacklyn Cock, "Deference and Dependence: A Note on the Self Imagery of Domestic Workers," *South African Labour Bulletin* 6 (1980): 9. See also Kastoor Bhana and Arvin Bhana, "Colour Concept Attitudes among Indian Preschool Children as a Function of Black Nannies," in *Journal of Behavioral Science* 2.3 (1975): 115–120. This contemporary study of Indian preschoolers found that their personal relationships with their African nannies did not prevent them from having negative cultural bias toward Africans in general. Contact per se was not enough to reverse or modify the prevailing attitudes they received at home and in the social environment. The authors conclude that the nature of the particular contact milieu between Africans and non-Africans is more influential in determining attitudes than the fact of contact.

12. On environmental knowing generally, see Roger Downs and David Stea, eds., *Cognitive Mapping and Spatial Behavior* (Chicago: Aldine Publishing Company, 1973); Douglas Pocock and Ray Hudson, *Images of the Urban Environment* (New York: Columbia University Press, 1978); Kevin Lynch, *The Image of the City* (Cambridge: MIT Press, 1960); Gary T. Moore and Reginald Golledge, *Environmental Knowing: Theories, Research, and Methods* (Stroudsbourg, Pa.: Dowden, Hutchinson & Ross, 1976); Peter Gould and Rodney White, *Mental Maps* (New York: Penguin Books, 1974). Although some authors make distinctions between the terms, I use the terms "maps" and "schemas" interchangeably.

13. Terrence R. Lee, "Psychology and Living Space," in *Cognitive Mapping*, edited by Down and Stea, 99; Gould and White, *Mental Maps*, 51–52.

14. See, for example, A. R. Luria, *Cognitive Development: Its Cultural and Social Foundations*, translated by Mortin Lopez-Amorillas and Lynn Solotaroff (Cambridge: Harvard University Press, 1976); A. R. Luria, *The Making of Mind: A Personal Account of Soviet Psychology*, edited by Michael and Sheila Cole (Cambridge: Harvard University Press, 1979); and L. S. Vgotsky, *Mind in Society: The Development of Higher Psychological Processes*, edited by Michael Cole et al. (Cambridge: Harvard University Press, 1978). For a useful discussion on various approaches to the study of childhood development, see William A. Corsaro, "Social Theories of Childhood," in his *The Sociology of Childhood* (Thousand Oaks, Cal.: Pine Forge Press, 1997).

15. N. Herman, *My Kleinian Home* (London: Quartet Books, 1985), 19, quoted in Wulfsohn, "South African Nanny," 11.

16. Josie W., interview by author, tape recording, Johannesburg, August 8, 1996.

17. See, for example, Robert Coles, *The Moral Life of Children* (Boston: Atlantic Monthly Press, 1986), 30, on what he calls the "garden" stage of early life.

18. John Kotre, *White Gloves: How We Create Ourselves Through Memory* (New York: Free Press, 1995), 127–128; M. H. Matthews, *Making Sense of Place: Children's Understanding of Large-Scale Environments* (Savage, Md.: Barnes and Noble Books, 1992), 12–16, 181–185; Pocock and Hudson, *Images of the Urban Environment*, 88–89; Hart and Moore, "Development of Spatial Cognition," in *Cognitive Mapping*, edited by Downs and Stea, 286–287.

19. Kotre, *White Gloves*, 128; Colin Ward, *The Child in the City* (New York: Pantheon Books, 1978), 24; Gary T. Moore and Reginald G. Golledge, "Environmental Knowing: Concepts and Theories," in *Environmental Knowing*, edited by Moore and Golledge, 10; Matthews, *Making Sense of Place*, 148; Lee, "Psychology and Living Space," 98.

20. Anonymous, "The Surrogates," *Leadership South Africa* 6.5 (1987): 127.

21. Eugenia Bowden, quoted in Susan Tucker, *Telling Memories among Southern Women: Domestic Workers and Their Employers in the Segregated South* (New York: Schocken Books, 1988), 65.

22. David P. interview by author, tape recording, Johannesburg, August 5, 1996.

23. Josie W., interview, speaking of her uncle.

24. David Milner, *Children and Race* (Harmondsworth: Penguin Books, 1975), 28–45. See also Pocock and Hudson, *Images of the Urban Environment*, 28.

25. Milner, *Children and Race*, 28–45.

26. On children and the development of racial or ethnic awareness, see Frances Aboud, *Children and Prejudice* (London: Basil Blackwell, 1988), ix, 22–52; Davey, *Learning to Be Prejudiced*, 41–56; Peter Dominic Stephen Stewart, "The Social Context of Political Attitudes among Middle-Class English-Speaking Whites in Johannesburg, in a Situation of Political Polarization," Ph.D. dissertation, University of the Witwatersrand, 1994, 21–22; Milner, *Children and Race*, 2; Don Foster, "The Development of Racial Orientation in Children," in *Growing up in a Divided Society: The Contexts of Childhood in South Africa*, edited by Sandra Burman and Pamela Reynolds (Ravan Press: Johannesburg, 1986), 159, 164.

27. Unidentified white mother, quoted in Wulfsohn, "South African Nanny," 170.

28. Unidentified white mother, quoted in Wulfsohn, "South African Nanny," 169.

29. Karen Horwitz, "White South African Kinship and Identity," M.A. thesis, University of the Witwatersrand, 1997, xii.

30. See, for example, Horwitz on catching glimpses of smog-covered Alexandra township. "White South African Kinship and Identity," xii.

31. Unidentified white mother, quoted in Wulfsohn, "South African Nanny," 169.

32. Unidentified white mother, quoted in Wulfsohn, "South African Nanny," 169.

33. Unidentified white mother, quoted in Wulfsohn, "South African Nanny," 171.

34. Jill Janvier, quoted in Tucker, *Telling Memories*, 184.

35. Cynthia Berg, quoted in Tucker, *Telling Memories*, 244.

36. Amy F., interview by author, tape recording, Rivonia, August 12, 1996.

37. Unidentified white mother, quoted in Wulfsohn, "South African Nanny," 165.

38. Wulfsohn, "South African Nanny," see esp. 160–187.

39. Unidentified white mother, quoted in Wulfsohn, "South African Nanny," 166.

40. Unidentified white mother, quoted in Wulfsohn, "South African Nanny," 167.

41. Unidentified white mother, quoted in Wulfsohn, "South African Nanny," 167.

42. Vincent Crapanzano, *Waiting: The Whites of South Africa* (London: Granada, 1985), 41.

43. Anonymous, "The Surrogates," 126–127.

44. Carol Gillian, *In a Different Voice: Psychological Theory and Women's Development* (Cambridge: Harvard University Press, 1982).

45. Felicity R., interview by author, tape recording, Johannesburg, August 3, 1996.

46. Hap X., personal communication, Johannesburg, 1996.

47. Crapanzano, *Waiting*, 42 note.

48. Unidentified white child, quoted in Wulfsohn, "South African Nanny," 168.

49. Tucker, *Telling Memories*, 61.

50. Mary Douglas and Baron Isherwood, *The World of Goods* (New York: Basic Books, 1979).

51. Sieverts, "Perceptual Images of Berlin," 285.

52. Matthews, *Making Sense of Place*, 202.

53. N. Herman, 30, quoted in Wulfsohn, "South African Nanny," 12.

54. Anonymous, "The Surrogates," 127.

55. Technically, this would not have been true, since most domestic workers came from the rural areas and their children remained in the countryside in the care of relatives.

10

Children and the Rosenwald Schools of the American South

MARY S. HOFFSCHWELLE

"Experiment Satisfactory," proclaimed a headline in the *New York Age* of June 25, 1914. The "experiment" was the construction of six one-teacher schools for African American children in rural Alabama by a partnership of local school patrons, Tuskegee Institute staff, and Sears, Roebuck and Company tycoon Julius Rosenwald. Booker T. Washington, principal of Tuskegee Institute and one of the most prominent African American leaders in the United States, had now convinced Julius Rosenwald to expand their experiment into a regional school-building program for black children across the American South. As the press release in the *New York Age* explained, "One of the crying needs in the South is good schoolhouses in the country districts where a majority of our people live. . . . Every time a schoolhouse is built in one of these country communities it will bring new hope and confidence to the people."[1]

Why did a self-proclaimed African American race leader, a self-made Jewish merchant prince, and legions of anonymous black southerners place their hope and confidence for racial advancement in rural school buildings? What did they expect would happen when children entered what would soon be known as "Rosenwald schools"? Even for an era in which Progressive educators saw schools as laboratories of democracy, the idea that children's experiences in new school buildings could cure poverty, ignorance, and racism was ambitious indeed. This chapter examines the Rosenwald school building program, which operated throughout the American South from 1912 until 1932, as a cooperative effort to create landscapes of childhood that would benefit African American families and communities and simultaneously promote racial harmony. Rosenwald schools were purpose-built learning environments designed by professionals with their own agendas for black schoolchildren and their communities. They also were community institutions for the children of "the people," hence this essay explores the experiences of Rosenwald school community members and their children. Rosenwald schools and the recollections of Rosenwald alumni illuminate the multiple ways that people invest personal and social meanings in the material culture of childhood. Although children figure in most accounts of Rosenwald schools as the objects of adult intentions, they were actors in a community's effort to build a Rosenwald school and in the physical structure itself.

Booker T. Washington originated the school building program, and found an ideal supporter for it in Julius Rosenwald. By the time that these two men met in 1911, Washington had established himself as a leading spokesperson for African Americans to white Americans. His autobiography *Up from Slavery* and 1895 "Atlanta Compromise" speech, his most famous exhortations for black educational and economic advancement through self-help and accommodation with segregation, had found a ready audience among sympathetic and paternalistic whites, mostly northerners. Washington was the most popular African American leader among whites because his reassuring gospel of black self-help seemed to acquiesce in the restriction of black civil and political rights. Washington also had many black supporters, who hoped his strategy would address the pressing needs in their own lives but avoid the white backlash they feared from a more confrontational approach. His gospel of self-help also resonated with many African Americans' experiences of building their own schools and churches as key community institutions, a tradition going back at least to the Civil War and emancipation.[2]

Washington wanted to extend his philosophy of self-help and industrial (vocational) education from Tuskegee Institute into the South's public school systems. But most southern black children attended school for only a few weeks a year if at all, in dismal buildings staffed by teachers who were poorly paid and had limited training. His plan was to organize black school patrons to buy land and build schools that would then be turned over to the local school authorities. These schools would feature a Tuskegee-style practical curriculum combining basic literacy and numeracy skills with agricultural and trades programs for boys and home economics training for girls. White school officials would accept the facilities because black parents had largely paid for them, and because the schools would train black children as farm and domestic workers. For black parents and children, such schools offered immediate improvement in terms of health and comfort, as well as leverage to secure public funding for longer school terms and better teacher salaries that would improve the quality of education for their children.[3]

Most African American southerners, especially those who lived in rural areas, could not afford to tackle these projects without outside financial support. Washington had previously secured contributions for school buildings in Macon County, Alabama, from Anna T. Jeanes, a wealthy Quaker benefactress, and Henry Huttleston Rogers, a Standard Oil executive and industrialist, but the work faced an uncertain future after Rogers's death in 1909. Washington found the new patron he needed in Julius Rosenwald, who joined Tuskegee Institute's board of trustees in 1912. Rosenwald had orchestrated the massive expansion of Sears, Roebuck and Company into one of the premier retail corporations in the

United States. A long-time supporter of Jewish causes and social programs such as Jane Addams's Hull House settlement in Chicago, he had first demonstrated his developing interest in African American issues by offering challenge grants for construction of YMCA and YWCA facilities for urban blacks. After Rosenwald met Washington in 1911, their common belief in the power of individual self-improvement for community progress quickly fostered a warm personal relationship and cooperative action for black education.[4]

In 1912 the two men agreed first on a small pilot project for six rural schools in the Tuskegee vicinity. When this experiment met Rosenwald's expectations in 1914, as the New York Age reported, Rosenwald agreed to fund a regional program administered by Tuskegee Institute. Washington died unexpectedly the following year, but the program continued at Tuskegee until 1920. Then Rosenwald transferred the building program away from Tuskegee Institute in response to complaints from southern whites about having to take orders from the Institute's African American staff, problems with accounting methods, and inadequate design and construction standards. The Julius Rosenwald Fund, a Chicago-based philanthropic foundation Rosenwald had established in 1917, created a southern office in Nashville, Tennessee, to handle the building program. The Fund's white administrators imposed new standards for school construction and expanded the range of grants to elicit greater public funding of school construction with the promise of more local and Rosenwald Fund contributions.[5] Changes in the Fund's leadership and philanthropic goals, the onset of the Great Depression, and Julius Rosenwald's death in 1932 ended the school program in that year.[6] Over the twenty years of its operation, the Rosenwald school building program cooperated with African American communities and public education authorities to build 4,977 schools, 217 teachers' homes, and 163 vocational buildings at a total cost of $28,408,520, to serve 663,615 children across fifteen states.

Although the program was identified with Booker T. Washington and Julius Rosenwald, a broader cast of individuals shaped each Rosenwald school long before it welcomed black children. Professional educators associated with the Rosenwald school building program and southern state departments of education dictated the schools' designs and curricula. Clinton J. Calloway, director of Tuskegee's extension department, oversaw the building program from its inception in 1912 to 1920. A former teacher and 1895 graduate of Fisk University, Calloway had expanded the extension department's mission from agricultural projects to school and community improvement. Samuel L. Smith headed the Rosenwald school program in Nashville, and was the principal designer of its school plans from 1920 until its conclusion in 1932. A former county school superintendent, he had served as Tennessee state agent for Negro schools from 1914 to 1920.[7]

Calloway and Smith worked closely with two other groups of professional educators: state agents for Negro schools and Rosenwald building agents. State Negro school agents were white men who supervised black education for southern state

departments of education, their positions funded by John D. Rockefeller's General
Education Board. State agents for Negro schools set annual Rosenwald school construction goals, promoted the building program to local school authorities,
approved applications for Rosenwald grants, and inspected the completed
schools.[8] In nine states, Julius Rosenwald and the Rosenwald Fund offered salary
assistance for a Rosenwald building agent as well. The Rosenwald agent was a
black man, whose job was to promote the building program at the community
level and coordinate the efforts of black school patrons and white local school
officials, as well as to monitor construction standards.[9]

Joining these outside activists was a diverse group of insiders with their own
interests in shaping children's experiences in Rosenwald schools: the adults in
southern African American communities. Local black leaders—school principals,
teachers, Jeanes supervising industrial teachers, and ministers—often spear-
headed Rosenwald school campaigns.[10] They held rallies and mass meetings at
which they invited the Rosenwald building agent or state agent for Negro schools
to speak. At these events, other black citizens organized themselves into committees to raise money, to find and buy the land, to cut trees and saw the lumber for
the school, to haul the building materials to the school site, and even to build the
school. Those who pledged contributions of money and labor included rural
wage earners such as sawmill and domestic workers, farm owners and sharecroppers, and the members of church congregations and fraternal lodges. Armed with
promises of black contributions and Rosenwald assistance, black community
leaders and their state allies met with the county superintendent of schools,
spoke to school board meetings, and lobbied influential whites to garner
approval for the new school and any additional funds necessary.[11]

How did a Rosenwald school transmit all of these adults' intentions for black
children's futures? First, the school building program's administrators planned
a construction process that would pool black and white southerners' goals and
resources in a collective effort to improve black children's lives. Thus, in keeping
with Washington's self-help philosophy, local people had to match the amount of
a Rosenwald construction grant, which depended on the size of the school, with
equivalent contributions of cash, labor, or building materials. By creating a program that required local participation, the Rosenwald program gave black southerners a means to shape Rosenwald schools to their own community traditions
and expectations for children.

But self-help was not an end in itself, for Washington, Rosenwald, and their
allies intended to push white southerners to accept black schools as integral elements of their school systems funded by public dollars. Rosenwald building program administrators also used these schools as visible demonstrations of how
interracial cooperation could improve social and economic life in southern communities if African American children accepted a certain type of education and
whites accepted black children as worthy future citizens. Rosenwald program
advocates emphasized that these schools featured a practical curriculum, which

would replace classical education and rote instruction with learning activities "that will give to the Negro boys and girls that type of training that will improve health conditions, that will encourage obedience to the law, promote industrial efficiency, and establish right relations with all concerned."[12] Proper new school facilities for black children would improve the workforce and stabilize rural communities, they claimed, by producing a new generation of better-skilled, more disciplined, and productive African Americans who would be satisfied to live within the confines of white supremacy.[13] Consequently they insisted that Rosenwald schools had to stand on multi-acre sites deeded to public school authorities and operate for a minimum number of months each year, to extract higher levels of public funding for the education of black children.[14]

Rosenwald schools made black children seem safe as the contented, productive workers of the community's future. That security would come at the expense of white recognition that black children had been neglected and abused by southern public school systems, and that black children deserved better treatment if they and their parents were to remain productive members of the community. Rosenwald school planners and community members never expected Rosenwald schools to overturn the South's Jim Crow system that required racial segregation of schools by state law. And some African American southerners, who had built and funded most black schools themselves in the face of white neglect and violent attacks on their community institutions, found it difficult to turn over their hard-won school property to white-controlled public education authorities just to get a Rosenwald building. Many black school patrons sought Rosenwald schools, not for integration with whites but as the next modern step in a historic tradition of building independent African American community institutions.[15] Even so, they could all agree that Rosenwald schools posed a three-dimensional assertion of black children's right to a public education that was separate and truly equal. As an editorial in the New Orleans newspaper The National Negro Voice observed, despite the slow pace of change "one can notice plainly that there is a determined plan to gradually make the facilities for colored education equal to those provided for the whites."[16]

Rosenwald program staff also recognized that the school building itself was a tangible statement of adult intentions to use children's school experiences as a vehicle for reform, and carefully controlled the material environments created by Rosenwald schools. The idea that a school building expressed community identity and could exercise a benign influence over students and their parents was commonplace among Progressive educators and reformers in the United States. In the early twentieth century, southern states created their first extensive public school systems, paying particular attention to the needs of rural schools and constructing large numbers of new schools for white children.[17] The Rosenwald school program took the simple, yet potentially radical, step of applying the same new standards of Progressive design being used for white schools in the South to the region's African American school buildings.

One condition of the Rosenwald grant was that the building must follow an "approved" plan. Clinton Calloway and Samuel Smith sent out printed information explaining that matching grants were available for new schools (and later, vocational buildings and teachers homes) if built and equipped according to the Rosenwald program's own plans or similar modern designs. Both Tuskegee Institute and the Julius Rosenwald Fund's southern office distributed their own plans free of charge. Professional architects and educators prepared both sets of plans. Robert R. Taylor, director of industries at Tuskegee Institute and the designer of many of the Institute's buildings, prepared the early Rosenwald school plans in cooperation with Clinton J. Calloway and Alabama state agent for Negro schools James L. Sibley. Tuskegee Institute staff distributed these plans to Rosenwald school communities and published them in a 1915 treatise, *The Negro Rural School and Its Relation to the Community* (Figure 10.1).[18] In 1920, Samuel L. Smith developed his *Community School Plans* for the Rosenwald Fund in consultation with his mentor Fletcher B. Dresslar, a nationally recognized authority on rural school design who had critiqued the Tuskegee plans for Julius Rosenwald (Figure 10.2). These standardized plans, especially the many editions of the *Community School Plans* published in the 1920s and 1930s, embodied key concepts of Progressive school architecture, and made Rosenwald plan schools instantly recognizable.[19]

Whether a one-teacher frame building standing in open country or a twelve-teacher brick structure on a busy city street, Rosenwald school designs followed the same general principles (Figure 10.3).[20] The first principle was proper lighting to protect children's eyesight. Each school plan depicted a one-story building with tall narrow windows that stretched from about three feet above the floor up

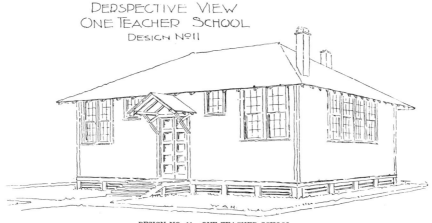

DESIGN NO. 11.—ONE TEACHER SCHOOL

FIGURE 10.1 "Perspective View, One Teacher School," Design No. 11.

From *The Negro Rural School and Its Relation to the Community* (Tuskegee, Alabama: Tuskegee Normal and Industrial Institute Extension Department, 1915).

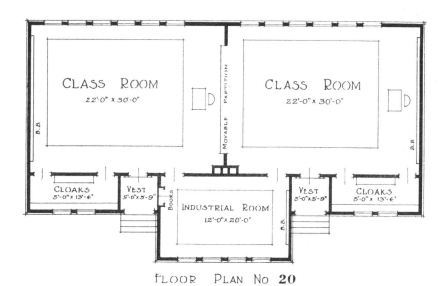

FIGURE 10.2 "Two Teacher Community School to Face East or West Only," Plan No. 20.
From *Community School Plans* (Nashville, Tennessee: Julius Rosenwald Fund, 1928), 26.

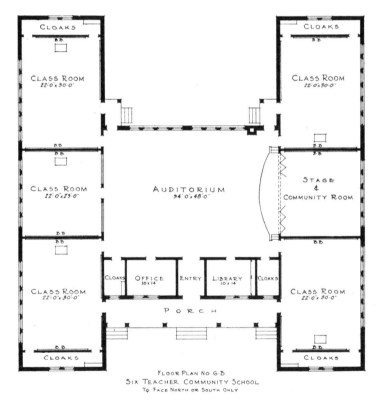

FIGURE 10.3 "Six Teacher Community School to Face North or South Only," Plan No. 6–B. By the time of this edition of *Community School Plans*, the Julius Rosenwald Fund offered matching grants for separate vocational buildings, hence the absence of the "industrial room" featured in earlier designs and smaller schools.

From *Community School Plans* (Nashville, Tennessee: Julius Rosenwald Fund, 1928), 13.

to the ceiling, grouped in "batteries" to provide a virtually unbroken stream of light from left to right across every student's desk. Smith's *Community School Plans* ensured that the window batteries provided the necessary light to conserve children's eyesight by preparing school plans specifically designed to orient the building on its site so that the classroom windows only faced east or west. The demand for proper lighting dictated the floor plan of the school, grouping classrooms in rectangular blocks or H-shaped forms.

The second principle was proper ventilation to keep children healthy. Obviously the windows facilitated this, but the building plans also provided careful directions for the placement and venting of wood stoves. Buildings stood just above the ground on short brick piers to avoid damp. The resulting crawlspace sometimes was left open in the Deep South to allow air to circulate under and up through the floor for coolness, but enclosed in large schools and the Upper South to keep children's feet warm. Ventilation was closely related to the third principle, sanitation. Each Rosenwald school had to have at least two privies and, whenever possible, a protected water supply.

The building's exterior was plain, with minimal hints of Arts and Crafts or Colonial Revival styling. A frame building was painted white, a reddish brown, or gray. Inside, rooms had to be ceiled and painted in dual-color schemes with a darker wainscot up to the base of the windows, and a lighter shade above to maximize light and minimize glare from the battery windows. Each classroom had at least one blackboard and thirty to forty modern desks. Additional innovative features included cloakrooms for boys and girls, to reduce classroom clutter; a mandatory industrial room for vocational subjects even in one-teacher schools; and, in larger schools, movable partitions and a stage in the classrooms or a full-fledged auditorium for school and community gatherings (Figure 10.4).

The designs of Rosenwald schools embodied more than the functional and aesthetic standards of Progressive school architecture. They also gave physical form to the educational and social meanings invested in them by reformers, educators, and African American community members that black children were expected to absorb. Observers recognized these messages, and their more subversive subtexts. Building even the most modest new school for black children sent a message about black aspirations that challenged white control, as the ever-cautious Booker T. Washington realized. In 1915 he warned Alabama Negro school agent James L. Sibley that "I think we will have to be very careful in putting up this large number of schoolhouses, not to put so much money into a building that it will bring about a feeling of jealousy on the part of the white people who may have a schoolhouse that is much poorer."[21] This concern was well placed. White arsonists repeatedly targeted Rosenwald schools, and other whites refused to sell land, protested plans to build Rosenwald schools near their neighborhoods, and pressured school officials to give priority to white schools. One contractor, who also chaired the white trustees' board for an Alabama school district, stopped work on a Rosenwald school "because it would be better than the white schoolhouse."[22]

FIGURE 10.4 Children in the auditorium of the Lake County Training School, Leesburg, Florida, constructed in 1922–1923.

Julius Rosenwald Fund Archives, courtesy of the Fisk University Franklin Library, Special Collections.

Although Rosenwald schools prevailed, opposition from whites signaled their understanding that black children would gain power within their new schools.

How these schools looked and felt to children in the 1910s and 1920s is difficult to document or recapture. The intense pride with which their parents and teachers wrote about Rosenwald schools at that time, and that former students still feel today, suggests that attending a Rosenwald school gave children a profoundly different material experience with important social as well as instructional benefits. Black children may not have discussed how many foot-candles of light or how much fresh air per cubic foot streamed through their classrooms—issues of central importance to designers—but they too found visual meaning in Rosenwald schools. First, these structures were unmistakably modern schools, whether small one- or two-teacher frame structures in rural districts or the brick buildings in the towns and cities where larger Rosenwald structures were erected in the late 1920s. They posed a striking contrast to the churches, lodge halls, old houses, or abandoned white school buildings in which most of the South's black children learned. A Rosenwald school looked different because it had been designed to meet children's physical and educational needs. It must have felt substantially different from every other place that black children experienced as well, especially children in rural neighborhoods. Rosenwald classrooms had many windows, all filled with glass and equipped with spring-loaded shades. They must have felt more open, airy, and bright than many rural African American children's homes and schools, photographs of which usually show only minimal window openings and often no glass (Figure 10.5). Inside, adjustable

FIGURE 10.5 First grade classroom at the Lake County Training School, Leesburg, Florida.

Julius Rosenwald Fund Archives, courtesy of the Fisk University Franklin Library, Special Collections.

patent desks with attached chairs surely made seatwork easier than the pews or rough plank benches typically found in black schools. Sanitary privies reinforced health lessons and the emphasis on order, light, and air in the classrooms at a time when few rural children of any sort had such facilities at home.

Progressive educators and school architects recognized these features as part of their campaign for standardized school plans that met specific standards for pupil health and instruction and that could be replicated over and over again. Although the *Community School Plans*' modest designs and industrial rooms identified them as schools for black children, these features also made them useful to states that were rapidly expanding their public school infrastructure and vocational education programs for white students. Professional educators and cost-conscious school administrators admired Rosenwald plans. Not only did they borrow freely from *Community School Plans* in developing their own state-approved school designs, but they used Rosenwald plans to build black schools that did not receive Rosenwald grants, and to build schools for white children as well.[23] Thus, although educated separately, many southern white and black children learned in classrooms that looked and felt the same, thanks to Rosenwald school designs. Going to a Rosenwald school meant being in the vanguard of modern education for African American children, and making a visual assertion of the equality of all children.

What did African American children really do in a Rosenwald school? Each state department of education mandated the curriculum for its public school system, making little or no allowance for the reality that African American schools typically lacked funding for a full school term, instructional materials, or enough room and teachers for a full elementary and secondary program. Rather than focusing on the underlying racism that produced these conditions, most white reformers interested in black education and African Americans who adopted Booker T. Washington's accommodationist strategy called for industrial education as the centerpiece of the Progressive black school curriculum.[24] The Rosenwald program, true to its origins at Tuskegee Institute, made classroom space for industrial education an essential component of each Rosenwald school's design.[25] Photographs of Rosenwald schools intended for white viewers reinforced such images by showing school farm projects or kitchen equipment.[26]

Nevertheless, vocational education never became fully entrenched in Rosenwald schools. Rosenwald building agent John S. Jones reported that "industrial training needs stressing in most of the schools visited" and that "little is done for the industrial training of boys" in Louisiana. He might have been describing Rosenwald schools in any state, many of which did not possess industrial equipment or neglected vocational instruction. The expense of vocational equipment and the lack of trained teachers limited industrial education in some schools; in others, the opening of a decent school building attracted so many new students that the industrial room had to be converted into a regular classroom. Elsewhere, teachers and patrons preferred academic instruction to vocational subjects for their children. State education officials and black school staff and patrons often disagreed about priorities. Louisiana state Jeanes supervisor Maggie Nance Ringgold observed that the Winterville Rosenwald school "presents a pleasing appearance, but the mistake of placing a valuable piano, instead of painting the interior and installing the necessary equipment, was made by the teachers and community people." She also complained that they had neglected their school garden. Likewise, state Negro school agents constantly complained about Rosenwald schools where children spent little or no time on vocational projects.[27] In the 1920s, the Rosenwald Fund repeatedly added new initiatives for vocational education, only to encounter the same limited results.[28]

Rosenwald program administrators clearly were more successful in determining the material environments in which southern black children learned than they were in shaping the content and practice of schoolchildren's lessons. Industrial education offers one avenue of insight into community standards for education set by local educators and parents, affirming African American southerners' long-standing commitment to education as a vehicle for achieving their own goals. Not surprisingly, then, Rosenwald students and faculty in later life recalled little about industrial training, and emphasized instead their perception that a Rosenwald school created a distinctive experience. Those who built or attended Rosenwald schools identified those buildings and their experiences in them as markers of their success in upholding a community tradition of educational activism.

For example, school histories written in the 1940s by African American educators in northern Alabama carefully designated which schools were Rosenwald schools and correlated a Rosenwald school with local achievement. "At this stage of the [Belle Mina] school's history, many parents and citizens of the community . . . saw the need of a new building, inquired about the Rosenwald Foundation, and learned what they would have to do to meet the requirements. As a result of their efforts, the present building was erected in 1927." The Blue Ridge school "burned in 1919 and in 1920 another was erected, financed through the Rosenwald fund. Since that time, through cooperative efforts of the county and the community, the school has made considerable progress."[29]

Although such accounts stress adult actions on behalf of children in a community, children were often directly involved in community campaigns for Rosenwald schools. Like their parents, they contributed to fundraising efforts to match a Rosenwald grant, albeit in small ways. Children raised funds for some of the original six Rosenwald schools by performing in a Tom Thumb wedding and a school concert, and holding a "candy contest"; a school children's club donated six dollars.[30] Children recited poems, gave speeches, and sang for their elders at many community school rallies. Older boys helped their fathers fell trees, saw lumber, and haul building materials. Girls helped teachers and community women prepare and serve the food at rallies or special entertainments. In some cotton-producing areas, sharecroppers and independent farmers pledged "Rosenwald acres" that probably were worked with family labor.[31] Children participated in annual Rosenwald School Day events, when they once again helped to raise money and participated in special work projects and celebrations.[32] When children acted in concert with, and at the behest of, their families, teachers, and neighbors for a Rosenwald school, they forged new links in the emotional and social bonds of their community.

Decades later, Rosenwald school alumni still located these schools within their personal and community traditions. Elizabeth Harris Pointer did not enter school until two years after the Rosenwald building program had ended, but she still recalled that the program had built schools across the state of Alabama, and identified her own Chehaw School and her husband's school in Mactama as Rosenwald schools.[33] The Chehaw School she attended was one of the last Rosenwald schools built in Booker T. Washington's lifetime. David Beasley, also a Chehaw alumnus, placed the school within a broader historic tradition of African American educational activism. His grandfather Jim Beasley had purchased land after emancipation and in the 1880s donated land for Chehaw's African Methodist Episcopal Zion church and then for the Chehaw School. "A man by the name of William [sic] Rosenwald from Chicago, used to be connected with Sears, Roebuck I believe," whom Beasley also recalled as a trustee of nearby Tuskegee Institute, "gave money to build the school. They called it the Rosenwald school." The one-teacher school had been enlarged to a two-teacher building by the time that David Beasley attended it, and eventually accommodated four teachers, including Beasley's spouse.[34]

Teachers and students at Rosenwald schools proudly described many positive features of their schools and their learning experiences. Faculty and alumni who contributed to Betty Jamerson Reed's study of the Brevard Rosenwald School in North Carolina spoke with "conviction that their Rosenwald experience was a positive one" and "remembered mostly happy times" bounded by strict codes of behavior monitored and enforced by teachers with support from their parents, and high expectations for their academic achievement (Figure 10.6). Alumni attributed success in their own adult lives to the lessons and values inculcated at their Rosenwald school. Their memories recognize the efforts that teachers and parents made to create a positive atmosphere that blended academic instruction with lessons in personal discipline and community responsibility. Although those efforts predated the Rosenwald building, the larger, upgraded facility "dominated the educational experience for black children" by consolidating smaller schools into a larger facility that allowed the staff to organize grades and classroom instruction more effectively. Children and parents strongly identified the Rosenwald school building with positive learning experiences and community events, and were devastated when it burned in 1941. The Brevard Rosenwald School was rebuilt and remains standing today, but alumni whom Reed interviewed resented that desegregation cost them their school, which was closed in 1966 and remodeled

FIGURE 10.6 Brevard Rosenwald School, now the Eugene M. Morris Education Center, Brevard, North Carolina.
Photo by the author.

into a teacher center. The loss of the Rosenwald name in 1981, when school authorities renamed the building for a prominent white educator, rankled as well.[35]

Alumni of the Mount Pleasant Rosenwald school in Dark Corner, south of Cotton Plant, Arkansas, shared similar experiences. Helen Howard recalled that the first school she knew there was a one-room school at the Mount Pleasant Church, but "after that the Rosenwald put in a school." The new building, like that at Brevard, was larger, with three classrooms that accommodated students from the first through eighth grades. Although most of her school memories recalled experiences most likely to resonate with children—singing, playing games, having to stand in a corner as punishment for something she did not do—she still linked the move to a larger and better new school building with "the Rosenwald."[36] Oliver Williams attended the Mount Pleasant School in the 1930s, by which time it had been expanded to seven rooms. His account identified several aspects of Rosenwald building design. One was the auditorium, which he described as having folding doors between it and the adjacent classroom to allow the entire student body to gather for devotions at the start of each school day. Rosenwald school plans commonly included large meeting spaces, created by dedicated auditoriums or by an opening between one classroom and another with a stage built at one end, to accommodate meetings and performances that would promote a common school and community identity. His memories also suggest the fate of many Rosenwald industrial rooms. One small, narrow room, Williams noted, was "supposed to have been a work shop" and was used as such for a while. But the lack of equipment resulted in the room being used as a teachers' room during the day and for a shop class at night.[37]

Proud as they were of their Rosenwald schools, students were well aware of the shortcomings caused by racial discrimination. Pupils in the Progress Rosenwald School in Jeff Davis County, Mississippi, learned in a classroom equipped with a stove, a blackboard, and good—if uncomfortable—desks. But instead of the forty students for whom Rosenwald classrooms were designed, eighty crammed themselves into the room in 1926. Children at the Belmont Rosenwald School in Hinds County, Mississippi, lacked basic school supplies and equipment. In the early 1930s they wrote on both sides of paper and on any sort of paper they could find: can labels, bags, wrapping paper. Students gleaned corn from harvested fields that they traded for writing tablets and pencils at a local store.[38]

Former Rosenwald students described the work ethic and discipline that parents and teachers instilled in them as positive life lessons, but they bitterly resented that white authorities continued to pay little attention to black children's needs. Cast-off textbooks from white schools and the lack of any high school program still burned in the memories of Brevard Rosenwald School alumni in the late 1990s.[39] Indeed, by the 1960s, many African American students realized that Rosenwald buildings had become outdated, and that the demand for local contributions to school construction let white school officials cheat black students out of their share of public school funds. A Wilcox County, Alabama, high school student complained in the 1960s "some years ago our parents were advised to buy some land upon which would be built a high school. Our parents gave fish frys and Saturday night jukes and bought the land and deeded it to the state and county. A school building was built for us which was not as good as some people's barn."[40] By this time, new generations of Rosenwald school students, teachers, and their communities were involved in grassroots civil rights activism, such as the students who went on strike to protest school conditions in Farmville, Virginia's Robert R. Moton School in 1951.[41]

Rosenwald schools transformed the rural landscape of the South in the early twentieth century. By the early 1930s, African American children could be seen walking to and from new school buildings and playing in school yards in places where schools for black children had never before stood, or where children had learned in churches, fraternal lodges, abandoned tenant houses. The architecture of Rosenwald schools, replicated across fifteen states, asserted black children's right to their own place on the landscape. As innovative design principles became commonplace, and as public school authorities retreated to the neglect from which the promise of grant money had lured them, Rosenwald schools lost some of their luster. Desegregation and integration closed many of them down or converted them to other purposes after the 1960s. Today, alumni have erected monuments to their schools and fought with varying success to hold on to the Rosenwald name. Surviving Rosenwald schools and their descendents, Rosenwald street signs, and alumni monuments still mark the landscape of the American South, reminders of the potential and the limitations of schools as agencies of change in children's lives.

NOTES

This chapter is derived from the author's book, *The Rosenwald Schools of the American South* (Gainesville: University Press of Florida, 2006). The author thanks Middle Tennessee State University and the John Hope Franklin Collection for African and African American Documentation at Duke University for supporting this research.

1. "Create Fund to Build Rural School Houses," *New York Age*, June 25, 1914, in "Education—1914 Common Schools, Improvement of," Tuskegee Clippings Files, University Archives and Museums, Tuskegee University, Tuskegee, Ala. (hereafter, Tuskegee Clippings Files).

2. Louis R. Harlan, *Booker T. Washington: The Making of a Black Leader, 1856–1901* (New York: Oxford University Press, 1972); Harlan, *Booker T. Washington: The Wizard of Tuskegee, 1901–1915* (New York: Oxford University Press, 1983); see also Carter G. Woodson, *The Education of the Negro Prior to 1861* (New York: G. P. Putnam's Sons, 1915); Henry Allen Bullock, *A History of Negro Education in the South from 1619 to the Present* (Cambridge: Harvard University Press, 1967); David Freedman, "African-American Schooling in the South Prior to 1861," *Journal of Negro History* 84.1 (1999), 1–47; James D. Anderson, *The Education of Blacks in the South, 1865–1935* (Chapel Hill: University of North Carolina Press, 1988), 4–32.

3. Anderson, *Education of Blacks in the South*; James L. Leloudis, *Schooling the New South: Pedagogy, Self, and Society in North Carolina, 1880–1920* (Chapel Hill: University of North Carolina Press, 1996); Eric Anderson and Alfred A. Moss, Jr., *Dangerous Donations: Northern Black Philanthropy and Southern Black Education, 1902–1930* (Columbia: University of Missouri Press, 1999).

4. Morris R. Werner, *Julius Rosenwald: The Life of a Practical Humanitarian* (New York: Harper & Row, 1939); Edwin R. Embree and Julia Waxman, *Investment in People: The Story of the Julius Rosenwald Fund* (New York: Harper and Brothers, 1949). Peter M. Ascoli's *JR: A Biography of Julius Rosenwald* (Bloomington: University of Indiana Press, 2006) sheds new light on Rosenwald's philanthropy, including his involvement with Tuskegee Institute and the school building program.

5. Anderson, *Education of Blacks in the South*; Thomas W. Hanchett, "The Rosenwald Schools and Black Education in North Carolina," *North Carolina Historical Review* 65.4 (1988): 387–444; Mary S. Hoffschwelle, *Rebuilding the Rural Southern Community: Reformers, Schools, and Homes in Tennessee, 1900–1930* (Knoxville: University of Tennessee Press, 1998), 61–89.

6. "Southern School Program," April 1932, and "Program for 1932–1933," box 331, folder 2, Julius Rosenwald Fund Archives, Special Collections and Archives, Franklin Library, Fisk University, Nashville, Tenn. (hereafter, Rosenwald Fund Archives).

7. "Clinton J. Calloway, A.B.," in *National Cyclopedia of the Colored Race*, edited by Clement Richardson (Montgomery, Ala.: National Publishing Company, 1919), 25; Samuel L. Smith, *Builders of Goodwill: The Story of the State Agents of Negro Education in the South, 1910 to 1950* (Nashville: Tennessee Book Company, 1950), 63–138.

8. Smith, *Builders of Goodwill*, 7–62.

9. Smith, *Builders of Goodwill*, 43–50.

10. Beginning in 1908, the Anna T. Jeanes Fund supported the work of industrial supervising teachers who taught vocational classes and organized community and school improvement projects in African American schools. On the key leadership roles of African American educators, see Kevin K. Gaines, *Uplifting the Race: Black Leadership, Politics, and Culture in the Twentieth Century* (Chapel Hill: University of North Carolina Press, 1996); Stephanie J. Shaw, *What a Woman Ought to Be and to Do: Black Professional Women Workers during the Jim Crow Era* (Chicago: University of Chicago Press, 1996); Adam Fairclough, "'Being in the Field of Education and Also Being a Negro . . . Seems . . . Tragic': Black Teachers in the Jim Crow South," *Journal of American History* 87.1 (2000): 65–91; Ann Short Chirhart, *Torches of Light: Georgia Teachers and the Coming of the Modern South* (Athens: University of Georgia Press, 2005); on Jeanes teachers, see Mildred M. Williams, et al., *The Jeanes Story: A Chapter in the History of American Education* (Jackson, Miss.: Jackson State University, 1979).

11. Carter G. Woodson, "The Story of the Fund," typescript, folder 1, box 33, series I, Julius Rosenwald Papers, Special Collections Research Center, University of Chicago Library.

12. J. T. Calhoun, "Negro Education," *Biennial Report and Recommendations of the State Superintendent of Public Education of the State of Mississippi for the Scholastic Years 1923–1924 and 1924–1925* (n.p., 1925), 19.

13. *Biennial Report and Recommendations of the State Superintendent of Public Education of the State of Mississippi for the Scholastic Years 1915–1916 and 1916–1917* (n.p., 1917), 17; Leo M. Favrot, *Aims and Needs in Negro Public Education in Louisiana*, Bulletin 2 (Baton Rouge: Louisiana State Department of Education, 1918), 14; O. H. Bernard, "The Julius Rosenwald Fund in Tennessee," [1927], box 76, folder 2, Rosenwald Fund Archives; J. S. Clark, "Colored Education," *Southern School Work* 7 (April 1919): 425.

14. David Strong, Pamela Barnhouse Walters, Brian Driscoll, and Scott Rosenberg, "Leveraging the State: Private Money and the Development of Public Education for Blacks," *American Sociological Review* 65.5 (2000): 658–681.

15. Betty J. Reed, *The Brevard Rosenwald School: Black Education and Community Building in a Southern Appalachian Town, 1920–1966*, Contributions to Southern Appalachian Studies

11 (Jefferson, N.C.: McFarland, 2004); Debra Herman and Althemese Barnes, *African-American Education in Leon County, Florida: Emancipation through Desegregation, 1963–1968* (Tallahassee, Fla.: John G. Riley Research Center and Museum of African American History, 1997); V. P. Franklin and Carter Julian Savage, eds., *Cultural Capital and Black Education: African American Communities and the Funding of Black Schooling, 1865 to the Present* (Greenwich, Conn.: Information Age, 2004).

16. "School Facilities for Colored People Expanding," *National Negro Voice*, November 20, 1926, in "Education—1926 Common Schools, Improvement of," Tuskegee Clippings Files.

17. See, for example, *Biennial Report and Recommendations of the State Superintendent of Public Education of the State of Mississippi for the Scholastic Years 1913–1914 and 1914–1915* (n.p., 1915), 6–14; Alabama Department of Education, *Consolidation of Schools and Transportation of Pupils*, Bulletin 56 (Montgomery: Brown Printing, 1917); *Biennial Report of 1913–'14 and 1914–'15, Part IV: Pictures of Public School Interests and Discussions of Public School Questions* (Baton Rouge: Ramires-Jones Printing, 1915), 62, 64.

18. Ellen Weiss, "Robert R. Taylor of Tuskegee: An Early Black American Architect," *ARRIS: Journal of the Southeast Chapter of the Society of Architectural Historians* 2 (1991): 3–19; Clarence G. Williams, "From 'Tech' to Tuskegee: The Life of Robert Robinson Taylor, 1868–1942," *MIT Archives and Special Collections*, <http://libraries.mit.edu/archives/mithistory/blacks-at-mit/taylor.html> (6 January 2004).

19. Fletcher B. Dresslar, *American Schoolhouses*, US Bureau of Education Bulletin 5 (Washington, D.C.: Government Printing Office, 1911); Dresslar, *Rural Schoolhouses and Grounds*, US Bureau of Education Bulletin 12 (Washington, D.C., 1914); Dresslar, *Report on the Rosenwald School Buildings* (Nashville: Julius Rosenwald Fund, 1920); Dresslar, *School Hygiene* (New York: Macmillan, 1925); Fletcher B. Dresslar and Haskell Pruett, *Rural School-houses, School Grounds, and Their Equipment*, US Office of Education Bulletin 21 (Washington, D.C.: Government Printing Office, 1930).

20. *The Negro Rural School and Its Relation to the Community* (Tuskegee, Ala.: Tuskegee Normal and Industrial Institute, 1915); Julius Rosenwald Fund, *Community School Plans* (Nashville: 1921, 1924, 1927, 1928, 1931); Julius Rosenwald Fund, *Community Schools: Paint Colors and Directions for Painting* (Nashville, 1922).

21. Booker T. Washington to James L. Sibley, May 26, 1915, SG15443, "W," Rural School Agent Correspondence, Alabama Department of Education Records, Alabama Department of Archives and History, Montgomery, Ala. (hereafter Alabama Department of Education Records).

22. Booker T. Washington, Jr., to James L. Sibley, October 29, 1915, SG15444, "W," Rural School Agent Correspondence, Alabama Department of Education Records.

23. *Rural School Houses and Grounds*, Bulletin 26 (Jackson: Mississippi Department of Education, 1921); T. H. Harris to Samuel L. Smith, September 24, 1925, box 339, folder 5, Rosenwald Fund Archives.

24. Anderson, *Education of Blacks in the South*, 78–109; Michael Dennis, "Schooling along the Color Line: Progressives and the Education of Blacks in the New South," *Journal of Negro Education* 67.2 (1998): 142–156.

25. Recommendations from the Conference of Rural School Agents for Negroes in the South and Rosenwald Schoolbuilding Agents, July 17, 1919, General Correspondence, box 51, folder 336, Robert Russa Moton Papers, University Archives and Museums, Tuskegee University (hereafter, Moton Papers).

26. "Interior View of the Arcadia Schoolhouse, Built with Aid from the Rosenwald Fund" and "One Acre of Cabbage and Tomatoes, Tallulah Colored School Garden, Madison

Parish," *Field Force Reports* (Baton Rouge: Louisiana Department of Education, May 1917), 47, 48.

27. J. S. Jones, "Report, Rosenwald Schoolhouse Building for Louisiana," October 1919, January 1920, April 1920, General Correspondence, box 51, folders 336, 340b, and 340c, Moton Papers; Maggie Nance Ringgold, "Report of Visit to Negro Schools of West Baton Rouge Parish, Louisiana," box 1, folder "Supervisors Reports Mch 18–1922," Department of Education Miscellaneous Records, Louisiana State Archives, Baton Rouge, La.; "Minutes of the Meeting of the Rosenwald Schoolhouse Building Agents," 1923, box 187, folder 12, and "Conference of State Agents for Negro Rural Schools" 1923, box 188, folder 4, Rosenwald Fund Archives.

28. On the Rosenwald Fund's urban industrial high school program, see Anderson, *Education of Blacks in the South*, 203–229.

29. *Retrospective Glances of Limestone County Negro Education* (n.p.: Limestone County Negro Teachers Association, 1947); see also Lake County Retired Teachers Association, *Through Schoolhouse Doors: A History of Lake County Schools* (Tallahassee: Rose Printing, 1983).

30. William Brown, "We the Building Committee of Brownsville School Number Two," 1913, box 14, untitled folder [1], and Fannie A. Wheelis to C. J. Calloway, May 27, 1913, box 14, untitled folder [2], Clinton J. Calloway Papers, Archives and Museums, Tuskegee University.

31. R. E. Clay to O. H. Bernard, August 31, 1929, folder 3; R. E. Clay to D. S. Tanner, May 31, 1930, and October 1, 1930, folder 4, box 269, Tennessee Commissioner of Education Records, microfilm reel 89, Tennessee State Library and Archives, Nashville.

32. A. C. Lewis and J. W. Bateman, *Rosenwald-Day Program*, Bulletin 102 (Baton Rouge: Louisiana State Department of Education, 1927); *Alabama Program of Julius Rosenwald Day Exercises* (n.p., [1930]), folder "Alabama," box 1, series 14, Georgia Department of Education Records, Georgia Department of Archives and History, Atlanta, Georgia; E. A. Duke, *Rosenwald School Day Program, March 6, 1931*, Bulletin 121-B (Oklahoma City: Oklahoma State Department of Education, [1931]), box 20, Department of Education Publications, Oklahoma State Archives, Oklahoma City; Division of Negro Education, *Rosenwald School Day in Arkansas* (Little Rock: Central Printing, [1930].

33. Elizabeth Harris Pointer, interview by Paul Ortiz, Tuskegee, Alabama, 22 July 1994, "Behind the Veil: Documenting African American Life in the Jim Crow South," Center for Documentary Studies at Duke University, Rare Book, Manuscript, and Special Collections Library, Duke University, Durham, N.C.

34. David Beasley, interview by Paul Ortiz, Tuskegee, Alabama, July 12, 1994, "Behind the Veil."

35. Reed, *Brevard Rosenwald School*, 35, 38, 52, 60–99, 117–119, 135, 136–159, 175–179.

36. Helen Howard, interview by Doris G. Dixon, Cotton Plant, Arkansas, July 19, 1995, "Behind the Veil."

37. Oliver Williams, interview by Doris G. Dixon, Cotton Plant, Arkansas, July 21, 1995, "Behind the Veil"; typescript list of Arkansas Rosenwald schools, box 337, folder 3, Rosenwald Fund Archives.

38. Fannie Styles Gayden, "Progress of an Elementary Teacher," and Freida Randall Powell, "Before the Days of Supplied Materials," in Mississippi Retired Teachers Association, *Bells Are Ringing* (Jackson, Miss.: Jackson Public Schools Print Shop, 1976), 124, 143.

39. Reed, *Brevard Rosenwald School*, 80–85, 107–109, 114–117.

40. National Education Association Commission on Professional Rights and Responsibilities, *Report of an Investigation: Wilcox County, Alabama: A Study of Social, Economic, and Educational Bankruptcy* (Washington, D.C.: National Educational Association, 1967), 9.

41. Kara Miles Turner, "'Getting it Straight': Southern Black School Patrons and the Struggle for Equal Education in the Pre- and Post-Civil Rights Eras," *Journal of Negro Education* 72.2 (2003): 217–229; see also David S. Cecelski, *Along Freedom Road: Hyde County, North Carolina, and the Fate of Black Schools in the South* (Chapel Hill: University of North Carolina Press, 1994); Vanessa Siddle Walker, *Their Highest Potential: An African American School Community in the Segregated South* (Chapel Hill: University of North Carolina Press, 1996).

11

The Geographies and Identities of Street Girls in Indonesia

HARRIOT BEAZLEY

Almost from the beginning, the presence of women in cities, and particularly in city streets, has been questioned, and the controlling and surveillance aspects of city life have always been directed particularly at women. Urban life potentially challenged patriarchal systems.

–Elizabeth Wilson, *The Sphinx in the City*

Since the Asian financial crisis began in August 1997, there has been a significant increase in the numbers of children living and working on the streets of Indonesia. Save the Children Indonesia puts the current population of Indonesian street children at 120,000, compared to a precrisis figure of 50,000, and street girls make up 20 percent of this figure.[1] Within the last few years there has been a dramatic increase in the numbers of female street children, particularly in the city of Yogyakarta, Central Java.

All street children in Indonesia are marginalized by a repressive state and society, and their social marginality is reflected in the marginality of the spaces that they occupy on the street. This chapter explores how street girls in particular suffer discrimination on the street, and how their social position is even more marginal than that of street boys.[2] This is because they are harassed not only by agents of the state but also by street boys and other men on the street.

Elsewhere I have discussed the street-boy community in Yogyakarta and the formation of their own subculture, the Tikyan, a name that derives from the Javanese *sithik ning lumayan*, meaning "just a little but enough."[3] In this chapter, I continue my analysis of the street-child subculture by examining how particular social processes influence behavior within the street-child social world, between street boys and street girls. By examining the lives and experiences of twelve street girls (aged between twelve and twenty) in Yogyakarta, I discuss how despite their subordinate street status, subcultural options are available to them. I explain the girls' behavior patterns as survival mechanisms and strategies of resistance, which are articulated through street girls' discourse, style, and income-seeking and leisure activities. I also explain how they negotiate different social and personal spaces for themselves, and how they have succeeded in creating their own gendered space on the street. I see this produced cultural space as a "microculture," meaning a small group within a subculture that exists beside, and interconnects with, the dominant male street-boy subculture.[4] I present these socio-spatial patterns as "geographies of resistance," and as a response to the pervasive patriarchal discourse within Indonesian society, a society which believes that girls should not be on the street.[5]

Girl Subcultures

Many feminist approaches to youth subculture have criticized subcultural theory for ignoring feminist issues, and point to the masculine and sexist elements of subcultures that marginalize girls.[6]

Among feminist subcultural theorists, central to the concept of a culture of femininity is the contention that girls negotiate a different social space from that of boys, and that those girls who enter male territory do so on male terms, as girlfriends, appendages, or whores.[7] McRobbie in particular has stated that subculture itself may not be the place for feminine excitement, where "Women are so obviously inscribed (marginalized, abused) within subculture as static objects (girlfriends, whores)."[8]

Street girls in Yogyakarta are also marginalized and abused by street boys, who call them Rendan, coming from *kere bedanda*, meaning "vagrants wearing makeup." Rendan is not a name used by the street girls, and they find the word offensive. This is because it is used as an insulting label by street boys, who liken street girls to prostitutes and consider them as subordinate. This is the way that street boys assert their difference from the girls, constituting them as powerless objects of sexist discourse and inferior others. Street girls in Yogyakarta are thus positioned at the bottom of the subcultural hierarchy, pushed to the margins of the street-child subculture by boundaries that are created from within. By drawing on arguments posited by Carrington and Miles, however, I contend that street girls are not mere appendages to street boys within the street-child subculture.[9] I argue instead that street girls actively attempt to subvert their inferior position on the street through various psychological, social, and spatial resistance strategies.

Recent studies in the United Kingdom have shown how the street provides an important social venue for young girls, as well as for boys, but that their use of space often conflicts with that of boys.[10] Girls in public spaces often find that they are conceptualized as "being the 'wrong' gender and being in the 'wrong' place." As Skelton argues, girls will frequently resist such a marginal positioning, especially through their friendships and the ways they use the street as a social space, in which they create their own social worlds.[11]

Ideological Discourse

The lives of street girls in Yogyakarta cannot be explained without first understanding the Indonesian state's ideological construction of femininity, which is reproduced through society's discourse and, subsequently, through the city's landscapes. More specifically, it is important to recognize how these ideological constructions are played out on the street, and how street boys have appropriated patriarchal attitudes, despite their own alienation from mainstream society. Such an understanding of gender inequality and patriarchal power relations in Indonesian society helps to explain the mainstream stereotyping of street girls as prostitutes, the mistreatment of society, and their subsequent need for "invisibility" on the street.

State Ibuism

Yogyakarta is the birthplace of former President Soeharto, who led the infamously repressive "New Order" regime until he was forced to step down from office in May 1998. During Soeharto's time in power (1966–1998), ideological indoctrination aided the state's attempts to create a culture of conformity for uniting a highly diverse and unequal society. One of the ideologies constructed by the New Order State in the pursuit of power was a sex and gender ideology, "State Ibuism."[12] State Ibuism represses women by emphasising their traditional role, placing them in a subordinate position to men, and defining them in narrow stereotypical roles of housekeepers and mothers (*ibu*).

As a result of this patriarchal ideology, girl children in Indonesia are not socialized to work in the public sector, or to spend time on the street, and are usually kept close to home and assigned domestic roles and duties from a very early age.[13] Such gender stereotyping excludes girls from the labor market and binds them to their future role as mother and caretaker of the family home. Mobility restrictions are also enforced, particularly once a girl reaches puberty. This is because girls in Indonesia are believed to need protection and guidance sexually, and their movements are restricted to the "safe" environment of the family home, a household, or a factory.[14]

Many girls, when they do work outside the home, do so with their mothers in the markets, as domestic servants, or in factories. These occupations are considered to be respectable positions in safe spaces that are appropriate for young girls.[15] As a result there are fewer girls working on the streets or in other informal-sector activities.

Consequently, girls in Yogyakarta grow up with a limited spatial experience, and an internalized fear of the streets, as they are frequently warned against its "dangers." Further, social stigma and stereotyping are key mechanisms that reinforce many of the restrictions placed on women in Indonesian society. For example, during my research, boys and girls on the street often mentioned how girls were supposed to behave. I asked them to tell me exactly what was expected of young women by Indonesian society. The children (both boys and girls) answered that women in Indonesia cannot go out after 9:30 P.M., they cannot go where they please, they cannot drink alcohol, they cannot smoke, they cannot have sex before marriage, they cannot wear "sexy" clothes, and they cannot leave the house without permission. They must be good, nice, kind, and helpful, and stay at home to do domestic chores and to look after their children or younger siblings. These answers from the children are a clear example of how gender roles are internalized at an early age.

Women are thus oppressed by this ideology, and there is a distinct distrust of women who break any of the unwritten rules, act independently, or leave the traditional sphere of the home and family. In Indonesia, a woman without a home defies all mainstream conventions. She is seen to challenge the patriarchal view of the ideal family and to represent chaos. Girls who do not conform to the female stereotype of staying at home, out of sight, being the passive "ideal girl," are regarded with suspicion and are stigmatized and labeled as "bad girls."[16]

Sphinx on the Street

Because of the nature of their existence, street girls are mistrusted by mainstream society. The moral message is that the city is a dangerous place for women, and the actions and lifestyles of street girls fall outside acceptable behavior. Any single woman seen on the street after 9:30 P.M. is viewed by society as sexually permissive and a "bad woman" or a prostitute, and prostitutes are officially labeled by the state as "women without morals" (*Wanita Tuna Susila* or WTS). The way the label "tramp" is interpreted when applied to women reflects similar stigmas in Western society.

Men on the streets of Yogyakarta also adhere to these same patriarchal beliefs that the street is fundamentally a male space, run by men. Along with other street codes, they pass these beliefs down to street boys, who subsequently hold a contemptuous and dismissive attitude toward street girls.

I frequently saw street boys mocking street girls, calling them names and sometimes even hitting or kicking them. The girls suffered this abuse from street boys more than from any other group of men on the street because street girls were one group over whom street boys actually had some control, and whom they felt superior to. Street boys felt very strongly that if girls want to be on the street, then they have to comply with their rules and values, which are necessarily masculine and tough. If they do not like it then they should not be there.

Producing Margins: Tikyan versus Rendan

During focus-group discussions I asked the boys to explain why they thought it was reasonable for them to be on the street, but not the girls. The overwhelming response was that the street was "no place for a girl." The boys felt that it is acceptable for them to be on the street, as it is a masculine space, but they strongly disapproved of girls living on the streets and thought that they should be at home. Many of the boys expressed this sentiment, and one boy said to me: "If my little sister lived like that I would kill my father for allowing it to happen."[17] The boys felt that the girls should seek good jobs that are "more honorable," such as a being a domestic servant. There were also boys who felt that the girls were "lazy to work," as all they did all day was "sit, eat, sleep, sit, eat, sleep . . . continuously."[18] This was exactly the same attitude many people in mainstream society have toward street boys.

Street boys, therefore, do not see street girls as being the same as themselves. They are considered to be a different group "other" to themselves, and as being more comparable to prostitutes than to street children. When I asked one boy about street girls, he said "there aren't any." I asked, "what about Rendan?," and he replied "Oh them! They're not street kids, they're Rendan . . . almost the same as prostitutes."[19] As McRobbie and Garber point out, males in most societies have divided the female world into "women-with-hearts-of-gold-who-look-after-them, and prostitutes."[20] This dichotomy is the focal point of the Indonesian state's gender ideology, and street girls are caught in its pitfalls and contradictions.

Ibu Kartini

The street boys' attitude toward street girls is clearly illustrated in a cartoon "zine," *Jejal*, which is produced by a local nongovernment organization, Humana, that assists street boys. The cartoon positions Rendan as being entirely "other" to an almost mythical figure in Indonesia, Ibu Kartini, a recognizd Indonesian feminist (Figure II.I). The cartoon reads:

STREET BOYS (TEKYAN): Mbah . . . are " 'Rendan" allowed to join in Kartini Day celebrations?

MBAH: Ssh! Who says they can't?

GIRL: Mbah . . . they say that Kartini wanted women to have the same rights as men. . . .

MBAH: BUT REMEMBER KARTINI WAS NOT A "RENDAN."

In the nineteenth century, Kartini lived in a town not far from Yogyakarta. She is represented in government discourse as the epitome of the "good woman" with a "heart of gold." She has been officially sanctioned by the Indonesian government as the ideal Indonesian woman, wife, and mother, and is perceived as having possessed all the nurturing, self-sacrificing qualities that a woman should desire.[21] The cartoon suggests that if a girl does not behave in the correct and proper way, in the way Kartini is believed to have behaved (by adhering to dominant patriarchal ideology), she has no rights, least of all equal rights to men.

FIGURE 11.1 Positioning street girls as "other."

From Dodo Kocomoto, "Kartini" *Jejal* 5 (April 1997): 30. Reprinted with permission from Humana NGO, Yogyakarta, Indonesia.

What is interesting about this cartoon is that the history of Kartini has been reworked and her words rearticulated by the state. In reality, Kartini was a young woman who wanted to rebel against the shackles of tradition, marriage, and family. She wanted to be free and independent and not to be dependent on her father or her husband, but only herself. She wrote these desires in her letters to a friend.[22] Kartini understood that it was wrong and "sinful" to have such yearnings and, eventually, she succumbed to the pressures of élite society, and a father she loved, by marrying a man she did not want and, subsequently, dying in childbirth when she was twenty-five years old. When reading the words of Kartini, "I long to be free, to be allowed, to be able to make myself independent, to be dependent on no one else . . . happiness is freedom," I am reminded of the same sentiments that were frequently expressed to me by street girls in Yogyakarta, almost a century after Kartini died.[23]

Regardless of the fact that street boys are powerless children, marginalized and ill-treated by representatives of an oppressive state, they are also perpetrators of patriarchal social relations, and street girls are one group to whom they feel superior. In this way the boys stake a claim to the mainstream, and create new margins within the street-child world. They do this by asserting their differences from street girls through male performance identities, and by labeling them as "Rendan" and "other," thus assuming a moral authority over the girls and seizing power. A process of shifting marginalities thus accommodates them while further alienating others and maintaining power at the center.[24] As Walkerdine asserts, "An individual can become powerful or powerless depending on the terms in which his/her subjectivity is constituted."[25]

Resistance to Patriarchal Social Structures

Women are not passive victims of circumstance locked into a private sphere. . . . Instead, women occupy multiple and shifting sites, employ a range of strategies, and experience a wide variety of spatial relations. . . . Some, as a strategy of resistance are able to breach the boundaries imposed on them.

–Shirlena Huang and Brenda Yeoh,
"Gender and Urban Space in the Tropical Third World"

The Indonesian state's attempts to keep women in the home are incompatible with real life. As Gerke emphasizes, such policies are merely an imposition of middle-class values that have molded traditional practices to suit the needs of dominant groups to create a passive, socialized workforce, and to control over-population and unemployment.[26] The ideologies only see women in relation to their husbands and children, ignoring their roles in the labor market, and do not recognize that many women are economically independent and dominant members of the household. Far from being idle, in reality, women in Java are traditionally economically independent, autonomous decision makers who have to cope with the problems of poverty, unemployment, and oppression in their families' everyday lives.[27] Such an actuality means that women cannot stay at home looking after their children, but must go out to work.

Further, the impact of the state's economic restructuring and the subsequent financial crisis created many social changes, which placed an enormous strain on the traditional patterns of family structure. Growing unemployment has seen many adults, both male and female, migrating to work on plantations in Malaysia. Significant numbers of young women have also started working in factories or as housemaids in Singapore and the Middle East, leaving their children in others' care, which has caused the desertion and dislocation of many families.[28] These changes have resulted in many more children needing to work on the streets to survive.

The traditional concepts of women's and children's roles in society as promoted by the state do not reflect the role of the majority of lower-class families in Javanese society. As the informal sector has grown, the street has become a reflection of serious economic imbalances and deep social inequalities that exist within Indonesian society. Street children can be seen as a visible indication of this disorder, because children living in poor, lower-class families have been affected by socioeconomic problems in the home.

There has been, therefore, a crucial gender dimension to the form of economic restructuring pursued by the Indonesian state. However, as Huang and Yeoh have identified in Singapore, and Desai in the slums of Bombay, poor urban women are not passive victims of circumstance but are able to cope with repressive situations by developing their own "diverse and subtle strategies to bring about change and enhance their lives."[29] These strategies are both social and spatial, and can be viewed as a form of informal politics that are crucially important as a form of empowerment for individuals, and that represent young women's citizenship in action.[30]

As a result of the social environment they live in, dominated by patriarchal discourse, street girls have similarly adopted behavior patterns, informal networks, and discourse in order to empower themselves. These subtle strategies are integrated into their lifestyle as survival strategies, and as strategies of resistance to their marginalization and sexual subordination in a male-dominated street world.

Street girls are very aware of existing social rules and the image that they create by being out alone at night, but the majority of them say it does not bother them. They say they "could not care less" and that people can "think what they like." Such responses can be understood as one way in which the girls resist the claims of dominant groups in mainstream society.

Many girls told me of how they left home because of violence or abuse at home, or because they were "bored of being stuck in the house all day" doing domestic chores, and not being allowed out. They wanted to escape to be "free as a bird," and they stressed how much they enjoyed living on the street with friends who feel the same way, being able to take their own decisions and living as they please. Similar to Skelton's findings with working-class girls in Wales, street girls in Yogyakarta are also "escaping from the home" to public streets, as an escape route from their domestic responsibilities.[31]

Tonight I was sitting with Ety (aged fourteen). . . . I asked Ety if she minded being called "Rendan." She said she didn't really care, but that the girls themselves don't call themselves Rendan, just *anak jalanan*, street kids. She said that mainstream society think that any girl who is out on the street at night "after 10'o'clock" is like all bad women, a prostitute. I asked her how that makes her feel, and she replied "let them!" She then said that although people thought that, it was still far better being on the street than being "stifled" at home in the house where you are "really, really feel fed up." I asked her what was so nice about living on the street, she replied: "On the street you're free and independent, there isn't anyone to tell you off. At home you are constantly busy; you have to do this job, do that job, working, working all the time. It's boring at home. When I went home I was shouted at so now I don't want to go home again.[32]

Leaving home can be seen as a rebellion, and as a street girl's first refusal of ideological constraints placed upon her. Most of the girls I met came from small towns and villages in the Central Java district. Young girls in rural areas are often excluded from public spaces and are forbidden from leaving the house and surrounding grounds. They compensate by watching television avidly. They are fascinated by soap operas, and consume media and TV images of the glamorous city lifestyles which seem more inviting to them than their boring domestic existence. With the pervasiveness of communication media in the villages, almost all girls in Indonesia have been exposed to the powerful and glamorous female images of the twenty-first century, who are portrayed as free and independent, such as Madonna, Britney Spears, and Dangdut and Bollywood stars. These women have become strong role models for young girls. Although it is difficult to assess the direct effect of mass media on the attitudes and behavior of individuals, the images of global youth culture in magazines and on TV are far more pervasive than even the government's ideological construction of femininity, and much more appealing as an agent of socialization to a young girl. The city offers attractions and more opportunity and freedom than the village, and is often a source of liberation for young girls, just as the factory was for Wolf's "factory daughters" in Jakarta.[33]

The phenomenon of "loose girls" (Perek) in Jakarta is an example of the way in which Indonesia's female youth is being affected by the process of globalization. Perek are middle-class girls who take control of their lives, emphasizing their autonomy, and who experiment with their sexuality and newfound independence. As Murray says of Perek, "These girls are influenced by the commodification of society and rising expectations created by the media and advertising, and reject the superficial morality which would curtail their ability to fulfil those materialistic expectations."[34]

There is little doubt that the economic and political crisis, and the events following September 11, have affected thousands of families throughout Indonesia in a detrimental way.[35] As a result, there are more girls living on the streets than ever before. One reason for this is that traditional family structures, which once kept girls more protected than boys, are breaking down in the face of long-term economic difficulties. I also believe that there are more girls living on the streets in Indonesia due to the impact of globalization. Girls, in particular, are restricted by the culture of conformity and sexist role stereotyping that exists in Indonesia, and are rebelling against it.

Spaces for Street Girls: Geographies of Resistance

Having escaped the stifling conditions at home, street girls find that they are still not as "free as a bird" from patriarchal ideology. They soon find that the street is not "magically protected" from dominant gender constructions, and end up embracing one form of oppression (the street culture) while escaping another (the home). What they find is the same ideology that rules the home rules the street, and that the relationship between street boys and girls is by no means egalitarian. As Miles suggests, however, "Sub-cultural space as such does not guarantee freedom from constraint, but for some it does provide a site of reflection and negotiation."[36]

On the street, girls are forced to negotiate their place and identity politics, by developing various strategies for survival and safety through different productions and uses of space in the city. As a response to their male-dominated environment they have erected and maintain a group boundary, which is physically located at the city park (Taman) in the south of the city. I had previously met some street girls when they were "visiting" the street boys at their gathering point in the center of the city, at the public toilet. At these times the girls were fairly passive and silent. It was not until I visited them in their own cultural space, the Taman, where they slept and hung out, that I really got to know them.

Due to the social environment they inhabit, street girls have specific ways of negotiating and using social and personal spaces for their everyday survival. Despite their stigmatization, street girls have managed to carve out niches in the city, as a resistance to the alienation they experience. One way they have done this is by constructing their own gendered gathering space at the Taman; a female-dominated space, to which they can retreat if they have had enough of the outside male world.

The Taman was a gathering place for a group of twelve street girls between twelve and twenty years old. These girls slept and kept their possessions in a small house at the gates of the park, and during the day they would hang out in a sheltered part of the building and in other parts of the park. The girls who lived in this park called themselves the "park kids" (*anak taman*). When they were in this space they were far more vocal, gregarious, and confident than they were outside it.

As Skelton found with the Rhondda Valley girls, by banding together street girls can enjoy relative safety, as they realize that the only way of protecting themselves on the street is to form a gang.[37] McRobbie who, in the past, commented on the fact that girls do not "need groups" or have the masculine desire to "hang around together," has more recently stated that: "Gangs are part of the disconnected fragmented expressions of dissent that characterize feminism in the Nineties."[38] This phenomenon is powerfully illustrated in Brinkworth's work on girl gangs and street violence in London. She notes that girls today are increasingly involved in street crime, robberies, and drug deals and, where in the past they would have been "hangers-on of notorious male gangs," today they form their own gangs and cultivate the reputation of being "hard" as a method of survival. As one seventeen-year-old "Peckham Rude Girl" said to Brinkworth: "If you can't work a reputation on the street, people will see you as a piece of dirt."[39]

Girl Power

Similarly, street girls in Yogyakarta have seen how aggression and the male approach command respect on the street and in the home, and they copy it, gaining more confidence and status on the street. In response to their social marginality on the street, the Taman girls adopt particular styles, behavior patterns, and discourse in their everyday lives. These are integrated into their lifestyle as strategies or resistance to what can be understood as resistance to their marginalization and sexual subordination in a male-dominated world. The girls almost always wear jeans and men's shirts and cut their hair short or hide it in baseball caps. This is partly to remain less conspicuous as a single girl on the street, but I also read it as an act of "refusal" to the constructions of femininity in Indonesian society.[40] The girls identify being female with being vulnerable, and reject female clothing for these reasons. This is also a survival strategy for the girls, as it makes them less visible and therefore less vulnerable to attack.

The Taman girls with whom I spent time smoked cigarettes, drank alcohol, and regularly took pills (such as Mogadon, Valium, or Rohipnol) as a form of diversion and escapism. They told me that they took these pills with cheap alcohol in order to "forget bad thoughts" and to relieve "stress." "Pills help you forget bad thoughts and problems. They make you fly, sometimes for as long as three days. When you wake up you can't remember anything of what you did. It's great!"[41]

The alcohol and pills help the girls release rage, frustration, and dissatisfaction with their circumscribed female role. Sometimes they also take morphine and heroine, administering it through razor cuts in their arms. They mix it with their blood and then suck. "It tastes really nice," they said.

Like street boys, most of the girls have tattoos and body piercing. The girls also have something that the street boys did not: numerous razor cuts, often in rows up the insides of their arms. These cuts, although sometimes used for taking drugs, are more significantly a sign of their subculture and present a tough and antifeminine image. The girls often said that they made the cuts in order to "feel the pain," but they also thought they looked "cool" (*hebat*). Almost all of the girls had these scarifications on their arms, and I read them as a "social inscription," which can be understood as a "public collective" social category, in modes of inclusion or membership. It was a sign of belonging to their group.[42] When discussing female punks, Miles refers to Hebdige's work on semiotic readings and acts of refusal (insubordination).[43] "Here the female body was viewed as a site of empowerment, a place where the power can be appropriated within sexual discourse . . . and if the body is the bottom line, then piercing becomes an act of refusal—a tactical block, a place to regain control."[44]

Piercing, tattooing, and scarification can be understood as an act of refusal by the street girls, and as an objection to dominant ideology which seeks to control their bodies (Figure 11.2). By wearing men's clothes, drinking alcohol, smoking

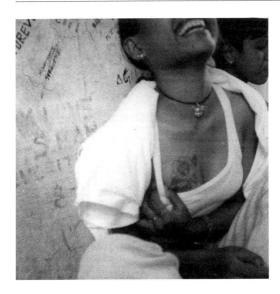

FIGURE 11.2 An "Act of Refusal." A street girl flaunts the tattoo of a rose on her breast.

Photo by the author.

cigarettes, taking pills, and cutting her arms, a girl is displaying how hard she is, "working a reputation on the street," and placing herself on a level more equal to both her female and male peers, who respect such a display.

Sources of Income

Most girls would like the same livelihoods as street boys, and to earn their own money (particularly by busking or shining shoes). However, in Yogyakarta, street girls are ostracized from these positions (and spaces to work in) by street boys, and public attitudes also make it difficult. Subsequently, they survive by taking boyfriends to look after them. Boyfriends are local boys or other street boys, who provide them with food, clothing, and protection in exchange for regular sex.

Although street girls are seen to be indistinguishable from prostitutes, sex work is only an occasional way of obtaining income for street girls. It is not something practiced on a regular basis, and some girls never do it. It is simply one survival strategy, and the girls do not regard themselves (or each other) as prostitutes if they occasionally trade sex for money, or more often, a meal. Boyfriends, however, are the principal form of income and protection for the street girls. They are sought after to buy the girls clothes and regular meals, and to protect them. Usually boyfriends sleep with the girls at the Taman. This is thought to be totally unacceptable behavior in Indonesia, where sex before marriage is taboo, and living together out of wedlock is considered indecent.

Gendered Geographies

The effects of these geographies of resistance are multiple, fluid, dynamic
and in some ways uncontainable or at least unintended.

–Steve Pile and Michael Keith, eds., *Geographies of Resistance*

Street girls occupy different areas in the city from those of street boys, because
the girls use the city differently from the boys. For example, they sleep and gather
at the Taman, but they also visit different places in the daytime and at night,
including a tourist bar where sex workers operate and where they can perhaps
meet foreign men; the mall, where street boys are often refused entry; and a hotel
on the main street, Malioboro, where they hang out at night.

Street girls also operate differently from street boys. Although they gather in
a fairly large group at the Taman, when they are not there they move around the
city in twos or threes, unlike the boys, who move about in larger groups. This is
partly to be less visible in the street due to the threat of violence or rebuke.
Besides the need for invisibility, however, girls also move around the city in small
groups because they do not have the same dependency on groups or solidarity as
street boys. This is something that McRobbie and Garber note when discussing
the reasons for the "invisibility" of girl subcultures.[45] As mentioned earlier, however, McRobbie has more recently noted the tendency for girls to adopt masculine styles and form gangs as an expression of dissent, and also because of their
need for protection and to survive on the street.

During the daytime the girls are much less mobile than street boys. This is
partly due to their lack of income-earning activities; they hang out and sleep at
the Taman, eat at one of the street stalls in the city square, or wander around the
shopping area for entertainment. At night, however, they are highly mobile and
move around the city far more than the street boys. This is because, unlike street
boys, who usually only mix socially with each other at night, street girls move
between different social groups in the city in order to find different boyfriends
and sources of income.

An integral part of street girls' daily survival strategies involves moving
across social spaces to socialize with different groups in their own territories.
These groups include *becak* (cycle rickshaw) drivers outside the shopping center;
buskers in the market, at bus stops, or in the city square; university and college
students on Malioboro, the main street; "uncles" (men who offer the girls a meal
or money, in exchange for sex) outside the hotel; and local *kampung* (poor urban
housing) boys at the entertainment park. When they are out at night the girls go
dancing at the entertainment park, where they look for boyfriends, and they
sometimes go on trips away with university or kampung boys on their motor-
bikes, to "Paris" (the nickname for the beach Parangtritis, forty kilometers away).
They may also go for a ride in a becak, around the city. One girl, Sylvie

(aged fourteen), explained to me how each girl at the Taman has her own becak driver friend, a "special friend," who takes her around the city. When I asked how the girls pay for these rides, she said, "well the becak drivers have money and we don't right? So they give us money or something to eat in exchange for our friendship, and we compromise."

All these different groups of boys and men are potential sources of income, alcohol, drugs, or a meal, and every night, the girls move around the city creating and maintaining these contacts. They also shift their identities according to where they are in the city, and with which groups they hang out. As well as forming relationships with these males, the girls also form friendships with female stall owners on Malioboro, and in the markets. These stall owners are useful for credit and protection.

Street girls do sometimes visit the street boys at their gathering place on Malioboro, but they seldom visit the toilet where the street boys congregate at night, unless invited, because they do not feel welcome there, and they are often treated with contempt. There are some spaces which the girls share with street boys, including the entertainment park. They also share a food stall on Malioboro.

Due to their social and spatial exclusion, street girls are forced to create spaces within which they can survive. Such socio-spatial patterns can be seen as survival strategies for the street girls. Further, their movements through the city across different social spaces, although perhaps "unintended" as geographies of resistance, do mean that the girls blend into the city and are harder to detect than street boys.[46]

Conclusion

This chapter has argued that street girls particularly encounter abusive discrimination on the streets of Indonesia, because they are seen to be committing a heretical geography by violating ideas of femininity in state discourse, and by invading the street that is fundamentally a male space.[47] I have shown how although street boys are themselves powerless children, suppressed by the control of an oppressive regime, street girls are one group to whom they feel superior and over whom they have power. For these reasons street girls suffer ill-treatment from many street boys, who believe that girls should not be on the street.

Street girls endure a type of multiple stigmatization, as they are victims of contempt not only from mainstream society but also from within the street subculture itself. Through the Tikyan discourse, street boys use difference to divide and rule, by accommodating themselves and alienating street girls; thus they create boundaries of shifting marginality within the street-kid subculture. This is done by refusing girls their status as street kids and by labeling them as Rendan or "other." Consequently, a street girl's existence on the street is even more marginal than that of a street boys, as she is at the bottom of the subcultural hierarchy, pushed to the margins of the street culture by boundaries that are created from within an already marginalized group.

Such reproduction of mainstream patriarchal attitudes has affected social processes and everyday street behavior in Yogyakarta. I have shown, however, that street girls are not passive victims of the male gaze, or mere appendages of street boys, but have been successful in negotiating the street-child subculture to produce their own gendered sense of space. In response to their social exclusion, street girls actively attempt to subvert patriarchal ideology by rejecting the sexist label Rendan, identifying themselves instead as "street kids" and the same as the boys. This is achieved by drinking, smoking, taking drugs, having tattoos and razor slashes, wearing boy's clothes, and talking and acting tough, thus refusing the conventional notions of femininity in dominant discourse. The girls are participating in the spectacle of street-child subculture, by "working a reputation" for themselves and by seeking visible identities and styles that are at once similar to the style of street boys, and outside mainstream respectable behavior.

In addition to these general resistance strategies, there are also spatiotemporal geographies of resistance involved in the range of survival mechanisms adopted by street girls in Yogyakarta, and the girls negotiate a different production and use of space from that of their male counterparts in order to survive. The girls with whom I spent my time had attached themselves to a particular site in the city, the Taman, and refer to themselves as the Taman kids, thus creating a positive self-identity for themselves as a street-girl culture. I see this place attachment as a survival mechanism and geography of resistance. The Taman is a site of liberation for the girls, where they can dress and act as they like, because it is their own space, a place that gives them a feeling of belonging, and where they can go to if they feel unsafe. In addition to this place attachment, the girls experience a wide variety of spatial relations over a number of different social sites. These socio-spatial patterns are survival strategies, as well as additional geographies of resistance in a society that seeks to restrict the mobility of single women in the city, especially at night. These tactics of resistance that street girls have adopted in the face of their multifaceted marginalization can be recognized as a production of their own separate culture, which exists beside and interacts with the street boy, Tikyan, subculture. It is a microculture within the street-child subculture of Yogyakarta.

NOTES

A longer version of this essay was published in *Urban Studies* 39.9 (2002): 1665–1687 by Blackwell Publishing.

1. "Indonesian Street Girls Coming Out of the Dark," *Straits Times.* Available at http://www.straitstimes.asia1.com.sg/mnt/html/women/archive/issues/13.html, 2002.

2. This chapter is based on material from my doctoral dissertation: Harriot Beazley, "'A Little but Enough': Street Children's Subcultures in Yogyakarta, Indonesia," Ph.D. dissertation, Australian National University, Canberra, 1999. Fieldwork was conducted over fourteen months in the city of Yogyakarta, Central Java. The girls no longer live in the city park, but nevertheless to protect their identities their names have been changed.

3. Harriot Beazley, "'Home Sweet Home?': Street Children's Sites of Belonging," in *Children's Geographies: Playing, Living, Learning*, edited by Sarah Holloway and Gill Valentine (London: Routledge, 2000), 194–210; Beazley, "Voices from the Margins: Street Children's Subcultures in Yogyakarta," *Children's Geographies* 1.2 (2003): 181–200; Beazley, "The Construction and Protection of Individual and Collective Identities by Street Children in Indonesia," *Children, Youth and Environments* 13.1 (2003): Available online at http://cye.colorado.edu.

4. See Helena Wulff, *Twenty Girls: Growing up, Ethnicity and Excitement in a South London Microculture*, Stockholm Studies in Social Anthropology 21 (Stockholm: Almqvist & Wiksell International, 1988).

5. Steve Pile and Michael Keith, eds., *Geographies of Resistance* (London: Routledge, 1997).

6. See, for example, Angela McRobbie and Jenny Garber, "Girls and Subcultures: An Exploration," in *Resistance through Rituals: Youth Subcultures in Post-war Britain*, edited by Stuart Hall and Tony Jefferson (London: Routledge, 1976), 209–222.

7. Kerry Carrington, "Cultural Studies, Youth Culture and Delinquency," in *Youth Subcultures: Theory, History and the Australian Experience*, edited by Rob White (Hobart: National Clearinghouse for Youth Studies, 1993), 27–34.

8. Angela McRobbie, *Feminism and Youth Culture: From "Jackie" to "Just Seventeen"* (Boston: Unwin Hyman, 1991), 25.

9. Carrington, "Cultural Studies," 30; Cressida Miles, "Spatial Politics: A Gendered Sense of Place," in *The Clubcultures Reader: Readings in Popular Cultural Studies*, edited by Steve Readhead (Oxford: Blackwell, 1997), 66–78.

10. See for example, Huge Matthews, Matthew Taylor, Barry Percy-Smith, and Melanie Limb, "The Unacceptable Flaneur: The Shopping Mall as a Teenage Hangout" *Childhood* 7.3 (2003): 279–274; Tracey Skelton, "Nothing to Do, Nowhere to Go: Teenage Girls and 'Public Space' in the Rhondda Valleys, South Wales," in *Children's Geographies: Playing, Living, Learning*, edited by Sarah Holloway and Gill Valentine (London: Routledge, 2000), 80–99.

11. Skelton, "Nothing to Do," 80.

12. Julia Suryakusuma, "The State and Sexuality in New Order Indonesia," in *Fantasizing the Feminine in Indonesia*, edited by Laurie J. Sears (London: Duke University Press, 1996), 92–119.

13. Norma Sullivan, *Masters and Managers: A Study of Gender Relations in Urban Java* (St. Leonards: Allen & Unwin, 1994).

14. See also Cindy Katz, who had similar findings in Sudan. "Growing Girls/Closing Circles," in *Full Circles: Geographies of Women over the Lifecourse*, edited by Cindi Katz and J. Monk (London: Routledge, 1993), 88–106.

15. See Diane Wolfe, *Factory Daughters: Gender, Household Dynamics, and Rural Industrialization in Java* (Berkeley: University of California Press, 1992); Katherine Robinson, "Housemaids: The Effects of Gender and Culture on the Internal and International Migration of Indonesian Women" in *Intersexions: Gender, Class, Culture, Ethnicity*, edited by Gill Bottomley, Marie de Lepervanche, and Jeannie Martin (Sydney: Allen and Unwin, 1991), 33–51.

16. See Valerie Walkerdine, *Schoolgirl Fictions* (London: Verso, 1990), 5.

17. Personal communication with Eko, age 14.

18. Personal communication with Budi, age 15.

19. Personal communication with Rahmad, age 13.

20. McRobbie and Garber, "Girls and Subcultures," 217.

21. Sylvia Tiwon, "Models and Maniacs: Articulation of the Feminine in Indonesia," in *Fantasizing the Feminine in Indonesia*, edited by Laurie J. Sears (London: Duke University Press, 1996), 47–70.

22. Tiwon, "Models and Maniacs," 56–57.

23. Tiwon, "Models and Maniacs," 55.

24. See Alison Murray, *Pink Fits: Sex, Subcultures and Discourses in the Asia Pacific* (Melbourne: Monash Asia Institute, 2001), 154–156.

25. Walkerdine, *Schoolgirl Fictions*, 5.

26. Gerke, "Indonesian National Development Ideology and the Role of Women," *Indonesian Circle* 59/60 (November 1993): 47–48.

27. Sullivan, *Masters and Managers*, 111.

28. Harriot Beazley, "The Malaysian Orphans of Lombok," in *Young Rural Lives: Global Perspectives on Rural Childhood and Youth*, edited by Ruth Panelli, Samantha Punch, and Elsbeth Robson (London: Routledge, 2007), 107–120.

29. Huang and Yeoh, "Gender and Urban Space," 105–112; Vandana Desai, "Informal Politics, Grassroots NGOs and Women's Empowerment in the Slums of Bombay," in *Rethinking Empowerment*, edited by Jane L. Parpart, Shirin M. Rai, and Kathleen Staudt (London: Routledge, 2003), 374–407.

30. Desai, "Informal Politics," 374.

31. Skelton, "Nothing to Do," 92.

32. Author's fieldnotes, Yogyakarta, July 1997.

33. Wolfe, *Factory Daughters*.

34. Murray, *Pink Fits*, 36–37.

35. These events, including the Bali and Jakarta bombings of 2002, 2003, and 2005 were followed by a steep decline in foreign investment and a significant slump in the number of tourists visiting Indonesia (a major form of income for Yogyakarta, a traditional tourist destination). More recently the devastating Java earthquake of May 2006, which killed over 6,000 people, has also had a detrimental impact of the number of tourists visiting the city.

36. Miles, "Spatial Politics," 69.

37. Skelton, "Nothing To Do," 80.

38. McRobbie and Garber, "Girls and Subcultures," 221; the second statement is quoted in Brinkworth, "Twisted Sisters," *Harpers & Queen*, April 1997, 131–133.

39. Brinkworth, "Twisted Sisters," 132.

40. See Dick Hebdige, *Subculture: The Meaning of Style* (London: Methuen, 1979).

41. Personal communication with Novi, age 15.

42. See Elizabeth Grosz, *Volatile Bodies: Towards a Corporeal Feminism* (St. Leonards: Allen and Unwin, 1994), 140–141.

43. Miles, "Spatial Politics," 68–69, citing Hebdige, *Subculture*, 17.

44. Miles, "Spatial Politics," 69.

45. McRobbie and Garber, "Girls and Subcultures," 221–222.

46. See Pile and Keith, *Geographies of Resistance*, 27.

47. See Tim Cresswell, *In Place/Out of Place: Geography, Ideology, and Transgression* (Minneapolis: University of Minnesota Press, 1996), 29–146.

PART FOUR

Consumption, Commodification, and the Media

Material Culture and Contemporary Childhoods

12

Coming of Age in Suburbia

Gifting the Consumer Child

ALISON J. CLARKE

Children's social worlds, according to an expanding cohort of scholars, are threatened by the escalating, degenerate force of consumer culture materialized in the form of toys, games, and clothing carefully designed and marketed for maximum appeal to fickle childhood tastes and desires.[1] With the emergence of modern consumer culture in late-nineteenth-century North America, educators and moralists, religious leaders and parents condemned the gamut of "dresses, toys, wagons and other playthings which . . . would corrupt the nation's youth."[2] But it is since the postwar period that the "child" has become a specific facet of the market to be addressed with an increasingly complex series of objects, games, and clothing, designed using a range of child-centric aesthetic genres.[3] An array of commodities from Barbie dolls through remote-control cars, microscooters, and character figures (Power Rangers, Mutant Ninja Turtle, Disney, Pokémon, Bratz, etc.) have built up a cosmology of contemporary childhood based on fads and crazes, fashions and gimmicks. This pernicious corporate-controlled toy culture is, according to some critics, as significant an aspect of global exploitation in the twenty-first century as child labor was in the nineteenth.[4]

In his critique of television marketing to children, Stephen Kline compares the "ingénue" child of the Victorian era (content to play with folk toys, found objects, and homemade items) with the market-manipulated child of the late twentieth century: "Children can become obsessed with wanting particular video games or toys and exceptionally persistent in their demands for them. On the other hand, they can treat very expensive or special gifts with total disrespect or disdain. If a particular article of clothing, a toy, or even a pencil is not designed with the right motifs accepted by their peers, children will refuse adamantly to use them."[5]

In Kline's analysis, the contemporary child, in contrast to the innocent pre-consumer child, is a commodity-obsessed being, manipulated by a corporate toy industry to the point of losing all sense of the value of things (and by extension, of social relationships themselves). While some academics advocate a more affirmative approach to children's consumption of mass-produced toys and games, in which the child's appropriation of images and material culture is viewed as a more proactive and heterogeneous process,[6] others have considered such consumption as a crucial part of socialization.[7]

The most recent and popularized studies, however, continue to condemn the "passivity" and "noncreativity" of contemporary play, and the demise of authentic childhood social relations as a requisite of commercialization. "Brands and products," laments Juliet Schor in *Born to Buy*, "have come to determine who is in and who is 'out,' who is hot and who is not, who deserves to have friends, or social status."[8] Within the field of marketing itself, popular literature identifies the contemporary "tween" (a child aged between eight and twelve years) as a new type of child: a technologically astute, information-loaded and brand-literate product of an advanced consumer culture.[9]

Over the last decade, some academics have questioned methodologies and approaches within the social sciences that have allowed only the "muted voices" of children to emerge within research.[10] Children have most often been constructed as "proto-adults" considered largely in terms of socialization and the context of their caregivers. While children have been construed as peripheral objects of study, childhood itself has been considered as a static entity within social theory; "sociological accounts locate childhood in some timeless zone standing as it were to the side of the mainstream (that is adult) history and culture."[11] It is perhaps this tendency toward the disavowal of children's agency that explains the neglect, within the bulk of critical literature around contemporary children's consumption, to socially contextualize the acquisitive behavior of children and their highly nuanced tastes for specific styles and typologies of goods.[12]

In Western industrial culture, children from an early age engage in the practices and sociality of gift giving, through attendance at birthday parties and ritualized events such as Christmas.[13] In contrast to their involvement in everyday provisioning, such as supermarket food shopping, where the parent might elicit a response from even the youngest infant over the selection of a favorite cereal or yogurt,[14] by the age of nine to eleven children's practices of gift-giving extend beyond the immediate child-parent relation. Despite their limited access to monetary resources and retail outlets, many children participate in a range of gift relations requiring discernment over the value of various forms of material culture. Children's activity in the arena of contemporary consumption is generally considered as a facet of socialization, or, as previously outlined, a symptom of the ever-expanding impact of the market on otherwise "authentic" childhood practices.[15] Forms of provisioning (ranging from a trip to the local shop to attendance at a birthday party) are used in an explicitly instrumental way to "teach" children about the values of things and relations. Beyond the commonly held model of socialization, this chapter considers the agency of children and objects in the construction of social relations and moral worlds. Contrary to the burgeoning discourse around children, brands, and consumer culture, it argues that it is through a dialectical relationship with the universal and particular nature of commodities and gifts that children generate a dynamic relationship with adults and peers around the value of "things" and social relations. Stylistic minutiae of toys, clothing, and artifacts are scrutinized by children as they begin to make evaluations regarding appropriate or desired objects and relations. Although they incorporate adult discourses (for example, the concept of "being spoiled"), children themselves, through their own investment and intricate exchanges in goods and values, generate their own moral economies external (but closely connected) to the household. Furthermore, these microdiscourses around contemporary consumer toys and goods evolve as a crucial means by which households participate in a broader public culture of "the child."

"Spaces" of Children's Play in North London

Jay Road, the ethnographic field site of this research project, is a street in North London consisting of mixed rented and owner-occupied state and private housing. The area itself can be described loosely as "semi-suburban" in that it lies a half mile equidistant from an overtly middle-class suburban enclave and a densely populated urban, inner-city area. The street was specifically identified by residents as offering a good compromise for child-rearing in London, as it offered all of the benefits of urban living and some of the popularly perceived advantages of suburbia (reduced pollution, greener space, quieter neighborhood).[16]

With the exception of small groups of older teenagers gathering toward the less residential end of Jay Road, near the local fish-and-chip shop and public telephone boxes, there is rarely any presence of children as a group on the street. This observation corroborates what academics have described as "a progressive retreat from the 'street'" by children over the last decades.[17] Generalized assumptions regarding the demise of children's presence in public urban space has been questioned by some academics,[18] but the ethnographic evidence of Jay Road supports the general contention that contemporary childhood worlds are shifting to the domestic sphere.

Parents, wary of the lack of control they can assert over their children who are playing in public, limit or entirely disallow their children's participation in outdoor play in the immediate area. Unlike the socializing that children take part in at school (beyond the gaze of neighbors and parents), in the locality there is a pronounced fear of children being seen "getting in with the wrong crowd," and that this might reflect unfavorably on parents or the household as a whole. The notion of "the neighbors" (acting as a form of interiorized "superego" controlling behavior) compels otherwise liberal or relaxed parents to intervene, as a parental obligation, in their child's "playing-out" activities. The presence of children and their play in an otherwise quiet and generally orderly environment adds to the potential for the behavior to be viewed as a "polluting presence" in an ordinarily adult space, "discrepant and undesirable."[19] Any group of children playing in or around Jay Road is viewed as "alien" and a potential threat to the residents' safety or comfort.

One parent on the street, Jane, described having the most ideal summer as her two eldest children, girls aged ten and eight, spent weeks "running in pink tutus . . . through the gap in the fence to and from each other's gardens." In keeping with what cultural geographers have referred to as the "pure space" adults construct around idealized depictions of a country upbringing, Jane equates these simple childhood pleasures and this level of freedom and with her own country childhood in southern Ireland.[20] The "naturalness," and the safe intra-household relations generated through "kids playing with the neighbors' kids in the fresh air," was placed in opposition to the otherwise contrived and heavily policed approach to children's play in London in general.

In keeping with the popular discourse around computers and children, several mothers expressed concern that their children were jeopardizing educational pursuits or avoiding more "active outside games" in preference to computer games.[21] However, in keeping with a general view of parenting in Britain, they still preferred their children to confine their activities to the domestic sphere.[22]

The domestication of middle-class children, and the use of toys as a means of bringing children in "from the street" and managing "extraordinarily powerful [child/parent] discourses" have a strong historical precedent.[23] But it is across the range of housing and social groups on Jay Road that the contradictory expectations of contemporary caregiving are experienced. On the one hand, there is the desire to allow children "freedom of expression," associated with contemporary notions of child development, in the context of a safe collective, community life. On the other hand, there is the social obligation to limit risk and protect children from potentially hazardous social and physical situations, as well as the cultural imperative to maintain privacy. This, as Holloway and Valentine contend, is not merely a practical dilemma but an historical shift with significant ideological ramifications; "childhood . . . has been increasingly domesticated over the course of the past two centuries. This process is not simply a material one, in the sense that children are spending increasing amounts of time in the home, but is also ideological, in that there is a sense in which this is where children should spend their time."[24]

As the risk taking of childhood is moved even further from the unsupervised physical geography of the park and the street, consumption and the exchange of related knowledge becomes the key means through which children generate an autonomous, risk-filled "space" of negotiation and social interaction. In this respect, the "currency" and temporality of brands, goods, and designs takes on a crucial role in the formation of middle childhood.[25]

Object Lessons: The Temporal World of Children's Goods

What I'm going to tell you [confiding to ethnographer] is a bit embarrassing—so you're not to tell nobody, right? My mum got me some Power Rangers pajamas for Christmas! Can you believe that? I'm ten years old and she goes and gets me Power Rangers. . . . She thought I liked them so I was pretending to be pleased but then she asked me if I wanted to take them [the pajamas] on holiday and I said "no" and pretended the other pair was more comfortable.

Certainly, according to fieldwork in north London, children have an intense and exacting relation to the commodity world expressed in an avid interest in the accumulation and acquisition of "things." But as shown in child-focused studies of play, a child's relation to the commercial product presents a model far more complex than the vision of the "stereotypical tabulae rasae of the modern commercial world."[26] Rather, as revealed in the preceding excerpt taken from a conversation with ten-year-old Jake regarding his "embarrassing" Power Ranger pajamas, all goods are incorporated into the microcosm of individual children's social worlds and the tentative moral economies of their households and parental relations.

Although the latest merchandizing offshoot might be eagerly sought after as a birthday present at one moment, its appeal quickly wanes as the style and age association becomes a source of social embarrassment within the broader peer group, as described by ten-year-old Shelley: "I got some annoying pajamas for my birthday—I got Care Bear pajamas [laughing] from my aunty! I pretended I liked them when she was there but then I got my mum to take them back [to the shop]."

Children's "annoyance" and "embarrassment" with receiving inappropriate styles of gifts is framed in a sense of knowing fondness of adult incompetence in such matters, rather than avaricious intent. Indeed, children identify "the embarrassing" relative's gift as part of a repertoire of adult gifts they will receive annually for Christmas or birthdays.[27]

Ten-year-old Phoebe recalls, with playful hilarity, one of the consistently "bad" items of clothing she received from her Aunty in Ghana: "My Aunty Margo, she sent me down this horrible body suit. It was all different types of green and I haven't wore [sic] it at all because it was really horrible and it made you feel 'yuk.' It was ghastly. I didn't tell her I didn't like it because it might have upset her. I said I loved it and I'd love to wear it but I'd use it for special occasions. And I never did [laughing]!"

While homemade goods are understood as encapsulating a thoughtful gesture, they are the most likely items to be pilloried as inappropriate gifts, as illustrated in this quote from Kelsey: "My grandma makes clothes for me but they're not very nice, like nighties and things. But they're not very nice. . . . I've never said to my grandma [that] I don't like them—but they're all covered with horrid pictures or patterns." Eleven-year-old Philip was much happier with his Auntie's gift because he informed her exactly what brand of microscooter to buy: "I wanted a Huffy because they're the best at the moment and so I gave her the product code number and price and everything in case she got it wrong."

On the surface, such ethnographic insights might substantiate critiques of children's consumption as materialistic, superficial, and brand dominated. But in each of the quotes cited what is clear is the child's sensitivity to the actual relationship in which the particular good is framed. Children describe the great lengths they go to disguise their disappointment with, or embarrassment at, a particular gift; from hiding age-inappropriate "uncool" soft toys at the back of the drawer to pretending to play enthusiastically with a computer game that's already "past its sell-by date" and an embarrassment to peers.

Adults' general inability to "correctly" select a desirable gift without due guidance is seen as part of a successful and normative child/adult relationship. Similarly, parents and caregivers themselves frequently express dismay at their children's inability to identify appropriately desirous goods as a symptom of some broader anomie.

Bob and Judy, living in a two-bedroom maisonette on Jay Road, discuss their concern over their son's recent birthday gift request and resort to using a widely distributed shopping catalogue in an attempt to "correct" their son's choice of toy: "The eldest one he wanted a 'Mr. Frosty.' I mean he's ten year old and he wants a Mr Frosty! Because last year in the summer on the way home from shopping we'd stop at the sweet shop at the top [of the street] and get what they call a Slush Puppy. Well, Mr. Frosty does the self-same thing . . . so he wanted one of them and he couldn't think of anything else, so as we're going through the Argos [shopping] catalogue we saw some Power Rangers so we got him that as well." These particular parents find the request for a soft-drink maker so incongruous as a gift appropriate to the normal desires of a preadolescent boy that they supplement his choice with plastic figures representing "action" characters from a popular children's television show. The choice of Mr. Frosty as a birthday gift challenges the parental perception of their child's development in terms of gender and age; in so doing it crucially undermines their role as parents and the "success" of the household.

For some parents (irrespective of income) providing their child with the most recent computer game is deemed an imperative of respectable parenting and caring. For others, faddish games and expensive technology are avoided as part of a conscious effort to resist what one parent described as the "escalating gift wars" indicative of an increasing media- and consumer-literate generation of children. More frequently, the gifting of children is positioned (through the choice of goods or an adherence to a notionally appropriate budget) between the extremes of providing a gamut of extravagant treats and a limited range of instructive or educational presents. In keeping with popular discourse regarding the commercialization of childhood, many parents complained about the pressure they felt to provide an increasing array of goods for their children. But the most distraught parents are not those whose children show a preoccupation with consumer goods but rather those whose children express minimal or negligible interest in contemporary toys or games.

Helen and Jim live in a two-bedroom flat on Sparrow Court state housing complex. Both have been unemployed for three years and so rely on welfare support and consumer credit to support their family. They have four children ranging from four to ten years of age. The most recent Christmas celebration caused great concern for the couple, as their children showed little interest in writing lists for Santa Claus. Although such lists often contain fantastical requests, they are used by parents to gain some idea of a child's desired repertoire of gifts.[28] Traditionally floated up the chimney over an open fire, more recent variations involve caregivers encouraging children to post their Christmas lists to a fictional address in Lapland or leave them pinned to the mantelpiece or equivalent domestic focal point. Similarly, visits to "Santa Claus's Grotto" in department stores is a secular pre-Christmas custom in which children are expected to articulate their material desires in exchange for good behavior. This is typically followed up after Christmas by an adult (relative or friend of the family) asking of a child "what did Santa get you?"—a question intended to elicit a response in which the child lists their favorite gifts and toys received. Children's articulation of material desires is, then, at least in terms of popular culture viewed as a positive indication of burgeoning selfhood.

It is unsurprising then, that even though Helen and Jim live on a limited income, shopping for their children's ideal gifts remains paramount. Despite financial restrictions, they are keen to see their children enjoy the anticipation involved in daydreaming about, and then excitedly opening, their presents in a manner that constitutes a "normal" family Christmas.

In response to their children's obvious apathy in identifying potential gifts, the parents desperately resorted to purchasing a fairly arbitrary range of toys from Argos (bulk retail outlet), Toys R Us, and Poundstretchers (budget store) in an attempt to cover all facets of a generalized notion of children's needs and desires:

> [We got] two little sets of police things, helicopter, four Power Rangers [plastic figures] from Toys R Us. It didn't matter because they ended up with stocking-fillers which were: a tangerine; a car; some small toys so when they get up in the morning they know they can have them. We got the police sets from Poundstretchers. We got John a Haunted Castle [game] and something to do with art. Then the youngest, all he wanted was a digital watch and he gave us no idea of what he wanted, that was as far as his mind would go. She's so small [four-year-old daughter] so we got her a doll, some hair bands, and a toy telephone.

In the absence of the children's desire, Helen and Jim were compelled to buy a collection of normative gifts in keeping with the age and gender range of their children, and then offset this with more "educational" articles in an attempt to stymie any negative affects of what they perceive as their children's passive consumption and malaise.

As preadolescent children gain greater autonomy, they invert the established child/parent relation, whereby the child poses a risk of social liability.[29] They begin to suffer the embarrassment of their affiliations with adults in the form, for example, of inappropriate gifts such as out-of-fashion toys and hand-made sweaters. In this way, children and parents engage in a tentative and dynamic process of morality making, mediated by the normative as constructed through strategies of child/parent gift giving. Commodities, mass-produced and easily accessible, offer the ideal form around which the normative is constructed. Items, such as highly expressive or homemade artifacts, which have maximum value in the nonmarket sphere of the household, hold minimal currency in the public realm of the children's playground, as they defy the requisite normativity.[30] Consequently, readily available shop catalogues, such as Argos, a widely distributed British publication listing a vast array of toys and general wares, is a vital medium bridging household and playground, through which children accumulate and circulate child-specific knowledge around goods.

Argos shopping catalogue, a full-color publication delivered free to homes or collectable from the local Argos store, provides an expansive overview of available consumer goods, and an exciting glimpse into the adult world of shopping, and a format for developing an intensely focused, child-specific culture around commodities. But the particular currency of the Argos catalogue (there are two seasonal editions each year) is its temporality; each season's edition features the plethora of "latest" toys and games. Even in households in which consumerism is overtly discouraged by parents, this particular catalogue is used by the household as a rationalized means of pricing goods and choices.[31]

Browsing and consulting the pages of catalogues, children and parents chart the temporality of contemporary material culture. Postman Pat bedspreads swiftly supersede Tele-Tubby bed linen, as the popularity of children's fictional television characters peaks and wanes. A Mega-Drive eagerly sought after one week may become entirely redundant as a current children's gift a few months later. In this context, catalogues such as Argos, in this particular locality of north London, provide a medium through which children can bring the information and culture of their interaction with other children to bear upon their parents.

JEROME: I love catalogues—I like looking at computer games, bikes, and some other stuff.

CINDY: I look in my mum's catalogues and I always put a mark round which ones I like and I wish I was old enough to get those things and I go to my mum "can I get that?"

MATTHEW: Get this. My mum's been looking at this catalogue yesterday and so there's two big catalogues I got—right—and I was looking at one of them and mum was looking at the same things and I was just looking in the kids section.

NOAH: I like the Argos catalogue—to see if there are any new computer games—and watches I bought one in there with my pocket money.

JAMIE: I looked in the Argos catalogue and there was a very nice picture of it [a remote-control car] so I looked at that a lot daydreaming about it.

RADHA: I look in Argos catalogue near Christmas. If my mum and dad can't think of anything they just ask me and I look through it.

NATALIE: I got a ring, I looked with mum and dad—I like those, I like those—sovereign ring from the catalogue and a chain with a Jesus cross out of the catalogue.

The Argos catalogue, in terms of its physical and cultural location, at once occupies space in the domestic sphere (it is a staple across households on Jay Road) and the playground. It is used in the home with adults and siblings, and conceptually (if not physically) in the playground with peer groups. Many children in this age group are able (and proud) to recite from memory page numbers that feature particularly "hot" goods. It might be easy to assume that a child's use of domestic forms, such as the Argos catalogue among peers, simply involves the reproduction or mimicry of a household's "philosophy" or parental opinion.[32] Children use domesticated objects and information, such as the Argos catalogue, however, in a way that frequently defies or contests adult provisioning.

In her ethnographic study of primary school children, Allison James considers the ways in which children create distinct social relations at home and at school. In this context, the "lunch box" acts as an object bringing messages directly from home into the child's social relations of the school; "the packed lunch in its confusing of two important domains in a child's social experience, is a potentially highly charged and emotive commodity. It represents food from the social context of the home which is eaten within the cultural context of school and in the company of other children."[33] Due to its domesticated status, children strategize around this poignant object and its contents, hiding, for example, food substances considered normal within the home but vilified by children at school. The pressure of the normative in this context has serious ramifications for children requiring "special" foods or diets, or for the negotiation of religious or ethnic difference made visible.

Similarly, in an inversion of the lunch-box scenario described by James, the repertoire of objects and meanings from the Argos catalogue is taken home from the peer-group associations of the playground and brought into the context of adult social relations. Despite the critical academic discourse around children and consumption, ethnographic evidence reveals the ways in which adults anticipate and encourage children as the purveyors of in-depth and sophisticated knowledge around "modern" goods, toys, and technologies. In the home, adults strategize around familiar media such as catalogues in an attempt to appropriately provision their children, particularly in the construction of "age."

Birthdays and birthday parties are the most prominent means by which stages of childhood and children (and their mothers) is expressed in British culture.[34] This attention to age as an ordering principle is, according to James, a crucial facet of the social construction of children; "each year lived through is recorded by the number of candles on the birthday cake, for it is this past upon which the child's future is deemed to rest."[35] Children continue, through schooling and educational and social achievement, to be judged and organized through the abstract concept of "age," the underpinning of social reproduction within capitalist Western societies. This belief system is intrinsically tied to the notion of children as constituting "the future," an idiom used in popular parlance and images from insurance company advertising campaigns to environmental debates. While children represent a "future" (the next generation), they also represent a past connoted by the way in which "childhood" is construed as a static condition as opposed to an experience bounded by temporal and spatial context.[36] Childhood exists in relation to the future and the past but is, according to James and Prout, rarely acknowledged as a having a present; "[children's culture] is a vibrant, adaptable culture responsive to the nuances of the adult world. There appears, then, to be a tension here between a mythical past and a modern present."[37]

The temporality accorded children's objects is not merely a reflection of children's biological age but is constitutive of the culturally specific construction of age described above. The provisioning of children with "brand new" items, for example, is indicative of a notion of "future" ascribed to a child. The idea of "brand newness" becomes particularly significant in relation to gifts that mark a visible transition in a child's development, such as learning to ride a two-wheel bicycle or "tell the time" with a wristwatch. In this way, objects such as bicycles and watches are often set apart from other toys and child-related items in their being conferred a special status most appropriately communicated in their state as pristine commodities. Ink pens might be given as markers of a rite of passage into "big" [high] school, and a geometry set signals entry to a particular class and educational stage. However, as revealed previously in the case of the Mr. Frosty drink maker and the disapproval of the child's parents regarding this gift, there is rarely such a delineated or functional facet to goods as markers of age; it is a far more complicated cultural process tentatively negotiated by adults and children.

The cosmology of children's goods, often faddish and ephemeral, is a vital part of "the processes through which reputations are acquired, mediated or lost within the social world of children."[38] Just as the telling of a playground rhyme with a skill that at once reveals consummate knowledge and innovative flair (negotiating what James describes as the constant tension in children's social relations between conformity and individuality) accords a child higher status, so too does the adroit articulation of material culture.

Children have historically expressed the particularity of their relationship with the ephemera of commodities in the act of collecting. Since the turn of the twentieth century, collecting has been encouraged as a normative aspect of childhood. In North America during the early part of the twentieth century children's collections (differing slightly according to gender) included objects such as rocks, cigar bands, birds' eggs, marbles, seashells, advertising cards, buttons, stamps, paper dolls, and pieces of cloth.[39] Studies carried out in industrial cultures throughout the twentieth century have shown collecting as a consistent feature of children's culture, with the period between nine and ten years of age revealing a peak in collecting activity.[40] Although the artifacts collected vary according to location and historical period, the phenomenon, according to Belk, is intrinsically tied to the rise of consumer culture; moreover, it is "in the process of collecting [that] collectors rehearse and imitate the market-based economy in which we are increasingly embedded."[41]

Eight-year-old Andrew, for example, has an extensive collection of samples of designer aftershave ranging from Gucci to Issey Miyake, which he keeps as prized objects, in a miniature papier-mâché portable model of an Egyptian sarcophagus he made for a school history project. Although the collection of these items is in keeping with traditional genres of childhood collecting, part of the attraction to these objects is their relation to the recognizably adult (and in this case male) world of consumption. Andrew carries his box of aftershaves to and from school and boasts of being able to discern, through smell, one item from another. Andrew relies on his mother Anne, rather than friends, to supply his collection. Anne finds it quaintly amusing and incongruous that her son should take an interest in aftershave at such a young age, but nevertheless makes frequent excursions to West End shops of London in order to persuade shop assistants in cosmetic departments to hand over free samples.

Marketing theorists and popularized critiques of children's consumption describe such activities as a pressured preadolescent desire to "fit in."[42] Similarly, this literature suggests that children also mimic the consumption behavior of adults. Certainly, children incorporate "rules" from other adult genres of consumption, such as collecting or masculine display, but they are used in keeping with the meanings of their own social relations. In this way objects, and the gift relations children have with adults, are a means of asserting and actively forming their personhood.

Children's involvement with provisioning, particularly as recipients of gifts within the household, is a far from a passive relation of socialization or a mere extension of the established (adult) moral economy of the household. Just as adults strive to mediate their children's tastes in the realm of the normative, so too children work with adults in establishing that same normativeness, as witnessed in the intricacies of ten-year-old Tessa's description of shopping with her parents:

> I like to go [shopping] with my mum and dad really because then they help me choose and they say if they liked me in something or what they prefer—well we both sort of like have a debate over it. Like if I like one thing and my mum likes it, and my dad doesn't like it, then two against

one. So we have to buy it, and he's, like, going off sulking. But if my dad likes it and wants to buy something and my mum wants to buy something and I want to buy something then it's all right. If you want to buy separate things then you go to separate shops because me and mum sort of have, like, the same taste.

Conclusion

Stylistic minutiae of toys, clothing, and artifacts are scrutinized by children as they begin to make evaluations regarding appropriate or desired objects and relations. Children's gifts and gifting practices are not merely devices of socialization and extensions of a household's moral economy. Rather they become the crucial means by which households participate in a broader public culture of "the child."

Children bring to bear their own moral economies (formulated through goods and values circulating in the context of their own social relations) on the domestic world of adults. In the power relations of gifting between adults and children, each generation is aware of projecting itself onto the other and, in this process, adults and children decide whether or not to collude with or denounce the other. For example, although many children embrace the ideal of the "home-made" they clearly draw the line at accepting (except through tolerance and good grace) unfashionable or "out-of-date" items that challenge the temporality of their material cultural worlds. Children may at once willingly respect the intentions of adults and wilfully assert themselves against them, mocking "embarrassing" presents while also making strenuous efforts to hide their parents' shame. Both can chose to point out the discrepancies or respect them, and they might do either depending on the state of play of the relationship itself, because the potential to sanction either by humiliation is great.

Children's normative gift culture, by incorporating brands and the temporality of designed goods, constitutes a form of space in which the contradictory expectations of contemporary caregiving are enacted. With the increasing domestication of children's lives, this "space"—of objects and the minutiae of design—replaces the public space of "the street" as a key arena of knowledge making and risk taking crucial to the construction of children's personhood and moral worlds.

NOTES

1. David Buckingham, *After the Death of Childhood: Growing up in the Age of Electronic Media* (Malden, Mass.: Polity, 2000); Gary Cross, *Kids' Stuff: Toys and the Changing World of American Childhood* (Cambridge: Harvard University Press, 1997); Stephen Kline, *Out of the Garden: Toys, TV, and Children's Culture in the Age of Marketing* (London: Verso, 1993); Susan Linn, *Consuming Kids: The Hostile Takeover of Childhood* (New York: New Press, 2004); Sue Palmer, *Toxic Childhood: How The Modern World Is Damaging Our Children And*

What We Can Do About (London: Orion, 2006); Neil Postman, *The Disappearance of Childhood* (New York: Random House, 1994); Juliet Schor, *Born to Buy: The Commercialized Child and Consumer Culture* (New York: Scribner, 2004).

2. Susan Matt, "Children's Envy and the Emergence of the Modern Consumer Ethic, 1890–1930," *Journal of Social History* 36.2 (2002): 283–302.

3. Thomas Daniel Cook, *Commodification of Childhood: The Children's Clothing Industry and the Rise of the Child Consumer* (Durham: Duke University Press, 2004); Cross, *Kids' Stuff.*

4. Paula Fass, "Children and Globalization," *Journal of Social History* 36.4 (2002): 963–977.

5. Kline, *Out of the Garden*, 12.

6. Allison James, *Childhood Identities, Self and Social Relationships in the Experience of the Child* (Edinburgh: Edinburgh University Press, 1993); Lydia Martens, Dale Southerton, and Sue Scott, "Bringing Children (and Parents) into a Sociology of Consumption: Towards a Theoretical and Empirical Agenda," *Journal of Consumer Culture* 4.2 (2004): 155–182; Ellen Seiter, *Sold Separately: Children and Parents in Consumer Culture* (New Brunswick: Rutgers University Press, 1993); B. Sutton-Smith, *Toys as Culture* (New York: Gardner Press, 1986).

7. Daniel Miller, "How Infants Grow Mothers in North London" in *Consuming Motherhood*, edited by Janelle S. Taylor, Linda L. Layne, and Danielle F. Wozniak (New Brunswick: Rutgers University Press, 2004); Mihaly Csikszentmihalyi and Eugene Rochberg-Halton, *The Meaning of Things: Domestic Symbols and the Self* (Chicago: University of Chicago Press, 1981).

8. Schor, *Born to Buy*, 11.

9. Martin Lindstrom and Patricia Seybold, *Brainchild: Remarkable Insights into the Minds of Today's Global Kids and Understanding Their Relationship with Brands* (Sterling, Va.: Kogan Page, 2003).

10. Pia Christensen and Allison James, eds., *Research with Children: Perspectives and Practices* (London: Falmer, 2000); Alan Prout, *The Future of Childhood* (London: Routledge, 2005)

11. Allison James and Alan Prout, "Re-presenting Childhood: Time and Transition in the Study of Childhood," in *Constructing and Reconstructing Childhood: Contemporary Issues in the Sociological Study of Childhood*, edited by Allison James and Alan Prout (London: Falmer, 1990), 220.

12. An exception to this is Elizabeth Chin, *Purchasing Power: Black Kids and American Culture* (Minneapolis: University of Minnesota Press, 2001). Chin's ethnographic study of African American fifth-grade children challenges the popular racialized and social class stereotype of "black kids" as "combat consumers" who express unthinking desire for a gamut of branded goods.

13. Christmas is identified in this study as the principal descriptive term for a festival or holiday period during which the gifting of children took place, as described by the subjects of the ethnography themselves. However, it should be noted that "Christmas" was commonly added to or conflated with celebrations of other religious and ethnic origin, most typically Hanukkah and Eid in families on the street, and was most commonly referred to as a secular event. For analysis of Christmas as a secularized child-centric festival of gift giving, see Claude Lévi-Strauss, "Le Père Noël supplicié," *Les temps modernes* 77 (1952): 1572–1590, translated as "Father Christmas Executed" in *Unwrapping Christmas*, edited by Daniel Miller (Oxford: Oxford University Press, 1993), 38–51; Adam Kuper, "The English Christmas and the Family: Time out and Alternative Realities" in *Unwrapping Christmas*, edited by Miller, 157–175; Russell. W. Belk, "Materialism and the

Making of the Modern American Christmas," in *Unwrapping Christmas*, edited by Miller, 75–104.

14. Daniel Miller, *A Theory of Shopping* (London: Polity, 1998); James McNeal, *Children as Consumers* (Austin: University of Texas, 1987).

15. Pierre Bourdieu, *Distinction: A Social Critique of the Judgement of Taste* (Cambridge: Harvard University Press, 1987); Kline, *Out of the Garden*; Linn, *Consuming Kids*; Schor, *Born to Buy*.

16. For a more detailed discussion of the field site in relation to child rearing and the ways in which values around maternity are materialized through the consumption of goods and space, see Alison J. Clarke, "Maternity and Materiality: Becoming a Mother in Consumer Culture," in *Consuming Motherhood*, edited by Janelle S. Taylor, Linda Layne, and Danielle F. Wozniak (New Brunswick: Rutgers University Press, 2004), 55–71; and Clarke, "Mother Swapping: The Trafficking of Nearly New Children's Wear," in *Commercial Cultures: Economies, Practices, Spaces*, edited by Peter Jackson, Michelle Lowe, Daniel Miller, and Frank Mort (Oxford: Berg, 2000), 85–100.

17. Hugh Matthews, Melanie Limb, and Mark Taylor, "The 'Street as Thirdspace,'" in *Children's Geographies: Playing, Living, Learning*, edited by Sarah Holloway and Gill Valentine (London: Routledge, 2000), 63.

18. Tracey Skelton, "Nothing to Do, Nowhere to Go? Teenage Girls and 'Public Space' in the Rhondda Valleys, South Wales," in *Children's Geographies*, edited by Sarah Holloway and Gill Valentine (London: Routledge, 2000), 80–99. See also Paul Watt and Kevin Stenson, "*The Street*: 'It's a Bit Dodgy around There'; Safety, Danger, Ethnicity and Young People's Use of Public Space," in *Cool Places: Geographies of Youth Cultures*, edited by Tracey Skelton and Gill Valentine (London: Routledge, 1998), 249–265.

19. Matthews, Limb, and Taylor, "The 'Street as Thirdspace,'" 63.

20. Owain Jones, "Melting Geography: Purity, Disorder, Childhood and Space" in *Children's Geographies*, edited by Holloway and Valentine (London: Routledge, 2000), 29–47.

21. Daniel Miller and Don Slater, eds., *The Internet: An Ethnographic Approach* (Oxford: Berg, 2000); Gill Valentine, "Transforming Cyberspace: Children's Interventions in the New Public Sphere," in *Children's Geographies*, edited by Holloway and Valentine (London: Routledge, 2000), 156–173.

22. Jane Ribbens, *Mothers and Their Children: A Feminist Sociology of Childrearing* (London: Sage, 1994), 83.

23. David Hamlin, "The Structures of Toy Consumption; Bourgeois Domesticity and the Demand for Toys in Nineteenth-century Germany," *Journal of Social History* 36.4 (2003): 857–869. See also J. H. Plumb, "The New World of Children in Eighteenth-century England," in *The Birth of a Consumer Society: The Commercialization of Eighteenth-Century England*, edited by Neil McKendrick, John Brewer, and J. H. Plumb (London: Europa Publications, 1982), 286–315, for an exploration of constitution of childhood and the growth of a eighteenth-century consuming middle class.

24. Sarah Holloway and Gill Valentine, "Children's Geographies and the New Social Studies of Childhood," in *Children's Geographies*, edited by Holloway and Valentine (London: Routledge, 2000), 15.

25. My initial research did not set out to consider "children" as a distinct category within consumption practise, but in the course of participant observation, and informal interviews and discussions, children emerged as a key part of the study. Walking children to and from local schools, attending school fairs and nearly-new sales, offering impromptu childcare and babysitting, playing with children in their homes, attending

(with mothers) child-related activities such as gymnastics and dance, library visits, park visits, and walks all formed part of my interaction with children. The data extrapolated from the broader participant observation was supplemented by specific research in the form of small discussion groups regarding children's gifting practices, conducted at a state primary school local to the field site. Interviews at the local primary school were conducted with the entire cross-section of classes on the nine-to-eleven age range, with the full consent and support of parents and teachers.

26. Gilles Brougère, "Le jouet: Valeurs et paradoxes d'un petit object secret," *Autrement* 133 (Paris, 1992), 16–27; Gary Cross, *Toys in the Making of American Children* (Cambridge: Harvard University Press, 1996). The quote is from B. Sutton-Smith, *The Ambiguity of Play* (Cambridge: Harvard University Press, 1997), 153.

27. The possibility of an adult misgauging the "correct" gift acted as a potential inversion of normal child-adult power relations. It is precisely this capacity for embarrassment that renders homemade or unique gifts a potential source of vulnerability for the adult in the child-adult gift relation. As Daniel Miller has argued extensively, contemporary commodities offer themselves as more appropriate gifts than the classic Maussian "inalienable" object due to their ability to generate low-risk, socially mediated salience and rationalized price-related value. See, for example, Daniel Miller, "Alienable Gifts and Inalienable Commodities," in *The Empire of Things: Regimes of Value and Material Culture*, edited by Fred R. Myers (Santa Fe: School of American Research Press, 2001), 91–115.

28. Asking children to write "pretend" Christmas wish lists for Santa Claus is also a research technique used by market researchers in ascertaining the currency of specific toys; see Kline, *Out of the Garden*, 187.

29. Sara Ruddick, "Maternal Thinking," in *Rethinking the Family: Some Feminist Questions*, edited by Barrie Thorne and Marilyn Yalom (New York: Longman, 1982), 76–94; Ribbens, *Mothers and Their Children*.

30. The term "playground" is used here to describe a cultural space (rather than a literal place) in which children meet and exchange with other children. This chapter goes on to describe how children themselves are used culturally as a "public space" that allows both private (household) affiliation and a broader transcendent relation to "society."

31. Alison J. Clarke, "Window Shopping at Home: Classifieds, Catalogues and New Consumer Skills," in *Material Cultures*, edited by Daniel Miller (Chicago: University of Chicago Press, 1998), 73–99.

32. Sandra Wallman, *Eight London Households* (London: Tavistock, 1984).

33. James, *Childhood Identities*, 144.

34. For a discussion of the gift-giving and social aspects of children's birthday parties in contemporary Britain, see Alison J. Clarke, "Making Sameness: The Commerce and Culture of Children's Birthday Parties," in *Gender and Consumption: Material Culture and the Commercialisation of Everyday Life*, edited by Emma Casey and Lydia Martens (London: Sage, 2007), in press.

35. James and Prout, "Re-presenting Childhood," 221.

36. For the cultural and historical construction see Harry Hendrick, *Children, Childhood and English Society, 1880–1990* (Cambridge: Cambridge University Press, 1997); Christopher Jencks, *Childhood* (London: Routledge, 1996).

37. James and Prout, "Re-presenting Childhood," 228.

38. James, *Childhood Identities*, 152.

39. Granville Stanley Hall, *Aspects of Child Life and Education* (Boston: Ginn, 1907).

40. Russell W. Belk, *Collecting in a Consumer Society* (London: Routledge, 1995); John Newson and Elizabeth Newson, *Four Years Old in an Urban Community* (Chicago: Aldine, 1968); Brenda Danet and T. Kateriel, "No Two Alike: The Aesthetics of Collecting," *Play and Culture* 2.3 (1989): 253–277. On the peak ages for collecting, see A. McGreevy, "Treasures of Children: Collections of Then and Now, or Treasures of Children Revisited," *Early Child Development and Care* 63 (1990): 33–36.

41. Belk, *Collecting in a Consumer Society*, 55.

42. Susan Linn, *Consuming Kids*; Schor, *Born to Buy*; Alissa Quart, *Branded: The Buying and Selling of Teenagers* (London: Arrow Books, 2003).

13

Inscribing Nordic Childhoods at McDonald's

HELENE BREMBECK

When going for a stroll in any Swedish city on a Saturday afternoon, one will find that the McDonald's restaurants are crowded with parents and children, especially at drive-ins near shopping malls. This is where a lot of Swedish parents relax on their way home from their weekly shopping expedition, knowing that stopping at the restaurant will allow them a break and a chat together while their children are occupied eating hamburgers and fries, examining their Happy Meal toys, mounting the climbing frame, or jumping in the ball room. Sweden is, in fact, the European country with the highest rate of McDonald's establishments per inhabitant, giving the company 150 million visitors a year, most of them teenagers or families with young children.

New phenomena contributing to McDonald's attractiveness among parents with kids are birthday parties. They were introduced in the 1980s, but are becoming increasingly popular as working life becomes more stressful, and parents experience less and less time for everyday chores. Most Swedish parents (mothers) take their time to arrange birthday parties at home for family and close relatives, and generally also bring ice cream to the day-care center or school to celebrate their child's big day. Many of them are therefore thankful for the possibility of arranging the third expected party, a children's birthday party for the friends of the child's own age, from McDonald's. On observing several birthday parties during the spring of 2003, it was obvious that one of the highlights of these parties was the treasure hunt in the kitchen, ending at the big freezer, where the children finally find their treasures—Happy Meal boxes including a toy, and generally also some discount coupons. The children joyously came jumping out of the kitchen waving their boxes, and soon the unpacking and putting together started. On opening the boxes, and finding the toy, the children always looked happy. They took up the toy and examined it carefully, alone or together with other children, and sometimes with their parents, trying to find out the way it worked, and its special features.

Pinocchio as Mediator of Child Subjectivities

During some weeks in the spring of 2003, the included toy was Pinocchio, targeting the Swedish release of the Disney film of the same name. In the McDonald's version, Pinocchio was transformed into a soft toy with its bottom half in the shape of a coil spring. The idea was to compress the coil spring and then to release it in order to make it jump. One could say that the toy carried a script in terms of its design, or a blueprint inscribed on the object, its shape, and expected handling.[1] Pinocchio was obviously designed to connect to the child in certain ways—the child should grab its upper parts and press the coil spring down to make it jump. The toy was not good for dressing, or walking, or sitting down. The children observed this right away, and they then spent a considerable time trying to make their Pinocchios jump. Thus one might argue that Pinocchio facilitated a certain kind of child subjectivity—an activity-seeking, pleasure-hunting type of child. Inscribed on Pinocchio is thus not only an idea of how to make an attractive toy but also a blueprint of a child supposed to be attracted by this jumping plaything— supposedly a child embracing activity, happenings, speed, and experience.

Pinocchio was, however, not very good at doing his thing—jumping—since the spring soon became shapeless and limp. One could easily argue that Pinocchio was quite bad at producing active pleasure hunters. One little girl, however, then started to carry her Pinocchio in her arms like a baby, an activity the fluffy and seemingly useless body might invite, thus inspiring other children to do the same. In doing so, the children transformed "Pinocchio the crazy jumper" to "Pinocchio the cuddly baby." In this transformation Pinocchio himself, or rather his limp coil spring, played an active part, making this transformation possible. One might argue that the coil spring destroys the idea of the toy as a mere representation, or materialization of discourse, to reveal itself instead as a mediator taking an active part in modifying, displacing, and translating messages to the child.[2] Subjectivity turns out to be not just a product of discourse but also a result of the subject's relations to other actors, or "actants," human as well as nonhuman,[3] where discourses can be conceived as merely one of the resources in the attempt to enroll others.[4] The competencies and subjectivities released at the meeting between Pinocchio and the little girl were obviously care and tenderness connecting to play with dolls and soft toys, and other ways of behaving and being a child that she had encountered in other parts of her life.

Using the term of Mike Michaels, one can conceive of the child and the toy as an occasional "co(a)gent," a hybrid of human and nonhuman, a child-toy, momentarily acting as a unified entity.[5] Artifacts "quietly and tacitly evoke suggestions and embody indistinct possibilities," Michaels argues, at the same time as individuals deploy various sorts of discourses trying to figure out a specific kind of use.[6] Toys like Pinocchio suggest the array of possible doings, at the same time as they distribute and extend the human in unpredictable ways.[7] Michaels sees this as a reduction of possible uses, but in the case of children this process can just as well be seen as an enlargement of the possible significations and uses of the toy due to children's imaginative and fluid way of handling objects. That children are active in shaping childhood, and ways of being a child, is mundane knowledge in childhood studies.[8] The objective of this essay is instead to argue that the boxes and toys also take an active part in the constantly transforming chain of events and actors, human as well as nonhuman, where modern childhood is being designed. Maybe it is time to "stop opposing words and world," and give the boxes and toys their rightful agency in shaping childhood.[9]

My way of highlighting this process is to follow processes of translations of the Happy Meal from an international (mainly American) context, into a Swedish (and to some extent Nordic) context. McDonald's is no doubt an international company. However, much research has proven that there is little truth in arguing that the restaurants and the menus look the same all over the world.[10] Instead, an active process of translating the global to fit local expectations, tastes, and circumstances is ongoing. In the company language this is called "localizing" or "creating local windows," and this is an important part of McDonald's worldwide success, as is the standardization of products, technologies, and staff training. And in this translation, inscriptions of local—in this case Swedish—childhoods become visible.

The Inscribed Happy Meal Child: From Happy and Grateful to Demanding and Choosy

The red Happy Meal box with its yellow handle and white text was introduced in Sweden in 1979, and was then called the "tasty-and-fun-box" (*Gott-och-skoj lådan*). On this simple object a scenario of children's (and parent's) competencies, preferences, and subjectivities were already inscribed.

The design of the box made it resemble a parcel, with the golden arches as an airy bow, a parcel bought by the parent to be opened by the child. The prime inscription was a giving parent, who presented the child with the gifts of consumer culture, and a receiving child. What was presupposed, or "put in a black box," to use Latour's words, was an unchanged generational structure.[11] Generational structuring or "generationing," according to Leena Alanen, is "the complexity of social process through which people become 'children' while other people become 'adults.'" This process involves agency of both children and adults, and is best understood as a "practical, and even material process, and can be studied as a practice, or a set of practices."[12] Much in accordance with Latour's thinking, the parental position cannot exist without the child position, in this case the more powerful giving parent and the less powerful receiving child.[13]

Yet another subordinating inscription was the surprise effect. The child was supposed to open the box with expectation, and be overjoyed with surprise, and it was this surprise effect and the thrill it created that constituted a great part of the value of the Happy Meal box. In "the black box" was the representation of the child joyously opening presents which, according to Ellen Seiter, is the oldest convention in toy advertisements, and which also includes the feelings of gratitude that will be directed at the giver/the parent, when the child opens the present.[14] Giving children presents is a way to create happiness and a spirit of community in the family, but also a way to confirm the prevailing generational structure. The child is considered a child in an obviously subordinate position in relation to adults: a predictable child, glad about little things, a child whose prime responsibility it is to rejoice at gifts from adults. One can assume that it was this expectation, or inscribed surprise effect, that contributed to the fact that the first Happy Meal toys were not particularly remarkable: tiny plastic objects that you could hardly do anything with except put on a shelf or in a box.

Increased Pleasures

During the nineties, something happened to the Happy Meal box and its contents. The times of small, simple, plastic toys were long gone. From 1998 on, the Happy Meal included Barbie and Hot Wheels. Barbie had four different outfits to change into, and the Hot Wheels cars could spark, spin, and "roar their engines." When Hot Wheels turned up again in 2002, this time in combination with Diva Stars, the cars were accompanied by different parts of a car track that could be put together to make a linked race track. To the yellow car belonged, for example, a curved piece, and a start device for pushing the car away with the aid of a small button. Diva Stars not only had various outfits to change into; they also had movable arms and legs, and a mechanical screw enabling them to move their heads and blink their eyelids.

The little red Happy Meal boxes with their simple illustrations were seen less and less; instead, the boxes came decorated with colorful pictures of the toys inside. The increasing hybridity of the toys also led to their tendency to grow out of their packages, and the boxes were often replaced with spacious decorated bags. One could question why Happy Meal boxes were needed at all, when everyone already knew what was inside. Probably first because they bestowed some dreamy and fabulous quality on the artifacts; their character as commodities, and their connection to monetary transactions, is veiled if they are put in a nice package.[15] The package also makes it possible to cling to the family illusion, and the love theme of the restaurants, that the Happy Meal is a gift from the company to the children, a reminder of how much McDonald's consider and care about each individual child. But it is also about enhancing the experience value. The packages often show the toys in action; they are not dead things but alive, and acting in magic worlds to which the child is allowed entrance with the help of the toy. This is about utilizing intertextuality, the fact that images move between various media—a Disney film, a T-shirt, a mug, a Happy Meal box, and so on.[16] Packaging is thus coproducer of the commercial world of images where children are at home. Toy and package are turned into a momentary co(a)gent, where the integral parts are both dependent on and exceed each other. The little plastic

Barbies and Hot Wheels are put into settings of action, romance, and fantasy, and the imagery on the outside of the boxes may be extended and "become alive" with the help of the toys inside and the child playing with them.

This reminds us that an object is designed both materially and semiotically. In Latour and Ackrich's wording, objects are "polysemic," where the "semic" refers as much to the material as to the semiotic.[17] The package serves to enable particular relations to the environment, and such enablement is not simply a matter of its "function" but also a reflection of its role as a cultural artifact, which signifies (that is, expresses) "fashion" regarding, for example, views on childhood, the child, and parenthood. The prescription (or affordance, following Michaels) of an object—what it allows or forbids from actors, what it anticipates—also gives it a certain kind of morality, both negative (what it proscribes), and positive (what it permits).[18]

The child "anticipated" by the boxes was a child eagerly expecting larger and more elaborate toys displayed on the package—at least this was what the new child inscription prescribed. The new inscription was of a media-wise child, familiar with the commercial world, a rather choosy child, not easily satisfied, a demanding child whom adults must make an effort to please.[19] The level of what counted as an experience was constantly raised: bigger toys, in several parts that could be handled in ever more refined ways. This was a child more equal to adults, no longer living in the protective cocoon of the home, but in the same commercialized, media-saturated society as the parents—a child with the right to consume experiences, the right to consume his or her subjectivity. It was also a child dispersed on a global level. The Disney films, gadgets, television series, and toys acted as co(a)gents at once cogent and distributed; only now the distribution extended further on a global market, and the heterogeneity was more opulent.[20] Increasingly this inscription started to clash with Swedish ideas of children, childhood, and child rearing.

Translations to Swedish

Decreasing sales for the company worldwide in the beginning of the new millennium opened up the opportunity for each national McDonald's, like McDonald's Sweden, to localize in order to get more in tune with the demands of their own market. Translations of products and activities adapted to Swedish values were ongoing. The attentiveness to guidelines of national experts as well as the voices of ordinary people was heightened. Not least important, executives were themselves mothers and fathers, and had a "gut feeling" of what was okay for Swedish parents. A process of adding values was noticeable semiotically in marketing but also materially in the range of products on offer that targeted the Swedish customer. The original inscriptions of the Happy Meal were transformed by adding values supposed to be attractive to both parents and children, such as learning, safety, and health.

Learning

In 2001, Swedish McDonald's launched its own Happy Meal programs, introducing learning as a new added value. The management argued that in Sweden "play value is not enough, something more is needed, some utility value, something causing an urge to learn." A first example was Learn for Life (*Lära för livet*), in Cupertino with the nonprofit association Movement for Reading (*Läsrörelsen*), resulting in a Happy Meal with children's books, small booklets with covers, of which one and a half million copies were distributed to all the McDonald's restaurants in Sweden during the spring of 2001. The books were all by respected Swedish authors of children's books and considered good reading for children, and the only obvious promotional quality of the books was that their good reputations were supposed to spill over onto the McDonald's brand.

In 2002, the campaign was followed by Play & Learn CD-ROMs. During three weeks, six educational CD-ROMs were included in the Happy Meal, with titles like Math, Preschool, First Grade, and English. The CD-ROM Happy Meal was an immediate success, and during the autumn of 2002 it was later followed by the Clever and Fun Happy Meal, consisting of six different activity books that taught children "useful facts" such as how to make a kite and the best way to equip your bike. Late in the summer of 2003, yet another pedagogical Happy Meal appeared. Six different discs, released two by two, were supposed to teach reading, spelling, and comprehension for children five to nine years old. Once again McDonald's was cooperating with the Movement for Reading association, and once again connections were made between learning, play, and desire, as play was stressed as an absolute condition to "really learn for life." It is important to note that the books and CDs where indeed polysemic. They were associated with pedagogy, and their physical shapes as books and CDs made them pedagogic devices rather than mere toys, and thus something Swedish parents might be interested in letting their children play with.

On the Danish home page, pedagogic added value is so far seen in, for example, the computer game McDonaldland that is marketed as "fun and educating." On the home pages in many countries, McDonaldland exists as a set of games heavily promoting the McDonaldland characters. Not only are they guides to the various digital attractions but you are also supposed to memorize their faces in the Memory game, draw them by connecting numbers, or paint them using a digital brush. In most countries these characters are well known to children, but in the Scandinavian countries these characters have always been met with suspicion, probably for being too openly branded in an American way. They have never been properly introduced, although attempts have been made. In the Danish McDonaldland, Ronald McDonald is indeed the guide, but the rest of the McDonaldland characters are absent, and the games contain no promotional characters. Walking around McDonaldland, the child will learn not only letters and numbers but also about plants and animals, and facts about different countries—games where the educational value equals the entertaining. These games are, in fact, very similar to the ones on the Swedish Play and Learn CD-ROM. Computer games are also pedagogic devices, and computer technology is often presented as having an enormous potential for informal learning by children, and moreover in a way that questions traditional generational structuring. Children are often seen as superior to adults in relation to computers, acting as their guides to the new digital worlds.[21]

McDonald's chooses to prolong these new, supplementary values via the packages themselves. On the bags with the educational CD-ROM games, the words Play & Learn are repeated in large letters, and the paper is filled with drawings seemingly made by children, all in order to elucidate and prolong the value of the disc. Another kind of child subjectivity is inscribed; another type of action is presupposed. The urge to learn is emphasised, as well as values such as curiosity, imagination, and creativity. The fanciful, creative child in the new knowledge society, in the new experience economy, is the ideal. Maybe the child script produced by McDonald's during the late nineties was giving birth to a child that was regarded as too fastidious, too spoiled, and too competent to agree with a Swedish audience—a child regarded as having too many traits of the "cool child." Gary Cross argues this child has followed the child characterized by "wondrous innocence," a child script that needed to be supplemented by a design of a child defined as learning, growing, put in place in relation to adults with the aid of pedagogical games and activities.[22]

Safety

Introducing CD-ROMs also invites children out of the secluded childhood garden of Rousseau to the adult world. New fears have to be dealt with, and safety precautions taken. This is addressed by the Danish McDonaldland, which should, therefore, not only be fun and educating but also a safe place for children. Different parental fears about children and computer games, following in the footsteps of the digital revolution that threatens to turn the generational order upside down, are cleverly met. Parents may limit the time spent in McDonaldland by setting a clock for the time the game closes down, "to prevent discussions at bedtime." And the game opens in full screen, preventing the child from clicking his or her way out into the dangerous cyberspace on his or her own.[23] Fears of children "getting stuck" in the game, or making the acquaintance of pedophiles or other dangerous persons on the net, are also frequent in the Swedish debate, although this has not resulted in any special warnings on McDonald's home page.[24]

Danish McDonald's moreover takes care of the children's bodies. Too much sitting in front of the computer causes pains in arms, neck, and back for adults, and children are even more at risk, the home page warns. Their bodies might "grow into unhealthy positions," giving them lasting pains almost impossible to get rid off. The new childhood materiality of the computer is hazardous, and might transform not only children's subjectivities but also their bodies in unpredictable ways. The childhood garden is turned into a workplace, and the child into a flexible worker and lifelong learner. To prevent physical disaster, signs for gymnastic breaks appear every fifteenth minute. "Healthy and fun exercises" for children made by a physiotherapist appear on the screen. The home page also gives children good advice on how to be sure to avoid getting hurt working in front of the computer—for example, always to sit facing the window to avoid reflections on the screen that could hurt the eyes. Here we see a new added value appearing side by side with amusement and learning: the healthy body—not surprising, since much attention has recently been given to overweight children in bad physical shape, and the fast-food industry, and especially McDonald's, have been pointed out as scapegoats. Thus equipped and safeguarded, the Danish child may enter on an entertaining and instructive expedition in McDonaldland, at least until the screen shuts down.

Health

Another way of connecting to health in the wake of the rising moral panic about sugar, fat, and overweight children, was the introduction by Swedish McDonald's in the spring of 2003 of baby carrots as an alternative to French fries. At McDonald's restaurants in many countries customers have long been able to add to their meals foil bags filled with small pieces of apple, obviously considered a snack or a desert. But this was the first time in McDonald's history you were able to change the fries altogether for something else: baby carrots, and it first happened in the Happy Meal. "Straight from the garden plot, with loads of vitamins and healthy fibers," ads in the daily papers announced.

Of course carrots are easy to put in little bags and transport all over the country, but so are quite a lot of other vegetables and fruits. And likewise, there are other root vegetables that could just as well serve as replacements for French fries. The naturalness by which the carrot had popped up in the minds of the McDonald's officials had its causes: it was rooted in the position of the carrot in traditional Swedish cooking and, more generally, in Swedish culture, for both adults and children. The point to be made here is that even such mundane objects as baby carrots incorporate ideologies, discourses, histories, and moralities, but that these ideologies, discourses, histories, moralities, and so on are always transformed by the materiality, the physical shape of the mediating object. The carrot connects children to great chunks of Swedish history and morality, and these discourses are translated by the appealing physical shape of the baby carrot. Carrots are thus considered good co(a)gents to Swedish children.

The carrots are certainly not just about health. Neither are they just about morality. They also have texture, taste, and materiality. They have a sweetish taste that children are supposed to be fond of. They are almost like candies. In fact, the Swedish producer markets them as "slim-candies" for children. They have a bright appealing color, rendering them funny and toylike. Making the carrots very small, cutting large ones into small pieces, turning them into cute little "babies," are supposed to be especially appealing to children, at the same time as the orange color signifies safety for parents, acting almost like a life jacket for the juicy content. And of course the size also makes them just right to put into children's mouths, already peeled and washed, easily chewed, echoing Zygmund Bauman and his prophesy about today's children losing the capacity for commitment.[25] American children can't even commit themselves to an orange long enough to peel it, he regrets, but want to consume it as juice: the baby carrot could also be counted in this line of easy consumable goods.

A number of interviews with parents at McDonald's reveal that this quality of the baby carrot might be even more desirable to parents than to children. Working couples with young children live in a state of constant stress and lack of time, and are, indeed, in need of products not needing too much commitment. Swedish parents are also generally convinced that children have the right to a good childhood, including the right to get their needs and wishes fulfilled, and moreover that it is their duty as parents to see to this. Parents thus become mediators of a lifestyle of low product commitments for their children, and the baby carrot is a perfect vehicle. Not only is it cute, fun, candylike, easily consumable, healthy, and safe but it also holds definite pedagogical associations.

To sum up, the baby carrot can be regarded as a hybrid of taste, health, safety, fun (safety vest, toy, enjoyment, pedagogical device, nourishment)—a perfect mediator of the fears, hopes, and enjoyments of our time. It imbues a certain childscript: children as valuable, in need of protection, children as persons with special needs—for example, concerning nutritional content and child-size pieces—but also as persons with rights to enjoyment, fun, bright colors, and sweet, nice tastes. It is not certain that children will adopt this subjectivity. The materiality of the baby carrot also gives children a certain kind of independence and confidence, doing away with the generational order—at least if they are old enough to open the stubborn plastic bags that keep them in a subordinate position to adults. The easily consumed character of the carrot crunches also position consumption as easy and enjoyable, making the impatient consumer instantly ready for new enjoyments.

Objects are not one and the same, but are given different roles and agencies, or rather co(a)gencies, in the different settings or networks they pass. On one hand, products like baby carrots are ways of commodifying parent's fears for children's health, their needs for relief in everyday chores, and their belief in children's right to a good childhood, including fun and tasty food. They are also the socially reliable company's way of listening to the demands of children, parents, nutritional experts, and governmental boards the corporate way, to answer the call from authorities to do their share in promoting healthier lifestyles. For children, the child/carrot co(a)gent might imbue independence: always being able to treat yourself to nice, tasty, ready-to-eat mouthfuls of healthy food without adults present; or increased dependence, since the bags, "mediating" the carrots to the child, are made of an especially stubborn, "breathable" plastic difficult for small children to open without adult assistance. Webs of co(a)gency are not always easy to spot or delimit: to know where to look, where to stop, what the important connections are. According to Latour, it is all a matter of taste or of framing.[26]

The Dog—An Example of a Bad Fit

The carrots, books, and CD-ROMs have all been accepted by Swedish parents and children. Successful translations have occurred. To be accepted and used, objects and ideas must be recognizable by the intended audience. They must resemble what is already known and taken for granted. Things that do not match our preconceptions are met with suspicion, and might not be used at all. And this is what happened to the Happy Meal promotion called "The Dog."

"The Dog" was launched in April 2004 to celebrate the twenty-fifth birthday of the Happy Meal, and was supposed to reach and unite children worldwide. It was designed to "capture the hearts and imaginations of kids, and delight collectors of all ages." The inspiration was a Japanese puppy photography franchise consisting of more than seventy different breeds of puppies photographed with exaggerated proportions, where the heads of the puppies were "charmingly enlarged." The twelve breeds selected by McDonald's featured the same exaggerated characteristics. "McDonald's is thrilled to bring the most desirable new toys, and characters to our young guests," exclaims McDonald's director of kids and family marketing.[27] Each Happy Meal Dog featured colorful plastic collars that transformed into clips, so children could walk their favorite dogs on backpacks, belts, zippers, or purses. In addition, each dog came with a hand tag with a picture of the dog, and a checklist helpful for collecting all twelve breeds.

But these heartbreaking global puppies were not considered possible to "read" or "describe" in Sweden,[28] and they were never introduced in this country. The exaggerated features and extended noses did not resonate very well with Swedish ideas of cuteness and childhood. Within such a framework they seemed unfamiliar, and almost hostile. The enlarged noses seem almost intrusive, and could not be interpreted using recognizable categories relating to Swedish childhood. Likewise, Manga-like figures like Hello Kitty has had a hard time getting acceptance in Sweden because of their large eyes and immobile faces (kind toys should smile). In fact Hello Kitty, who is one of the favorites in Southeast Asian McDonald's restaurants for girls of all ages, has never been introduced in Sweden.[29] This is just one example of the vanity of some "global" toys and appeals.

Jafar—An Example of a Good Fit

Although The Dog was not accepted, there are other truly global toys that are accepted by Swedish children and their parents, not least Disney characters. Films and promotions of Disney have a special place in the heart of Swedish parents,[30] who remember from their own childhood films like Snow White and Cinderella. They are possible to interpret, to translate using existing frames and categories. This good reputation also spills over to new films and to creatures that can be said to be no more appealing than The Dog, for example the wizard Jafar from Disney's "Aladdin."

Jafar was included in the Fantillusion Parade Happy Meal that succeeded Pinocchio at the birthday parties discussed in the beginning of this chapter, and to which we will now briefly return. The Fantillusion Parade mimicked the parade by the same name of thirteen Disney characters on moving platforms at Disneyland Paris. The Happy Meal included six of these platforms, all of them with buttons and sticks to manipulate. If you press the button on Jafar's platform, out jumps a dragon, which is fired by the use of a spring. Together with Ursula, the witch from Disney's "The Little Mermaid," who came jumping out of her "sea platform" when her button was pressed, Jafar was a very popular gift at the birthday parties. Considerable commitment was given to this toy, which demanded a lot of cunning and dexterity to put together. The children often collaborated, trying to find out how to assemble it and how to make it work. The boys were especially insistent. There was a lot of pressing at buttons and manipulating of springs, and lots of laughter and comparisons of skills, and inventive ways to use the toys. However there was a considerable difference in the children's abilities to assemble and manipulate the toys. Especially the younger ones retreated to their parent, and the act of assembling often became a family project, with parents and older siblings bending their necks over miniature blueprints and stubborn plastic bags with obscure toy pieces.

This is a reminder that inscribing subjectivities is not enough to make them happen, just as researching practices of inscription is not enough to understand today's childhood. Ethnography, too, is needed. Participant observation shows that children might not want to carry on the chain of translations, or they might transform things and ideas, targeting them in unpredictable ways, using categories that they are accustomed to. Obviously the subjectivities released in the meeting of the child and the Happy Meal toy could be far from the inscribed learning of the millennium child—for example, traditional gender roles of female care (Pinocchio) and male engineering (Jafar). They could release cooperation (and competition) among friends as well as traditional family values, which assert that parents know best. However unpredictable, materiality, such as the coil spring of Pinocchio and Jafar's button, nevertheless enable particular relations to the environment, afford a range of actions, make certain trajectories possible, and thus play an active part in shaping childhood. It is obvious that not only childhood but also its artifacts matter. As the child passes from one context to the next, fragments of agency and identity from preceding co(a)gencies are brought, be it with Pinocchio or Jafar, giving also these mundane objects a role in shaping modern childhoods.

NOTES

Participant observations at McDonald's restaurants were made as a part of the "Commercial Cultures" project at the Center for Consumer Science (CFK), Göteborg University, www.cfk.gu.se. The article furthermore draws on data from the home page of Swedish McDonald's, including the digital Happy Meal archive; visits to collectors' exhibitions; books on McDonald's collectibles, such as Ruby and Ray Richardson and David and Lesley Irving, *McDonald's Collectibles: The Definitive Guide* (London: Apple Press, 1997); and interviews with executives, staff, and customers.

1. Madeleine Akrich, "The De-Scription of Technical Objects," in *Shaping Technology/ Building Culture. Studies in Sociotechnical Change*, edited by John Law and Wiebe Bijker (Cambridge: MIT Press, 1992), 205–225.

2. Bruno Latour, "On Recalling ANT," in *Actor Network Theory and After*, edited by John Law and John Hassard (Oxford: Blackwell), 23–34.

3. Michel Callon and Bruno Latour, "Unscrewing the Big Leviathan: How Actors Macro-structure Reality and How Sociologists Help Them to Do It," in *Advances in Social Theory and Methodology: Towards an Integration of Micro and Macro-Sociology*, edited by Knorr-Cetina and Cicouvel (London: Routledge, 1981), 116–132. According to Callon and Latour, actants may be individuals (human) as well as objects, organizations, documents, narratives, and so on (nonhuman).

4. Iver B. Neuman, *Mening, materialitet, makt: en innföring I diskursanalyse* (Oslo: Fagboksforlaget, 2001).

5. Mike Michaels, *Reconnecting Culture, Technology and Nature. From Society to Heterogeneity* (London: Routledge, 2000).

6. Michaels, *Reconnecting Culture, Technology and Nature*, 60.

7. For the argument that objects and technologies are extensions to children, see Nick Lee, *Childhood and Society: Growing up in an Age of Uncertainty* (Buckingham: Open University Press, 2001).

8. For example, Allison James and Alan Prout, eds., *Constructing and Reconstructing Childhood: Contemporary Issues in the Sociological Studies of Childhood* (London: Falmer Press, 1990); and Allison James, Chris Jenks, and Alan Prout, *Theorizing Childhood* (Cambridge: Polity Press, 1998).

9. Latour, "On Recalling ANT," 31.

10. For example, Barry Smart, "Digesting the Modern Diet: Gastro-porn, Fast Food and Panic Eating," in *The Flâneur*, edited by Keith Tester (London: Routledge, 1994), 79–91; James Watson, ed., *Golden Arches East: McDonald's in East Asia* (Stanford: Stanford University Press, 1997); Melissa Caldwell, "Domesticating the French Fry: McDonald's and Consumerism in Moscow," *Journal of Consumer Culture* 4.1 (2004): 5–26.

11. According to Callon and Latour, "black boxes" are those matters which are not called into question, "that which no longer needs to be considered, those things whose contents have become a matter of indifference." See Callon and Latour, "Unscrewing the Big Leviathan," 285.

12. Leena Alanen, "Explorations in Generational Analysis," in *Conceptualizing Child-Adult Relations*, edited by Leena Alanen and Barrie Mayall (London and New York: Routledge/ Falmer Press, 2001), 129.

13. Leena Alanen and Barrie Mayall, "Introduction," in *Conceptualizing Child-Adult Relations* (London and New York: Routledge/Falmer Press, 2001), 19.

14. Ellen Seiter, *Sold Separately: Children and Parents in Consumer Culture* (New Brunswick: Rutgers University Press, 1993), 55.

15. James G. Carrier, *Gifts and Commodities* (London: Routledge, 1994).

16. Anna Sparrman, *Visuell kultur i barns vardagsliv—bilder, medier, praktiker* (*Visual Culture in Children's Everyday Life—Images, Media and Practices*) (Linköping: Tema University, 2002), 149 ff.

17. Bruno Latour and Madeleine Akrich, "A Summary of Convenient Vocabulary for the Semiotics of Human and Nonhuman Assemblies," in *Shaping Technology/Building Culture: Studies in Sociotechnical Change*, edited by John Law and Wiebe Bijker (Cambridge: MIT Press, 1992), 259. In their redefinition of semiotics, Akrich and Latour state that it is "the study of how meaning is built, (where) the word 'meaning' is taken in its original nontextual and nonlinguistic interpretation: how a privileged trajectory is built, out of an indefinite number of possibilities; in that sense, semiotics is the study of order building or path building and may be applied to settings, machines, bodies and programming languages as well as texts."

18. Michaels, *Reconnecting Culture, Technology and Nature*, 67.

19. David Buckingham, *After the Death of Childhood: Growing up in the Age of Electronic Media* (Cambridge: Polity Press, 2000).

20. Michaels, *Reconnecting Culture, Technology and Nature*, 67.

21. Also see Barbro Johansson, "*Kom och ät!*" "*Jag skall bara dö först.*" *Datorn i barns vardag* [*"Time to eat!"* "*Okay, I'll just die first."* *The computer in children's everyday life*] (Göteborg: Etnologiska föreningen i Västsverige, 2000).

22. Gary Cross, "Valves of Desire: A Historian's Perspective on Parents, Children, and Marketing," *Journal of Consumer Research* 29.3 (2002): 441–447.

23. The U.S. home page also includes safety precautions, but only to the extent that parents are advised to keep an eye on their children's doings, and children are requested to ask their parents before answering any attempt to contact them on the net.

24. Johansson, "*Kom och ät!*" "*Jag skall bara dö först,*" 126.

25. Zygmund Bauman, "Consuming Life," *Journal of Consumer Culture* 1.1 (2001): 9–29.

26. Bruno Latour, *On Technical Mediation: The Messenger Lectures on the Evolution of Civilization*, Cornell University, Institute of Economic Research Working Paper Series (Ithaca, 1993).

27. McDonald's International, press release March 9, 2004.

28. Latour and Akrich, "A Summary of Convenient Vocabulary," 259.

29. Helene Brembeck, "Tracing Parent-Artefact-Child Relations at McDonald's: Attempts at Multilocal Feldwork," paper presented at the conference "Sociology of Childhood: Revisions and Challenges for the Future," 8th Annual Meeting of the Sociology of Childhood section of the German Sociological Association (Berlin, May 31 and June 1, 2002).

30. Gisela Eckert, Wasting Time or Having Fun?: Cultural Meanings of Children and Childhood (Linköping: Tema University, 2001).

14

"Board with the World"

Youthful Approaches to Landscapes and Mediascapes

OLAV CHRISTENSEN

Today's children and young people increasingly encounter the world with knowledge based on experience gained from the media and not from participatory practice. "Being a modern child and a modern young person means learning by learning, not learning by doing," says Kirsten Drotner, Danish media researcher.[1] In a complex day-to-day life where young people are constantly shifting between such different spheres as school, home, and recreation, the media have become important sources for understanding each area of knowledge and their relationships. The range of knowledge areas has also increased dramatically, and the recreation sphere alone comprises a rich selection of traditions we become familiar with even in our childhood. The field of sports provides a great number of choices with wide acceptance in the general public across major regions of the world, and continuously sprouts new trends. Traditional forms are reinterpreted, and technologies arise in response to the desire to challenge the basic elements of water, air, and snow in new ways.

The snowboard was a technological answer to the desire to transcribe bodily experiences from surfing waves to surfing snow. This was not a new dream in the 1960s, but the vision and the culture surrounding snowboarding developed parallel to the gradual technical development. The alternative approach to snow lost none of its appeal when snowboarders were denied access to the alpine skiing centers. Snowboarding was born as a deviation, living on the fringe and edges of an upper-class-dominated slalom culture.[2] Until the mid 1980s, snowboarding was more or less exclusively a North American practice with very limited acceptance. Then came the technological breakthrough that opened the way for the soaring virtuosity we now know as snowboarding.[3] This included a cultural diversification made possible by the emergence of internal media, and the basis for communication between various groups of snowboard freaks on the North American continent was created. By thematizing marginalization and exclusion, the media reinforced and fortified the subculture element.

Snowboarding had its breakthrough in America's mainstream media in the winter of 1987, appearing as a rebellious youth culture fronted by stars whose behavior was not unlike that of punk rock artists. Snowboarding had a very young image, and this was presented in visual media dominated by internal codes. As a lifestyle and sport, snowboarding became a new American export commodity in an increasingly globalized world, and its success was formidable in other parts of the world, such as Scandinavia. Children were also captivated by the magic of this new synthesis of bodily patterns of movement, style, and counter-cultural positioning as presented by the media. Here was a form that played to the wishes of children and young persons for positioning their identity in a globalized consumer society, a form that transcended limitations tied to place and tradition.

Methodological Reorientations

Until the wave of affluence in the 1980s, slalom skiing was a sport for the more well-to-do social groups. Snowboarding was initially derided as a mutation that would be short lived, but young Norwegians who acquired their snowboards toward the end of the 1980s were riding on the American boom. While working on a master's thesis on the nationalization of winter and skiing in Norway early in the 1990s, I began to notice these newcomers and their American-influenced preferences.[4] The predominantly alternative aspect of this approach aroused my curiosity, and when I defined my doctoral thesis project in 1995, the innovative nature of snowboarding appealed to me.[5] But I quickly found that it was difficult to acquire knowledge about this new field. My searches in literature databases and on the Internet yielded no results, and I was unaware of the existence of American snowboarding magazines. I had planned as my methodology to use surveys and formal interviews in contexts where I met snowboarders—in and around the alpine skiing hills. However, when I asked my questions among snowboarding young people, the answers were invariably "huh?" or "no time"; or I was simply ignored. The only result was that suddenly I felt much older.

I had much the same experience that sociologist Belinda Wheaton had with her field work in her doctoral research on windsurfers; I found that young people did not want to spend time answering my questions.[6] But to be honest, I must also admit that I was so clueless about this environment that my questions might have been less than stimulating. My sense of failure at least led me to recognize that if you want to ask interesting questions about a topic, you need special knowledge. What I found most uncomfortable was that I felt that people were suspicious of me: Snowboarders were young boys, and "hunting" them down on the slopes and lifts and in cafés led to suspicions that I was some kind of pedophilic predator rather than someone with serious academic curiosity. Before I realized that other approaches were necessary, I experienced my share of discomfort.

My methodological reorientation initially led me to give up on using interviews, and I now also understood that trust needed to be built. I contacted a journalist I knew who worked for one of the major Norwegian newspapers, presented my project, and argued that snowboarding was outdoor recreation on a par with cross-country skiing, and that this new tradition was deserving of our interest and attention. The outcome was an interview with me and a group of young snowboarders in a skiing center outside Oslo, and an article that for the first time presented the new sport seriously and critically. This gave me renewed confidence, so I returned to the Norwegian alpine Mecca of Hemsedal, where I put my new skis aside and rented snowboarding gear. With my body as the field instrument, I anticipated the required change of method. Acquiring knowledge from a closed room requires an ethnographic approach. Booted and boarded, I experienced the alpine slopes in ways thus far unknown, including experiences from not-so-elegant horizontal positions. Even though I was a slow learner, and I painfully experienced this with my body, the situation could nevertheless be considered as substantially improved.

Now there was a breakthrough: I was surprised to find an acquaintance from my younger days on the slopes. He was a post-hippie who had found happiness as a full-time senior snowboarder. He took the time to demonstrate the basic skills and techniques, and told me all he knew about snowboarding. I was given to understand that snowboarding was a complex practice, and the idea struck me that editing an introductory manual on snowboarding would give me a great opportunity to learn about it. The senior snowboarder liked the idea, and introduced me to a group of young persons who lived and breathed snowboarding. He pointed out two, a self-taught photographer and a snowboarding electrician's apprentice. With me as the ghostwriter and editor, we landed a contract with a Nordic publishing house, the book was published the same autumn, and I never again had any problems finding motivated informants.[7]

"Word" in a Norwegian Tribe

The roughly forty young snowboarders I came into contact with lived in worn-out trailers at a trailer camp called Totten Camping, at the bottom of the alpine skiing center in the small Norwegian mountain community of Hemsedal. Some of them were there for their fifth year in a row. Not all were living there on a permanent basis; some commuted on a weekly basis from Oslo, where they had a job. Four out of five were boys. To the extent that they had vocational experience, it was as craftsmen and laborers, and many told me about difficulties with concentration and problems with school and sitting still in the classroom. These young persons were seventeen to twenty-four years of age, and most came from the working-class dominated eastern sections of Oslo. Even though many of them came from divorced homes and had experienced various problems, all of them had at least one responsible caregiver.

FIGURE 14.1 A skateboarder at Totten. The group camping was inspired by Third World primitivism and popular heroic mythologies.

Photo by Einar Johansen.

In the center of this trailer camp a group of mobile homes were placed in a circle, focusing on a roughly shaped totem pole, an old sofa, and a barbecue (Figure 14.1). In the early evenings there were many activities, including ball games, trampoline jumping, and lots of games and laughter. Many of them had little money, making do with pancakes, instant soup, and simple food. But once the seasonal pass for the lift had been bought and the winter's rent for the mobile home site had been covered, then a box of instant noodle soup could lengthen the stay. Those who had the least funds might live for most of the week on leftovers from the commuters, returning empty bottles for the deposit and doing simple odd jobs.

Naturally, I was a person they were very curious about, and initially I encountered some skepticism and even wonder. Why had I started to hang around the camp, and what was I actually doing? I explained patiently again and again that I was studying for a doctoral degree. Many of them thought this meant that I was studying medicine and that I was interested in ligament injuries and broken bones, and I came to realize that this was not popular. It turned out that the local doctor had made negative statements to the press, and presented snowboarding as dangerous and hazardous. I therefore put much effort into explaining to these young persons that I was a kind of anthropologist, that I was not

FIGURE 14.2 During the eight years of the THCs existence, different tribal signs and logos were in use. This "psychedelic" card was used as an entrance ticket at the local disco, and was not part of a free-drugs campaign, but rather a mixture of irony and protest.

a doctor, but that my business was text. This earned me the nickname "Doctor Word," later just "Word."

In the course of the three winter seasons I conducted my fieldwork (1996–1998), I registered many expressions of the social and cultural conflicts between the dominant group of well-to-do skiers and "poor" snowboarders at Totten camping. A gallows outside one of the mobile homes had a ski hanging from it, and the head of the totem pole was for a long time capped with a German helmet from World War II. The group called themselves Totten Happy Campers and Totten Hard Core (rendered in English), but the logo THC had an added value: it referred both to the banned drug cannabis (THC) and the prototypical snowboard tribe Mt. Baker Hard Core (MBHC) (Figure 14.2).

You need a car to get to Hemsedal, but cars cost money, both to buy and to drive. Only a very few could afford such a luxury, so much energy and ingenuity was put into filling up the available cars. The three-hour trip to Hemsedal was therefore undertaken with many changing constellations of passengers. This kept the seats in the cars always full, but also made the travel experience a collective affair. Hence an internal folklore arose. You had to honk the car horn when passing a special house along the road, but nobody could explain why. There was another ritual when crossing cattle grids: Everyone had to lift their feet off the floor of the car, and whoever forgot would become a "cow." Typically the cow ritual was practiced most assiduously on the way to Hemsedal. A cattle grid is only capable of stopping the most awkward of creatures, and the mild cud-chewing slowness of cows is the complete opposite of snowboarders' artistic ideals of soaring flight in the mountains.

Linguistic Barriers

Snowboarders used a special jargon, an in-group argot with terms for tricks and moves, experiences and adventures these young people shared. The origin of these terms was American slang, particularly from surfing and skateboarding communities. The terms were learned through the internal media and through foreign "colleagues" they spent time with. The language referred to in-group values. A key term was the Norwegian *baile*, which was taken directly from *to bail*, used by American snowboarding to mean "to fall in a controlled manner." Among these risk seekers, falling in a controlled manner was not an action deserving of respect—rather the opposite. To bail was synonymous with not daring, being a coward, or chickening out.

To bail was part of a scale of values where the brave ones do not bail, but go for it all out—they *rule* (the Norwegian term *ruler* again coincides with the American term). A person who rules is *aggro*, that is, aggressive, and goes hard, fast, and on the edge, *gunning* or *burning* away (*gunner* and *burner* in Norwegian). *Burning* is a term borrowed from drag racing on the western seaboard of the United States, while *gunning*, needless to say, relates to the energy of a gunshot. Not only the most fearless ones but also technical masters will be designated as snowboarders who rule. In Norwegian tradition, being radical (*radikalitet*) means being in favor of change in a political sense, but for snowboarders at Totten radical refers to physical expressiveness, the power to act, and courage. A *rad* (*radikal* in Norwegian) is a person who will do things that are too extreme for normal persons. Having *cred* (from credibility, Norwegian *kred*) is another common expression, borrowed from American, but with a very special meaning because it has been brought "home to Norwegian" in a subcultural context. Having cred is connected to internal knowledge and status.

Special terms were used to express the intense emotions accompanying running flat out at high speed and with great risk, which were the kinds of thrills the young people at Totten were chasing. Being *stoked* (*stoka*) describes the sense of being excited and exalted, sensing the rush of having challenged one's own limits to the fullest. This term is derived from burning, as in stoking the fire, and apparently comes from the surfing community. This emotional state follows from the so-called *adrenalin rush* or *adrenalin kick* (the same words and spelling in Norwegian). These terms have a special brilliance because they reflect, albeit weakly, the intense and sought-after adventures on the slopes. Tracks that others would associate with avalanche danger were potential adventures for the snowboarders.

Many terms are tied to being together and being social, such as *hooking up with* (*hooke opp med*—meeting) or *hanging out with* (*henge ut med*—be together with). A slang term describing enjoyment together and communicating well is *to jazz* (*jazze*). This suggests improvization, playfulness, harmony, and togetherness, but also something that is on the move. These terms are used frequently, an indication of the importance of the social community. This language is dominated by traditional masculine values, which elevate courage, resoluteness, and overcoming fear, and praise friendship and community. My experience was that the important words and terms I learned at Totten were also used in other snowboarding communities. Mastering the lingo that was central to the American "mother culture" was essential to prove that one was on the inside, and it made it easier to communicate with like-minded foreigners. The use of American slang and American terms pronounced as Norwegian words gave status in this community, also marking distance from other young people.

Powder Dreams

Snowboarding may roughly be divided into two traditions, the skateboarding-inspired freestyle and the outdoor-oriented free ride. What drew snowboarders to Hemsedal were the large untouched areas with steep downhills and large drops in altitude. The adventure could be experienced in the so-called back country. At Totten most were willing to do what the first snowboarders in the United States had done when they were declared unwanted in the alpine skiing facilities: They would walk to reach the highest peaks. That gave them more elevation to ride down, and they found tracks and slopes beyond the reach of the ski lifts.

The optimal conditions were those with a great deal of powder (*pudder* in Norwegian) and steep virgin slopes, preferably at the same place and the same time. The snowboarders spoke of how "cruising the powder" gave an "adrenalin rush," and for many it was natural that such experiences would be accompanied by singing, shouting, and yelling. Snow absorbs not only noise and sounds but also aggression and frustration. Powder snow was generally looked upon as the thing that powered their daily lives in the most perfect way. Powder could also be called new snow or loose snow, or they would use the English word "powder"; one has many names for favorite things. The snow is soft and wet to run in, and the snowy landscape changes character. Where in summer there are stones and sharp angles, snow rounds them into soft curves. Seen through male eyes, it is easy to think that snow makes the landscape female and sensual, a phenomenon that is also thematized in the snowboarding media. In the same vein, untouched powder is also spoken of as "virgin" and "untouched," and it is not without reason that running powder is compared to sex, orgasm, and ecstasy. Sociologist Mark Stranger refers to this phenomenon in surfing, where the wave is compared to a beautiful woman lifting her skirts.[8]

In some places snow piles up high, while in other places it will create drifts and so-called lips. This term comes from surfing, where the lip is the crest of the wave. Such formations are ideal places for take-offs. Cutting turns in such "frozen waves" has the same name as in water sports: cut backs. The snow landscape is alive—not quite like the sea, but almost. The quest for powder creates a state of exception, and snowboarders would compete to find the best places first. This was materialized in the English saying "No friends on a powder day," which the snowboarders know and live by. There is a strong desire connected to the consumption of powder. Powder is a limited good; in part because snow changes its texture relatively quickly, and in part because the most attractive areas will be quickly used up. Nonetheless, the competition for the best tracks never stood in the way of the joy of common experiences. Cutting the first track through a snowy landscape is a typical sensuous experience, but it also has cultural dimensions.

The track is like a signature in the snow, and performing this kind of "inscription" is a form of body calligraphy. Reading such a track is also interesting and challenging, and experts can collect a great deal of information about the moves and experiences that made such a track. Some even claim they can identify the person who cut the track.

Landscape Conquests

The snowboarders felt a clear ownership of their landscape of experiences. The consequences of this were continuously discussed. "Just where you find the rock by Totten-skogen (Totten wood) there's a cool drop," Hanne told me. "We were on our way there one day this winter, and then we met two telemark skiers, and they asked if we knew where the drop was. Yeah right, heh heh. We just left, and when we were down, they were still standing there looking." This sense of ownership is reminiscent of what researchers at the Center of Contemporary Cultural Studies at the University of Birmingham found in their subculture studies on territories, street corners, and so on.[9] The emotional component in this attachment to locations also has clear similarities with what sociologist Yu Fu Tuan calls "topophilia."[10]

The construction of the landscape occurs through the production of memories that follow from experiences and adventures in it and narratives about it. Giving a place meaning not least involves naming it. Names are synonyms for mental images of what they represent, and they transform surroundings into something that is historically and socially experienced. On the basis of their own tracks, patterns of moves, traditions, and values, the snowboarders developed their own sets of names. "Bush," an area dominated by birch and other vegetation, was attractive, and it was claimed that trees are less dangerous than skiers; "you know where you have the trees." Thrills can be found in Eventyrskogen (Adventure Forest), Farthingwood, and Caravanskogen (Caravan Forest), favorite areas and examples of snowboarders' naming customs. Places where nature has made the perfect terrain for jumps and airy rides have been dubbed Backsiden (the Backside), Vindlippen (the Wind Lip), and Tinenlippen (the Tinden Lip). These names refer to special natural formations or the tricks they lend themselves to. Steinen (the Stone) and Varden (the Cairn) are important meeting places and reference points in the landscape.

Nature has made some places particularly perfect for tracks, and the first requirement is a good foundation of snow. Various formations are suitable. Snow has generally been blown away from peaks and ridges, and the highly prized powder will usually collect in the lowest areas of landscapes, such as ravines, gulches and rounded U formations. Peaks have their charm and interest for reasons other than snow. "You feel powerful up on peaks," Marius emphasized. "Peak hunting is challenging and means overcoming hardship" (Figure 14.3). While overcoming is tied to getting up there, the challenge is in the ride down the mountain. The

FIGURE 14.3 The extreme snowboarding in Hemsedal takes place in dramatic scenery, famous for its many narrow and frightfully steep routes and drops. Marius is taking an overview of the valley.

Photo by Einar Johansen.

ideal condition is a frozen base of packed snow and thick layers of powder. Tottenbollen (Totten Basin), Mandagsbollen (Monday Basin) and Sukkerbollen (Sugar Basin) are mountain hollows, as suggested by their names, where the snow does not get blown away but rather collects. Here conditions may be good even if the overall amount of snow is low. Gullies and ravines also collect snow and offer perhaps the most challenging and potentially most dramatic tracks. Annalen (the Anus) and Roni-renna (Roni Gully) are narrow and frightfully steep. Below Matterhorn (local name) there is a spot offering three different descents, called De tre brødre (the Three Brothers). Some names recall physical experiences and mental adventures. Kyllingspranget (Chicken Run) suggests a lower limit for courage, while Angsthang (Dread Wall) and Manndomsprøven (Manhood Test) suggest the opposite end of the bravery scale.

In a landscape, the distance between two places is perceived as a trip, a bodily movement from one place to another. Paths (and tracks) can be understood as media tying together places where people move, and on the basis of these experiences and adventures narratives are created. The snowboarders' perceptions of landscape and their bodily experiences are expressed in narratives, often starting with a particular place or track, and relating to who took part, or the crew: "Andy and I had one of the boys from the lift run us up to Totten 2. Found powder and virgin track down Reidarskaret (Reidar Gully). Right there in the middle of the gully my mobile went off, from my mother: 'Don't have time to talk to you now, mum, am standing in the middle of a rock wall,'" Lars explained on one occasion. Spectacular jumps, drops, and falls are recurrent themes. Narratives are often succinct and concern single incidents, of the type "B-ern had a serious fall in the Anus. He just tumbled right down and didn't stop before the narrowest place [in the gully]. We found his goggles 500 meters further down." Peter Donnelly and Kevin Young write the following about such narratives: "Narrow escapes become even more famous because they indicate that there is always hope of survival."[11]

These narratives cover a wide range of themes, including comical events, accidents, bad weather, avalanches, and incidents with wild animals. The repertoire presents incidents that have occurred and their topographical location in the landscape. There is also a type of "mythical" narrative dealing with how a new off-piste track was discovered, challenged, and conquered. Three of the young snowboarders found a first descent west of the ski lift on the road toward Lærdal. They had seen a gully from the floor of the valley, and spent half the day trudging up. The run down took all of two minutes, but in return they were high on this run the rest of the day. At the bottom of the run they met some people staying in a cabin. "They had used this cabin for more than twenty years and never seen anybody or even tracks coming down that gully." This track was named Gwandarrenna (Gwandar Gully), after the name Gwandar they found in a porn magazine.

The landscape's potential for presenting meaning was also used by the young persons at Totten. Only hours after an avalanche accident where two snowboarders were seriously injured, some of the remaining snowboarders took me along on a car trip that initially appeared incomprehensible. The destination for the trip was Gwandar Gully, and we parked below it and sat looking at the conditions in the perilously steep slope. I later decided that by seeking out a location where courage and audacity really had been tested, the snowboarders had found renewed motivation while processing the shock of the accident. The car trip to Gwandar was a statement that the snowboarding game would continue as before. This particular location pinpointed values that it was interesting to be reminded of precisely there and then.

Nature Identification

The ideal of snowboarders is to "merge" with the surroundings, become one with them.[12] The very act of riding a snowboard suggests how. On a snowboard, the body posture must be to stand with one foot forward in a fixed and strapped-down position. The weight distribution is between the forward leg and the rear leg; the shoulders and the head are in the direction of running, and this way of moving through the terrain gives snowboarders a feeling that could be associated with a speeding animal. Wild animals have their habitat in the landscapes loved by snowboarders, and are hence assigned special status. While people walking on their skis are just skiers, snowboarders are riders. Snowboarding attire is the "armor" and the board is the "mount" in the game where one transcends into the mimetic universe. This may be the reason why French snowboard legend Regis Rolans claimed that the "snowboard gives you power in the mountain."

"Sometimes when we've been gunning down in the forest we've actually overtaken a hare," Einar told me one evening at Totten. "You get the special qualities an animal might have had. Our days are not quite human. We're not sitting in an office, we're using our bodies the way it was done in the old days." Snowboarders have special qualities, animals have special qualities, and this creates special relationships. Nevertheless, not all living things are as fascinating as others; the fascinating ones are those creatures that appear independent and strong. The snowboarders share the world with these creatures. In the wild, these animals have superior qualities it is exciting to imagine having. Bearing this in mind, predators and birds of prey are admired and respected. There are continuous references to these cool and radical "relatives" in statements, advertisements, feature articles, and videotapes. Many of the young people at Totten cruise through the mountain landscape with the sticker "Wolves are protected but not saved" on their snowboards.

The Gripping Beast, the dragon depicted on Norwegian stave church portals, was used as visual identification. This mythological creature has the qualities of a predator, and body control is its form—a good summary of what makes identification with the realm of animals interesting. The uncompromising radicalism of a predator coupled with bodily elegance, power, and control is what snowboarders seek in their game. Snowboarding becomes like a game with animal elements, not only in the surroundings but also in oneself. The qualities of the animals impress them, and young people learn about animals from nature shows on television. In popular culture, particularly in cartoons and comic books, we find animal characters with human qualities, and these animals are both hero characters and idols (Figure 14.4).

The final and decisive step, nevertheless, is the sense of intensity, what has been called flow (in Norwegian as well). The intensity of emotions in the mountain erases the distinction between the rider and the surroundings; actions and

FIGURE 14.4 During most of the nineties, the young Norwegian Terje Haakonsen ruled the half-pipe, pushing the limits of the sport. His ability to land on his feet, even when it seemed he would fall on his back or neck, gave him the reputation of being a "cat-man." Advertisement for Volcom / Terje Haakonsen.

awareness merge, the sense of time passing by ceases, and all extraneous impulses, thoughts, and reflections are put on hold. Sociologist Nancy Midol suggests that this state qualifies for the designation "animal or even 'non human.'"[13] Could it be that it is the "animal" inside that snowboarders (re)discover out there in the winter landscape?

In the Universe of the Sub-mass Media

In addition to the lived-experience dimension, with the rich symbolic and ritualistic field I have suggested above, I found that these young people were substantial consumers of media such as magazines and movies. What interested these young persons were snowboard media dominated by understanding of their world and internal reference frameworks, what Sarah Thornton designates sub-mass media.[14] The content relationship between printed media and film was striking, focusing on the same persons, locations, and events. The most important source of inspiration appears to be road movies with a clear documentary nature. While the films were accompanied by (rock) music, short texts supplemented the picture-dominated magazines and (eventually) the Web sites.

By taking part in the life and times of others, particularly pro runners, a cultural sky was elevated over the snowboarders' lives, undoubtedly an important part of the explanation of the self-sufficiency of their community. Bill Nichols points out that "[d]ocumentary offers access to a shared, historical construct. Instead of *a* world, we are offered access to *the* world."[15] In *the* world, reality is not distant or abstract, but action has real consequences in that it may create guidelines for one's own actions. Snowboard media, and not only film, apply a form of demonstrative rhetoric by being "proof-based" on demonstration, and this is precisely what makes them interesting to watch and read. This form of realism is based on how events appear for us on film as they do in day-to-day life, thus presenting life as we otherwise see it. Events are specific with reference to a world of shared experience. Dealing with this world of shared experience creates common aims for bodily action (snowboarding), while it supports the sense of being a real community, not just an imagined one.

At the campsite in Hemsedal, watching videotapes of snowboarding was one of the most common forms of relaxation after the lifts stopped running in the afternoon. Watching videotapes constituted a special form of social togetherness, which might be advertised and arranged in advance or just happen by impulse on the spur of the moment. The nickname *kino-vogna* (the movie car) was used for one of the smallest mobile homes, where the furniture consisted of almost nothing but a double bed where up to ten persons might lie or sit for short or long sessions watching videotapes (Figue 14.5). Snowboarding videotapes provide enjoyment of the moment, where each move is a short narrative. This fascination with details means that selected highlights or fuzzy moments are repeated. The story line itself is so simple, stylized, and standardized that it does not require concentration, being there only as a metanarrative within which all the other small narratives have their place. Matter-of-fact or joking comments, exclamations of surprise, enthusiasm, disappointment, or irritation, even discussions and conversations are part of the context for watching the videotapes. The fact that the medium creates a visual representation of their bodily expression makes it possible to enjoy experiences that last for tenths of a second in peace and quiet, while bodily experiences, style, and technical details can be discussed. Discussions about locations, landscape formations and snow conditions, landings, moves, and style illustrate the scope of the field of knowledge, and the importance of pictures in this subcultural universe.

Snowboarding magazines were studied with the same enthusiastic approach as movies, and were discussed and assessed according to the same criteria. Snowboard photos are not "snapshots" and "fast food" for those who buy the magazines. Studying pictures stimulates creativity. In the April 1998 issue of *TransWorld Snowboarding* magazine, one snowboarder describes his way of studying

FIGURE 14.5 The *kino-vogna* (movie car).

Photo by Einar Johansen.

pictures: "First, I like to track the action taking place in a shot, then I scan every scaled-down foot of terrain in the frame. You can envision any number of things: Where would I go? Would I be hittin' that thruway with much edge-pressure, stay still and drift it, or would I suck it up, then pop? Why the hell didn't he go over there?" The young snowboarders at Totten told how some photographs had stuck on the retina and become established as synthesized expressions of social stunts, summing up drama and power in a movement, in turn giving guidelines for action.

The local snowboarders spent a great deal of time on the magazines. While reading a copy of *TransWorld Snowboarding*, one kept studying a picture of his hero Johan Olofsson halfway down one of the extremely steep mountains of Chugach, Alaska. "Here's a picture from Johan's [video] part in TB 5," he explained: "This is a cool picture, it is pleasing to see. Seeing these long tracks [he follows the track along a ridge] you can see from his tracks what has happened. You can see the speed." I wanted to know more about this. "You can see whether he was going fast, whether he has *ollied* (jumped) in the turns, you can see *drops*, and you can see avalanches, how the avalanches are falling. It makes me happy to see such pictures," the boy said, emphasizing that the picture was an enjoyment worth dwelling on. The next page showed the same movie shoot and another crazy ride down a vast mountain. "When the track is short the run down the mountain has just started. Then the runner has everything to look forward to. Then it's cool to sit and watch details, see where you could have gone."

An exciting snowboard picture not only contains visible elements but also stimulates speculations about what comes next. Films and photographs show the same persons, heroes the young snowboarders at Totten called by their first names. When one is practicing the same moves as one's idols, the idols take on special importance. The desire to imitate the tricks and moves of the heroes is expressed, and no one finds it difficult to see oneself imitating them. This is how snowboarding has developed quickly and in similar ways in different places during the last ten or fifteen years. The phenomenon is similar to radio waves: From each idol emanate rings of inspiration presented by the media. Thus thousands of young snowboarders on several continents have practiced the same tricks and moves simultaneously.

Approaching Mediascapes through Co-creator Roles

The young people at Totten were in ambiguous positions in many ways, between fragmentation and globalization, between subjection and influence, between consumption and production. This ambiguity also dominated their relationship to the media, which they on the one hand admired almost uncritically, but which they also could have ambitions to surpass. Many were active producers, using digital video cameras, Super 8 or Video 8 equipment, or a regular camera. Most of their material was initially intended for in-group use, but when the first Norwegian snowboarding magazine *Playboard* was launched in 1998, several members of the Totten clan joined as editors, and pictures from this environment became part of the magazine's visual profile (Figure 14.6). One of the first commercial Norwegian snowboarding videotapes released in the market (Fall 1999) was created on the initiative of another person in the Totten group. Moreover, some participated in the animation and production, while many of the better snowboarders had so-called "parts" in the film.

The idea of producing a movie was not new in 1999; in the winter of 1996 Vebjørn lived at the campsite for most of the winter to realize movie plans. An uncommonly low amount of snowfall put an end to this project, but did not stop talk about it, and many offered input. Not the least, his friends' ambitions were high:

> When Vebjørn was going to make a movie, then he said that he counted on us to drop from cliffs of fifteen or twenty meters. Yeah, sure, no big deal, we'd do that! Now we're going to rev it up, we ain't gonna make any shit! We'll outdo the Americans, at least when it comes to madness! Vebjørn had spotted lots of places, was going to make drops himself too. We talked a lot and planned while he was waiting for the snow. It's not certain it would have been good, but then it would have been better to fill the movie with old stuff, old cult movies, stunts from black and white movies or something, like jazz it up. You need to think it's cool if you do it, Hatchett (of Standard Films) doesn't, but "Creatures of Habit" do, they

FIGURE 14.6 Several members of the community at Totten played a part when *Playboard Magazine* was launched in 1998. One of the regular girls at Totten, Hanne, shows her courage on the first cover of the magazine.

Cover photo by Einar Johansen.

jazz it up with motocross. It's not important what it is, only that it's radical. A movie must be planned if it's to be any good. You should have seen the computer animation we had planned! Totally psycho! The movie would start with *this* gang of dudes going to Hemsedal. Just before you reach Hallingporten (the gate to Hallingdal) by Lake Krøderen, Midgardsormen (a mythical dragon encircling the earth in Norse mythology) comes up behind us, spewing flames after us when we go through the tunnel, so we shoot like projectiles out of the tunnel, up in the air, take off, and there Thor with the Hammer comes up beside us and POW!— straight into a snowboarding movie! Vebjørn had photographed and prepared for Pål to create an animation. There were lots of plans.

Producers of snowboard media are not only snowboarders but also experts who know and comply with the cultural values that are in force and sanctioned. Innovation and creativity also occur within such a framework. All encoding processes occur in keeping with internal cultural frames: Those who photograph, film, and write are insiders who are linked by identity to snowboarding. They are the community biographers. At all times they must refer to a cultural whole that emphasizes the subelements that are the theme.[16] For the expert snowboarder, decoding is relatively unproblematic: regardless of where you are on the globe, familiarity with the standardized system for visual representation is general, while (most) bodily movements are within the horizon of experience.

Conclusion: Sublime Experiences

Snowboarders have no collective ideology in the regular sense of the term, nor do they accept any formal organization. For this movement, actions are central. Through the collective activity the group's cultural community is strengthened, while the community also becomes a driving force behind the activity. The *form* itself is a message, a symbolic challenge of the prevailing values. Precisely this building of group-specific *action fields* is the basis for establishment of modern collective identities, according to sociologist Alberto Melucci. In this process the relations between the communicating actors are activated, and emotional investments are made in actions that bind the community together.[17] Snowboarding subcultures idealize individualism and special characteristics, while cultivating the sense of belonging to the group, and the collective creates security. Even if bans, persecution, and marginalization are part of the history, the narratives about this mythical time strengthen the sense of solidarity. Many young people are attracted to this way of creating their own cultural space, because it relates to the perceptions of marginality associated with being young, and subcultures have a high status in many young people's communities.

The most important factor defining social position in the snowboarding subculture is knowledge. The bodily and expressive competence related to games on the board is one aspect of this knowledge; another is intimate familiarity with the sub-mass media. Knowledge about what exists within the frameworks of the snowboarding subculture is the basis for conscious decisions related to idols, but these decisions are also related to taste. This in turn is the basis for choice of style related to the technical aspects of riding technique, clothing, and what is otherwise emphasized when it comes to appearance, language, and so on. All of these nevertheless relate to knowledge: Somebody who only imitates external features such as style will always, on closer inspection, be unmasked as fake and a "wanna-be."

The background for snowboarding having "conquered" youth culture in areas such as the Scandinavian countries relates to the dynamics that follow from the processes outlined above. There is, however, one aspect I have neglected to mention, which might go a long way toward explaining why the sub-mass media are so important in snowboarding. There is significant similarity and linking between the body-based perception of flow and the media-presented perception of what is sublime. While visual representations of perception normally are characterized by distance between subject and object, a snowboarder experiences the sublime in a way that has been acquired through flow experiences of the same type that trigger the sublime. The hunger for new kicks makes reading magazines or watching videotapes a source of intense enjoyment which, given the lack of possibility for bodily realization, satisfies the need, at least to a point. The mediated perceptions and the bodily experiences do not belong in separate spheres but in the same sensing individual. This point may also be stated in another way: When reality is not fragmented through analytical approaches in an academic universe, it appears as holistic and universal, not least for a snowboarder at Totten.

NOTES

1. Kirsten Drotner, *Unge, medier og modernitet—pejlinger i et foranderligt landskab* (Valby: Borgens forlag, 1999), 15.

2. Duncan Humphreys, "'Shredheads Go Mainstream': Snowboarding and Alternative Youth," *International Review for the Sociology of Sport* 32.2 (1997): 149.

3. Suzanne Howe, *(Sick) A Cultural History of Snowboarding* (New York: St. Martin's Griffin, 1998).

4. Olav Christensen, "The Nationalization of Winter and Skiing in Norway," *ARV Nordic Yearbook of Folklore* 50 (1994): 81–101.

5. Olav Christensen, "'Absolutt snowboard': Studier i sidelengs ungdomskulturer," Ph.D. dissertation, University of Oslo, Acta Humaniora, 2001. Papers in English by Christensen: "The Tales of the Tribes. Communication and Consumption in Snowboard Subculture," in *Younger than Yesterday, Older than Tomorrow; Cultural Perspectives on Contemporary Childhood and Youth*, vol. II of Nordic Network of Folklore Publications, edited by Marit Hauan and Gry Heggli (Turku: Nordic Network of Folklore, 2002), 75–99, and "The Playing Collective: Snowboarding: Youth Culture and the Desire for Excitement," *Ethnologia Scandinavica* 29 (1999): 106–119.

6. Belinda Wheaton, "Consumption, Lifestyle, and Gendered Identities in Post-modern Sports: The Case of Windsurfing," Ph.D. dissertation, University of Brighton, 1997.

7. Lars Eriksen, *Snowboard: En innføring* (Oslo: Cappelen, 1996).

8. Mark Stranger, "The Aesthetics of Risk: A Study of Surfing," *International Review for Sociology of Sport* 34.3 (1999): 273.

9. Stuart Hall and Tony Jefferson, eds., *Resistance through Rituals: Youth Subcultures in Post-war Britain* [1975] (London: Routledge, 1998).

10. Yu Fu Tuan, *Topophilia: A Study of Environmental Perception, Attitudes and Values* (Englewood Cliffs, N.J.: Prentice Hall, 1974).

11. Peter Donnelly and Kevin Young, "The Construction and Confirmation of Identity in Sport Subcultures," *Sociology of Sport Journal* 5.3 (1988): 234.

12. Nancy Midol and Gerard Broyer, "Towards an Anthropological Analysis of New Sport Cultures: The Case of Whiz Sports in France," *Sociology of Sport Journal* 12.2 (1995): 207.

13. Nancy Midol, "Cultural Dissents and Technical Innovations in the 'Whiz' Sports," *International Review for Sociology of Sport* 28.1 (1993): 27.

14. Sarah Thornton, *Club Cultures: Music, Media and Subcultural Capital* (Cambridge: Polity Press, 1995).

15. Bill Nichols, *Representing Reality. Issues and Concepts in Documentary* (Bloomington: Indiana University Press, 1991), 109.

16. Elizabeth Edwards, "Beyond the Boundary: A Consideration of the Expressive in Photography and Anthropology," in *Rethinking Visual Anthropology*, edited by Marcus Banks and Howard Morphy (New Haven: Yale University Press, 1997), 59.

17. Alberto Melucci, *Challenging Codes: Collective Action in the Information Age* (Cambridge: Cambridge University Press, 1996).

15

Migrating Media

Anime Media Mixes and the Childhood Imagination

MIZUKO ITO

At least since the rise of television in the fifties, children's popular culture has been a haven for imagining alternative realities, ghettoized and (partially) contained by the "naturally" imaginative life stage of childhood. Even before the advent of mass media, childhood provided a repository of difference both intimate and strange, but recent years have seen childhood fantasy becoming both a more fantastic and more capitalized site of cultural production in Japan and elsewhere. The contemporary move toward "home entertainment" as a focus of childhood amusement has meant that popular children's media have been largely framed by the space of the home and the institution of the family. Yet particularly since the advent of the television, and even more with the advent of the Internet, children's media have become a mechanism for kids to get "out" more, in virtual and imaginary spaces produced through media networks. The imaginary spaces of children's media are also moving "in" more to structure the subjectivities of children, domestic micropolitics, and a growing industry. Morphing from the *Mickey Mouse Club* to *Teenage Mutant Ninja Turtles*, children's popular culture is becoming more fantastic, more culturally hybrid, and more "far out," even as it is becoming an utterly unremarkable aspect of everyday life for children—and, increasingly, for adults as well.[1]

One focus of my work has been on *Yugioh*, a *manga* (comic) and *anime* (animation) series that also creates a multireferential fantasy world interpenetrated with the everyday social lives of children. In this paper, I describe how the fantastic and otherworldly characters and narratives of the Yugioh pantheon are part of the everyday constructions of identity and social relations among children, adult fans, and media industries in Japan. I first locate Japanese media mixes within the contemporary context of children's media culture. Then I describe three ethnographic "sitings" where the imaginary of Yugioh manifests in the everyday lifeworlds of children and youth. In addition to making the fantasy of Yugioh manifest across a wide range of settings, the practices that I track also have the effect of rendering different versions of childhood, gender, and economic relations.

Mediated Childhoods

As Gutman and Coninck-Smith describe in their introduction to this volume, the production of space of modern childhood as uniquely innocent and deserving of protection has gone hand-in-hand with increasing adult engineering of childhood, ranging from formal schooling to the proliferation of media designed for children. Yugioh and other contemporary media mixes in children's content need to be located within this production of childhood as a distinct social arena and market. Just as schools, playgrounds, and children's hospitals have defined modern frames for childhood, popular culture has also become a mechanism for defining a distinct age-specific cultural domain. With the growing consumerism and sophistication of children's media, popular culture has become a mechanism for articulating a counterhegemonic subculture of children in opposition to adult values. In *Sold Separately*, Ellen Seiter writes about how commercials depict children's products as a vehicle to critique and escape adult worlds and accountabilities: "Anti-authoritarianism is translated into images of buffoonish fathers and ridiculed, humiliated teachers. The sense of family democracy is translated into a world where kids rule, where peer culture is all. Permissiveness becomes instant gratification: the avid pursuit of personal pleasure, the immediate taste thrill, the party in the bag."[2]

Much as the counterculture of the sixties and seventies provided powerful advertising tropes in creating a new youth-oriented market, the growth of the children's culture market has rested on differentiation from adult sensibilities and everyday accountabilities.[3] In Japan, antagonistic discourses between children and adults are somewhat less pronounced, but children's popular culture has reflected a similar escapist and fantastic element.[4] Japanese anime has provided a unique vision of childhood as charmed, cute, but not innocent, an imaginary that has proved compelling both in Japan and overseas.[5] This particular imaginary has been increasingly integrated into international media markets, particularly in the past decade, when anime became a major international commodity. In the later years of the nineties, Japan stole center stage in transnational marketplaces of children's media by innovating in media forms that create a hybrid relation between analog and digital media, a merging of the strengths of broadcast media with the communicative and performative power of the Internet and video games. *Pokemon* revolutionized the workings of media technology. By linking content in multiple media forms such as video games, card games, television, film, manga books, toys, and household objects, Pokemon created a new kind of citational network that has come to be called a "media mix."

The media mix of Pokemon, and subsequent series such as *Digimon* and Yugioh, create a virtual world that manifests in multiple media forms, producing synergy between different media types.[6] Kids can engage with narratives and characters through television and manga, as with traditional children's media, but they can also produce their own unique narratives and game play through electronic and card gaming and collection. Further, these media-mix series provide a pantheon of hundreds of collectible monsters with unique characteristics that can be combined with different monsters and props to produce an endless variety of game play strategies. This is a networked world of expanding reference that destabilizes the prior orthodoxy of children's media.[7] Rather than spoon-feed stabilized narratives and heroes to a supposedly passive audience, Pokemon and Yugioh invite children to collect, acquire, recombine, and enact stories within their peer networks, trading cards, information, and monsters in what Sefton-Green has called a "knowledge industry."[8] These media mixes challenge our ideas of childhood agency and the passivity of media consumption, highlighting the active, entrepreneurial, and technologized aspects of children's engagement with popular culture. They also create a proliferating set of contact points between practice, media, and imaginings, as players perform and identify with media characters in multiple and often unexpected ways.

Yugioh

Yugioh was the most popular media-mix content among elementary-age boys in Japan in the years from 2000 to 2002. Launched in 1996, the Yugioh manga series has also spawned a television animation, its own immensely popular card game, over ten different video game versions, and character goods ranging from T-shirts to packaged curry to pencil boxes. One survey in 2000 of three hundred students in a Kyoto elementary school indicated that by the third grade, every student owned some Yugioh cards.[9]

The hero of Yugioh, Mutou Yugi, is a high-school boy with a split personality. Yugi's original personality is one of a small, weak, skinny, and unpopular kid, whose one strength is his skill in playing games. One day, he solves a complex ancient Egyptian puzzle and unlocks a hidden spirit of an Egyptian pharaoh within it, who becomes a second personality for him, Yami Yugi (Yugi of darkness), powerful, secure, decisive, and ruthless. The two Yugis use their game expertise to combat forces of greed and evil, battling with adults as often as with other children. The series pivots around the rivalry between two master duelists, Yugi and Kaiba, with Yugi representing one pole of kindness and fraternity and Kaiba representing an opposing pole of ruthless individualism. Occasionally the two find themselves united against forces of evil such as the shadow corporation "the Big Five" or a group of "Card Hunters" that use cheating and counterfeiting to rob others of their rare cards.

The series focuses on a card game *Magic and Wizards*, a thinly veiled reference to *Magic the Gathering*, the card game that swept the United States in the early nineties. In the manga and anime, players engage in lengthy duels where they pit monster, magic, and trap cards against each other in dramatic play, often involving technologies that render the dueling monsters in three dimensions. The monsters include creatures derived from an entire spectrum of fantasy genres: outer-space, medieval, occult, mythological, cartoon, magical. Red-eyed dragons blast robot warriors and a Venus on a half shell casts spells on penguin soldiers and carnivorous hamburgers. In the narratives of the manga and anime, the monsters leap out from the cards with the help of virtual reality technologies, often inflicting real pain on the human duelists depicted in the series. These holographic monsters, springing into action when played in a duel, function as a metaphor for the imaginative projection that real-life kids engage in when they play with their own card or video games.

Yugioh is similar to the media mixes of Pokemon and Digimon in that they involve human players that mobilize otherworldly monsters in battle. Unlike Digimon and Pokemon, however, the monsters in Yugioh inhabit the everyday world of Yugi and his peers in the form of trading cards that the players carry with them in their ongoing adventures. The humans in Pokemon travel with actual monsters, not cards depicting the monster. By contrast, Yugi carries around trading cards, just like kids in real life. The activities of children in our world thus closely mimic the activities and materialities of children in Yugi's world. They collect and trade the same cards and engage in play with the same strategies and rules. Scenes in the anime depict Yugi frequenting card shops and buying card packs, enjoying the thrill of getting a rare card, dramatizing everyday moments of media consumption in addition to the highly stylized and fantastic dramas of the duels themselves. Trading cards, Game Boys, and character merchandise create what Anne Allison has called "pocket fantasies," "digitized icons . . . that children carry with them wherever they go," and "that straddle the border between phantasm and everyday life."[10]

Just as in the anime, the focus of dramatic action for kids is moments of card play. The boys that I encountered in the course of my fieldwork engaged with Yugioh at multiple levels. Most owned versions of the Game Boy game, read the manga at least periodically, and watched the TV show. Some participated in Internet groups that exchanged information and Yugioh goods. But the most popular is the card game. All of the boys I encountered had some kind of collection of cards that they treasured; they ranged from kids with large boxed collections and playing decks in double-encased sleeves to kids with a single dog-eared stack of cards held together by a rubber band. The standard process of game play is one-on-one, where duelists pit monster, magic, and trap cards against one another. Each player makes a playing deck of forty or more cards that reflects a personal style of play. Children develop certain conventions of play among their local peer groups, and often make up inventive forms of game play, such as team play or play with decks mimicking the characters in the manga series. Rules are negotiated locally, among peers, who acquire knowledge through extended peer networks, television, and manga.

Yugioh was a ubiquitous fact of life for kids in Japan during the years that I was conducting fieldwork in Tokyo. Boys would appear at playgrounds with their favorite cards displayed in cases worn around their necks. As I picked up my three-year-old daughter from day care, I saw two tots with wielding dominoes, striking a characteristic duelist pose. "Time to duel!" one of them announced. Conversations about dark witches and white dragons peppered talk that I over-heard on trains and on the street. At a McDonald's I saw a little girl, maybe five years old, excitedly tearing open a pack of new Yugioh cards under the supervision of her puzzled parents. "What do you do with these?" they asked. "They are just cool." Even children not old enough to play the card game enjoyed the anime series and were energized by the palpable electricity of competitive play that coursed through the networks of kids' play and imaginings. Yugioh was truly a mass phenomenon, creating an alternative imaginary and exchange economy that alternately alarmed, perplexed, and amused older generations.

In the remainder of this essay, I describe three uncommon contact points between the fantasy worlds of Yugioh and the worlds of child and adult players, sites that direct some of this electricity into more concentrated spectacles of the Yugioh imagination. I illustrate some of the ways in which the other world of Yugioh, embedded in a variety of media technologies such as trading cards, the internet, and anime, become mobilized as concrete material and symbolic resources in the lives of committed Yugioh players and fans. These sites of trans-lation between fantasy and reality are sites of consequential subject formation, social negotiation, and the production of childhood as a particular cultural domain.

Siting I: Yugi Incarnate

In the course of my fieldwork, I had the good fortune to meet Yugi incarnate, an eleven-year-old Yugioh expert. I will call him Kaz. My research assistants and I had been frequenting one hobby shop in central Tokyo that hosted weekly Yugioh tournaments. We were usually the only female participants in these events domi-nated by guys in their teens through their twenties. Kaz, a sixth grader, was one of the regulars at this event, generally beating the adults that competed regularly, and taking home the weekly gift-certificate prize. It was unusual to see elemen-tary-aged kids frequent these mostly adult-oriented spaces, and Kaz stood out even more in being the most skilled Yugioh player of the bunch. This despite a substantial financial handicap compared with the adult players, who could afford to buy all the cards that they needed to play. He lived in a single-parent household headed by his father, and had an unusual amount of freedom in traveling through the city after school and on the weekends.

Kaz's play with the older duelists in the tournaments had overtones of Yugi that other players remarked upon. One of the leaders of one of the powerful adult gaming teams called him a prodigy of immense talent. Another player described how he was "like Yugi" in that he always managed to draw the right card at just the right time. Another player explained to me that Kaz did not always have the best strategy, but he was fearless in his attacks and relied on his intuition, having "the heart of the true duelist" often ascribed to Yugi. I often marveled at his composure as he trounced older players in duel after duel. He was a ruthless player, and after defeating his opponents would often rub it in with an understated but cocky self-confidence.

Nobody was surprised when Kaz won in the Tokyo regional junior championship hosted by Konami, the company that makes Yugioh cards. Konami sponsors separate tournaments for adults and children, and Kaz was just below the cut-off for the junior category. I was among the small group of his fans that followed Kaz to this event and the subsequent national championship held at the Toy Show.

Upon entering the huge hall of the trade show, we quickly spot the Yugioh booth. It is dedicated to the national championship, and the center of the booth has a large enclosed structure that spectators enter in from one side. It is a replica of the stage that was the setting for the second duel between Yugi and Kaiba. The center of the space has a glass box containing a table and just enough space for two duelists. Along the periphery is seating for the spectators and a booth with two commentators giving blow-by-blow descriptions of play.

Before long, the final duel of the junior "King of Duelists" tournament is announced. Of course, Kaz has made it to the finals and his name is trumpeted together with his opponent's. The two boys walk through a set of double doors that open with clouds of smoke pouring out to announce their entry. In contrast to the spectacle of plexiglass and smoke being produced on the corporate side, the players and spectators are strikingly mundane. Kaz is dressed in the same black Puma jogging suit that I see him wearing almost every time I see him, and even Kaz's close friends alternate between watching the duel and chatting and playing with their Game Boys, barely attentive to the action on center stage. As is typical of the duels of more experienced players, there is little dialogue between players, and all action is understated. In contrast to younger children who might mimic the turns of phrase of the manga characters and boast about the cards they are playing, professional duelists communicate with gesture and expression more than verbal bravado, making the emotional undercurrents of the duel detectable only to the experienced observer. Kaz wins, and his friends are blasé, declaring it was "a foregone conclusion." In the award ceremony that follows, the press snaps pictures of a grinning Kaz, and he appears in the next edition of *Shonen Jump Comics* together with the next installment of Yugioh.

Kaz's relationship to Yugi is less surface mimicry than performance of a resonant subjective and social location. Kaz's virtuosity at the card game and the grudging respect of his adult opponents mirror the narrative of Yugioh. Like Yugi, too, Kaz had two faces, the face of the ruthless duelist and the childish persona of a sixth grader. My research assistants describe in their fieldnotes how they think he is adorable, and I feel the same. He has pudgy pink cheeks and an embarrassed and shy smile that appears when he is talking about anything other than Yugioh. After winning the national championship with his characteristic swagger, he blushes beet red when one of my research assistants congratulates him and gives him a small gift. For Kaz and his cohort, performing Yugi means performing in competition; persona, age, dress, and language are secondary to proficiency at the game. Yugi is a role model for a practices bounded by the parameters of a form of game play.

Kaz channels the narrative of Yugioh into the referents of our world, making them consequential and meaningful in the competitive negotiations among children and between children and adults. Kaz, like Yugi, inverts the power dynamic between adult and child within the virtual world of Yugioh play. He is a figure of a child elevated to heroic proportions in a national cultural imaginary, backed by an immense media apparatus that provides the cultural resources for his performances. Kaz provides an example of engagement with Yugioh that demonstrates the agentive potential of children when given the resources to compete with adults, as well as evidence of the growing appeal of "child's play" in the world of adult recreation. Although Kaz's precocious performances challenge some of the power hierarchies between adult and child, his play also reinscribes the domain of play as authentically childlike, a domain bracketed from the "real" consequentiality of work and mainstream achievement.

Siting 2: Card *Otaku* and the Resignification of Value

Unlike Kaz, who is an uncommon but legitimate subject in the narratives of Yugioh and the competitive spectacles produced by game industries, many adult gamers are in an uneasy relationship to the dominant narratives of Yugioh. Adult game and anime fans are often described by the at times pejorative term otaku, which roughly translates to "media geek," with hints of connoisseurship associated with the American term "cult media."[11] Otaku are often objects of suspicion because of what are perceived as dangerous boundary crossings between reality and fantasy, adult and child. Unlike children, who are the "normal" audience for animated content, the cultural category of otaku has regressive, obsessive, erotic, and antisocial overtones for the cultural mainstream. Recently the term has migrated to Euro-American contexts as a way of celebrating forms of media and techno-fetishism associated with Japanese popular culture and technology. Key to its popularization in the United States, the premier issue of *Wired* described otaku as "a new generation of anti-social, nihilistic whiz-kids," or "socially inept but often brilliant technological shut-ins."[12] In Japan, the terms is used more broadly to refer to individuals or specific groups as well as a certain cultural style; *otaku-kei* (otaku-like) events, fashions, magazines, and technologies that may or may not be shunned by the mainstream.

Like most popular forms of anime content, Yugioh has an avid following of adult fans. Adult otaku communities are the illegitimate offspring of the Yugioh media empire, and are in an uneasy relationship with the entertainment industries that create Yugioh content. They exploit gaps in dominant systems of meaning and mainstream commodity capitalism, mobilizing tactics that are a thorn in the side of those relying on mass marketing and distribution. Card otaku, who buy and sell cards through alternative networks, even to the extent of creating counterfeit or original cards, are considered a threat to normalized capitalist relations. Let me give you one example of the tension between mainstream industry and otaku, how they intervene in the flow of symbolic and monetary capital between producers and consumers.

Yugioh cards have been released in a variety of forms, including ready-to-play packs, vending machine versions, and limited-release versions packaged with Game Boy software, in books, and distributed at trade shows. The most common form of purchase is in five-card packs costing ¥150. A new series of these five-card packs is released every few months. When purchasing a pack of cards, one doesn't know what one will get within the fifty or so cards in a series. Most card packs have only "normal" run-of-the-mill cards, but if you are lucky you may get a "rare," "super-rare," "ultra-rare," or perhaps even an "ultimate-rare" card in one of your packs.

One kind of otaku knowledge is known as *sa-chi*, "searching," which consists of methods by which card collectors identify rare-card packs before purchase. Collectors meet with each other on rounds of convenience stores, sharing tips and techniques. Now these tips are posted on numerous Web sites soon after the new packs hit the shelves. These Web sites post detailed photos highlighting and describing minute differences in packaging, such as the length of the ridges along the back of the card pack, or slight differences in printing angle and hue.

I find myself out at one A.M. with a group of card collectors, pawing through three boxes of just-released cards. The salesperson is amused but slightly annoyed, and it takes some negotiating to get him to open all three boxes. My companions pride themselves on their well-trained fingertips that enable them to identify the key card packs. They teach me a few tricks of the trade, but clearly this is a skill born of intensive practice. After identifying all the rare, super-rare, and ultra-rare cards in the store, they head out to clear the other neighborhood shops of rare cards before daybreak, when run-of-the-mill consumers will start purchasing.

Single cards, often purchased in these ways, are sold at card shops and on the Internet. In city centers in Tokyo such as Shibuya, Ikebukuro, and Shinjuku, there are numerous hobby shops that specialize in the buying and selling of single cards, and which are frequented by adult collectors as well as children. These cards can fetch prices ranging from the equivalent of pennies to hundreds of dollars for special-edition cards. Street vendors and booths at carnivals will also often have a display of single-sale Yugioh cards that children flock to. The

Internet, however, is probably the site that mediates the majority of these player-to-player exchanges. The total volume is extremely large. One collector I spoke to said he purchases about 600 packs of cards in each round of searches and could easily make his living buying and selling Yugioh cards.

Some of these adult traders are in it for the money, but all that I encountered in the card shops that I frequented proclaimed their love for Yugioh and their commitment to the game. They face off with Kaz and each other in high-tension competition, groaning in frustration at their losses. They organize themselves in regional teams that compete in official competitions that Kaz and other kids would participate in. They generally associate with each other with pseudonyms like Yellowtail or White Moon that they use only in the context of card-game play, bracketing their more mundane identities in the moments when they sit at the duel table. For these Yugioh teams, the Internet provides the primary sites for affiliating with chat rooms, bulletin boards, card trade areas, and virtual duel spaces. Their real-life meetings are called *offukai* or "offline meetings," a term similar to what U.S. virtual communities call "flesh meets."

Children share the same active and entrepreneurial stance, cultural fascinations, and interests as the adult gamers, but they lack the same freedom of movement and access to money and information. The rumor mill among children is very active, though often ill informed. All the children that I spoke to about it had heard of search techniques, and some even had some half-baked ideas of how it might be done. Children create their own microeconomies among peer groups, trading, buying, and selling cards in ways that mimic the more professional adult networks. Despite adult crackdowns on trading and selling between children, it is ubiquitous among card-game players.

Konami has been rumored to have tried, unsuccessfully, to pressure some card shops to stop the sale of single cards. They have also tried to exclude the members of at least one adult gaming team from the official tournaments. Konami makes their business out of selling card packs to regular consumers in mainstream distribution channels. At the same time, Konami plays to multiple markets by mobilizing mass-oriented strategies as well as fodder for otaku and entrepreneurial kids. They have both an official and unofficial backchannel discourse. They continue to generate buzz and insider knowledge through an increasingly intricate and ever-changing set of rules and the release of special-edition cards and card packs. The market for media-mix content is becoming organized into a dual structure, where there are mainstream, mass-distribution channels that market and sell to run-of-the-mill consumers, and an otaku zone of exchange that blurs the distinction between production and consumption, children and adults.

This backchannel discourse of the card otaku is the mostly unsung but often performed story of Yugioh as a case of new economy commodity capitalism and an entrepreneurial and wired childhood. Unlike the spectacular narratives told at official tournaments and on the TV screen, the furtive rounds of collectors in the shadow of the night, and the flow of cards through Internet commerce and street-level exchange, point to alternative material realities in the symbolic exchange of Yugioh cards. These are entrepreneurial narratives involving forms of virtuosity and negotiation that are morally complicated and subversive, in contrast to the heroic narrative of good versus evil and spectacular competition gracing the pages of the manga series and official tournaments. The symbolic capital of Yugioh refuses to be contained within the sanctioned networks and contact points of mainstream industrialists marketing stabilized narratives to masses of children.

Siting 3: Appropriating Yugi

In December of 2002, I made one of my yearly pilgrimages to Comic Market, the largest trade show in Japan and the epicenter for a certain type of manga-otaku. The show occupies Tokyo Big Site twice a year, an immense convention hall located on new landfill in the plastic port entertainment town of Daiba at Tokyo Bay. As usual, I arrive in the late morning, and miss the crowds of fans that camp at the site at the crack of dawn to purchase manga fan-zines, or *doujinshi*, the self-published manga, video, and game software that reshape mainstream anime and manga narratives. The site is always packed, and millions of yen exchange hands as fans purchase magazines ranging from a few U.S. dollars to the equivalent of $30.00 (US) for the high-end glossy publications. An organizing team with militaristic precision keeps up to 300,000 attendees in line, shooing throngs away from fire zones with megaphones, distributing flyers on how photos are or are not to be taken, issuing press badges, selling telephone-book-sized catalogs for the equivalent of $20.00 (US). Magazines by the most popular writers are always in short supply, and buyers line up for hours in the cold and heat to purchase copies—scarce commodities that are often resold at shops and on the Internet. Unlike events catering to video-game otaku or aficionados of other forms of technology, Comic Market is dominated by young working-class women, though there is a respectable male contingent as well.[13] There are an estimated 20,000 to 50,000 amateur manga circles in Japan.[14] Children are rarely present at this event dominated by teens and young adults.

Unlike prior years, where there were only a handful of booths devoted to Yugioh renditions, this year Yugioh content dominates four long rows in the main convention room. The most popular theme is romance between Yugi and Kaiba, the two rivals, but some also depict liaisons between Yugi and his best friend Johnouchi, Kaiba and Johnouchi, or other less central characters. In a somewhat different vein, some artists render Yugi as a girl, with the enormous doe-like eyes typical of girl characters, in sexy but childlike poses. I wander through the aisles, purchasing a few magazines, some Yugioh letterhead, postcards. Like most content featuring *bishounen* (beautiful boys), Yugioh doujinshi are generally created and consumed by women and follow the "June" genre of erotic manga featuring boy-boy relationships (named for the magazine *June*, which popularized this genre).[15] I don't see any men on either the buying or selling side of the Yugioh booths. Some women avoid my gaze as I browse through their manga. Others I hear chatting openly and gaily about the liaisons between their characters in the latest works.

More striking than the orderly rows of booths selling doujinshi are the cosplay (costume play) participants, decked out with wigs, plastic space suits, and other trappings of their favorite manga and anime characters. Doujinshi, video game, and anime events are all occasions for cosplayers to strut their stuff, striking poses for conventioneers toting professional camera equipment specifically for cosplay shots. The cosplayers are like Digimon and *Pocket Monsters* warping into our real world, colorful but routine additions to every manga and anime related event. I spot three different groups of Yugioh cosplayers in my meandering of the convention halls. All groups have the central figure of Yugi, a cosplay challenge with red, black, and blonde hair spiked out in all directions. Kaiba is the second favorite, generally in his signature floor-length leather jacket with dark hair swept over his eyes. Jounouchi rounds out the basic trio, though more dedicated groups will also feature peripheral characters such as Kaiba's brother Mokuba or Yugi's girlfriend Anzu. These characters are all performed by women, as is the case with the majority of cosplay acts. Web sites of cosplayers often have front pages with a warning: "This site is devoted to otaku content and gay content for women. Don't enter if you don't like this kind of stuff." Or more simply: "Men keep out!" Favorite photos are posted of cosplayers at events like Comic Market or smaller Yugioh-only fan events.

Like the doujinshi artists, cosplayers vary in their openness about their alternative identities. Most conceal their cosplay activities from classmates, family, and workplace colleagues, seeing their cosplay lives and friends in high tension with the normalcy of their everyday lives. On these cosplay Web pages, and in the halls of the Comic Market, I encounter another incarnation of Yugioh, but one with strikingly different properties from Kaz and his cohort of card addicts. These are women otaku resignifying a series of imaginings coded as competitive, male, and child-oriented in the cultural mainstream, taking pleasure in claiming it for a women-dominated space of desire, camaraderie, and play. With their bodies and their pens, these cosplayers and artist reinscribe Yugioh as a form of play different from the status economy of duels and card collecting. This is fantasy made manifest in places devoted to alternative identities and practices resolutely differentiated from the mainstream cultural imagination.

As in the case of Yugioh card traffic, these otaku activities grow out of the everyday practices of children engaging with popular media. As part of my fieldwork, I made regular visits to a public children's center that runs an after-school program for elementary-aged kids. I spent most of my time in the arts and crafts room and the library on the second floor, foraying down to the first-floor gym only during the occasional Yugioh tournaments hosted there. The library had a substantial collection of novels and reference books, but also stocked the latest manga magazine for elementary-aged boys and girls, as well as well-thumbed archives of popular series that are later released in paperback book format. There was always an array of kids sprawled on the library floor and sofas with manga in hand. In the arts and crafts room, they copied and traced their favorite manga characters from coloring books, or drew them from memory in their notebooks. When there wasn't a structured activity in the arts and crafts room, small groups of girls would often be drawing their own pictures of characters from popular anime. Pokemon monsters and *Hamtaro* hamster characters were the most popular, and girls would often delight in showing me and other girls how skilled they were at drawing a particular Pokemon or hamster from the pantheon.

The children frequenting this center were mostly first- and second-graders, just beginning to use the visual culture of manga as part of their own form of personal expression. When I spoke to older girls and women in other contexts, many described how this early drawing practice evolved into "pencil manga," or the drawing of manga frames and narratives in the late elementary through high-school years. For those who came to be more "serious" or fan-identified, they might aspire to become a professional manga artist, or to participate in the vibrant doujinshi scene. In this sense, there is a continuity between the informal and everyday practices of growing up in a manga-saturated childhood and the more "hardcore" or otaku practices of aspiring to be a manga artist. At the same time, the identity shift from a girl who can draw manga characters to a "manga fan" or otaku who aspires to writing her own manga is a shift from a normative to an alternative or subcultural identity. Just as in the case of Yugioh fandom, where otaku knowledge and card economies are bifurcated from the mainstream economies, "regular" girls don't participate beyond the reading of manga and casual drawing of favorite characters. Doujinshi artists and cosplayers take up the same cultural resources as the girls in the after-school center, but reshape and redirect them into alternative worlds of meaning and performance.

The Symbolic Economy of Yugioh and Children's Media

In this chapter, I have described some of the heterogeneous networks of narrative and materiality that produce the imaginary of Yugioh as a social fact. Yugioh achieves its status as otherworldly fantasy manifesting in everyday reality through the complicated interplay between competitive play, exchange, and media production and connoisseurship. The trajectories between representation, practice, meaning, and value are by no means direct; the dominant narrative of corporations marketing culture to receptive masses of child consumers is only the beginning of the webs of relationships built with the materials of popular culture enmeshing the everyday and fantastic.

Children's media provide repositories of value, signification, and exoticized imagining that morphs across multiple regimes of value.[16] In the mainstream but ghettoized regime of sanctioned children's media, Yugioh becomes a vehicle for children to imagine and sometimes perform with greater competence than adults at complex games. The penumbra to these mainstream spectacles is the grey market of trading-card exchange that unites the ludic with real-life economies in a regime of value that threatens mainstream forms of capitalist exchange. In a radically different domain, female artists and cosplayers inhabit parallel lives that invert the dominant regimes of age as well as gender identity. These are plays between multiple marginalities, the marginal status of children, grey markets, and adult subcultures mobilizing mass culture in particular ways.

One important aspect of the relation between our world and the other world of Yugioh is the role of children as the literal and symbolic mediums for translation. Yugioh and still the majority of anime content is coded and marketed as children's culture despite adults' role in its creation, consumption, and resignification. Just as Yugi's immature frame harbors the spirit of a powerful adult pharaoh, Yugioh content is a celebration of triumphs of childhood over adult norms of responsibility, deferred gratification, discipline, work, and academic achievement. Sharon Kinsella suggests that one reason for the popularity of child-identified and cute products among young adults is that it represents resistance to mainstream adult society.[17] Yugi is representative of the depiction of children in anime as pure and uncorrupted, and as having unique powers, the ability to cross over between mundane and otherworldly realities. Children engage with this culture as a form of peer identification and empowered immersion in a world where "kids rule." Youth and young adults engage with this culture as a way of deferring their entry into adult subjectivity, or maintaining a parallel life of child-identified play even as they lead professional lives. I often saw salarymen at card shops pulling their neckties off as they sat down at the duel table. They would often self-deprecatingly talk about themselves in infantilized terms. As one adult gamer told me, "You're probably wondering why an adult like me is wasting all his money on kid stuff like this." Attributes associated with childhood—commitment to play and the fusion of fantasy and reality—become ideals for a disaffected counterculture of young adults.

The symbolic separation of childhood as a unique cultural and subjective space is a cultural obsession in Japan as elsewhere, even as it is being challenged by the practical intersections between adult and children's worlds. Only when the object of childhood is reified and idealized can we experience a sense of that object in violation and at risk. Childhood functions as a compelling cultural export outside of the domain of actual children, precisely because of the value placed on an uncorrupted sphere of childhood. Otaku culture, associated with the Japanese media mix of children's media, has become a prominent adult subculture in other parts of Asia, Europe, and the United States. A media fan culture has existed in the United States around certain types of adult-oriented content such as *Star Trek*. But the Japanese otaku culture has unique characteristics because of its focus on child protagonists and child-identified media.

The international spread of Japanese otaku culture is normalizing adult consumption of children's media even as it continues to depict childhood as a uniquely
gifted life stage.

Recent articulations of childhood studies have posited that the category of
"child" is produced and consumed by people of all ages, within the power-laden
hierarchies of child-adult relations.[18] Following on this, I argue that adults are
increasingly not only mobilizing tropes of childhood in political and personal
arenas but are also consuming childhood as an alternative identity formation. In
his study of advertising images in the sixties and seventies, Thomas Frank
describes what he calls the conquest of cool, the appropriation of hip, youthful,
countercultural images in selling commodities that broadcast resistance to the
square mainstream of work and discipline.[19] I believe we are seeing a similar
process in the conquest of cute in the commodification of images and products
of childhood. Childhood play is becoming fetishized and commodified as a site of
resistance to adult values of labor, discipline, and diligence, as well as a site for
alternative forms of symbolic value and economic exchange. It becomes a receptacle for our dissatisfactions about rationalized labor, educational achievement,
stabilized economic value, and mainstream status hierarchies. For adults, these
images of childhood are a colorful escape from the dulling rhythms of salaried
work and household labor. For children, these popular cultures become mechanisms for them to engage in newly activist, extroverted, and intergenerational
media cultures.

NOTES

A longer version of this essay was published with the title "Intertextual Enterprises:
Writing Alternative Places and Meanings in the Media Mixed Networks of Yugioh" in *ET
Culture: Anthropology in Outerspaces*, edited by Debbora Battaglia and published by Duke
University Press in 2005. This research was funded by a postdoctoral fellowship from
the Japan Society for the Promotion of Science, the Abe Fellowship, and the Annenberg
Center for Communication at the University of Southern California. It has benefited
from feedback from Ning de Coninck-Smith and Marta Gutman, as well as comments
from Debbora Battaglia, who organized the session at the American Anthropological
Association meetings where this paper was presented, and comments by discussants
Jodi Dean and Susan Harding.

1. Gary Cross, *Kids' Stuff: Toys and the Changing World of American Childhood* (Cambridge:
Harvard University Press, 1997).

2. Ellen Seiter, *Sold Separately: Parents and Children in Consumer Culture* (New Brunswick:
Rutgers University Press, 1995), 117–118.

3. Thomas Frank, *The Conquest of Cool: Business Culture, Counterculture, and the Rise of Hip
Consumerism* (Chicago: University of Chicago Press, 1997).

4. Merry White, *The Material Child: Coming of Age in Japan and America* (Berkeley: University
of California Press, 1994).

5. Sharon Kinsella, "Cuties in Japan," in *Women, Media, and Consumption in Japan*, edited by
Lise Skov and Brian Moeran (Honolulu: University of Hawaii Press, 1995), 220–254;
Anne Allison, "Cuteness and Japan's Millennial Product," in *Pikachu's Global Adventure:*

The Rise and Fall of Pokémon, edited by Joseph Tobin (Durham: Duke University Press, 2004), 34–52.

6. Anne Allison, "The Cultural Politics of Pokemon Capitalism," in *Media in Transition 2: Globalization and Convergence* (Cambridge: MIT Press, 2002), 290–294. This is a conference presentation available on the web at http://web.mit.edu/cms/Events/mit2/Abstracts/AnneAllison.pdf. Also see Joseph Tobin, ed., *Pikachu's Global Adventure: The Rise and Fall of Pokémon* (Durham: Duke University Press, 2004).

7. Tobin, ed., *Pikachu's Global Adventure*.

8. Julian Sefton-Green, "Initiation Rites: A Small Boy in a Poké-World," in *Pikachu's Global Adventures: The Rise and Falll of Pokémon*, edited by Joseph Tobin (Durham: Duke University Press, 2004), 141.

9. "Otousan Datte Hamaru," *Asahi Shinbun*, January 7, 2001, 24.

10. Allison, "Cuteness and Japan's Millennial Product," 42.

11. Sharon Kinsella, "Japanese Subculture in the 1980s: Otaku and the Amateur Manga Movement," *Journal of Japanese Studies* 24.2 (1998): 289–316; Karl Taro Greenfeld, "The Incredibly Strange Mutant Creatures Who Rule the Universe of Alienated Japanese Zombie Computer Nerds," *Wired* 1.01 (1993), 66–69; Toshio Okada, *Otakugaku Nyuumon* [Introduction to Otakuology] (Tokyo: Ota Shuppan, 1996); Joseph Tobin, "Masculinity, Maturity, and the End of Pokémon," in *Pikachu's Global Adventure: The Rise and Fall of Pokémon*, edited by Tobin (Durham: Duke University Press, 2004), 241–256.

12. Greenfeld, "Incredibly Strange Mutant Creatures."

13. Kinsella, "Japanese Subculture in the 1980s," 289–316.

14. Frederik L. Schodt, *Dreamland Japan: Writings on Modern Manga* (Berkeley: Stonebridge, 1996); Kinsella, "Japanese Subculture in the 1980s," 289–316.

15. In an interview in Schodt's *Dreamland Japan*, June founder Toshihiko Sagawa explains the appeal of this genre for women. "The stories are about males, but the characters are really an imagined ideal that combines assumed or desired attributes of both males and females. Thus the heroes can be beautiful and gentle, like females, but without the jealousy and other negative qualities that women sometimes associate with themselves." See Schodt, *Dreamland Japan*, 122. Although these works are similar to the "slash" genre of fan fiction in the United States, Japanese doujinshi take even greater creative license in repackaging established content, sometimes even changing characters' gender and often ignoring the mainstream plot entirely. Henry Jenkins, *Textual Poachers: Television Fans and Participatory Culture* (New York: Routledge, 1992); Constance Penley, "Brownian Motion: Women, Tactics, and Technology," in *Technoculture*, edited by Constance Penley and Andrew Ross (Minneapolis: University of Minnesota Press, 1991), 135–162.

16. Arjun Appadurai, "Introduction: Commodities and the Politics of Value," in *The Social Life of Things: Commodities in Cultural Perspective*, edited by Appadurai (New York: Cambridge University Press, 1986), 3–63.

17. Kinsella, "Cuties in Japan," 243.

18. Allison James, Chris Jenks, and Alan Prout, eds., *Theorizing Childhood* (New York: Teachers College Press, 1998); Allison James and Alan Prout, eds., *Constructing and Reconstructing Childhood: Contemporary Issues in the Sociological Study of Childhood*, 2nd ed. (Philadelphia: RoutledgeFarmer, 1997).

19. Frank, *The Conquest of Cool*.

Epilogue

The Islanding of Children–Reshaping the Mythical Landscapes of Childhood

JOHN R. GILLIS

Two German scholars, Helga and Hartmut Zeiher, have recently directed our attention to what they have chosen to call the "islanding" of children in contemporary Western society. By this they mean not only the insulation of children's spaces from those of adults but also the separation of one child's space from another's. Today's homes, day-care facilities, schools, playgrounds, juvenile detention centers, and sports facilities are "scattered like islands in a functionally differentiated urban landscape."[1] As they describe it, each child journeys from island to island on his or her or her own customized itinerary, different from that of every other youngster. "The 'modern' model," writes Helga Zeiher, "is that of the insulated individual life space."[2] Each child now has his or her own schedule as well as his or her own geography. There is no longer a shared time or territory of childhood, no mainland of childhood, only infinite archipelagoes of stranded children, ever more dependent on adults to transport them from island to island and to keep them on schedule in their increasingly hurried lives.

Children have been systematically excluded from the former mainlands of urban and suburban existence, especially the streets and other public spaces. What has been described as a "sanitized childhood, without skinned knees or the occasional C in history" is evident in both the United States and Western Europe, even as terrifying images of "street children" proliferate; and more and more children are under surveillance or locked up.[3] Parks and playgrounds, once the free space of childhood, are increasingly supervised. Even the suburban neighborhood, once a territory of spontaneous encounter, is now a series of oases, connected by caravans of SUVs. For many children, their most immediate environment is a blur seen from car or bus. The full range of sensual and social experiences afforded to earlier generations is denied to those who no longer walk or ride bikes in their immediate environments.[4] To be sure, there are real dangers confronting children in today's public spaces. Yet, as a historian, I must question whether these are greater than in the past, when life was a good deal more uncertain and unhealthy for everyone. And it is important to keep in mind that the home remains the single most dangerous place for both women and children. It is there, not the street or playground, where they are most likely to be injured or abused. As Karen Fog Olwig and Eva Gulløv have suggested elsewhere, the "child-safe" places so favored by adults are not necessary good for children themselves.[5]

We are therefore left with the question of what else contributes to the islanding of children. I want to suggest that islanding it is part of a larger cultural process, which has more to do with the ways adults, and especially adult males, think about, or rather think *with*, childhood. We carve out of the flow of life something called childhood, which, according to Elizabeth Goodenough, is "both a chronological stage and a mental construct, an existential fact and a locus of desire, a mythological country continuously mapped by grownups in search of their subjectivity in another time and place."[6] Childhood is perceived as stable point in an otherwise topsy-turvy world. As Fog Olwig and Gulløv point out, "childhood bears this heavy burden of providing a source of identification and rootedness for adults."[7]

Modern life is full of child-centered moments—Christmases, birthdays, summer holidays—elaborate rituals created by adults both to connect with children and gain reassuring access to memories of their own childhoods. The modern home is purpose built as an islanded place to produce and preserve those memories, a museum of childhood even when there are no longer any children in residence.[8] Photographs and memorabilia make them a presence even in absence. As Carolyn Steedman has observed, "accounts of children's space relate most directly to lost or unexplored concepts of the adult self."[9] The islanding of children must be considered a creation of adults, a response to their own needs rather than to those of children. Islanding children is a way that adults have developed to cherish their angels and exorcise their demons.

Adults have not only islanded children physically but have also constructed mythical landscapes that sustain childhood it in its idealized forms, even when it is no longer sustainable in the real world. Mircea Eliade has written that what he calls mythical geography is "the only geography man could never do without."[10] Mythical geography consists of the mental maps that orient us in the world where physical landmarks and signposts are often obscure or absent. The mythical landscapes of childhood constitute a kind of parallel universe, one that bears a similarity to physical geography but has the virtue of being invulnerable to both temporal and spatial changes that are constantly transforming the real world. The mythical landscapes of childhood reassure adults that things are what they wish them to be. It is a geography to live *by* as opposed to a geography to live *in*. It does not exist on maps but is present in literature, in art and photography, and is alive in popular culture. Each family has its own mythical geography, sustained by stories they tell about themselves, captured in the treasured photographs and immaculately maintained "home places," often separate from the family place of residence, better to keep there activities and memories of childhood safe from the encroachments of real life. Mythical geography requires the investment of large amounts of time and energy, not to mention money, all to the purpose of creating and maintaining islanded worlds capable of sustaining the desired image of childhood.

Mythical Isles of Childhood

The mythical geography of childhood emerged simultaneously with the physical islanding of children in the nineteenth century. It has played a vital role in sustaining modern notions of childhood ever since, becoming even more significant in recent decades as the physical islanding of children has become increasingly difficult to sustain. The isles conjured by literature, art, and popular memory provide children to live *by*, even for those who no longer live *with* actual children.

In the later twentieth century, islands, particularly summer islands but also winter islands, have come to be thought of as places ideal for children. They are deemed safe places for preserving childish innocence, and they also serve to create memories of childhood that sustain adults through the rough seas of later life and that are an invaluable source of renewal and revitalization in contemporary society. Such islands are increasingly precious to those parents and grandparents who can afford to invest in island vacations or maintain second homes on islands or in islanded places. There they not only have periodic access to their children and grandchildren but, when these retreats remain in the family over several generations, they also become depositories for memories of their own childhoods and thus a source of personal, familial, and communal identity.

Photographer Eliot Porter spent his first summer on Maine's Great Spruce Head Island when he was eleven in 1913. Fifty years later he returned with his sons and grandchildren for a multigenerational reunion. He tells of approaching the island with trepidation, "anxious as well as excited, as though I feared that the Island out there in the bay might no longer exist, and perhaps had never existed outside my imagination." Arrival produced enormous relief. "At last, unbelievably, I was on the Island. It had not changed: everything was the same." The perceived timelessness of Great Spruce Island allowed Porter to close the distance between present and past, to connect not only with his own children and grandchildren but also with his own childhood. "For if one is privileged to live through the cycle of two generations, he has the opportunity to gain a perspective on his life, first through the emotional attachment to his children, and later through a more detached involvement with his grandchildren."[11]

The emergence of the seasonal island is a notable feature of the contemporary developed world. It became possible in the wake of the catastrophic drop in the number of year-round islands over the past hundred years. In the Gulf of Maine, there were once three hundred of these, where there are now only fifteen.[12]

And the pattern is similar in Canada and Europe, where islands have also become places of sojourn rather than residence. By and large, small islands are no longer places to bring up children. Having lost their economic base, they cannot provide the schooling and opportunities offered to mainland children. But these deficiencies are precisely what make them so attractive to those who have bought up island property in search of the quiet, unhurried refuges they despair of finding on the mainlands of modern existence. Islands inhospitable to real children have thus become the favored locations for the endangered ideal of childhood.

To be sure, the summer (or winter) island experience is the domain of the privileged few. Yet its presence in literature, art, and, more recently, the visual media of advertising, film, and television is disproportionate to the numbers of people who have access to such places. Many millions live *by* islands they will never visit, locating there images of ideal childhood that neither they nor their progeny have never experienced, a childhood that, in fact, has never existed and never will apart from their imaginations.[13] And the mythical landscapes of childhood proliferate even as their physical counterparts disintegrate. As the physical islanding of children grows more problematic, and islands with children become exceedingly rare, modern societies expend ever-greater resources to sustain this parallel universe. Appreciation of the historical relationship between the real and imagined islanding of children is vital to an understanding of contemporary childhood itself.

Spaces of Childhood

The process of the physical islanding of children had its origins in the nineteenth century, when those institutions designed specifically for that age group first emerged on a mass scale. The development of universal schooling ultimately led to ever more refined systems of age grading and the segregation of younger from older children. By the end of the century, new categories like "baby," "infant," and "adolescent" found institutional expression in the nursery, kindergarten, and the secondary school. In the twentieth century, these were further augmented by the addition of day care and junior high school. As Annmarie Adams and Peter Gossage have shown, health-care systems also came to embrace specialties that treated children separately from adults.[14] The innovative open-air schools described by Anne-Marie Châtelet reflected the new discipline of pediatrics, while the children's hospitals studied by David Sloane were the product of a trend toward age grading that also shaped the criminal justice system, islanding the juvenile delinquent from the adult criminals.[15]

Often age segregation moved apace with, and was inseparable from, gender and racial separation. Rebecca Ginsburg's research on the backyards of Johannesburg's white suburbs demonstrates how apartheid itself was age graded.[16] The familiarity allowed between black nannies and white infants could not be tolerated as those children grew older. The Rosenwald schools discussed by

Mary Hoffschwelle represent another kind of islanding, in this case of benefit to black children in the segregated American South.[17] In a similar way, the insistence on the separation of girls and boys after a certain age became a feature in many North American and European countries. This went furthest in boarding schools, but was a feature of even those sex-integrated school systems where sports and extracurricular activities were defined as gendered activities. The islanding of children thus served many different purposes, reinforcing a hierarchical class system while sustaining boundaries of sex and race.

The essays collected in this volume also show how the landscapes of play were reshaped in the name of the safety and protection of children. Effectively, new play landscapes segregated children from the adult world, as Anéne Cusins-Lewer and Julia Gatley show to be the case in New Zealand. Even the radically new junk playgrounds described by Roy Kozlovsky assumed the separate status of children.[18] Sport became increasingly age segregated in the twentieth century, as did all kinds of leisure activities that had once brought together children and adults. The emergence of summer camps described by Abigail A. Van Slyck are but one illustration of a trend that not only separated the spaces of children from those of adults but also created distinctive calendars for each age group.[19] Until the advent of universal schooling, summer had been a time that brought adults and children together in work as well as play. In the twentieth century, summer became the preeminent season of childhood, an island of time often associated with camps and vacation homes located on islands or in remote, islanded places as far as possible from the mainlands of adulthood. Though subject to increased adult supervision in school and on the playground, children came to have far less access to the times and places of adults in general. Excluded by protective labor laws from most workplaces, children and juveniles were less likely to be in the company of their elders except within the precincts of domestic space. The street, previously the mainland of social life, became off limits to them; and the establishment of drinking and driving ages, bans on juvenile smoking, and stricter enforcement of laws governing sexuality had the effect of temporal as well as spatial islanding.

But even as children, and then juveniles, were excluded from the mainlands of adulthood, they were rapidly incorporated in the expanding realms of consumption. By the early twentieth century, there was a multitude of products designed specifically for these age groups. Highly specialized children's food, furniture, clothing, and toys were on offer.[20] At first affordable only by affluent parents, they ultimately became a mass market of huge proportions. Stores added children's departments, as advertising increasingly targeted children themselves. In the wake of World War II, teenagers became consumers in their own right, prompting the development of a new teenage economy, segmented by sex and class, but a model for other age-graded niche markets to follow. Since that time children have entered into consumption at ever earlier ages, encouraged by marketing strategies aimed at building product and brand loyalty even among preschoolers. As Alison

Clarke and Helene Brembeck have shown, this process is now worldwide, fine-tuned to cultural variations, but highly successful in commodifying virtually every aspect of child life in developed countries.[21]

Access to children is made ever easier by the multiplication of media aimed at younger and younger audiences. Children's books and magazines proliferated at the end of the nineteenth century, part of a larger effort to protect children from the supposedly corrupting effects of adult literature and even, as in the case of the recurrent panics about the evils of the comic book, publications originally aimed at younger readers. The advent of movies immediately presented a perceived challenge to the reigning ideal of childhood innocence, but the film industry soon learned to island its audiences, creating a whole new genre of cartoons and features for children, and establishing special viewing times for younger audiences. Radio and, later, television programming also attempted to segregate child from adult listeners and visitors. Children's hours were established and content was carefully regulated, though it has become increasing difficult to prevent access to adult media since the 1980s and 1990s, when children came into possession of their own televisions and gained access to video. Now, with the advent of the Internet, the cultural islanding of children faces yet another test; and in a wireless world, where access is even less subject to regulation, it is as if all the boundaries have been washed away and everyone inhabits the same electronic mainland.

Times of Childhood

The islanding of children has always proceeded at an uneven pace, however. It was most pronounced among the European and North American middle classes, the first group to internalize in a systematic way ideas about the distinctiveness of childhood. The idea of the child had existed in earlier periods, but did not become a social norm and an imperative of social existence until the later nineteenth century. The urban bourgeoisie were the first to organize their family life around children, to redesign their households to provide special spaces for children. Having removed their children from the world of work, bourgeois families reorganized their daily routines around children's time—school time, meals, and bedtimes—and established new calendars marked by children's birthdays, graduations, rites of passage, and holidays. The bourgeois family year came to revolve around the summer vacation, but above all it pivoted on Christmas, which in the course of the nineteenth century became the preeminent celebration of childhood.[22]

The islanding of children proceeded much more slowly among the working classes. A large part of the population could not afford to give up the earnings of their children and resisted the arrival of compulsory schooling. Their over-crowded households had no space or time for bourgeois notions of childhood or adolescence. Working-class children entered early into adult work and leisure activities; and it was not until after World War II that falling family size, higher wages, and improved housing allowed them access to secondary schooling and to the world of mass consumption. By the 1960s, class divisions had eroded so significantly that it was possible to talk about broadly based child and youth cultures. Although gender and racial distinctions within age groups remained pronounced, there was by then an unprecedented degree of synchronization across class lines. In advanced Western societies, children and juveniles entered and exited schooling in lock step; the transition to work became more uniform, and even the age of marriage, which had previously been heterogeneous, converged toward a certain norm.[23] Never had the life course been so uniform and the temporal and spatial islanding of age groups so complete.

Islanding has been a feature of the developed world. The landscapes and timescapes of today's developing worlds remind us of the landscapes of childhood that once existed in Europe and North America before massive urbanization and industrialization. The Indonesian street cultures described by Harriot Beazley are not unlike those that once existed in Dickens's London and nineteenth-century Paris.[24] To find parallels to the lives of the nomadic children of Senegal we would have to search in much earlier periods, but we would surely find them in pastoral regions of preindustrial Spain and among nineteenth-century Native Americans of the great plains.[25]

Modernization theories popular after 1945 once confidently predicted the convergence of world patterns of family, marriage, and aging as industrialization and urbanization spread around the globe. But in the past thirty years the processes associated with globalization have produced more diversity than similarity. We now live in an era when modernity takes many forms, and childhood comes in many varieties. Instead of declining, child labor has increased in many underdeveloped countries; in what Mike Davis calls a "planet of slums" ever larger generations of unschooled street children engage in crime and violence; child prostitution is on the rise, and child soldiers have become commonplace in Africa and Asia.[26] Although Zeynep Kezer's study of childhood in early republican Turkey suggests just how powerful the Western model can be, there is no reason to think that it will continue to shape the world as it once did.[27] There exist in the world today many varieties of childhood, many different ways of being a child, and we cannot afford to ignore these possibilities, even when they clash with our own deeply held values.

Virtual Childhood

Today the islands of childhood are under pressure from many different sources. The questioning is most intense in the affluent societies of Europe and North America, where in recent decades it has become increasingly difficult to sustain the isolation of children from the influences of the adult world. Like those low-lying Atlantic and Pacific islands that are now threatened by the rising waters occasioned by global warming and devastated by the frequent storms occasioned by climate change, the islands of childhood that once seemed so secure are currently under threat from high tides of social and cultural transformations that have been altering the physical landscapes of childhood for the last thirty years, and which show no sign of receding. In North America and Europe the worlds of adults and children are now in much greater proximity than they once were, the gap bridged by a communications revolution that gathered strength over the twentieth century and has become particularly evident since the 1970s.

As Joshua Meyrowitz observed in the 1980s, physical separation no longer guarantees psychological or social isolation. Children have gained access to the previously segregated mainlands of adulthood, while adults were invading the places previously reserved for younger age groups. In the past, "each stage of socialization has been associated with its own physical location," notes Meyrowitz, but now "the idea of special places for special stages of life is fading."[28] Over the past thirty years, the physical landscapes that had earlier sustained not just age but also gender, race, and ethnic distinctions have been radically eroded, creating deep anxieties expressed not only in the extensive literature on the "disappearance of childhood," "children without childhoods," and the "adult-like child" but also in concern about the eclipse of adult identities, focused on the multiplication of midlife crises and the emergence of the childlike adult, particularly childlike men.[29] According to Mizuko Ito, the blurring of boundaries is already occurring in the realm of video games, where adults enter fantasy worlds on an equal footing with children.[30] It seems as if both the gender and generational order, constructed around distinct landscapes of work and home, public and private spheres, is crumbling. In an era when home became work and work became home not only for men but for an ever larger part of the adult female population, it is as if a tsunami was washing over the familiar archipelagoes of everyday life, threatening to undermine the geographies of both age and gender.[31]

Yet the eclipse of the physical boundaries does not mean that the islanding of children has ceased to be a central feature of the social and cultural life of contemporary Western societies. For even as children have become less isolated in a physical sense, they have come to occupy an even more central place in the mythical land- and timescapes that adults live by mentally and emotionally. Europe and North America have become extraordinarily child-centered societies, even as children become an ever smaller portion of the population. Never have children been so valued, but also never have so many adults lived apart from children, especially those resident in retirement and gated communities. Only a third of the households in the United States now contain children; and voluntary childlessness is on the rise. Because we now live so much longer, we spend a lesser part of our lives with children. Yet never has the image of the child been so pervasive in our politics, commerce, and culture. It has become ever more luminous in the absence of actual children.[32]

Family life has become vicarious. When families no longer share a here and now, but are scattered widely nationally and internationally, they must depend on high levels of conscious coordination if they are to retain a semblance of continuity and connection. The home has ceased to be a place of residence, but it has become a collective memory for the generations which for one brief moment cohabited there.[33] Marjorie Garber notes how "the house becomes an unlived life, the place we stage the life we wished we had time to live."[34] In this fragmented world, nothing is left to chance, nothing happens that is not planned.[35] The children of the affluent now carry the same palm pilots and day planners as their parents. They coordinate their play dates by the same wireless technology that executives use to organize their busy schedules. Family time is no longer something that happens, but rather a special occasion that must be organized, planned, and, if it meets the high expectations we have come to expect of such moments, recorded and commemorated.[36]

If the amount of ordinary time and space shared with children has greatly diminished, the number of special occasions devoted to them has increased enormously. Much of what we call "family life" today is spent either in anticipation of these moments or in remembering them. What has come to be called "quality time" with children has come to be associated with set of specially designated locations, most of them islanded, if only momentarily, from everyday existence. Some of these take place in commercial venues, such as the McDonald's discussed by Helene Brembeck in her revealing study of the celebration of birthdays in Nordic countries.[37] Commercialized playrooms, children's museums, and theme parks fall into this category, and so does the domain of highly privatized second homes and weekend retreats where so much of the contemporary family life of the affluent classes now takes place, and where the precious images of childhood are captured and preserved for posterity.

This virtual landscape of childhood is created and sustained by a unique set of rituals and narratives that have developed in the modern era. Photographs of children, especially young children, taken almost exclusively on festive occasions and in holiday settings, have become the favored means of sustaining an idealized, highly stereotyped images of childhood that seems never to change from generation to generation. "Children—and especially girl children—must learn to present themselves *as* an image," writes Patricia Holland.[38] In an era when children are so rarely present in the everyday lives of adults, they are on call at those special times and places that have been set aside for them. Childhood itself has become performative, on stage at those moments and in those places where children are supposed to act like children. Even as the time allotted to childhood erodes, and the children cease to be children at ever earlier ages, the ideal is sustained by a set of occasions (birthdays, Christmases, summer vacations) and in islanded places (camps, weekend and holiday houses). There children act out prevailing notions of children before an appreciative audience of adults, eager not only to confirm their ideal of what childhood should be but eager to revisit their own imagined childhoods vicariously.

To achieve the intended results, the contemporary performance of childhood is best enacted at a time and in a place that, like a theatrical stage, is removed from everyday life. A visit to a fantasy theme park is one way of achieving this but, for those who can afford them, private venues are far preferable. The home has traditionally served as the site of child-centered rituals, but the invasion of domestic space by activities once kept at a distance has caused families to turn elsewhere for space more suitable to these purposes. In the late twentieth century, the weekend or seasonal place in the countryside has become a favored location. The more remote and islanded the better, with islands themselves the most desirable locations of all. As Eliot Porter discovered, islands are the perfect stage for the enactment and reenactment of childhood.

Recovery of Lost Childhood

For centuries, islands have been the favored locus of Western imaginings. "The island seems to have a tenacious hold on the human imagination," writes Yi-Fu Tuan. "But it is in the imagination of the Western world that the island has taken the strongest hold."[39] Powerful images of both good and evil have been projected onto islands, whether landlocked or sea-moated. Eden, the ultimate source of innocence as well as original sin, was initially imagined as an islanded place somewhere in the deserts of the East. The Greeks and Romans regarded islands with both fear and longing; and the medieval Saint Brendan voyaged to isles that were both holy and hellish. Nurtured on such myths and legends, Columbus was prepared to find both paradise and hell on the islands he encountered. Sir Thomas More located the first modern utopia on an isle, but Europeans also dumped their undesirables on islands. Even as they reimagined Eden in the tropics, they turned the Caribbean into the world's first gulag of prison and slave labor. The first modern fictional hero, Robinson Crusoe, made his appearance on an island; and, for a time, islands were the prize possession of the colonial powers.[40]

For centuries, islands were associated with origins, with new beginnings. The earth itself was imagined as an island, surrounded by impassable waters. In the eighteenth century, island peoples were thought to be the nearest thing to the first people of world, living links to uncorrupted humanity. The exploration of islands, especially the remote islands of the Pacific, was a new form of time travel, a passage into a past that supposedly no longer existed on the mainlands of Europe and America.[41] In the nineteenth century, evolutionary theory placed island peoples at the earliest stages of human development, analogizing them to children. Seen uncivilized but unspoiled, islands came to be imagined as the few places where the original innocence and vitality of mankind had been preserved and could be recovered by a civilization grown old and flaccid through the effects of massive urbanization and industrialization.

Islands had become the repository of all that seemed threatened by modern progress, the ultimate symbols of lost worlds and thus the focus of unprecedented nostalgia. It was then that the association of children with islands took firm hold of the Western imagination. Islands became places were it was possible to visualize a family life that was becoming increasingly unimaginable in modern urban society. Parson Wyss created the patriarchical fable of Swiss Family Robinson for his children at precisely the moment when patriarchalism itself was on the wane in Europe. By the end of the nineteenth century the family idyll was replaced by fictions of islands of children, free from adult control and parental supervision. Only on islands was it possible to imagine a world of Peter Pans, of a lost but uncorrupted childhood.[42]

Such were the fictions created largely by a generation of middle-class male writers, whose nostalgia for childhood has placed such an indelible stamp on Western culture. That longing was a product of that moment in the history of urban, industrial Europe when paid work was separated from the home, and adult masculinity demanded a radical separation from the domestic sphere, from the world of women and children. For these men, growing up was the equivalent of the expulsion from the Garden of Eden. Among them, paradise lost had become child-hood lost, producing an intense nostalgia that resulted in the creation of new child-centered traditions, the most enduring of which is Christmas. "God has given us each our own Paradise, our own old childhood, over which old glories linger—to which our hearts cling, as all we have ever known of Heaven upon earth," wrote Anthony Froude.[43] The overpowering sense of loss compelled these men to expend enormous time and energy on connecting with and recovering that which would always remain just beyond their grasp.[44] As Catherine Robson has suggested, male sense of loss found expression an obsession with young children, particularly with young girls. Men like Lewis Carroll attempted to recover connection to their own lost feminized selves through photographing female children.[45]

In Western cultures childhood remains a prime a source of selfhood, especially for men, the thing they use to explain themselves to themselves and to others. In a secular age that has ceased to believe in eternity, childhood has become a guarantee of immortality, the one solid thing left when everything else seems to melt into thin air. It is the most photographed and immortalized of all of life's phases. "We fend off death's terrors, snapshot by snapshot," observes Anne Higonnet, "pretending to save the moment, halt time, preserve childhood intact."[46] In the latest phase of Western cultural development, the favorite image is that of the unborn child, stranded on its fetal island, the ultimate representation of pristine origins, the original uncorrupted self.

Islands are particularly congenial for imagining the originary self because, in the words of David Harvey, "the internal spatial ordering of the island strictly regulates and controls the possibility of social change and history."[47] In our mythical geography, history is associated with mainlands, stasis with islands. "Islands are better at creating and preserving memories, particularly youthful ones," writes Thurston Clarke, "and the best islands for doing this are simple and uncluttered ones."[48] "Islands infantilize people," explains James Hamilton-Patterson, a theme played on by the tourist industry and real estate developers.[49] Their small scale makes us feel safe in a world of gigantism; their boundedness has taken on additional value in the recent era of globalization when physical distance no longer offers real or psychic security. In a culture that fears the disappearance of childhood itself, the search for our "lost" childhoods has colonized not only sea-moated islands but all those islanded places were have constructed to preserve childhood, even in the absence of real children.

Returning to the Mainland

Islands and childhood remain inseparable in the land- and timescapes of the modern imagination. But, while family occasions are child centered, they are clearly adult created; and are often contested by the children themselves.[50] We need to keep in mind that "*the time of childhood*," a time defined by adults, is different from "*time for children*—children's experience of and participation in the temporal rhythms of childhood through which their lives unfold."[51] And just as the adult-constructed time of childhood is not the same as the time that children make for themselves, so the spaces adults map for childhood are not necessarily the same as the territories children wish to occupy.[52] The Norwegian snowboarders described by Olav Christensen have created their own real and mythical landscapes in conscious opposition to adult skiers.[53] We have become less trustful of children, and subject them to ever-greater control. Children resent their loss of autonomy and transgress the boundaries adults have set for them. When they do not conform to our idealizations, children are perceived as fallen angels or, worse, as little monsters. Therefore we should not be surprised when adults express wildly opposite reactions to children, on one hand excessive protectiveness and, on the other, chronic indifference and episodic abusiveness. As John Demos has argued, in a situation where adult identities are so tied up with idealized notions of childhood, childish misbehavior becomes especially threatening, producing anger and violence directed to otherwise beloved children.[54]

This helps explain the ambivalence expressed toward islanded children. On one hand, they are perceived as the epitome of innocence and goodness; on the other hand, they can stand for that which is uncivilized, even savage. As Marina Warner has pointed out, the mythical landscapes of children are populated by little devils as well as little angels.[55] It was only a matter of time before images of islanded innocence were challenged by the demonic visions of William Golding's *Lord of the Flies*. Already associated with the primal and the primitive, islands were a ready receptacle for adult nightmares about the disorder they feared lurked just beyond the mainlands of civilization. Today, islands continue to function as mirrors to the light and dark sides of the human spirit. Their remoteness as well as their boundedness provide the perfect depository for the ambivalence toward children that cannot be expressed closer to home.

I would suggest that the islanding of children is not particularly healthy for society at large. Islanding makes it difficult for adults to know children as complex beings, the compounds of goodness and badness, that they really are. As daily contact diminishes, adult views are increasingly filtered through lenses, rosy and dark, that are inevitably distorting. That so many of these lenses are crafted by the media makes the situation even worse. In turn, children learn less and less about the adult world they are fated to enter, leading to obvious problems in teenage and afterward.

Would it not be better to bring children back to the mainlands that they must inevitably share with adults? Unfortunately, this solution ignores the degree to which those mainlands have become inhospitable for many adults as well as children. Creating new mainlands configured to the needs of both adults and children is a daunting challenge, but it is a project that demands our attention, not only in the name of children but for the good of adults as well. It is comforting that we have available to us a rich repertoire of childhoods past as well as the anthropological record of age relations around the world to work with. We should be able to draw on this vast experience to rethink the time- and landscapes best suited to children, always conscious of the fact that no one model suits all. We also need to heed Marina Warner's caution that "without paying attention to adults and their circumstances, children cannot begin to meet the hopes and expectations of our torn dreams about what a child and childhood should be."[56] At a time when so much public policy is dedicated to making the world safe for children, we must also consider initiatives that make it safe for adults.

NOTES

1. Hartmut Zeiher and Helga Zeiher, *Orte und Zeilen der Kinder: Soziale Leben im Alltag von Grossstadtkindern* (Weinheim/Munich: Juventa, 1991), chapter 1.

2. Helga Zeiher, "Children's Islands in Space and Time: The Impact of Spatial Differentiation on Children's Ways of Shaping Social Life," in *Childhood in Europe: Approaches-Trends-Findings*, edited by Manuela du Bois-Reymond, Heinz Sünker, and Heinz-Hermann Krüger (New York: Peter Lang, 2001), 148.

3. Hara Estroff Marano, "A Nation of Wimps," *Psychology Today* (December 2004): 58–70, 103.

4. Gary Naban and Stephen Trimble, *The Geography of Childhood: Why Children Need Nature* (Boston: Beacon, 1994).

5. Karen Fog Olwig and Eve Gulløv, "Towards an Anthropology of Children and Place," in *Children's Places: Cross-Cultural Perspectives*, edited by Karen Fog Olwig and Eva Gulløv (London: Routledge, 2003), 3.

6. Elizabeth Goodenough, "Introduction to Special Issue on the Secret Spaces of Childhood," *Michigan Quarterly Review* 29.2 (2000): 180.

7. Fog Olwig and Gulløv, "Towards an Anthropology of Children and Place," 2.

8. John Gillis, *A World of Their Own Making: Myth, Ritual, and the Quest for Family Values* (New York: Basic Books, 1996), chapter 11.

9. Quoted in Allison James, Chris Jenks, and Alan Prout, *Theorizing Childhood* (Oxford: Polity, 1998), 57.

10. Mircea Eliade, *Patterns in Contemporary Religion* (New York: New American Library, 1964), chapter 11.

11. Eliot Porter, *Summer Island, Penobscot Country* (New York: Sierra Club, 1966), 90–94.

12. Philip Conkling, *Islands in Time: A Natural and Cultural History of the Islands of the Gulf of Maine* (Camden, Me.: Downeast Books, 1999), chapter 1.

13. John Gillis, *Islands of the Mind: How the Human Imagination Created the Atlantic World* (New York: Palgrave/Macmillan, 2004), Introduction.

14. Annmarie Adams and Peter Gossage, "Sick Children and the Thresholds of Domesticity: The Dawson-Harrington Families at Home," in this volume.

15. Anne-Marie Châtelet, "A Breath of Fresh Air: Open-Air Schools in Europe," and David C. Sloane, "A (Better) Home Away from Home: The Emergence of Children's Hospitals in an Age of Women's Reform," both in this volume.

16. Rebecca Ginsburg, "The View from the Back Step: White Children Learn about Race in Johannesburg's Suburban Homes," in this volume.

17. Mary S. Hoffschwelle, "Children and the Rosenwald Schools of the American South," in this volume.

18. Anéne Cusins-Lewer and Julia Gatley, "The 'Myers Park Experiment' in Auckland, New Zealand, 1913–1916," and Roy Kozlovsky, "Adventure Playgrounds and Postwar Reconstruction," both in this volume.

19. Abigail A. Van Slyck, "Connecting with the Landscape: Campfires and Youth Culture at American Summer Camps, 1890–1950," in this volume.

20. Gary Cross, *Kid's Stuff: Toys and the Changing World of American Childhood* (Cambridge: Harvard University Press, 1997).

21. Alison J. Clarke, "Coming of Age in Suburbia: Gifting the Consumer Child," and Helene Brembeck, "Inscribing Nordic Childhoods at McDonald's," both in this volume.

22. Gillis, *A World of Their Own Making*, chapter 5.

23. Gillis, *A World of Their Own Making*, chapter 11.

24. Harriot Beazley, "The Geographies and Identities of Street Girls in Indonesia," in this volume.

25. Kristine Juul, "Nomadic Schools in Senegal: Manifestations of Integration or Ritual Performance?" in this volume.

26. Mike Davis, *Planet of Slums* (New York: Verso, 2006), chapter 8.

27. Zeynep Kezer, "Molding the Republican Generation: The Landscapes of Learning in Early Republican Turkey," in this volume.

28. Joshua Meyrowitz, *No Sense of Place: The Impact of Electronic Media on Social Behavior* (New York: Oxford University Press, 1988), vii, 157.

29. Meyrowitz, *No Sense of Place*, 233; Meyrowitz, "The Adultlike Child and the Childlike Adult: Socialization in an Electronic Age," *Daedalus* 113.3 (1984): 19–48.

30. Mizuko Ito, "Migrating Media: Anime Media Mixes and the Childhood Imagination," in this volume.

31. Arlie Hochschild, *Time Bind: When Work Becomes Home and Home Becomes Work* (New York: Metropolitan Books, 1997).

32. John Gillis, "Birth of the Virtual Child: Origins of Our Contradictory Images of Children," in *Childhood and Its Discontents*, edited by Joseph Dunn and James Kelly (Dublin: Liffey Press, 2002), 31–50; Patricia Holland, *What Is a Child? Popular Images of Childhood* (London: Virago, 1992).

33. Gillis, *A World of Their Own Making*, 234–235.

34. Marjorie Garber, *Sex and Real Estate: Why We Love Houses* (New York: Pantheon, 2000), 207.

35. Helga Zeiher, "Children's Islands in Space and Time," 149.

36. John Gillis, "Never Enough Time: Some Paradoxes of American Family Time(s)," in *Minding the Time in Family Experience: Emerging Perspectives and Issues*, ed. Kerry J. Daly (Amsterdam: Elsevier Science, 2001), 19–36.

37. Brembeck, "Inscribing Nordic Childhoods at McDonald's," in this volume.

38. Holland, *What Is a Child?*, 17.

39. Yi-Fu Tuan, *Topophilia: A Study of Environmental Perception, Attitudes, and Values* (Englewood Cliffs, N.J.: Prentice Hall, 1974), 118.

40. For a survey of changing ideas about islands, see Gillis, *Islands of the Mind.*

41. Gillis, *Islands of the Mind*, p. 115.

42. Alain Corbin, *The Lure of the Sea: The Discovery of the Seaside in the Western World, 1750–1840* (Berkeley: University of California Press, 1994), chapter 6; Martin Green, *The Robinson Crusoe Story* (University Park: Pennsylvania State University Press, 1990), chapters 6, 11.

43. Gillis, *A World of Their Own Making*, 103–104.

44. Anne Higonnet, *Pictures of Innocence: The History and Crisis of Ideal Childhood* (London: Thames and Hudson, 1998), chapters 1, 4.

45. Catherine Robson, *Men in Wonderland: The Lost Childhood of the Victorian Gentleman* (Princeton: Princeton University Press, 2001).

46. Higonnet, *Pictures of Innocence*, 95.

47. David Harvey, *Spaces of Hope* (Edinburgh: Edinburgh University Press, 2000), 160.

48. Thurston Clarke, *Searching for Crusoe: A Journey among the Last Real Islands* (New York: Ballantine, 2001), 147.

49. James Hamilton-Paterson, *The Great Deep: The Sea and Its Thresholds* (New York: Random House, 1992), 175.

50. On one such contest, see Regine Sirota, "The Birthday: A Modern Childhood Socialization Ritual," in *Childhood in Europe: Approaches-Trends-Findings*, edited by Manuela du Bois-Reymond, Heinz Sünker, and Heinz-Hermann Krüger (New York: Peter Lang, 2001), 117–135.

51. Allison James, Chris Jenks, and Alan Prout, *Theorizing Childhood* (New York: Teachers College Press, 1998), 61; emphasis in original.

52. This theme is more fully developed in John Gillis, "Childhood and Family Time: A Changing Historical Relationship," in *Children and the Changing Family: Between Transformation and Negotiation*, edited by An-Magritt Jensen and Lorna McKee (London: Routledge, 2003), 149–164.

53. Olav Christensen, "'Board with the World': Youthful Approaches to Landscapes and Mediascapes," in this volume.

54. John Demos, *Past, Present, and Personal: The Family and the Life Course* (New York: Oxford University Press, 1986), 84–87.

55. Marina Warner, *Six Myths of Our Times: Little Angels, Little Monsters, Beautiful Beasts, and More* (New York: Vintage, 1995), 57, 60

56. Warner, *Six Myths*, 62.

NOTES ON CONTRIBUTORS

ANNMARIE ADAMS is William C. Macdonald Professor at the School of Architecture, McGill University, in Canada. She is the author of *Architecture in the Family Way: Doctors, Houses, and Women, 1870–1900* (1996) and the co-author, with Peta Tancred, of *Designing Women: Gender and the Architectural Profession* (2000).

HARRIOT BEAZLEY completed her doctorate in human geography at the Australian National University. She is a lecturer in the Faculty of Behavioral Sciences at the University of Queensland, Australia, and a consultant for Save the Children and UNICEF. Her current research focuses on children, young people's participation, and feminine subcultures and female transgressions in Indonesia.

HELENE BREMBECK is senior lecturer at the Department of Ethnology and research leader at the Center for Consumer Science (CFK) at Göteborg University in Sweden. Her area of research is childhood and parenthood, and she has published several articles and books in this field, most recently *Beyond the Competent Child: Exploring Contemporary Childhoods in Nordic Welfare Societies* (2004), with Barbro Johansson and Jan Kampmann.

ANNE-MARIE CHÂTELET is associate professor of architectural history at the School of Architecture in Versailles, France. The focus of her research is school architecture, and she has published several works on this topic, including *La naissance de l'architecture scolaire* (2000) and *Open-Air Schools: An Educational and Architectural Venture in Twentieth-Century Europe* (2003), co-edited with Dominique Lerch and Jean-Noël Luc.

OLAV CHRISTENSEN is a cultural historian, currently working as postdoctoral researcher at the Department of Cultural Studies and Oriental Languages, University of Oslo, Norway. His current research project is "Children and Commercial Youth Cultures: Studies in Sub-Cultural Career Choices." He has published several books and articles on youth cultures, ethnicity, and nationalism.

ALISON J. CLARKE is professor in design history and material culture at the University of Applied Arts, Vienna, Austria. She is co-editor of *Home Cultures: Journal of Architecture, Design and Domestic Space* and has published widely in the area of domestic ethnography, design, consumption, and material culture.

NING DE CONINCK-SMITH is associate professor, Ph.D., at the School of Education–Arhus University. She has written extensively on the social and cultural history of education, primarily in Denmark during the nineteenth and twentieth centuries. Her publications in English include *Education and Moral Regulation: A Social History of Schooling*, co-edited with Kate Rousmaniere and Kari Dehli (1997), and *Industrious Children: Work and Childhood in the Nordic Countries 1850–1990*, co-edited with Bengt Sandin and Ellen Schrumpf (1997). She was one of four editors of the *Encyclopedia of Children and Childhood in History and Society*, with Paula S. Fass as editor-in-chief. Her current research includes the history of children's architecture in Denmark.

ANÉNE CUSINS-LEWER is a doctoral candidate in the School of Architecture at Victoria University of Wellington, New Zealand. Her thesis, "Exchanges: Architecture and Medicine," investigates an interdisciplinary discourse on "health" and the constructed environment occurring in New Zealand history. Anéne is a practicing architect in Wellington.

PAULA S. FASS is the Margaret Byrne Professor of History at the University of California at Berkeley in the United States. Her books include *Outside In: Minorities and the Transformation of American Education* (1989), *The Damned and the Beautiful: American Youth in the 1920s* (1977), *Kidnapped: Child Abduction in America* (1997), and *Children of a New World: Culture, Society, and Globalization* (2006). She is the editor of the award-winning *Encyclopedia of Children and Childhood in History and Society* (2004) and (with Mary Ann Mason) of *Childhood in America* (2000). She is currently working on a book that examines generational relations in the United States.

JULIA GATLEY is a lecturer in history, theory, and design in the School of Architecture and Planning at the University of Auckland, New Zealand. Her research is focused on twentieth-century architecture and urban planning, including modern and postmodern architecture and the advent of modern town planning.

JOHN R. GILLIS is a social and cultural historian with transatlantic interests who has worked on the history of age relations, marriage, and family cultures. Most recently, he has turned his attention to cultural geography, focusing on islands and coasts. His latest book is *Islands of the Mind: How the Human Imagination Created the Atlantic World* (2004). John recently retired from Rutgers University and lives in Berkeley, California.

REBECCA GINSBURG teaches African architecture, American cultural landscapes, and plantation landscapes in the Department of Landscape Architecture at the University of Illinois, Urbana-Champaign in the United States. She is the co-editor of *Slave Space: The Environments of North American Slavery* (2008) and is completing a manuscript about domestic service in South Africa during the apartheid era.

PETER GOSSAGE is professor of history at l'Université de Sherbrooke in Sherbrooke, Quebec, Canada. He is an historian of family, population, and private life in Canada, the author of *Families in Transition: Industry and Population in Nineteenth-Century Saint-Hyacinthe* (1999), and a former editor of the *Canadian Historical Review*.

MARTA GUTMAN is associate professor at the School of Architecture, Urban Design, and Landscape Architecture, The City College of the City University of New York, where she teaches architectural and urban history. In addition to co-editing this volume, she is preparing for publication *What Kind of City: The Charitable Landscape that Women Built for Children in Oakland, California*.

MARY S. HOFFSCHWELLE is the author of *The Rosenwald Schools of the American South* (2006) and professor of history at Middle Tennessee State University in the United States. Her previous work on Rosenwald schools includes *Rebuilding the Rural Southern Community: Reformers, Schools, and Homes in Tennessee, 1900–1930* (1998), and *Preserving Rosenwald Schools* (2003).

MIZUKO ITO is a cultural anthropologist examining young people's changing relationships to media and communications in the United States and Japan. She is co-editor of *Personal, Portable, Pedestrian: Mobile Phones in Japanese Life* and is a research scientist at the Annenberg Center for Communication at the University of Southern California in the United States, and a visiting associate professor at Keio University in Japan.

KRISTINE JUUL is associate professor at the Department of Geography, Roskilde University in Denmark. After completing doctoral work focused on the effects of drought and migration on pastoralists in Senegal, she has worked on decentralization and local politics in northern Senegal. She is co-editor of *Negotiating Property in Africa* (2002).

ZEYNEP KEZER received her doctorate in architecture from University of California at Berkeley. She is a lecturer at the University of Newcastle upon Tyne, in England, and her primary research interests include the history of modern architecture and urban cultural landscapes, with emphasis on the state and space. Currently, she is writing a book about the construction of Ankara, the Turkish capital city, and its place in mediating the country's transition from an empire to a modern nation-state.

ROY KOZLOVSKY is an architectural historian and a doctoral candidate at the Princeton University School of Architecture in the United States. His dissertation, "Reconstruction through the Child: English Modernism and the Welfare State," examines the architecture of childhood in England during the aftermath of World War II.

DAVID C. SLOANE is professor in the School of Policy, Planning, and Development at the University of Southern California. His research examines issues of urban and medical history, focusing on evolving cultural landscapes as well as contemporary concerns about health disparities in community health planning.

ABIGAIL A. VAN SLYCK is the Dayton Associate Professor of Art History at Connecticut College in the United States and the author of *Free to All: Carnegie Libraries and American Culture, 1890–1920* (1995) and *A Manufactured Wilderness: Summer Camps and the Shaping of American Youth, 1890–1960* (2006).

Index

Italicized page numbers refer to illustrations. **Bolded** page numbers indicate authors of selections.

Senegalese nomads, 10, 152–168; and colonialism, 161–164, 169nn8,11; and formal education, 152–157; and learning to be herders, 157–160, 158, 159, 160; and postdrought strategies, 164–168, 170n25

September 11 terrorist attacks, 241, 249n35

servants, 71. See also nannies

Seton, Ernest Thompson, 25, 27–29, 31–32, 34, 37–38, 41n16

sexual abuse, 183

sexuality, 92, 235–236; and gay content, 311

Shonen Jump Comics, 306

Sibley, James L., 218, 221

sick rooms in private homes, 7–8, 61–77; and child as connection, 69–71; and shared spaces, 71–76; and sick child at home, 66–69. See also children's hospitals

Skelton, Tracey, 234–235, 240, 242

slalom culture, 282–283, 286, 289. See also Norwegian snowboarding

Sloane, David C., 8, 42–60, 319

slums: and children's hospitals, 43; and evictions and clearance, 85, 101n21; and Myers Park experiment, 82–83, 84–85, 84, 93, 97, 99, 101n21; and play centers, 182–184, 189n28. See also town planning; urban renewal

Smith, Samuel L., 215, 218, 221

Snell, Henry Saxon, 75

snowboarding. See Norwegian snowboarding

Snow White, 279

social capital, children as, 86

social class and childhood, 2–6, 10–11, 56–57, 320, 322

socialization of children, 4–5, 7; and apartheid-era South Africa, 193, 209n2; and gifting of children, 254–255, 263; and Indonesian street girls, 235, 241; and summer camps, 25

Soeharto, 235

Sold Separately (Seiter), 302

Sørensen, Carl Theodor, 173–174, 176

South Africa. See apartheid in South Africa; black domestic spaces (Johannesburg); Northern Suburbs (Johannesburg)

Souvenirs de la maison de verre (Lacapère), 122

Spain, Daphne, 42

Spickendorff, Walter, 109, 112

Spiller, Barbara, 91

Sponge Bob Squarepants, 1

sports fields, 96

Standard Oil, 214

Star Trek, 313

Statten, Taylor, 37

Stearns, Peter, 2–3

Steedman, Carolyn, 317

Stephens, Sharon, 2, 6

stereotyping, 172, 235–236

sterilization, 49, 53

Stranger, Mark, 289

Strathcona Medical Building (McGill Univ.), 75

street culture, 316, 322; and gifting of children, 255–256; and Indonesian street boys, 233–234, 248n3; and Indonesian

street girls, 11, 233–247, 247n2; and play centers, 182–183

Study of the Country and Geography (Turkey), 134

subcultures: and Indonesian street girls, 234–235, 242–243; and Norwegian snowboarding, 282, 287, 289, 298

subjectivity and children, 317; and adventure playgrounds, 171–172, 176, 185–186, 187–188n6; and Indonesian street girls, 239; and McDonald's "Happy Meal," 270–271, 273, 275, 277, 279

sub-mass media, 293–296, 298–299

summer camps, 4, 7, 320; Camp Ahmek (Ontario), 37; Camp Alanita for Girls (Ala.), 32; Camp Becket (Mass.), 25; campers' perspectives on, 37–38; and child-saving ideals, 7–8, 23–39; Camp Greenkill (Kingston-on-Hudson, N.Y.), 29; Camp Mary Day (Natick, Mass.), 32, 33; Camp Mishawaka (Grand Rapids, Minn.), 29, 30, 32; Camp Ojiketa (Minn.), 32; Camp Siwanoy (Dutchess County, N.Y.), 29; Camp Tuxis (Conn.), 26; Camp Wigwam (Harrison, Maine), 32; Hillaway-on-Ten-Mile-Lake (Hackensack, Minn.), 23, 38; and Indian council ring, 25, 27–33, 28, 30, 33, 37–39, 41n16; interwar years and, 25–32, 38; and lessons of campfire, 38–39; and postwar campfire circles, 25, 33–36, 34, 36, 39; Wohelo (Maine camp), 30–32, 31, 38; Wyndygoul (Cos Cob, Conn.), 28, 28, 32, 37; and YMCA, 25–27

summer homes, 67–68, 74

sunlight: and Myers Park experiment, 86, 95, 95; and open-air schools, 107, 109–112, 116, 122; in operating rooms, 49–50, 50, 56; and Rosenwald schools, 218–221, 218, 219, 220, 222

surfing, 282, 286–287, 288, 289

Sweden. See McDonald's "Happy Meal"

Switzerland. See open-air schools

synagogues, 97

Tait, Arthur Fitzwilliam, 25, 26

tattoos, 243, 244

Taut, Bruno, 150n9

Taylor, Andrew, 62, 74, 76, 78–79nn9,13

Taylor, Robert R., 218

teachers: and Myers Park experiment, 88–89; and open-air schools, 108, 110–111, 118, 122–123; and Rosenwald schools, 214–216, 218, 224, 226–227, 229n10; and schools in Senegal, 156–157, 161, 166–167; and summer camps, 24; and Turkish Republic, 131–132, 134–135, 135, 140, 142–145, 143. See also curricula; education

Teaching Geography in Elementary Schools (Turkey), 140

Tele-Tubby bed linens, 260

textbooks: and schools in Senegal, 153; and Turkish Republic, 129, 131, 134–135, 136, 140, 142, 143, 144–145, 147–148, 151n35. See also curricula; education

Thompson, Mary, 43